IMPROVISATION
FOR THE THEATER

A HANDBOOK OF TEACHING AND DIRECTING TECHNIQUES

VIOLA SPOLIN

ORIGINATOR OF **THEATER GAMES**

NORTHWESTERN UNIVERSITY PRESS

EVANSTON, ILLINOIS

Northwestern University Press
625 Colfax Street
Evanston, Illinois 60208-4210

First edition 1963
Second edition 1983
Third edition 1999

Second paperback printing 2000

Printed in the United States of America

ISBN 0-8101-4008-X

Design and composition by
Wilsted & Taylor Publishing Services

Library of Congress Cataloging-in-Publication Data

Spolin, Viola.
Improvisation for the theater : a handbook of
teaching of directing techniques / Viola Spolin. — [3rd ed.]
p. cm.
Includes bibliographical references.
ISBN 0-8101-4008-X (pbk.)
1. Improvisation (Acting). 2. Amateur theater. I. Title.
PN2071.I56 1999
792'.028—dc21   99-27042
CIP

The paper used in this publication meets the
minimum requirements of the American National
Standard for Information Sciences—Permanence of Paper
for Printed Library Materials, ANSI z39.48-1984.

To Neva Boyd, Ed Spolin, The Young Actors Company,

and my sons Paul and Bill Sills

EDITOR'S NOTE

In this edition, we have attempted to be faithful to Viola Spolin's writings. Such changes that the reader will find reflect Viola's own desire for a revised edition which would update the exercises, use gender-inclusive language, and present procedures for each theater game that provide focus, description, side-coaching, and evaluation. The source was her own published work[1] or Paul Sills' knowledge of her later work: for instance, beginning the Where sessions with EMERGING WHERE, an exercise not published before.

All her later exercises are included in this edition either in the body of the book or in Appendix I. Cross-referencing has been used to connect related exercises, and Appendix I has its own alphabetical listing. Exercises are now listed in the contents as well as in the alphabetical listing of games, which will be of major assistance in planning workshops.

New to this edition is a glossary of side-coaching phrases, with Viola's definitions of their meaning and value. Also new to this edition is a collection of the traditional games played most frequently as warm-ups or to heighten energy. They are included in the alphabetical listing and appear in Appendix II in alphabetical order following a short introduction. No workshop of Viola's was ever held without the playing of such games, most of which come from Neva Boyd's *Handbook of Recreational Games*.[2]

1. Viola Spolin's *Theater Game File*, *Theater Games for Rehearsal: A Director's Handbook*, and *Theater Games for the Classroom*, all published by Northwestern University Press.

2. Neva L. Boyd, *Handbook of Recreational Games* (New York: Dover, 1975; reprint of *Handbook of Games* [Chicago: H. T. Fitzsimons, 1945]).

In previous editions, whole series of exercises, such as MIRROR, GIB-
BERISH, SPACE WALKS, or WHAT'S BEYOND, were numbered, which led
to confusion. Now, in most series, each game is named, after its heading,
which is clearer when one is searching in the alphabetical lists for a particular exercise.

Renaming of any exercise helps this edition to correspond with Spolin's
later published work, or to correct gender confusion, as in the case of MAN
ON THE STREET, which we renamed ROVING REPORTER.

Published for the first time are important speech exercises such as
EXTENDED SOUND and VOWELS AND CONSONANTS. Most of Viola's
speech games are now assembled in Chapter X, which is retitled "Speech
and Rounding-Out Exercises," and includes the speech exercises formerly
found in Chapter VIII. Speech exercises found in the appendixes are cross-
referenced in the text and included in the alphabetical list.

In Viola's *Handbook of Theater Games for the Classroom*, also published
by Northwestern University Press (1986), she presents a theater game curriculum for six-to-eight-year-olds, as well as for older children, an approach
which differs from that of this book, first published in 1963. In revising this
edition, we decided to leave these contents (Chapters XIII to XV) basically
unchanged, since these are the techniques that were used successfully
with her companies of young actors in Hollywood and Chicago. Exploration of both texts is recommended for those working with children.

Paul Sills' work on this edition began in 1994, eleven years after Viola's
previous revision, when she and I sat together in her home in the Hollywood Hills, seeking to add her then latest concepts on theater space and
transformation to the original book. Paul's lifelong knowledge of Viola's
work provided the confirmation needed to edit this volume. Together we
trust that Viola Spolin's *Improvisation for the Theater* will continue to serve
the theater and the community beyond the theater.

Mary Ann Brandt, the late Robert Martin, and Robert Kolmus Greene,
her husband, must also be acknowledged for their great commitment to
assisting Viola prepare work for publication over many years.

Carol Bleackley Sills
1999

PAUL SILLS' INTRODUCTION

Viola Spolin died in her home in Los Angeles, November 22, 1994, at the age of eighty-eight.

This third edition of her book contains many new games. The editing has been done by Carol Bleackley Sills, who worked with Viola on the previous edition published in 1983, as well as on some of her other books, and myself.

In editing this new edition we find ourselves astonished, Carol and I, to realize certain games have not been included before. If Viola said *"Slow motion"* once to me she said it a thousand times. Viola was a true believer in what she called "the many, many benefits of slow motion. Use slow motion!" she advised. "The intuition is directly empowered."

SLOW MOTION was not formerly in *Improvisation for the Theater*, nor was it really in the *Theater Game File*, except as a way of playing freeze tag.[1] But she did develop a game called SLOW/FAST/NORMAL as early as 1963 which now appears in this edition on p. 213, prefaced by an introduction.

Also in this edition we have added important games for voice and speech: EXTENDED SOUND, VOWELS AND CONSONANTS, MIRROR SOUND, MIRROR SPEECH, UNRELATED CONVERSATION, SPELLING, ECHO, and BUILDING A STORY. These theater games can help us to lift our voices in speech while putting players in true relation, a gift of intuition.

It is on intuition, by the way, that Viola is an authority; intuition being the direct knowing of something without the conscious use of reasoning. It is a way of knowing other than intellectual knowing. The entire thrust of

---

1. See SLOW MOTION/FREEZE TAG, p. 212.

her work activates the intuitive, which she preferred to call the "X-area."[2] It might be useful to remember that in the myth, Ceres wandered the world searching for her daughter, Persephone, carrying two torches: Reason and Intuition. The intuitive way of knowing is neglected in our education in favor of reason (intellect). And yet what we prize—love, faith, art, and insightful knowledge—all reach beyond the intellect and depend on intuitive knowing and its great attribute, certainty. One of Viola's sayings is "With intuitive awareness comes certainty."[3] The sense of self is intuitive, relation is intuitive, and when they occur: certainty.

It is not simply a matter of switching from intellectual, logical knowing to this other way of knowing. It cannot be found easily; intuition is as inaccessible as the glass mountain in fairy tales. Viola says we must be thrown off-balance and must blank out the intellect (the known): "break through the walls that keep us from the unknown, ourselves and each other." Our vehicle must be focus. "Focus is a fresh start. The past is made to loosen its grip." It is focus that rests the mind and overcomes the distractions of intellect. It is a form of "meditation in action," as Viola called it, and "acts as a springboard into the intuitive."[4]

In each of the exercises she selected, her voice can be heard intending to help us become present, liberated from what she called the approval/disapproval syndrome that keeps us in the past and obscures the self. As she is quoted in the "Sayings of Viola" that I have collected and which follow this introduction, "The fear is not of the unknown, but of not knowing." She speaks of this fear and identifies its source as approval/disapproval or authoritarianism. Looking for approval, fearing disapproval, "we are creatively paralyzed. We see with others' eyes and smell with others' noses," wailing "Who am I?" like Clever Elsie in the Grimm Brothers' fairy tale of that name. Viola's problem-solving games and her non-judgmental meth-

---

2. See pp. liv–lv.

3. See p. 9.

4. Pages 20–25 are the source of the above quotes on the subject of focus. In this edition, the term FOCUS replaces POINT OF CONCENTRATION; see Viola's "Preface to the Second Edition" for a discussion regarding this change.

ods help the player to come forth and, "with an awakening sense of self, authoritarianism drops away."[5] In an unpublished article written in the 1980s, she wrote, "Theater games do not inspire 'proper' moral behavior (good/bad), but rather seek to free each person to feel his or her own true nature, out of which a felt, experienced, actual love of neighbor will appear."

Of all her spontaneous sayings, the one I most often recall was told me by Robert Kolmus Greene, her husband and companion of many years. An interviewer asked her, "In what way does Second City still fulfill your vision, and in what ways has it disappointed you?" Viola responded, "My vision is a world of accessible intuition."

1999

5. See p. 9.

PAUL SILLS' SAYINGS OF VIOLA SPOLIN

Viola Spolin and I engaged in a long dialogue about improvisation and so I was sometimes present when her discoveries took a precise verbal form. Many of the sayings of Viola compiled here come from this dialogue. Besides those clearly recollected, I went to letters she wrote and to quotes jotted down during telephone conversations. For the sake of emphasizing key ideas, her published writing also became a source.

What is emerging? I hit for emerging.

Were they acting? Get them to play.

When it bogs down, play a game.

Always throw them off-balance.

Approval/disapproval is keeping you from a direct experience.

Success/failure is a side product of the approval/disapproval syndrome. Trying to succeed or giving in to failure drains us.

That which is not yet known comes out of that which is not yet here.

With intuitive awareness comes a feeling of certainty.

Don't initiate! Follow the initiator! Follow the follower.

When you are in a state of reflection you are including another; when you initiate you deny yourself.

I played all the games.

See things through the eye, not with the eye. Keep it in flow.

I'm changing mind to body. Body includes mind.

The fear is not of the unknown, but of not knowing.

Involve the audience as a fellow player; together hand in hand (one body).

The improvisor is in waiting, not waiting for.

What is the mind? The mind is a side-coach.

When the player escapes the trap of character, story, and emotion, the game ends and theater begins.

The head has no energy. The X-area is the source of energy.

We are working on two levels: the obvious, the story, the scenario, the characters. The other is the invisible, the luminous, the spirit-world.

Shut off the mind. When the rational mind is shut off, we have the possibility of intuition.

Let the magic of the focus work for you. Stay out of it.

Focus is a fresh start. The past is made to loosen its grip.

Focus is not the content of focus; it is the effort to stay on focus.

Focus is an anchor. It holds you to your self.

Focus dissolves ambivalence, time-lag, should I, shouldn't I? The whole thing is to get out of the head.

Put the focus in no motion.

When we bring space into existence, we come into existence.

It should read life, liberty and the pursuit of harmony. It is harmony we seek.

Education is to train for crisis, to reach intuition and self.

Games and story bring out self rather than ego.

Authoritarians lean on discipline and goals. Involvement is goal. Discipline is involvement.

Involvement belongs to the sphere of the non-directive.

Will has little to do with it. Will keeps the ego-centered organism directing its efforts towards maintaining the structure.

Moderation is an art form; in it past and future come together.

Change is not enough. This body of work asks more: transformation.

Movement, interaction, transformation.

Theater games do not inspire "proper" moral behavior (good/ bad), but rather seek to free each person to feel his or her own true nature, out of which a felt, experienced, actual love of neighbor will appear.

CONTENTS

CHILDREN AND THE THEATER

ALPHABETICAL LIST OF EXERCISES

IMPROVISATION FOR THE THEATER

ACKNOWLEDGMENTS

I wish to thank Neva L. Boyd for the inspiration she gave me in the field of creative group play. A pioneer in her field, she founded the Recreational Training School at Chicago's Hull House, and from 1927 until her retirement in 1941 she served as a sociologist on the faculty of Northwestern University. From 1924 to 1927 as her student at her house, I received from her an extraordinary training in the use of games, story-telling, folk dance, and dramatics as tools for stimulating creative expression in both children and adults, through self-discovery and personal experiencing. The effects of her inspiration never left me for a single day.

Subsequently, three years as teacher and supervisor of creative dramatics on the WPA Recreational Project in Chicago—where most of the students had little or no background in theater or teaching—provided the opportunity for my first direct experiments in teaching drama, from which developed a non-verbal, non-psychological approach. This period of growth was most challenging, as I struggled to equip the participating men and women with adequate knowledge and technique to sustain them as teacher-directors in their neighborhood work.

I am also grateful for the insights I have had, at sporadic times throughout my life, into the works of Constantin Stanislavsky.

To my son, Paul Sills—who with David Shepherd founded the first professional improvisational theater in the country, the Compass (1956–1958)—I owe the first use of my material, and I am grateful for his assistance in the writing of the first manuscript a dozen or so years ago and his experimental use of it at the University of Bristol while a Fulbright Scholar. From 1959 to 1964 he applied aspects of this system with actors at the Second City in Chicago. The final revision of this book could only take place after I came to Chicago, observed his work with his company, and sensed his vision of where it could go.

I wish to thank all my California students who nagged me over the years; and my assistant Robert Martin, who was with me during the eleven years of the Young Actors Company in Hollywood where most of the system was developed; and Edward Spolin, whose special genius for set design framed the Young Actors in glory.

My grateful thanks to Helene Koon of Los Angeles, who helped me through the second rewrite of the manuscript, and all my dear Chicago friends and students who helped in every way they could during the arduous task of completing the third and final draft of the manuscript.

Viola Spolin

VIOLA SPOLIN'S PREFACE
TO THE FIRST EDITION

The stimulus to write this handbook can be traced back beyond the author's early work as drama supervisor on the Chicago WPA Recreational Project to childhood memories of delightful spontaneous "operas" that were performed at family gatherings. Here, her uncles and aunts would "dress up" and through song and dialogue poke fun at various members of the family and their trials and predicaments with language and jobs as newcomers to America. Later, during her student days with Neva Boyd, her brothers, sisters, and friends would gather weekly to play charades (used as WORD GAME in this book), literally tearing the house apart from kitchen to living room as pot covers became breastplates for Cleopatra and her handmaidens and drapes from the window became a cloak for Satan.

Using the game structure as a basis for theater training, as a means to free the child and the so-called amateur from mechanical, stilted stage behavior, she wrote an article on her observations. Working primarily with children and neighborhood adults at a settlement-house theater, she was also stimulated by the response of school audiences to her small troupe of child improvisers. In an effort to show how the improvising game worked, her troupe asked the audience for suggestions which the players then made into scene improvisations. A writer friend who was asked to evaluate the article she wrote about these activities exclaimed, "This isn't an article — it's an outline for a book!"

The idea for a book was put aside until 1945, when, after moving to California and establishing the Young Actors Company in Hollywood, the author again began experimenting with theater techniques with boys and girls. The creative group work and game principles learned from Neva Boyd continued to be applied to the theater situation in both workshops and rehearsal of plays. Gradually the word "player" was introduced to replace "actor" and "physicalizing" to replace "feeling." At this time, the problem-solving and point-of-concentration approach was added to the game structure.

The training continued to develop the form that had appeared earlier in the Chicago Experimental Theater—scene improvisation—although the primary goal remained that of training lay actors and children within the formal theater. The players created scenes themselves without benefit of an outside playwright or examples by the teacher-director while they were being freed to receive the stage conventions. Using the uncomplicated guiding structure labeled Where, Who, and What, they were able to put the full range of spontaneity to work as they created scene after scene of fresh material. Involved with the structure and concentrating upon solving a different problem in each exercise, they gradually shed their mechanical behaviorisms, emoting, etc., and they entered into the stage reality freely and naturally, skilled in improvisational techniques and prepared to act difficult roles in written plays.

Although the material has been drafted for publication for many years, its final form was reached after the author observed how improvisation works professionally—at the Second City in Chicago, the improvisational theater of her son, director Paul Sills. His further development of the form in use professionally brought new discoveries and the introduction of many newly invented exercises in her Chicago workshops. The manuscript underwent total revision to include the new material and to present the clearest use of the form for professional as well as community and children's theater.

The handbook is divided into three parts. The first is concerned with the theory and foundations for teaching and directing theater, the second with an outline of workshop exercises, and the third with special comments on children in the theater and directing the formal play for the community theater.

The handbook is equally valuable for professionals, lay actors, and children. For the school and community center it offers a detailed workshop program. For directors of community and professional theater it provides insight into their actors' problems and techniques for solving them. To the aspiring actor or director it brings an awareness of the inherent problems which lie before him.

1963

VIOLA SPOLIN'S PREFACE
TO THE SECOND EDITION

Over my past twenty years of living with the games/exercises, of working to keep them constantly alive and exciting, several of their key ideas have emerged as essential, and I have tried to stress them as much as possible in this new edition.[1] (1) The importance of group response, in which players see themselves as an organic part of the whole, becoming one body through which all are directly involved in the outcome of the playing. Being part of the whole generates trust and frees the player for playing, the many then acting as one. (2) The need for players to see themselves and others not as students or teachers but as fellow players, playing on terms of peerage, no matter what their individual ability. Eliminating the roles of teacher and student helps players get beyond the need for approval or disapproval, which distracts them from experiencing themselves and solving the problem. There is no right or wrong way to solve a problem; there is only one way—the seeking—in which one learns by going through the process itself. (3) The need for players to get out of the head and into the space, free of the restricted response of established behavior, which inhibits spontaneity, and to focus on the actual field—SPACE—upon which the playing (energy exchange) takes place between players. Getting out of the head and into the space strengthens the player's ability to perceive and sense the new with the full body. My years of working with the games have shown that this living, organic, non-authoritarian climate can inform the

1. Some of the thinking included in this preface was developed while compiling my *Theater Game File* (Evanston, Ill.: Northwestern University Press, 1989).

learning process and, in fact, is the only way in which artistic and intuitive freedom can grow.

When I started this work forty or more years ago, one of my most difficult problems was to capture the non-verbal essence of my approach to drama in words. Words can easily become labels, dead and useless. The word or the subject matter should not take the place of the process; it is the process of solving a problem that releases intelligence, talent, and genius. Just as in my teaching practice I change the focus when a game isn't working, so here, in this edition, I've changed some terms in order to reflect new understanding and workshop practice. Most significantly, I now use "focus" instead of "point of concentration" (although it was not possible to change this term throughout the book). Point of concentration suggests a set object. It can be a blinder, like a magnifying glass held over one object or an absent-minded professor falling off his chair while concentrating on a thought. "Focus," on the other hand, suggests to me a moving energy, like a ball in a constant state of movement, the players all acutely conscious of everything going on around them while keeping their eye on the ball. Similarly, whereas "relationship" is static and implies role playing, "relation" is a moving force—seeing, hearing, perceiving. "Motivation," a commonly used term, I have replaced with "integration." Motivation is limited and subjective; it cuts the players off from ongoing stage life, and it implies that you have to have a reason for everything. I also now even further de-emphasize mime and conscious muscular memory, and I no longer recommend visualization or memorization of invisible objects/props. Instead of visualization and memorization, which are in the head (the intellect, the known) and not in the space (the intuitive, the unknown), to make the invisible visible I refer to "space" substance or objects. Space objects are projections of the unknown, the inner self, into the visible world. When one player throws an invisible ball (space object) to another, the activity makes visible the player's sharing and connecting with the player who catches the invisible ball. Here there is no time lag between facing a problem and solving it. There is no time for thinking about playing—the player plays. I use "X-area" to supplement "intuition." "Intuition" is an over-used term which means many things to countless other schools. "X-area" emphasizes the undefined and perhaps undefinable nature of intuition, the hidden well-springs, the unlabeled, beyond intellect, mind, or memory, from which the artist (the player) draws inspiration.

The most significant change in the games themselves is the addition of "Follow the Follower" (p. 62), a variation on the "Mirror" game in which no one initiates and all reflect. This game quiets the mind and frees players to enter a time, a space, a moment intertwined with one another in a non-physical, non-verbal, non-analytical, non-judgmental way. Played daily, this exercise can bring miraculous unity and harmony to a group of players; it is a thread woven through the entire fabric of the theater game process.

The changes in this new edition will, I hope, enable players to be present to the moment they are present to, to directly see and be seen, touch and be touched, know and be known. The games, I hope, will awaken the natural talent within everyone. I would like to thank Carol Sills for her assistance in preparing this edition.

1983

THEORY AND FOUNDATION

CHAPTER I

CREATIVE EXPERIENCE

Everyone can act. Everyone can improvise. Anyone who wishes to can play in the theater and learn to become "stageworthy."

We learn through experience and experiencing, and no one teaches anyone anything. This is as true for the infant moving from kicking to crawling to walking as it is for the scientist with equations.

If the environment permits it, anyone can learn whatever he or she chooses to learn; and if the individual permits it, the environment will teach everything it has to teach. "Talent" or "lack of talent" have little to do with it.

We must reconsider what is meant by "talent." It is highly possible that what is called talented behavior is simply a greater individual capacity for experiencing. From this point of view, it is in the increasing of the individual capacity for experiencing that the untold potentiality of a personality can be evoked.

Experiencing is penetration into the environment, total organic involvement with it. This means involvement on all levels: intellectual, physical, and intuitive. Of the three, the intuitive, most vital to the learning situation, is neglected.

Intuition is often thought to be an endowment or a mystical force enjoyed by the gifted alone. Yet all of us have known moments when the right answer "just came" or we did "exactly the right thing without thinking." Sometimes at such moments, usually precipitated by crises, danger, or shock, the "average" person has been known to transcend the limitation of the familiar, courageously enter the area of the unknown, and release momentary genius within. When response to experience takes place at this intuitive level, when a person functions beyond a constricted intellectual plane, intelligence is freed.

The intuitive can only respond in immediacy—right now. It comes bearing its gifts in the moment of spontaneity, the moment when we are freed to relate and act, involving ourselves in the moving, changing world around us.

Through spontaneity we are re-formed into ourselves. It creates an explosion that for the moment frees us from handed-down frames of reference, memory choked with old facts and information and undigested theories and techniques of other people's findings. Spontaneity is the moment of personal freedom when we are faced with a reality and see it, explore it and act accordingly. In this reality the bits and pieces of ourselves function as an organic whole. It is the time of discovery, of experiencing, of creative expression.

Acting can be taught to the "average" as well as the "talented" if the teaching process is oriented towards making the theater techniques so intuitive that they become the students' own. A way is needed to get to intuitive knowledge. It requires an environment in which experiencing can take place, a person free to experience, and an activity that brings about spontaneity.

The full text is a charted course of such activity. The present chapter attempts to help both teacher and student find personal freedom so far as the theater is concerned. Chapter II is intended to show the teacher how to establish an environment in which the intuitive can emerge and experiencing take place: then teacher and student can embark together upon an inspiring, creative experience.

SEVEN ASPECTS OF SPONTANEITY

Games

The game is a natural group form providing the involvement and personal freedom necessary for experiencing. Games develop personal techniques and skills necessary for the game itself, through playing. Skills are developed at the very moment a person is having all the fun and excitement playing a game has to offer—this is the exact time one is truly open to receive them.

Ingenuity and inventiveness appear to meet any crises the game presents, for it is understood during playing that a player is free to reach the game's objective in any style chosen. As long as we abide by the rules of the game, we may swing, stand on our heads, or fly through the air. In fact, any unusual or extraordinary way of playing is loved and applauded by fellow players.

This makes the form useful not only in formal theater but especially so for actors interested in learning scene improvisation, and it is equally valuable in exposing newcomers to the theater experience, whether adult or child. All the techniques, conventions, etc. that the student-actors have come to find are given to them through playing theater games (acting exercises).

> Playing a game is psychologically different in degree but not in kind from dramatic acting. The ability to create a situation imaginatively and to play a role in it is a tremendous experience, a sort of vacation from one's everyday self and the routine of everyday living. We observe that this psychological freedom creates a condition in which *strain* and *conflict* are dissolved and potentialities are released in the spontaneous effort to meet the demands of the situation.[1]

Any game worth playing is highly social and has a problem that needs solving within it—an objective point in which each individual must become involved, whether it be to reach a goal or to flip a chip into a glass. There must be group agreement on the rules of the game and group interaction moving towards the objective if the game is to be played.

Players grow agile and alert, ready and eager for any unusual play as they respond to the many random happenings simultaneously. The personal capacity to involve one's self in the problem of the game and the effort put forth to handle the multiple stimuli the game provokes determine the extent of this growth.

1. Neva L. Boyd, *Play, a Unique Discipline.*

Growth will occur without difficulty in students because the very games they play will aid them. The objective upon which the player must constantly focus and towards which every action must be directed provokes spontaneity. In this spontaneity, personal freedom is released, and the total person, physically, intellectually, and intuitively, is awakened. This causes enough excitation for the student to transcend himself or herself—he or she is freed to go out into the environment, to explore, adventure, and face all dangers unafraid.

The energy released to solve the problem, being restricted by the rules of the game and bound by group decision, creates an explosion—or spontaneity—and as is the nature of explosions, everything is torn apart, rearranged, unblocked. The ear alerts the feet, and the eye throws the ball.

Every part of the person functions together as a working unit, one small organic whole within the larger organic whole of the agreed environment which is the game structure. Out of this integrated experience, then, a total self in a total environment, comes a support and thus trust which allows the individual to open up and develop any skills that may be needed for the communication within the game. Furthermore, the acceptance of all the imposed limitations creates the playing, out of which the game appears, or as in the theater, the scene.[2]

With no outside authority imposing itself upon the players, telling them what to do, when to do it, and how to do it, each player freely chooses self-discipline by accepting the *rules of the game* ("it's more fun that way") and enters into the group decisions with enthusiasm and trust. With no one to please or appease, the player can then focus full energy directly on the problem and learn what he or she has come to learn.

Approval/Disapproval

The first step towards playing is feeling personal freedom. Before we can play (experience), we must be free to do so. It is necessary to become part of the world around us and make it real by touching it, seeing it, feeling it,

2. In education, the release of intelligence—learning!

tasting it, and smelling it—direct contact with the environment is what we seek. It must be investigated, questioned, accepted or rejected. The personal freedom to do so leads us to experiencing and thus to self-awareness (self-identity) and self-expression. The hunger for self-identity and self-expression, while basic to all of us, is also necessary for the theater expression.

Very few of us are able to make this direct contact with our selves. Our simplest move out into the environment is interrupted by our need for favorable comment or interpretation by established authority. We either fear that we will not get approval, or we accept outside comment and interpretation unquestioningly. In a culture where approval/disapproval has become the predominant regulator of effort and position, and often the substitute for love, our personal freedoms are dissipated.

Abandoned to the whims of others, we must wander daily through the wish to be loved and the fear of rejection before we can be productive. Categorized "good" or "bad" from birth (a "good" baby does not cry too much) we become so enmeshed with the tenuous threads of approval/disapproval that we are creatively paralyzed. We see with others' eyes and smell with others' noses.

Having thus to look to others to tell us where we are, who we are, and what is happening results in a serious (almost total) loss of personal experiencing. We lose the ability to be organically involved in a problem, and in a disconnected way, we function with only parts of our total selves. We do not know our own substance, and in the attempt to live through (or avoid living through) the eyes of others, self-identity is obscured, our bodies become misshapen, natural grace is gone, and learning is affected. Both the individual and the art form are distorted and deprived, and insight is lost to us.

Trying to save ourselves from attack, we build a mighty fortress and are timid, or we fight each time we venture forth. Some in striving with approval/disapproval develop egocentricity and exhibitionism; some give up and simply go along. Others, like Elsa in the fairy tale, are forever knocking on windows, jingling their chain of bells, and wailing, "Who am I?" In all cases, contact with the environment is distorted. Self-discovery and other exploratory traits tend to become atrophied. Trying to be "good" and avoiding "bad" or being "bad" because one can't be "good" develops into a way of life for those needing approval/disapproval from authority—and the investigation and solving of problems becomes of secondary importance.

Approval/disapproval grows out of authoritarianism that has changed its face over the years from that of the parent to the teacher and ultimately the whole social structure (mate, employer, family, neighbors, etc.).

The language and attitudes of authoritarianism must be constantly scourged if the total personality is to emerge as a working unit. All words which shut doors, have emotional content or implication, attack the student-actor's personality, or keep a student slavishly dependent on a teacher's judgment are to be avoided. Since most of us were brought up by the approval/disapproval method, constant self-surveillance is necessary on the part of the teacher-director to eradicate it in himself or herself so that it will not enter the teacher-student relationship.

The expectancy of judgment prevents free relationships within the acting workshops. Moreover, the teacher cannot truly judge good or bad for another, for *there is no absolutely right or wrong way to solve a problem*: a teacher of wide past experience may know a hundred ways to solve a particular problem, and a student may turn up with the hundred and first.[3] This is particularly true in the arts.

Judging on the part of the teacher-director limits our own experiencing as well as students', for in judging, we keep ourselves from a fresh moment of experience and rarely go beyond what we already know. This limits us to the use of rote-teaching, of formulas and other standard concepts which prescribe student behavior.

Authoritarianism is more difficult to recognize in approval than in disapproval—particularly when a student begs for approval, to get a sense of himself or herself. Although a teacher's approval usually indicates progress has been made, it remains progress in the teacher's terms, not the student's. In wishing to avoid approving we must therefore be careful not to detach

3. See "Evaluation," pp. 273–75.

ourselves in such a way that the student feels lost, feels that nothing is being learned, etc.

True personal freedom and self-expression can flower only in an atmosphere where attitudes permit equality between student and teacher and the dependencies of teacher for student and student for teacher are done away with. The problems within the *subject matter* will teach both of them.

Accepting simultaneously a student's right to equality in approaching a problem and a lack of experience puts a burden on the teacher. This way of teaching at first seems more difficult, for the teacher must often sit out the discoveries of students without interpreting or forcing conclusions on them. Yet it can be more rewarding for the teacher, because when student-actors have truly learned through playing, the quality of performance will be high indeed!

The problem-solving games and exercises in this handbook will help clear the air of authoritarianism, and as the training continues, it should disappear. With an awakening sense of self, authoritarianism drops away. There is no need for the "status" given by approval/disapproval as all (teacher as well as student) struggle for personal insights—with intuitive awareness comes certainty.

The shift away from the teacher as absolute authority does not always take place immediately. Attitudes are years in building, and all of us are afraid to let go of them. Never losing sight of the fact that *the needs of the theater are the real master,* the teacher will be cued, for the teacher too must accept the *rules of the game.* Then the role of guide will be easily found by the teacher-director, who after all knows the theater technically and artistically, and whose experiences are needed in leading the group.

Group Expression

A healthy group relationship demands a number of individuals working interdependently to complete a given project with full individual participation and personal contribution. If one person dominates, the other members have little growth or pleasure in the activity; a true group relationship does not exist.

Theater is an artistic group relationship demanding the talents and energy of many people—from the first thought of a play or scene to the last echo of applause. Without this interaction there is no place for the single actor, for without group functioning, who would one play for, what materials would one use, and what effects could one produce? A student must learn that "how to act," like the game, is inextricably bound up with every other person in the complexity of the art form. Improvisational theater requires very close group relationships because it is from group agreement and group playing that material evolves for scenes and plays.

For students first entering the theater experience, working closely with a group gives a great security on one hand and becomes a threat on the other. Since participation in a theater activity is confused by many with exhibitionism (and therefore with the fear of exposure), individuals fancy themselves "one against many," who must single-handedly brave a malevolent-eyed people sitting in judgment. The student, then, bent on proving self-worth, constantly watches and judges himself or herself and moves nowhere.

When working with a group, however, playing and experiencing things together, the student-actors integrate and find themselves within the whole activity. The differences as well as the similarities within the group are accepted. A group should never be used to induce conformity but, as in a game, should be a spur to action.

The cue for the teacher-director is basically simple: we must see that each student is participating freely at every moment. The challenge to the teacher or leader is to activize each student in the group while respecting each one's immediate capacity for participation. Though the gifted student will always seem to have more to give, yet if a student is participating to the limit of his or her powers and using abilities to the fullest extent, he or she must be respected, no matter how minute the contribution. The student cannot always do what the teacher hopes, but as progress is made, capacities will enlarge. Work with students where they are, not where you think they should be.

Group participation and agreement remove all the imposed tensions and exhaustions of the competitiveness and open the way for harmony. A highly competitive atmosphere creates artificial tensions, and when competition replaces participation, compulsive action is the result. Sharp competition connotes to even the youngest the idea that he or she has to be better than someone else. When a player feels this, energy is spent on this alone; a player becomes anxious and driven, and fellow players become a threat. Should competition be mistaken for a teaching tool, the whole meaning of playing and games is distorted. Playing allows a person to respond with his or her "total organism within a total environment." Imposed competition makes this harmony impossible, for it destroys the basic nature of playing by occluding self and by separating player from player.

When competition and comparisons run high within an activity, there is an immediate effect on students which shows in their behavior. They fight for status by tearing other people down or develop defensive attitudes, giving detailed "reasons" for the simplest action, bragging, or blaming others for their own deeds. Those who find it impossible to cope with imposed tension turn to apathy and boredom for release. Almost all show signs of fatigue.

Contest and extension, on the other hand, is an organic part of every group activity and gives both tension and release in such a way as to keep the player intact while playing. It is the growing excitement as each problem is solved and more challenging ones appear. Fellow players are needed and welcomed. It can become a process for greater penetration into the environment.

With mastery of each and every problem we move out into larger vistas, for once a problem is solved, it dissolves like cotton candy. When we master crawling, we stand, and when we stand, we walk. This everlasting appearing and dissolving of phenomena develops a greater and greater sight (perceiving) in us with each new set of circumstances. (See all transformation exercises.)

If we are to keep playing, then, natural extension must exist wherein each individual strives to solve consecutively more complicated problems.

These can be solved then, not at the expense of another person and not with the terrible personal emotional loss that comes with compulsive behavior, but by working harmoniously together with others to enhance the group effort or project. It is only when the scale of values has taken competition as the battle cry that danger ensues: the end-result—success—becomes more important than process.

The use of energy in excess of a problem is very evident today. While it is true that some people working on compulsive energies do make successes, they have for the most part lost sight of the pleasure in the activity and are dissatisfied with their achievement. It stands to reason that if we direct all our efforts towards reaching a goal, we stand in grave danger of losing everything on which we have based our daily activities. For when a goal is superimposed on an activity instead of evolving out of it, we often feel cheated when we reach it.

When the goal appears easily and naturally and comes from growth rather than forcing, the end-result, performance or whatever, will be no different from the process that achieved the result. If we are trained only for success, then to gain it we must necessarily use everyone and everything for this end; we may cheat, lie, crawl, betray, or give up all social life to achieve success. How much more certain would knowledge be if it came from and out of the excitement of learning itself? How many human values will be lost and how much will our art forms be deprived if we seek only success?

Therefore, in diverting competitiveness to group endeavor, remembering that process comes before end-result, we free the student-actors to trust the scheme and help them solve the problems of the activity. Both the gifted student who would have success even under high tensions and the student who has little chance to succeed under pressure show a great creative release and the artistic standards within the workshop rise higher when free, healthy energy moves unfettered into the theater activity. Since the acting problems are organic, all are deepened and enriched by each successive experience.

Audience

The role of the audience must become a concrete part of theater training. For the most part, it is sadly ignored. Time and thought are given to the place of the actor, set designer, director, technician, house manager, etc., but the large group without whom their efforts would be for nothing is rarely given the least consideration. The audience is regarded either as a cluster of Peeping Toms to be tolerated by actors and directors or as a many-headed monster sitting in judgment.

The phrase "forget the audience" is a mechanism used by many directors as a means of helping the student-actor to relax on stage. But this attitude probably created the fourth wall. The actor must no more forget the audience than lines, props, or fellow actors!

The audience is the most revered member of the theater. Without an audience there is no theater. Every technique learned by the actor, every curtain and flat on the stage, every careful analysis by the director, every coordinated scene, is for the enjoyment of the audience. They are our guests, fellow players, and the last spoke in the wheel which can then begin to roll. They make the performance meaningful.

When there is understanding of the role of the audience, complete release and freedom come to the player. Exhibitionism withers away when the student-actor begins to see members of the audience not as judges or censors or even as delighted friends but as a group with whom an experience is being shared. When the audience is understood to be an organic part of the theater experience, the student-actor is immediately given a host's sense of responsibility toward them which has in it no nervous tension. The fourth wall disappears, and the lonely looker-in becomes part of the game, part of the experience, and is welcome! This relationship cannot be instilled at dress rehearsal or in a last minute lecture but must, like all other workshop problems, be handled from the very first acting workshop.

If there is agreement that all those involved in the theater should have personal freedom to experience, this must include the audience—each member of the audience must have a personal experience, not artificial stimulation, while viewing a play. If they are to be part of this group agreement, they cannot be thought of as a single mass to be pulled hither and yon by the nose, nor should they have to live someone else's life story (even for one hour) nor identify with the actors and play out tired, handed-down emotions through them. They are separate individuals watching the skills of players (and playwrights), and it is for each and every one of them that the players (and playwrights) must use these skills to create the magical world of a theater reality. This should be a world where every human predicament, riddle, or vision can be explored, a world of magic where rabbits can be pulled out of a hat when needed and even the devil can be conjured up and talked to.

The problems of present-day theater are only now being formulated into questions. When our theater training can enable the future playwrights, directors, and actors to think through the role of the audience as individuals and as part of the process called theater, each one with a right to a thoughtful and personal experience, is it not possible that a whole new form of theater presentation will emerge? Already fine professional improvising theaters have evolved directly from this way of working, delighting audiences night after night with fresh theatrical experiences.

Theater Techniques

Theater techniques are far from sacred. Styles in theater change radically with the passing of years, for *the techniques of the theater are the techniques of communicating*. The actuality of the communication is far more important than the method used. Methods alter to meet the needs of time and place.

When a theater technique or stage convention is regarded as a ritual and the reason for its inclusion in the list of actors' skills is lost, it is useless. An artificial barrier is set up when techniques are separated from direct experiencing. No one separates batting a ball from the game itself.

Techniques are not mechanical devices—a neat little bag of tricks, each neatly labeled, to be pulled out by the actor when necessary. When the form of an art becomes static, these isolated "techniques" presumed to make the form are taught and adhered to strictly. Growth of both individual and form suffer thereby, for unless the student is unusually intuitive, such rigidity in teaching, because it neglects inner development, is invariably reflected in performance.

When the actor knows "in my bones" there are many ways to do and say one thing, techniques will come (as they must) from the total self. For it is by direct, dynamic awareness of an acting experience that experiencing and techniques are spontaneously wedded, freeing the student for the flowing, endless pattern of stage behavior. Theater games do this.

Carrying the Learning Process into Daily Life

The artist must always know where he or she is, perceive and be open to receive the phenomenal world in order to create reality on stage. Since theater training does not have practice hours in the home (it is strongly recommended that no scripts be taken home to memorize, even when rehearsing a formal play), what we seek must be brought to the student-actor within the workshop.[4] This must be done in such a way that it is absorbed, and carried out again (inside the self) to daily living.

Because of the nature of the acting problems, it is imperative to sharpen one's whole sensory equipment, shake loose and free one's self of all preconceptions, interpretations, and assumptions (if one is to solve the problem) so as to be able to make direct and fresh contact with the created environment and the objects and the people within it. When this is learned inside the theater world, it simultaneously produces recognition, direct and fresh contact with the outside world as well. This, then, broadens the student-actors' ability to involve themselves with their phenomenal world and more personally to experience it. Thus *experiencing* is the only actual homework and, once begun, like ripples on water is endless and penetrating in its variations.

When students see people and the way they behave when together, see the color of the sky, hear the sounds in the air, feel the ground beneath

4. See pp. 316–18.

them and the wind on their faces, they get a wider view of their personal world and development in the theater is quickened. The world provides the material for the theater, and artistic growth develops hand-in-hand with one's recognition of it and one's self within it.

Physicalization

The term "physicalization" as used in this book describes the means by which material is presented to the student on a physical, non-verbal level as opposed to an intellectual or psychological approach. "Physicalization" provides the student with a personal concrete experience (which can be grasped) on which further development depends; and it gives the teacher and student a working vocabulary necessary to an objective relationship.

Our first concern with students is to encourage freedom of physical expression, because the physical and sensory relationship with the art form opens the door for insight. Why this is so is hard to say, but be certain that it is so. It keeps the actor in an evolving world of direct perception—an open self in relation to the surrounding world.

Reality as far as we know can only be physical, in that it is received and communicated through the sensory equipment. Through physical relationships all life springs, whether it be a spark of fire from a flint, the roar of the surf hitting the beach, or a child born of man and woman. The physical is the known, and through it we may find our way to the unknown, the intuitive, and perhaps beyond to the human spirit itself.

In any art form we seek the experience of going beyond what we already know. Many of us hear the stirring of the new, and it is the artist who must midwife the new reality that we (the audience) eagerly await. It is sight into this reality that inspires and regenerates us. This is the role of the artist, to give sight. What is believed cannot be our concern, for these matters are of intimate nature, private to the actor and not for public viewing. Nor need we be concerned with an actor's feelings. We are interested only in direct physical communication. Feelings, personal to each of us, are of no use in theater. When energy is absorbed in the physical object, there is no time for "feeling" any more than a quarterback running down the field can be concerned with his clothes or whether he is universally admired. If this seems harsh, be assured that insisting upon this objective (physical) relationship with the art form brings clearer sight and greater vitality to the student-actors. For the energy bound up in fear of exposure is freed (no longer secretive) as the student intuitively realizes no one is peeping at his or her private life or cares where he or she buried the body.

A player can dissect, analyze, intellectualize, or develop a valuable case history for a part, but if one is unable to assimilate it and communicate it physically, it is useless within the theater form. It neither frees the feet nor brings the fire of inspiration to the eyes of those in the audience. The theater is not a clinic, nor should it be a place to gather statistics. The artist must draw upon and express a world that is physical but that transcends objects—more than accurate observation and information, more than the physical object itself, more than the eye can see. We must all find the tools for this expression. "Physicalization" is such a tool.

When a player learns he or she can communicate directly to the audience only through the physical language of the stage, it alerts the whole organism.[5] Players lend themselves to the scheme and let this physical expression carry them wherever it will. In improvisational theater, for instance, where few or no props, costumes or set pieces are used, players learn that a stage reality must have space, texture, depth and substance— in short, physical reality. It is creating this reality out of nothing, so to speak, that makes it possible for the actor to take a first step into the beyond. For the formal theater where sets and props are used, dungeon walls are but painted canvas and treasure chests empty boxes. Here, too, the player can create the theater reality only by making it physical. Whether with prop, costume, or strong emotion the actor can only *show* us.

5. "Direct communication" as used in this text refers to a moment of mutual perceiving.

CHAPTER II

WORKSHOP PROCEDURES

A system of work suggests that, by following a plan of procedure, we can gather enough data and experience to emerge with a new understanding of our medium. Those who work in the theater with any success have their ways for producing results; consciously or unconsciously they have a system. In many highly skilled teacher-directors, this is so intuitive that they have no formula to give another. While this may be exciting to observe, it narrows the field to the naturally "gifted" teacher-director only, and this need not be so. How often upon viewing demonstrations and lectures on the theater have we thought, "The words are right, the principle correct, the results wonderful, but how can we do it?"

All acting problems in this handbook are charted steps in a system of teaching/learning which is a procedure that begins as simply as the realization of the first step on a path or the knowledge that one and one make two. A "how to do it" procedure will become apparent with the use of the material. Yet, no system should be a system. We must tread carefully if we are not to defeat our aims. How can we have a "planned" way of action while trying to find a "free" way?

The answer is clear. It is the demands of the art form itself that must point the way for us, shaping and regulating our work and reshaping all of us as well to meet the impact of this great force. Our constant concern then is to keep a moving, living reality for ourselves, not to labor compulsively for an end-result. Whenever we meet, whether in workshops or in performance, in that meeting must be the moment of process, the moment of living theater. If we let this happen, the techniques for teaching, direction, acting, developing material for scene improvisation, or the way to handle a formal play will come from our very core and appear as if by accident. It is out of willingness to understand organic process that our work becomes alive. The exercises used and developed in this handbook grew out of this focus. For those of us who serve the theater and not a system of work, what we seek will evolve as a result of what we do to find it.

Especially in the new and exciting development of scene improvisations is this true. Only from meeting and acting upon the changing, moving present can improvisation be born. The material and substance of scene improvisation are not the work of any one person or any one writer but come out of the cohesion of player acting upon player. The quality, range, vitality, and life of this material are in direct ratio to the process the individual student is going through and is actually experiencing in spontaneity, organic growth, and intuitive response.

This chapter attempts to clarify for the teacher-director how to organize material for training in the theater conventions and how we can all stay away from rote teaching and meet in the area of the yet unknown. Though many may pull away, fearful of leaving the familiar cage, some of us will find each other and together preserve the vital spirit of the theater.

To come to this understanding, the teacher must keep a dual point of view towards himself or herself and the student: (1) observation of the handling of the material presented in its obvious or outward use as training for the stage; (2) constant close scrutiny of whether or not the material is penetrating and reaching a deeper level of response—the intuitive.

To keep the word "intuitive" from becoming a catch-all word which we throw around or use for old concepts, use it to denote that area of knowledge which is beyond the restrictions of culture, race, education, psychology, and age; deeper than the "survival dress" of mannerisms, prejudices, intellectualisms, and borrowings most of us wear to live out our daily lives.[1] Let us rather embrace one another in our basic humanness and strive in the workshops to release this humanness in ourselves and our students.

1. Today the area commonly referred to as "the right brain."

Here, then, the walls of our cage, prejudices, frames of reference, and pre-determined right and wrong dissolve. We look with an "inward eye." In this way there will be no fear that a system becomes a system.

Problem-Solving

The problem-solving technique used in workshop gives mutual objective focus to teacher and student. In its simplest terms it is *giving problems to solve problems*. It does away with the need for the teacher to analyze, intellectualize, dissect a student's work on a personal basis. This eliminates the necessity of the student having to go through the teacher or the teacher having to go through the student to learn. It gives both of them direct contact with the material, thereby developing relationship rather than dependencies between them. It makes experiencing possible and smoothes the way for people of unequal backgrounds to work together.

When one has to go through another to learn something, the learning is colored by the subjective needs of both student and teacher, often creating personal difficulties. The whole experience is altered in such a way that direct experiencing is not possible. The approval/disapproval critique of authority becomes more important than learning and students are kept in old frames of reference (their own or the teacher's). Behaviorisms and attitudes remain unchanged. Problem-solving prevents this.

Problem-solving performs the same function in creating organic unity and freedom of action as does the game and generates great excitement by constantly provoking the question of procedures at the moment of crisis, thus keeping all participating members open for experiencing.

Since there is no right or wrong way to solve a problem, and since the answer to every problem is prefigured in the problem itself (and must be to be a true problem), continuous work on and the solving of these problems opens everyone to their own source and power. How student-actors solve a problem is personal to them, and as in a game, they can run, shout, climb or turn somersaults as long as they stay with the problem. All distortions of character and personality slowly fade away, for true self-identity is far more exciting than the falseness of withdrawal, egocentricity, exhibitionism and need for social approval.

This includes the teacher-director or group leader as well. You must be constantly alerted to bring in fresh acting problems to solve any difficulties that come up. You become the diagnostician, so to speak, developing personal skills, first in finding what students need for their work and second, finding the exact problem that will work for each student. For example, if a group cannot handle being more than four together on stage, creating cluttered stage pictures and all talking at once, presenting GIVE AND TAKE, p. 149, will clear this up. Once the problem in GIVE AND TAKE is solved, it can only result in students organically understanding some of the problems of blocking. From then on, all you need to do (should the difficulty arise again) is to side coach "Give and Take!" for the players to understand and act accordingly.

And so with all the other exercises. Problems to solve problems, voice projection, characterization, stage business, developing material for scene improvisation—all are manageable through this way of working. Dogmatism is avoided by not giving lectures on acting; language is used for the purpose of clarification of the problem. This can be considered a non-verbal system of teaching insofar as the student-actor gathers data within a first-hand experience. This mutual involvement with the problem instead of each other frees the air of personalities, judgment values, recriminations, fawning, etc. and is replaced by trust and relationship making artistic detachment a strong probability.

When the youngest actors are told that they will never be asked a question that they cannot answer or given a problem that they cannot solve, they can well believe it.

Focus (The Point of Concentration)

Focus or Point of Concentration is central to the system covered in this handbook. In all previous editions of this book, point of concentration was the term used. But focus, the more active word, was ultimately chosen to replace point of concentration and this is reflected throughout the new edition. Focus releases group power and individual genius. Through focus, theater, the most complicated of art forms, can be taught to the young, the old, to plumbers, schoolteachers, physicists and housewives. Focus frees all to enter into an exciting, creative adventure, making theater meaningful in the community, neighborhood and home.

The focus of an exercise does the work for the student. It is the "ball" with which all play the game. While its uses may be manifold, the four following points help clarify it for use in workshops. (1) It helps to isolate segments of complex and overlapping theater techniques (necessary to performance) so as to thoroughly explore them. (2) It gives the control, the artistic discipline in improvisation, where otherwise unchanneled creativity might become a destructive rather than a stabilizing force. (3) It provides the student with a focus on a changing, moving single point ("Keep your eye on the ball") within the acting problem, and this develops the capacity for involvement with the problem and the relationship with fellow players in solving it. Both are necessary to scene improvisation. It acts as a catalyst between player and player and between player and problem. (4) This singleness of focus on a moving point used in solving the problem—whether it be the very first session where one counts the boards or chairs (EXPOSURE) or later, more complicated ones—frees the student for spontaneous action and provides the vehicle for an organic rather than a cerebral experience. It makes perceiving rather than preconception possible and acts as a springboard into the intuitive.

(1) Presenting material in a segmented way frees a player for action at every stage of development. It sorts theater experience into such minute (simple and familiar) bits of itself that each detail is easily recognizable and does not overwhelm or frighten anyone away. In the beginning a focus may be a simple handling of a cup, a rope, a door. It becomes more complex as the acting problems progress, and with it the student-actor will eventually be led to explore character, emotion, and complicated events. This focusing upon a detail in the over-all complexity of the art form, as in a game, gives everyone something to do on stage, creates playing by totally absorbing the players and shutting off fear of approval/disapproval. Out of this something to do (playing), teaching, directing, acting, and scene improvi-

sation techniques arrive. As each part (detail) unfolds, it becomes a step towards a new integrated whole for both the individual's total structure and the theater structure as well. By working intensely with parts, the group is also working on the whole.

With each acting problem intrinsically interrelated to another, the teacher keeps two, three, and sometimes more guide points in mind simultaneously. While it is most essential that the teacher be aware of the part of the theater experience explored in each acting problem and where it fits into the whole fabric, the student need not be so informed. Many stage techniques may never be brought up as separate exercises but will develop along with the others. Thus rendering of character, for instance, which is carefully and deliberately avoided in the early training, grows stronger with each exercise, even though the main focus is on something else.[2] This avoids cerebral activity around an acting problem and makes it organic (unified).

(2) The focus of an exercise acts as an additional boundary (rules of the game) within which the player must work and within which constant crises must be met. Just as the jazz musician creates a personal discipline by staying with the beat while playing with other musicians, so the control in the focus provides the theme and unblocks the student to act upon each crisis as it arrives. As the student need only work on focus, it permits direction of full sensory perception on a single problem so a student is not befuddled with more than one thing at a time, while actually doing many. Occupied with focus, the student moves unhesitatingly to anything that presents itself, functioning without fear or resistance. Because each problem is solvable and is also a focus outside the student which can be seen and grasped, each successive focus acts as a stabilizing force, soon freeing everyone to "trust the scheme" and let go, giving themselves over to the art form.

(3) All players, while individually working on the focus, must at the same time, as in a game, gather around the object (ball) and play together to solve the problem, acting upon the focus and interrelating. This makes a

2. See Chapter XII.

direct line from player to problem (similar to the line from teacher and student to problem). This total individual involvement with the object (event or project) makes relationship with others possible. Without this object involvement, it would be necessary to become involved with one's self or one another. In making ourselves or another player the object (the ball), there is grave danger of reflection and absorption. Thus we might push each other around the field (the stage) and exhibit ourselves instead of playing ball. Relations keep individuality intact, allowing breathing space (play) to exist between everyone, and prevent us from using ourselves or each other for our subjective needs. Involving ourselves in the focus absorbs our subjective needs and frees us for relation. This makes stage action possible and clears the stage of playwriting, emoting, and psychodrama. In time, when artistic detachment is a fact, we can then make ourselves or others the object without misuse.

(4) The point of concentration is the magical focus that preoccupies and blanks the mind (the known), cleans the slate, and acts as a plumb-bob into our very own centers (the intuitive), breaking through the walls that keep us from the unknown, ourselves, and each other. With singleness of focus, everyone is intent on observing the solving of the problem, and there is no split of personality. For both players and audience the gap between watching and participating closes up as subjectivity gives way to communication and becomes objectivity. Spontaneity cannot come out of duality, out of being "watched" whether it be the player watching himself or herself or being fearful of outside watchers.

This combination of individuals mutually focusing and mutually involved creates a true relation, a sharing of a fresh experience. Here old frames of reference topple over as the new structure (growth) pushes its way upwards, allowing freedom of individual response and contribution. Individual energy is released, trust is generated, inspiration and creativity appear as all the players play the game and solve the problem together. "Sparks" fly between people when this happens.

Unfortunately, understanding the focus of an exercise as an idea is not the same as letting it work for us (accepting it wholeheartedly). Time is needed if the principle of focus is to become a part of the total integration of ourselves and our work. While many people concede the value of using focus, it is not easy to restructure one's self and give up the familiar, and so some resist in it every way they can. Whatever the psychological reasons for this, it will show itself in refusal to accept group responsibilities, clowning, playwriting, jokes, immature evaluation, lack of spontaneity, interpretation of everyone else's work to meet a personal frame of reference, etc. Students with high resistance will try to manipulate fellow players to work for them and their ideas alone rather than entering into group agreement. It oftens shows itself in resentment of what is considered a limitation imposed by the teacher or sometimes in referring to the game exercises as "kid stuff." Exhibitionism and egocentricity continue as the student-actor ad-libs, "acts," plays "characters," and "emotes" rather than becoming involved in the problem at hand.

It is axiomatic that the student who resists working on the focus of an exercise will never be able to improvise and will be a continuous discipline problem. This is so because improvising is openness to contact with the environment and each other and willingness to play. It is acting upon environment and allowing others to act upon present reality, as in playing a game.

Sometimes resistance is hidden to the student-actor and shows itself in a great deal of verbalization, erudition, argument, and questioning as to "how to do it" within the workshops. With skilled and clever players this is often difficult to pinpoint and uncover. Lack of discipline and resistance to the focus of an exercise go hand in hand, for discipline can only grow out of total involvement with the event, object, or project.[3]

However, at no time is the student-actor to misuse the stage, no matter what the subjective resistance may be. A firm hand must be used, not to attack or impose one's will, but to maintain the integrity of the art form. If students train long enough, they will realize this way is not a threat to them, will not destroy their "individuality"; for as the transcending power

3. See "Discipline Is Involvement," pp. 264–66.

in keeping the focus of an exercise is felt by everyone and results in greater theatrical skills and deeper self-knowledge, their resistance will in time be overcome.

Evaluation

Evaluation takes place after each individual team has finished working on an acting problem. It is the time to establish objective vocabulary, and direct communication made possible through non-judgmental attitudes, group assistance in solving a problem, and clarification of the focus of an exercise. All the members of the workshop as well as the teacher-director enter into it. This group help in solving problems removes the burden of anxiety and guilt from the player. Fear of judgments (one's own as well as those from others) slowly leaves the players as good/bad, right/wrong reveal themselves to be the very chains that bind us, and they soon disappear from everyone's vocabulary and thinking. In this loss of fear rests release; in this release rests the abandonment of restrictive self-controls (self-protection) by players. As they abandon these and lend themselves willingly to a new experience, they trust the scheme and take a further step into the environment.

The teacher-director must also evaluate objectively. Was concentration complete or incomplete? Did they solve the problem? Did they communicate or interpret? Did they show or tell? Did they act or react? Did they let something happen?

Evaluation that limits itself to a personal prejudice is going nowhere. "Policemen don't eat celery," or "People don't stand on their heads in a situation like that," or "He was good/bad, right/wrong"—these are the walls around our garden. It would be better to ask: "Did he show us who he was? Why not? Did he stay with the problem? Whose good/bad, right/wrong— mine, Jonathan's, or yours? Did he keep his focus?"[4]

In time, mutual trust makes it possible for students to give themselves over to the evaluation. Able to keep a *single* purpose in mind, for they no

4. See p. 275.

longer need to watch themselves, they become eager to know exactly where the problem might have gotten away from them. When they are the audience, they evaluate for fellow actors; when players, they listen to the evaluation given by the student audience to them, for they stand with their peers.

The kind of evaluation made by the student audience is dependent upon their understanding of the focus of the exercise and the problem to be solved. If the student is to have a greater understanding of the stage work, it is most essential that the teacher-director does not make the evaluation but, rather, asks the questions which all answer—including the teacher. Did they playwrite? Did she pretend or make it real? Did he move the object or let the object move him? Did he cry with his feet? Did she make contact or make assumptions? Did they solve the problem?

The student audience is not to sit by and be entertained, nor are they to protect or attack the players. If they are to help one another, Evaluation must be on what was actually communicated, not what was "filled in" (by either the actor or the audience) and not any personal interpretation of how something should be done. This furthers the whole point of process as well, for it keeps the audience busy watching not a play or story but the solving of a problem. As the student audience come to understand their role, the communication lines from audience to actor as well as from actor to audience are strengthened. Those in the audience change from passive observers to active participants in the problem.

"Assume nothing. Evaluate only what you have actually seen!" This keeps throwing the ball back to the players and sharpens their eye and their hand in finer selectivity in clarifying the stage reality. The student audience does not compare, compete, or clown; they are there to evaluate the acting problem presented and not a performance of a scene. Thus audience responsibility for the actors becomes part of the organic growth of the student. When a scene does evolve, it is added pleasure for all.[5]

The point of accepting a direct communication without interpretation and assumption is difficult for students to understand in the beginning

5. See "Points of Observation," No. 4, in the BEGIN AND END exercise, pp. 126–27.

work. It may be necessary to work hard to get this point across. Asking each member of the audience, "What did the player communicate to you?" may clarify this point. It is at this time that what the student-audience "thought" the player did or assumed was done out of the student's frame of reference can be identified as interpretation rather than the receiving of a direct communication. A player on stage either communicates or does not. The audience sees or does not see the space objects held. This is all we ask. The very simplicity of this is what confounds most students. The player who did not make a direct communication to the audience will make every effort to do so, the next time on stage. If the audience did not receive a communication, they didn't—that is all.

Sometimes members of the student audience hold back on Evaluation, for the following reasons: first, they do not understand the focus of the exercise and so do not know what to look for; second, many students confuse Evaluation with "criticism" and are reluctant to "attack" their fellow students. Once it is understood, however, that Evaluation is an important part of the process and is vital to the understanding of the problem for both the actor and the audience, the reticence which some students might feel about expressing themselves will disappear. Third, the teacher-director may not truly "trust the scheme" and may be unknowingly squelching the students' Evaluation by taking it over. The teacher-director must become the audience together with the student-actors in the deepest sense of the word for Evaluation to be meaningful.

Side-Coaching

Side-coaching alters the traditional relationship of teacher-student, creating a moving relation. Side-coaching allows the teacher-director an opportunity to step into the excitement of playing (learning) in the same space, with the same focus, as the players.

It is a method used in holding the player to the focus of an exercise whenever he or she may have wandered away. (*Keep your eye on the ball!*) This gives players self-identity within the activity and allows functioning at a fresh moment of experience, and further, it makes the teacher-director a fellow player.

Side-coaching keeps the stage space alive for the student-actor. It is the voice of the director seeing the needs of the overall presentation; at the same time it is the voice of the teacher seeing the individual student-actor's needs within the group and on the stage. It is the teacher-director working on a problem together with the student as part of the group effort.

Side-coaching reaches the total organism, for it arises spontaneously out of what is emerging on stage and is given at the time players are in action. Because it is a further method of keeping the student and teacher relating and must therefore be objective, great care must be taken to see that it does not disintegrate into an approval/disapproval involvement instead—a command to be obeyed!

A simple, direct calling out is best. *Share the stage picture! See the buttons on John's coat! Share your voice with the audience! Write with a pen, not your fingers!* (When writing is done early in training, most players pretend by using fingers.) *You walked through a table! Contact! See it with your feet! No playwriting!* Such comments are worth a dozen lectures on blocking, projection, giving reality to space objects, etc., for they are given as part of the process, and the student-actor effortlessly moves out of a huddled position, gives the table space, and sees a fellow player. Our voice reaches the total self, and the player moves accordingly.

The player who looks out inquiringly when first hearing our Side-coaching need only be coached *Listen to my voice but don't pay any attention to it*, or *Listen to my voice but keep right on going. Just stay with the problem!*

Side-coaching gives the student-actor self-identity within the activity because it keeps players from wandering off into isolation within a subjective world: it keeps one in present time, in the time of process. It keeps each player aware of the group and the self within the group.[6]

6. See "Detachment," p. 358. See also the "Glossary of Side-Coaching Phrases," p. 374.

Do not confuse players with a barrage of Side-coaching. Wait for the emerging play. Remember you are a fellow player.

Side-coaching is also used to end an exercise when necessary. When "One minute!" is called out, the players must solve the problem they are working on within an approximation of that time.

Teams and Presentation of the Problem

All the exercises are done with teams chosen at random. Students must learn to relate with everyone and anyone. Dependencies in the smallest areas must be constantly observed and broken. This is related to the acting itself, for many actors become dependent upon mannerisms as well as on people and things. Removing crutches whenever they appear helps students to avoid developing these problems. This is why changing rooms, using circle staging as well as proscenium, and improvising in front of "cameras" and "microphones" are highly recommended.

"Counting off" is a simple device accepted by all age groups in dividing up for teams. If the teams fall into the same groupings too often, then alter the method of selection (vary numbers in counting), so that students are never quite certain just where to sit in order to fall in with their friends. This counting method eliminates the negative exposure which the slower members of a group may experience if the teams are chosen by the students themselves (captain system or whatever). It is very painful for a student to sit and wait to be asked to join a team, and such procedures should be avoided in the beginning workshops. This is as true of the student-actor of fifty as it is for one eight years old.

However, if there is a good deal of uneven development within the group in the beginning of workshops, it may be necessary to match players so as to keep everyone with as challenging partners as possible. Ways must be found to do this without pointing it up at all.

Presenting the Problem

The teacher-director is advised to present the acting problem quickly and simply. Clarify the focus of the exercise and cover the material given, just as you would present the playing of a game. Going into details now might become a way of *showing how* and prevent self-discovery in the students. Show no concern if all do not seem to "get it" immediately. Working on the problem itself and the group preparation (with teacher-director guiding when necessary) before doing the exercise will bring clarification to many students. If there is still confusion, Evaluation will make it quite clear for those who are slower to understand.

Along the same line, do not tell students why they are given a problem. This is particularly important with young actors and lay actors. Such verbalized predeterminations place students in a defensive position, and their concentration will be on giving the teacher what the teacher wants instead of working at the problem. Indeed, there should be no verbalization of "what we are trying to do" for the student personally. All language is to be directed to clarify the structure of the problem alone. Let the student-actor stay with what seem to be the simple externals of the problem to know in time what Neva L. Boyd termed "the stimulation and release that is happening to his full nature."

PHYSICAL SET-UP OF THE WORKSHOPS

Environment in Workshop Training

"Environment" in workshop training refers to both the physical set-up and the atmosphere existing within that set-up. Physically, whenever possible workshop sessions should be held in a well-equipped theater. While "well-equipped" does not mean an elaborate stage, the workshop area should have at least one lighting dimmer and a simple sound system (amplifier, speaker, phonograph, perhaps a microphone). If such a physical set-up is provided, then student-actors are given full opportunity to develop skills which add up to the total theater experience: acting, developing scene material, and creating technical effects.

The exercises in this handbook allow for set pieces, costumes, sound effects, and lighting to be used spontaneously during the solving of the problems. The elements needed to achieve these effects should be readily available to your student-actors as they prepare their situations. Large wooden set blocks are extremely useful, since they can be quickly transformed into counters, thrones, altars, sofas, or whatever called for. A costume rack with specially selected costume parts should be close at hand, loaded with hats of all types (chef, police, medieval, clown, etc.), cloaks, robes, scarves, and a beard or two. The sound corner should be equipped with some gadgets for creating manual sound effects (cowbells, wooden sticks or blocks, tin cans, chains, buckets, etc.) as well as a few sound-effects recordings such as autos starting, trains, sirens, wind and storms, etc. Each team should choose one member to act as technician and provide whatever sound or lighting effects may be needed while improvising (see Chapter VIII).

While it is true that improvisational theaters, for the most part, use few or no real props or set pieces, the actor who is training specifically for this form should handle real props as suggested by some of the exercises in the text. Learning to use sets, costumes, lights, etc. with no more time for planning than the actors have for structuring their scenes is simply a way of stirring up action in another area of the theater—another road to the intuitive.

The atmosphere during the workshop session should always be one of pleasure and relaxation. Student-actors are supposed to absorb not only the techniques they gain from the workshop experience but also the accompanying moods.

Preparation for the Acting Problem

The student-actors should make their own decisions and set up their own physical world around the problems given them. This is one of the keys to this work. The players create their own theater reality and become masters of their "fate," so to speak (at least for fifteen minutes).

Once you, the director or group leader, have introduced the acting problem, you must retire to and become part of the group, moving around from group to group during the early workshop sessions, clarifying the focus and procedures wherever necessary, and helping individual members to group agreement.

In Orientation, for example, even the simplest group decision on such things as group listening (p. 57) will be hard to come by. Individuals on the team will toss ideas back and forth. Some will try to tell everyone "how to do it." Moving from team to team, the teacher-director will be able to help them to come to group agreement.

This time may also be used to clarify any misunderstandings about the problem. In the first workshop, for instance, many will ask, "How do I show listening?" Do not allow anyone in the group to answer this and remain noncommittal yourself, for everyone physicalizes "listening" through their own individual structure and there should be no chance for imitation. Encourage them to "just listen." They will soon discover that they already know how to "listen" (or "see" or "taste").

The simple group agreement of the first exercise will open the way to far more complicated situations in later exercises. If the groundwork is carefully laid, agreement on later problems—such as place (Where), character (Who), and problem (What)—will come more easily with each successive exercise.

Again, for those interested in the development of scene improvisation, this is the only way of working. Because of the nature of this art form, the finding of and use of material for scenes must evolve out of the group itself, during the process of solving a problem along with every other technique the student-actors are developing.

Timing

An acting problem must be ended when the action has stopped and the players are simply ad-libbing, making jokes, etc. This is the result of not working on the problem or not playing with one another. Side-coaching "One minute!" will let students know they must finish their scene or end their problem. This sometimes accelerates action, and the scene may continue for a while. When this does not happen, it is sometimes necessary to then call, "Half-minute!" and sometimes it may be necessary to stop the improvisation immediately.

In the early work inform students that when "One minute!" is called, they must try to solve the problem they are working on within that time. This, then, revives the focus for them and usually accelerates the scene simultaneously, which becomes an excellent point to bring up in Evaluation. When players are working on the focus, "One minute!" rarely has to be called. Interest as to what is happening on the stage remains high, as in playing a game.

Calling "One minute!" develops an intuitive sense of pace and timing in players. For this reason it is sometimes useful to allow the student audience or chosen members of it to call time. When this is done, group evaluation on this point should be made. As a group develops this time sense, "One minute!" need rarely be called, for the players bring their scenes to their natural endings.

Timing is perceiving (sensing); it is an organic response which cannot be taught by lecture. It is the ability to handle the multiple stimuli occurring within a setting. It is the host attuned to the individual needs of the many guests. It is the cook putting a dash of this and a flick of that into a stew. It is children playing a game, alerted to each other and to the environment around them. It is to know objective reality and to be free to respond to it.

Labels and/or Concepts

The acting workshop is concerned with process, not information. And so, the teacher-director must avoid using labels in early sessions. Keep away from technical terms such as "blocking," "projection," etc. Instead, substitute phrases such as "share the stage picture," "share your voice," etc. Far from eliminating analytical thought, the avoiding of labels will free it, for it allows the player to "share" in his or her own way; for imposing a label before its organic meaning is fully understood prevents direct experiencing, and there are no data to analyze. For instance, only when "share your voice" is understood by the actor organically and dynamically after months of use as the responsibility to the audience (making them part of the game) should the term "projection" be introduced. A label is static and prevents process.

In some cases, the workshop will contain student-actors with previous theater experience who will initially use the conventional stage technology. However, these terms will gradually disappear as the teacher-director establishes the general vocabulary to be used throughout training. Because the whole workshop system is based on self discovery, the undesirability of labels should be very clear in the teacher-director's mind at the outset.

Avoiding the How

It must be clear in everybody's mind from the very first workshop session that How a problem is solved must grow out of the stage relationships, as in a game. It must happen at the actual moment of stage life (Right now!) and not through any pre-planning. Pre-planning how to do something throws the players into "performance" and/or playwriting, making the development of improvisers impossible and preventing the player in the formal theater from spontaneous stage behavior.

In almost every case a student new in the theater workshops thinks performance is expected. Sometimes the group leader also is confused on this point and mistakes "performance" for growth (although in some cases this can be true). With new students pre-planning results in awkwardness and fear; with the skilled, it continues their old patterns of work. In either case very little is learned, for at best whatever comes to the student must be but a trickle struggling its way through old frames of reference and set attitudes.

Performance is confused with learning, end result with process. No matter to what extent the need for spontaneity and the taboo of the planned How are stressed, it is a very difficult point to grasp and will require constant clarification for everyone. However, when everyone understands that How kills spontaneity and prevents new and untried experiences, they will avoid conscious repetition of old actions and dialogue and trite ideas, either "borrowed" from the current TV show or from old plays they themselves have been in.

Direct communication prevents How. This is why in Evaluation each individual student-audience member is asked to be open for communication. The player makes the communication or does not, the audience sees it or does not. This, then, continues to clear up the whole problem of How; for members of the audience cannot then decide How in their terms (interpretation) the player should have made the communication.

Pre-planning How constitutes the use of old material even if that material is but five minutes old. Pre-planned work on stage is the result of a rehearsal even if that rehearsal was but a few seconds of mental visualization. Any group of student-actors laughingly give up their hold on How when they realize that if they want to rehearse and perform they should be with a group doing a show instead of a workshop. For the unskilled, whose rehearsal can at best bring only anxious performance, a great sense of relief is evident when they realize all they have to do is play the game.

Real performance, however, opens players up for deeper experiences. When this moment arrives, it is apparent to everyone. It is the moment of the total organism working at its fullest capacity—right now! Like a flash fire, real performance is all-consuming, burning away all the subjective needs of the player and creating a moment of great excitement throughout the theater. When this occurs, spontaneous applause will come from the workshop members. (See "Performance," p. 365).

Pre-planning is necessary only to the extent that the problems should have a structure. The structure is the Where, Who, and What plus the focus. It is the field upon which the game is played that is pre-planned. How the game will go can be known only when the players are out on the field.

REMINDERS AND POINTERS

The following list of reminders and pointers for both teacher (or group leader) and student rightfully should be weighed after the exercises have been used. However, a quick glance at them now will alert everyone, and the list should be reviewed while a group is working through the exercises.

1. Do not rush student-actors. Some students particularly need to feel

unhurried. When necessary, quietly coach. "Take your time." "We all have lots of time." "We are with you."

2. Interpretation and assumption keep the player from direct communication. This is why we say *show*, don't *tell*. Telling is verbally or in some other indirect way indicating what one is doing. This then puts the work upon the audience or the fellow actor, and the student learns nothing. Showing means direct contact and direct communication. It does not mean passively pointing to something.

3. Note that many exercises have subtle variations. This is important, and they should be understood, for each variation is solving a very different problem for the student. As you go through the work, you as teacher-director will find that you may make your own variations to solve problems.

4. Repeat problems at different points in the work, to see how student-actors handle early work differently. Also, this is important when relationships with the environment become fuzzy and detail is lost.

5. How we do something is the *process of doing* (right now!). Pre-planning How makes process impossible and so becomes resistance to the focus of the exercise, and no "explosion" or spontaneity can take place, making any change or alterations in the student-actor impossible. True improvisation re-shapes and alters the student-actor through the act of improvising itself. Penetration into the focus, connection, and a live relation with fellow players result in a change, alteration, or new understanding for one or the other or both. In time, during the solving of the acting problem the student becomes aware of being acted upon and of acting, thereby creating process and change within his or her stage life. The intuition gained remains with the player in everyday life, for whenever a circuit is opened for anyone, so to speak, it is usable everywhere.

6. Without exception, all exercises are over the moment the problem is solved. This may happen in one minute or in twenty, depending on the growing skills of students in playing. The solving of the problem is the scene's life force. Continuing a scene after the problem is solved is *cerebration* instead of *process*.

7. Try always to keep an environment in the workshop where all can

find their own nature (including the teacher or group leader) without imposition. Growth is natural to everyone. Be certain that no one is blocked off in the workshops by an inflexible method of treatment.

8. A group of individuals who act, agree, and share together create strength and release knowledge surpassing the contribution of any single member. This includes the teacher and group leader.

9. The energy released in solving the problem, flowing through the Where, Who, and What, forms the scene.

10. If during workshop sessions students become restless and static in their work, it is a danger sign. Refreshment and a new focus is needed. End the problem immediately and use some simple warm-up (object) exercise or game. Skip around the handbook and use anything that will keep up the vitality level of the group. Just be careful not to use any advanced exercises until the group is ready for them. Be certain that Orientation and Where exercises are given students in the beginning work, however. This is as true for the professional company as it is for the lay actor and newcomer to the theater.

11. Become familiar with the many game books useful in this work.

12. Remember that a lecture will never accomplish what an experience will for student-actors.

13. Be flexible. Alter your plans on a moment's notice if it is advisable to do so, for when the foundation upon which this work is based is understood and you know your role as teacher, you can find an appropriate theater game and/or games to meet an immediate problem.

14. Just as you watch your students for restlessness and fatigue, so you must watch yourself. If following workshops you find yourself drained and exhausted, go carefully over your work and see what you are doing to create this problem. A fresh experience can only create refreshment.

15. While a team is working on stage, the teacher-director must observe audience reaction as well as the players' work. The audience (including yourself) should be checked for interest levels and restlessness; the actors must interrelate, communicate physically, and be seen and heard as they solve the acting problem. When an audience is restless, uninterested, the actors are responsible for this.

16. The heart of improvisation is transformation.

17. Avoid giving examples. While they are sometimes helpful, the reverse is more often true, for the student is bound to give back what has already been experienced.

18. If the environment in the workshop is joyous and free of authoritarianism, everyone will play and become as open as young children.

19. The teacher-director must be careful to always stay with the focus. The tendency to discuss character, scene, etc. critically and psychologically is often difficult to stop. The focus keeps both the teacher and the student from wandering too far afield.

"Did he solve the problem?"

"He was good."

"But did he solve the problem?"

20. No outside device is to be used during playing. All stage action must come out of what is actually happening on stage. If actors invent an outside device to create change this is avoidance of relation and the problem itself.

21. Actors in improvisational theater, like the dancer, musician, or athlete, require constant workshops to keep alert and agile and to find new material.

22. Act, don't react. This includes the teacher and group leader as well. To react is protective and constitutes withdrawal from the environment. Since we are seeking to reach out, a player must act upon environment, which in turn acts upon player, catalytic action thus creating interaction that makes process and change (building of a scene) possible. This is a most important point of view for members of the workshop to have.

23. If the student-actors are to develop their own material for scene improvisations, group selection and agreement on the simplest objects in the beginning work are essential to developing this group skill.

24. The response of an audience is spontaneous (even when the response is boredom), and with rare exception (as when large numbers of friends and relatives are present), can be considered just. If the actors realize that they do not face a "put-on" response, they can then play with the audience as they would with another team. An actor can be reassured,

"If they were a bad audience, then, of course, they deserve to be punished."

25. Watch for excessive activity in early sessions of workshop; discourage all performing, all cleverness. Students with previous training, natural leadership, or special talent will often ignore the focus just as the fearful one will resist it. Keep everyone's attention focused on the problem at all times. This discipline will bring the timid ones to fuller awareness and channel the freer ones towards greater personal development.

26. Let all scenes develop out of the agreed stage environment. The players must help each other "make do" with what is at hand if they are to truly improvise. As in games, the student-actors can play only by giving complete attention to the environment.

27. Discipline imposed from the outside (emotional tug-of-war for position) and not growing out of involvement with the problem produces inhibited or rebellious action. On the other hand discipline freely chosen for the sake of the activity becomes responsible action, creative action; it takes imagination and dedication to be self-disciplined. When the dynamics are understood and not superimposed, rules are abided by, and it is more fun that way.

28. Keep the fine line between emoting and perceiving always clear within the workshop by insisting upon concise physical expression (physicalizing) and not vague or stale feeling.

29. The sensory equipment of students is developed with every tool at our command, not to train for mechanical accuracy in observation, but for strengthening perception towards their expanding world.

30. Unless needed to solve a specific problem in a play, remembered experiences (recalls) are avoided as the group works for immediate (right now) spontaneous ones. Every individual has enough muscular memory and stored-away experience that can be used in a present-time situation without deliberately abstracting it from the total organism.

31. If student and teacher are freed from ritual and authoritarianism and allowed to share this freeing of their creativity, no one need dissect and examine their emotions. They will know that there are many ways of express-

ing something—that cups, for instance, are held differently by different people and different groups.

32. By helping to free the student-actor for the learning process and by inspiring communication in the theater with dedication and passion, it will be found that the average person will not fail to respond to the art form.

33. Warm-ups should be used before, during, and after workshop sessions when necessary. They are brief acting exercises that refresh the student as well as catering to particular needs as seen by the teacher-director during each session.

34. Stage life comes to the player by giving life to the object. Giving life to the object prevents the player from mirroring the self.

35. Invention is not the same as spontaneity. A person may be most inventive without being spontaneous. The explosion does not take place when invention is merely cerebral and therefore only a part or abstraction of our total selves.

36. The teacher-director must learn to know when the student-actor is actually experiencing, or little will be gained by the acting problems. Ask the player!

37. Never use the advanced acting exercises as a bribe. Wait until students are ready to receive them.

38. Allow students to find their own material.

39. Self-discovery is the foundation of this way of working.

40. Do not be impatient. Don't take over. Never force a nascent quality into false maturity through imitation or intellectualization. Every step is essential for growth. A teacher can only estimate growth, for each individual is a personal "center of development."

41. The more blocked, the more opinionated the student, the longer the process. The more blocked and opinionated the teacher or group leader, the longer the process.

42. Tread gently. Keep all doors open for future growth. This includes the teacher and leader of the group as well.

43. Do not be concerned if a student seems to be straying far from your idea of what should be happening to him or to her. When students trust

the scheme and have pleasure in what they are doing, they will give up the bonds that keep them from release and full response.

44. Everyone who involves himself or herself and responds with his or her total organism to an art form usually gives back what is commonly called talented and creative behavior. When players respond joyously, effortlessly, you will know that the theater is, then, in their very bones.

45. Always work to achieve the universal selection, the essence understood by all who see it.

46. Ad-libbing and wordiness during the solving of problems constitutes withdrawal from the problem, the environment, and each other. Verbalizing becomes an abstraction from total organic response and is used in place of contact to obscure the self, and when cleverly done, this is difficult to catch. Dialogue, on the other hand, is simply a further expression of a total human communication (connection) onstage.

47. Train actors to handle theatrical reality, not illusion.

48. Do not teach. *Expose* students to the theatrical environment through playing, and they will find their own way.

49. Nothing is separate. In the unity of things rests growth and knowledge. Technical facts about the theater are available to everyone through many books. We seek far more than information about the theater.

50. In the seed rests the flowering tree. So must the acting problems hold within them the prefiguring of their results from which "the individual in the art and the art in the individual" can flourish.

51. To evolve problems to solve problems requires a person with rich knowledge of the field.

52. Creativity is not rearranging; it is transformation.

53. Sentiment, tear-jerking, etc. are cultural weapons. On our stages, let us cry and laugh not from old frames of reference but from the sheer joy of watching human beings explore a greater beyond.

54. Imagination belongs to the intellect. When we ask someone to imagine something, we are asking them to go into their own frame of reference, which might be limited. When we ask them to *see*, we are placing them in an objective situation where reaching out into the environment can take place, in which further awareness is possible.

55. Tension should be a natural part of the activity between players without every scene ending in a conflict to make something happen (release can come out of agreement). This is not easily understood. A rope between players might set up opposite goals (conflict) in a tug-of-war, yet a rope between players pulling them all up a mountain could have similar tension with all pulling together towards the same goal. Tension and release are implicit in problem-solving.

56. For improvisational theater, a player must always see and direct all action to fellow players and not to the character being played. In this way each player will always know to whom to throw the ball, and players can help each other out. During performance and workshop, knowing this, when one has gone astray, the other can pull him or her back into the scene (game).

57. Some students find it very difficult to keep from "writing a play." They remain separate from the group and never interrelate. Their withdrawal blocks progress during the group-planning sessions and while working onstage. They do not enter into relationships but manipulate their fellow students and the stage environment for their own purposes. This "playwriting" within the group violates the group agreement, prevents process with the other players, and keeps the user from achieving an expanding creative personal experience. Playwriting is not scene improvisation. Scene improvisation can only evolve out of group agreement and playing. If playwriting continues as the session progresses, the players do not understand the focus. Sometimes a whole group, not understanding this point, will all be playwriting.

58. The player must be aware of himself or herself in the environment equally with other players. This gives self-identity without the need for exhibitionism. This is equally true of the teacher or group leader.

59. Work for equality in the workshops and retreat from imposing the teacher's authority. Allow the acting exercises to do the work. When students feel they "did it themselves," the teacher has succeeded in his or her role.

60. Caution: if students consistently fail to solve the problem and fall back on ad-libbing, playwriting, joke-making, and working separately,

with body and body movement misshapen and distorted, their whole foundation is shaky. They have been rushed, or the function of group agreement and the focus has never been understood. They must go back to the earlier exercises and work on the simplest object involvements until they are sure enough of the beginning material to advance successfully.

61. No one can play a game unless intent both on the object and the fellow player.

62. Improvising in itself is not a system of training. It is one of the results of the training. Natural unrehearsed speech and response to a dramatic situation are only part of the total training. When "improvising" becomes an end in itself, it can kill spontaneity while fostering cleverness. Growth ceases as the performers take over. The more gifted and clever the players, the more difficult it is to discover this. Everyone ad-libs every waking hour of the day and responds to the world through the senses. It is the enriching, restructuring, and integration of all of these daily life responses for use in the art form that makes up the training of the actor for scene improvisation and formal theater.

63. A moment of grandeur comes to everyone when they act out of their humanness without need for acceptance, exhibitionism, or applause. An audience knows this and responds accordingly.

64. It takes a penetrating eye to see the environment, one's self within it, and make contact with it.

65. All of us must constantly dig around, above, and below, cutting away the jungle to find the path.

66. In playing, for better or for worse we all throw ourselves into the same pool.

67. An audience is neither refreshed nor entertained when not included as part of the playing.

68. A fixed attitude is a closed door.

69. When urgency (anxiety) appears, find the focus and hang on. It is the tail of the comet.

70. Individual freedom (expressing self) while respecting community responsibility (group agreement) is our goal.

71. The game exercises train for formal theater as well. Keep students

working with both formal and improvisational theater for a rounded experience.

72. Rote response to what is going on is a treadmill.

73. Student-actors hang on to themselves out of sheer desperation, fearful they might "fall off the cliff."

74. Acting is doing.

75. Right of individual choice is part of group agreement.

76. No one player can decide that a scene (game) is ended even if his or her theater sense is correct. If for any reason a player wishes to leave the scene, it may be done by inciting action within the group to end the scene by solving the problem, or, failing that, the player may find a reason to exit within the structure of the scene.

77. Group agreement is not permissiveness; it simply keeps everyone playing the same game.

78. Let the object put us in motion.

79. It is difficult to understand the need for a "blank" mind free of preconceptions when working on an acting problem. Yet everyone knows that you cannot fill a basket unless it is empty.

80. Contact comes out of our sensory equipment. Self-protection (assumption, prejudices, etc.) keeps us from contact.

81. It takes courage to move out into the new, the unknown.

82. The theater games are interactive. If students do not show some integration of earlier exercises when working on new ones, the workshops may be pushing ahead too quickly.

83. When players are always alerted and willing to come to each other's aid as needed, each member of the cast is given a sense of security. This mutual support brings a feeling of well-being to the audience.

84. Any player who "steals" a scene is a thief.

85. A close-working group in improvisational theater often communicates on a non-verbal level with uncanny skill and swiftness.

86. Improvisation is not exchange of information between players; it is communion.

87. Any player who feels urgent about the game and plays it alone does not trust his fellow players.

88. Many want only to reaffirm their own frame of reference and will resist a new experience.

89. Players must learn to use any and every break made during the solving of problems for the onstage event. Breaks, for the most part, are momentarily pulling away from the stage environment and relationships. If this happens through laughter, for instance, the teacher-director simply side-coaches, "Use your laughter." This is easily picked up by the player, who utilizes the energy and "legalizes" it within the scene. A student-actor soon learns that there is no such thing as a break on stage, for anything that happens is energy that can be channeled into the mainstream of the playing.

90. On stage, one's *taking* is the other's *giving*.

91. Everyone, including the teacher-director, is strengthened and moves towards action and leadership when reasons for not doing something (or doing something) are not acceptable. The simple statement, "There is always a reason," keeps the student from verbalizing reasons further. It is important to know that each and every reason is valid, whether it be socially acceptable or not, whether it be in truth "a sick grandmother" or just dilly-dallying, for in every case the reason created the present problem, whether it be lateness to rehearsal or a quarrel between players. When the youngest actor knows that the only thing that matters is to keep the game going and that a reason is but a past step that holds up the playing, he or she is freed from the need to be servile. Reasons have value to us only when they are an integral part of and help us to understand the present situation. Any other reason is imposed. It is a private matter and therefore useless except for possible subjective reasons.

92. An object can be put in motion only through its own nature and will not respond to manipulation. To transform or alter an object requires total absorption without meddling. Let it happen! Stay out of it!

93. The question often arises, "Is the child more fanciful, freer than the adult?" Actually, when the adults are freed for the experiencing, their contribution to scene improvisation is far greater.

94. No one knows the outcome of a game until one plays it.

95. Without the other player, there is no game. We cannot play tag if there is no one to tag us.

96. Scene improvisation will never grow out of the artificial separation of players by the "star" system. Players with unusual skills will be recognized and applauded without being separated from their fellow players. Group harmony pleases an audience and brings a new dimension to the theater.

EXERCISES

The workshop sessions in this section
can be used in progressive sequence.

CHAPTER III

ORIENTATION

Orientation must be given to each new student, particularly in the case of beginners. The first exercise in EXPOSURE (p. 53) and the subsequent exercises in Involvement provide the foundations upon which all following problems are laid.

Included in this edition are the later SPACE SHAPING and SPACE WALK exercises (pp. 80–83) which are to be played at any time after EXPOSURE. FEELING SELF WITH SELF (p. 57) is the warm-up with which to precede SPACE WALKS when beginning sessions.

ORIENTATION PURPOSES

Orientation is not to be looked upon as a mere introductory or "getting acquainted" process. Indeed, players who do not receive a proper Orientation are generally much slower to grasp subsequent acting problems. This is particularly true when they have missed EXPOSURE. Even highly trained players benefit from the clarified communication and the definition of terms which the Orientation experience brings them.

1. It establishes the non-acting, problem-solving approach by bringing the first organic awareness of self, space, and environment to the student. It is the first step in removal of the subjective pretend/illusion response.

2. It helps the student begin to relate to Space Objects.

3. It takes the students over the first step in Involvement with Space Objects. It sets the reality of the Invisible among them.

4. It sets up the technique of theater games and brings fun and spontaneity into the acting exercises.

5. It encourages group agreement and individual participation in making decisions.

6. It establishes group agreement and the necessity of interdependent action to solve the problem.

7. It is the first step in breaking the student's dependency upon the teacher by establishing the teacher as part of the group.

8. It introduces the actors' responsibilities to the audience and shows them how to include the audience as part of the game.

9. It introduces the audience's responsibility towards the actors and presents the audience (students and teacher-director alike) as an evaluator, not as a judge, for it removes judgmental words from the evaluation. It eliminates personal interpretations and assumptions which spring from limited frames of reference and shows how to turn evaluation away from the personalities of both the actors and the audience. It creates mutual focus on the problem at hand.

10. It introduces the student-actor to the focus of an exercise and to the need for directed (focused) energy while on stage. "Keep your eye on the ball!"

11. It establishes a working vocabulary between the teacher-director and the student.

12. It induces the student to meet himself or herself and make the first physical analysis of personal "feelings" (in determining tensions) and reduces fears of the audience, the activity, and the teacher-director.

13. It gives each student the right to his or her own observations and allows selection of one's own material.

14. It sets the tone for the work to follow—adventuring and non-forcing, the awakening of the intuitive.

OUTLINE OF A THEATER GAME

If the following outline is thoroughly understood and absorbed into your reading attitude when going through this handbook, you will have no trouble in making the exercises your own. Simply stated, here are the components to bear in mind as you go through each exercise.

1. Focus
2. Description and Example
3. Side-Coaching
4. Evaluation
5. Points of Observation

The following exercise will begin Orientation.

EXPOSURE

▶ Divide the total group into halves. Send one half to stand in a single line across the stage, while the other remains in the audience. Each group— audience and on stage—is to observe the other. Coach: "You look at us. We'll look at you." Those on stage will soon become uncomfortable. Some will giggle and shift from foot to foot; others will freeze in position or try to appear nonchalant. If the audience starts to laugh, stop them. Just keep coaching: "You look at us. We'll look at you."

When each person on stage has shown some degree of discomfort, give the group that is standing a task to accomplish. Counting is a useful activity, since it requires focus: tell them to count the floorboards or the seats in the auditorium. They are to keep counting until you tell them to stop, even if they have to count the same things over. Keep them counting until their discomfort is gone and they show bodily relaxation. Then their bodies have a natural look, although at first they continue to show signs of years of held muscles.

When the initial discomfort has disappeared and they have become absorbed in what they are doing, reverse the groups: the audience is now on stage, and the actors have become the audience. Handle the second group just as you did the first. Do not tell them that you will give them anything to do. The direction to count (or whatever is useful) should be given only after they too have become uncomfortable.

EVALUATION: When both groups have been on stage, instruct all the students to return to the audience. Now question the whole group about the experience they have just had. *Be careful not to put words into their mouths.* Let players discover for themselves how they felt. Discuss each part of the exercise separately.

How did you feel when you were first standing on stage?

There will be few answers at first. Some might say, "I felt self-conscious" or "I wondered why you had us standing there." Such answers are generalities which indicate the student's resistance to the exposure just experienced. Try to break down the resistance. For instance, ask the audience:

How did the actors look when they first stood on stage?

The members of the audience will be quick to respond, since they will readily forget that they also were "the actors" themselves. Although they may also use generalities, they will speak up more freely when talking about the others.

Encourage the actors to describe their physical responses to their first experience on stage. It is far easier for them to say "The calves of my legs were tight" or "My hands felt bloated" or "I felt out of breath" or "I felt tired" than it is to admit "I was afraid." But you may not get even this physical description until you ask directly:

How did your stomach feel?

When these physical descriptions are flowing freely, then allow all the students to speak up in as much detail as they wish. You will find that the student who previously covered up and insisted he was comfortable when first standing on stage will suddenly remember that his lips were dry or the palms of his hands were moist. Indeed, as their concern about self-exposure subsides, they will speak about their muscular tensions almost with relief. There will always be a few who will remain resistant; but they will be influenced by the group's freedom in time and should not be singled out at the beginning.

Keep the discussion brief and on a group level. Steer them away from emotional responses and generalities. If a student says, "I felt self-conscious," just reply: "I don't know what you mean—how did your shoulders feel?"

When the first part of the exercise has been fully discussed, then move on to evaluation of the second part.

How did you feel when you were counting the boards?

Be careful not to refer to it as "when you had something to do." Let this realization come to each student in his or her own way, particularly when working with lay actors and children. (Presumably, all professional actors already know that "something to do" on stage is what we seek. This "something to do" allows the player to receive the environment.)

What about the fluttering in your stomach? What happened to your watery eyes? Did the stiffness leave your neck?

The answer will be, "It went away"; and why it went away will soon become evident: "Because I had something to do."

And it is this "something to do" (focused energy) that we call the actor's focus. Quickly explain to your students that counting the boards (their "something to do") will be replaced by a different acting problem each time they do an exercise; and that this acting problem, this something-to-do, will be called their focus.

SENSORY AWARENESS

At this point, the group should be greatly released and receptive—ready for a short discussion of the senses and their value as tools. When it is pointed out that, in stage life, mashed potatoes are often served as ice cream and stone walls are actually made of wood and canvas (indeed, in improvisational theater, props and scenery are rarely used at all), students will begin to understand how a player through sensory (physical) equipment must make visible for an audience what is not visible.

This physical or sensory involvement with objects should be firmly established in the student-actor in the beginning sessions.[1] It is a first step on the path to building other and more complex stage relationships. The object agreed upon is the *one* reality between the players around which they gather. This is the first step in group agreement. The following exercises provide the basis for developing this sensory awareness.

1. RANDOM WALK used with sensory-awareness exercises is especially valuable for children (Chapter IX).

SEEING A SPORT

FOCUS: on seeing.

▶ Two teams. Players divide by counting off in twos. This is the first random team grouping and is most important.

By *group agreement*, the team decides what sport they are going to watch. When group agreement has been reached, the team goes on stage. Players themselves are to call "Curtain!" when they are ready.

SIDE-COACHING: *See with your feet! See with your neck! See with your whole body! See it 100 times larger! Show us, don't tell us! See with your ears!*

POINTS OF OBSERVATION

1. Tell the students beforehand that the event they are going to watch is taking place some distance away from them (so they must concentrate on watching closely). This is the first step in getting them out into the environment. If distance is not stressed, they will sit with their eyes cast downward, never venturing away from their immediate surroundings.

2. While the group is watching, side-coach frequently. If students look at you wonderingly when you first call out, tell them to hear your voice but to keep focused on watching. If the focus (seeing) is sustained (as in the counting of the boards during EXPOSURE), tension will be released, fear will be well on the way out.

3. The individuals on a team are not to have any interplay during the "seeing" but are to individually watch the event. This is a simple way of getting single or individual work while all are still within the security of a group.

SEEING A SPORT, RECALL

FOCUS: on the whole scene—seeing the colors, hearing the sounds, watching the people, following the movement, etc.

▶ Full group. All sit quietly and think of a time when they were seeing a sport, whether ten years ago or last week.

SIDE-COACHING: *Focus on colors! Listen for sounds! Concentrate on smells! Now put them all together! See movement! Focus on what's above, below, around you.*

POINTS OF OBSERVATION

1. Recalls for the most part should be avoided, since they are more useful clinically than for the art form. Sensory exercises are given to provide the student-actors with a quick example of the vastness and availability of past experience. Present experience is the aim of the workshops, but recalls will arise and be spontaneously selected when needed. (See "Reminders and Pointers," No. 30, p. 40, and Definition of Terms.)

2. "Seeing" homework: Tell the students to take a few moments out of each day to concentrate on seeing the things around them, noticing colors, listening to sounds, observing the environment.

LISTENING TO THE ENVIRONMENT

FOCUS: on hearing the sounds around us.

▶ All are to sit quietly for one minute and listen to the sounds of the immediate environment. They then compare the sounds they heard: birds, traffic, creaking chairs, etc.

POINT OF OBSERVATION

Assign this exercise as homework, to be done a few minutes each day.

WHAT AM I LISTENING TO?

FOCUS: on listening.

▶ Two teams. Each team decides (by group agreement) what they will listen to. They are to choose either a lecture or a musical program and should decide specifically what type of lecture or concert it is to be (e.g., classical music, psychology, jazz).

See SEEING A SPORT, p. 56, for side-coaching and points of observation.

Listening homework: Tell the students to take a moment or two out of every day to concentrate on the sounds around them.

FEELING SELF WITH SELF

This exercise, which gives players a full body perception of self, can follow a traditional game to start workshops and may be used frequently, alone or leading into a SPACE WALK (pp. 80–83).

FOCUS: on feeling self with self.

▶ Entire group sits quietly. Players physically feel what is against their bodies with their bodies as side-coached. Side-coach continuously. If necessary, coach players to keep their eyes open.

SIDE-COACHING: *Feel self with self! Feel your feet with your feet. Feel your feet in your stockings and your stockings on your feet. Feel your slacks or skirt on your legs and your legs in your slacks or skirt! Feel your underclothing next to your body and your body next to your underclothing! Feel your shirt against your chest and your chest inside your shirt! Feel your ring on your finger and your finger in your ring! Feel the hair on your head! Your eyebrows on your forehead! Feel your nose against your cheeks! Your ears! Your tongue inside your mouth. Try to feel the inside of your head with your head! Feel all the space around you! Now let the space feel you!*

EVALUATION: Was there a difference between feeling your ring on your finger and feeling your finger in the ring?

IDENTIFYING OBJECTS GAME

FOCUS: on feeling the object.

▶ Players stand in circle and one is called to center, to stand with hands behind back. Coach then slips some object into the player's hands. Using the sense of feel, the player is to discover what the object is. It is best to use objects that are fairly recognizable, though not commonly used (e.g., poker chip, playing card, comb case, rubber stamp, etc).

SIDE-COACHING: *What color is it? How is it shaped? How big is it? What is it for?*

GROUP TOUCH EXERCISE #1

FOCUS: on feeling the object.

▶ The group feels a series of objects that they have all used hundreds of times, such as soap. Ask the players, *"Do you think your hand remembers the feel of soap?"* The answer will be a unanimous "yes!" Change objects after a time, keeping them familiar. Then, go directly into the next exercise.

SIDE-COACHING: *Let your hand remember!*

POINT OF OBSERVATION

Go directly into the next exercise after the players have solved this problem.

GROUP TOUCH EXERCISE #2

FOCUS: on an object or substance.

▶ Two teams. Each selects a familiar object or substance (sand, clay, etc.). When group agreement has been reached, one team goes on stage and all play simultaneously in the space, focusing all energy on the object—its size, shape, texture, etc.

SIDE-COACHING: *Feel the texture! Feel its temperature! Feel its weight! Feel its shape!*

EVALUATION: Audience, what was the object or substance?

POINT OF OBSERVATION

"Touch" homework: Tell the students to take a few minutes out of every day to pick up and handle an object, then put the object down and try to recall how it felt.

TASTE AND SMELL

FOCUS: on tasting and smelling the food.

▶ Two teams. Each is to select something very simple to eat. When group agreement has been reached, first team goes on stage and proceeds to eat, smelling and tasting the food as they go along.

SIDE-COACHING: *Chew the food! Feel its texture in your mouth! Taste the food! Let it go down your throat!*

EVALUATION: Audience, what were they eating? Players, is that right?

POINT OF OBSERVATION

"Taste" and "Smell" homework: while eating at home, students are to take a few minutes to concentrate on the taste and smell of their food.

Evaluation of All Sensory Exercises

Was players' focus complete or incomplete? It probably varied, since it takes time to learn concentration on stage. Stress that when focus on the problem is complete, we, the audience, can *see*.

What were they handling, seeing, listening to, etc.? Keep this discussion centered on the whole group effort, not on individuals.

Did they show us or tell us? Even if they did not speak but used very obvious physical actions rather than focusing energy on the problem, they were telling rather than showing.

For instance, a player who "pantomimed" what was seen while watching a baseball game was telling. On the other hand, a player who held on tightly to the problem of seeing made good use of the focus.

Showing becomes a physicalization of the focus and is not a pantomime. It grows out of the problem and is not imposed upon it. Telling is calculated and comes from the head; showing is spontaneous and comes from the intuitive.

Points of Observation for All Sensory Exercises

1. These exercises use the first random team-groupings which will be part of all subsequent workshop sessions. With two teams, count off in twos; for three teams, count off in threes, etc.

2. Each team must come to group agreement before going on stage. There is to be no interplay or dialogue between players during these exercises. In this way, premature situations and thus "acting" are avoided. Players are working alone together, you might say.

3. Do not ask single players to perform during these first sessions. The group security is essential if individuals are to release muscle holds (fear).

4. When "Curtain!" must be called by a team ready to start an exercise, rather than appointing someone, let players step spontaneously into the theater experience by calling for their curtain. As simple as this may seem, it is most important. The call for "Curtain!" is, in effect, the magical raising of the actual theater curtain, even though the theater may be nothing more than a row of chairs and an open space at the end of a large room.

5. If some look to see what fellow players are doing after "Curtain!" has been called, side-coach: *Everyone listens in his or her own way! Keep your focus on the problem, not on your fellow player!*

While a percentage of every age group will "peek" in this way, it is more prevalent among children. (See "The Uncertain Child," p. 266). Stopping momentarily to explain that it is not a MIRROR exercise (imitation) might clear it up for students. You must not point out the player who is peeking, who does it out of a need to "do right" and will soon learn that there is no right or wrong way to solve a problem.

6. Begin EVALUATION after all players have had their chance on stage. It is during EVALUATION that players' value judgments of good/bad–right/wrong are replaced with the impersonal terms of complete/incomplete.

7. Do not dwell on the problem too long. Sensory exercises are the first step in recognizing that physical memory exists within us and can be called up intuitively whenever we need it. They show us that we need not withdraw into a subjective world or move into a cloud of past memories when working in the theater or in the classroom.

8. Side-coaching should help to free bodily response in the players. If an individual resists the side-coaching, call out: *Don't think about what I'm saying! Let your body listen!*

9. It is advisable for you to end the exercises at this early stage rather than waiting for players to end them.

10. Discourage all jokes, premature situations, etc. by keeping players' focus on the reality.

11. Avoid the parlor-game attitude which these exercises might provoke. The audience is not to guess—the audience must know through what the players show (communicate).

MIRROR SERIES

Play WHO STARTED THE MOTION? (p. 68) and THREE CHANGES (p. 73) as warm-ups to the three MIRROR exercises, which follow.

MIRROR

FOCUS: on exact mirror reflection of the initiator's movements.

▶ Players count off into teams of two players. One player becomes A, the other B. All teams play simultaneously. A faces B and A reflects all movements initiated by B, head to foot, including facial expressions. After a time, reverse the roles, calling upon B to reflect A.

SIDE-COACHING: *B initiate! A reflect! Big full body movements! Reflect only what you see! Not what you think you see! Keep the mirror between* *you! Reflect fully—head to toe! Change! Now A initiate movement and B reflect! Know when you initiate! Know when you reflect!* (Call change again and again to keep game going.)

EVALUATION: Is there a difference between reflection and imitation?

Did you know when you were initiating? Did you know when you were reflecting?

POINTS OF OBSERVATION

1. Watch for assumptions which prevent reflection. For instance, if B makes a familiar movement, does A anticipate and assume the next move, or does A stay with B?

2. Watch for true reflection. If B uses right hand, does A use right hand or opposite hand? Do not bring this aspect of the game to players' attention cerebrally. Playing MIRROR/WHO IS THE MIRROR? will bring an organic understanding of reflection.

3. Changeover or reverse must be made without stopping the flow of movement between players.

MIRROR/WHO IS THE MIRROR?

FOCUS: on concealing from audience which player is the mirror.

▶ Teams of two. Before calling curtain, a team decides which player will be the initiator and which the Mirror. One player initiates all movement, the other reflects, and both attempt to conceal from the audience players which one is the mirror. When the two players are in motion, coach calls out the name of one player. Audience players raise hands if that player appears to be the mirror. Coach then calls for hands on second player. Both players continue playing through the voting until the vote is unanimous for one or the other or a stalemate is reached.

POINT OF OBSERVATION

This effort to confound the audience demands a heightened concentration and produces a penetrating involvement with each other. Players look and *see* their fellow player.

MIRROR/FOLLOW THE FOLLOWER

FOCUS: on following the follower.

▶ All teams of two players simultaneously play MIRROR. Side-coach calls

"Change!" at intervals for players to reverse positions. When players are initiating and reflecting with large movements, side-coach *"On your own!"* Players then reflect each other without initiating. Both are at once the initiator and the mirror (or follower), reflecting themselves being reflected. The flowing movement dissolves the walls between players.

SIDE-COACHING: (Begin calling changes, as in MIRROR. Side-coach may enter the playing area to check player initiations.) *Reflect! Know when you initiate! Heighten full body movements!* (When you see initiation and reflection with full body movements, begin *follow the follower* coaching:) *On your own! Follow the follower! Reflect only what you see! Keep the mirror between you! Reflect! Don't initiate! Follow the follower! Follow the follower! Don't initiate!*

EVALUATION: During actual play, to a moving player: Did you initiate? Or did you reflect what you saw?

POINT OF OBSERVATION

Start players on their own only when they are in full body motion.

PHYSICAL INVOLVEMENT

TUG-OF-WAR

FOCUS: on giving the space rope connection.

▶ The players must play tug-of-war with a space rope. The "rope" is the connection between them. Players should choose partners of equal strength.

SIDE-COACHING: *Pull! Pull! Stay in the same space!*

POINTS OF OBSERVATION

1. Body action must come out of the rope's connection. If full focus is put on the object between players, they will use as much energy as they would pulling an *actual* rope.

2. This exercise shows that—as in a game—almost all the problems players will work on can be solved through interaction with another player. It also shows the need to give the object space for the interaction to take place.

3. If players do not leave this game with all the physical effects of having actually played tug-of-war (i.e., warm, out of breath, pink cheeks, etc.) you may be sure that they were pretending!

PART OF A WHOLE ACTIVITY (WHAT)

FOCUS: on showing a whole general activity by taking part in it.

▶ Large teams of ten to fifteen players. One person goes on stage and begins a simple activity. Upon seeing this activity, other players join in one at a time until all are participating.

SIDE-COACHING: *Show! Don't tell! See what's going on. Join the activity! Avoid dialogue. Become part of the whole!*

EVALUATION: What was the activity? Players, were you part of the whole?

POINTS OF OBSERVATION

1. This group interaction should create flow and energy. Repeat the game until this takes place.

2. Fellow players are not to know what the first player's activity is ahead of time. Examples of activity are: painting a fence, scrubbing a floor, raking leaves, etc.

OBSERVATION GAME[2]

▶ A dozen or more real objects are placed on a tray, which is set in the center of the circle of players. After ten or fifteen seconds, the tray is covered and/or removed. The players then write individual lists of the names of as many of the objects as they can remember. The lists are then compared with the tray of objects.

PLAY BALL

FOCUS: on keeping the ball in space and out of the head.

▶ Divide group into two large teams; one of players, one of audience members. The first team plays with a ball made of space substance and standing in a circle decides on the size of the ball and then tosses the ball among themselves. Once the game is in motion, the coach calls out that the ball is becoming lighter or heavier or moving at various speeds. When the second team plays, the first team becomes audience.

SIDE-COACHING: *The ball is one hundred times lighter! The ball is one*

2. Neva L. Boyd, *Handbook of Games* (Chicago: H. T. Fitzsimons, 1945; reprinted as *Handbook of Recreational Games* [New York: Dover, 1975]), p. 84.

hundred times heavier! The ball is normal again! Use your full body to throw the ball! Throw the ball in slooow mootion! (Coach in slow motion too) *Catch the ball in verrry slooow motion! Normal speed! Keep your eye on the ball! Give the ball its time in space! Now, change! Speed it up! Triple Time! Throw and catch as fast as you can! Okay, now normal once more!*

EVALUATION: Players, was the ball in the space or in your heads? Audience, do you agree?

POINTS OF OBSERVATION

1. The player knows when the ball is in the space or in the head. When it is in the space it will "appear" to both player and audience alike.

2. Side-coach with energy! Emphasize use of full body to keep the ball in motion.

3. Following PLAY BALL, have the group play DODGE BALL, p. 382, JUMP ROPE, p. 387, and then introduce PLAYGROUND, p. 390.

INVOLVEMENT IN TWOS

FOCUS: on keeping the object (space) between them.

▶ Players agree on an object and begin an activity with it as in TUG-OF-WAR. The object they choose determines the activity. For example: spreading a sheet, pulling a blanket between them in bed, taffy pulling.

SIDE-COACHING: *Work together! Keep the object between you!*

POINTS OF OBSERVATION

1. One way to prevent students from planning How (see p. 35) is to have each team write the name of an object on a slip of paper. The slips of paper are then collected and placed in a hat and each team picks from the hat just prior to going on stage. This is enjoyable for everyone.

2. For this first involvement, suggest that the object be one which ordinarily brings forth a tactile response.

INVOLVEMENT IN THREES OR MORE

FOCUS: on keeping an object in space between players.

▶ Three or more players agree on an object which cannot be used without involving all of them. They are to participate in a joint action in which all move the same thing. For example: pulling a fishnet, tugging a boat, portaging a canoe, pushing a stalled car.

SIDE-COACHING: *Keep the object in space! Show! Don't tell!*

EVALUATION: Did they work together? If three people pushed a car and the fourth sat behind the wheel, the problem was not solved, for all did not physically move the car.

Did they need each other to solve the problem, or could one of them have managed the problem alone? If one of the players could have managed the problem alone, then the group's choice of an object was incorrect for the problem presented.

Did they work together or separately? If three people were using the activity of painting an object, then they were working separately even though they were working on the same project. However, if the people needed each other to move the object, then they would be working on the problem.

POINTS OF OBSERVATION

1. INVOLVEMENT IN TWOS will almost automatically keep players involved together. INVOLVEMENT IN THREES OR MORE may tend to confuse them. Do not give any examples, however; allow them to discover the solution to the problem themselves.

2. Watch to see that the students do not work separately while in the group.

INVOLVEMENT WITHOUT HANDS

FOCUS: on showing and manipulating an object between players without using hands.

▶ Two or more players agree on an animate or inanimate object between them, which they are to set in motion without using their hands. Some examples are: pushing a rock or a car, getting a toboggan to move, mountain climbing (rope tied to waists).

EVALUATION: Did they show us the object or tell us?

POINTS OF OBSERVATION

1. If the players take a built-in/no-hands agreement such as mashing grapes with the feet, this is resistance to the focus of the exercise. Ask them to make a new choice.

2. Watch for spontaneity and unusual ways of putting the objects in motion. Remember, giving examples is telling How to your students!

3. A first step in involvement without hands might be to give the entire group something that ties them all together such as a chain gang. A third step would be to play WHERE WITHOUT HANDS (p. 134) sometime after introducing Where.

MIRROR/SUB-TEAMS FOLLOW THE FOLLOWER

FOCUS: on exact mirror reflection of initiator's movements; then on follow the follower.

▸ Teams of four divide into sub-teams which reflect each other. Sub-team A is mirror; sub-team B initiates all movement. Sub-team that initiates must agree on an activity involving both players, for example: barber shaving customer. Sub-team A then becomes the reflection of the barber and customer and must follow the activity exactly. Play as in MIRROR, p. 61. After a time, reverse the teams, side-coaching "Change!"

POINT OF OBSERVATION

This exercise can be given again when players come to the problems on seeing.

PART OF A WHOLE OCCUPATION (WHO)

FOCUS: on becoming part of a whole occupational activity.

▸ One player goes on stage and starts an activity. Other players join at a time as definite characters (Who), and begin an action related to the activity. For example: first player is a surgeon; other players are nurse, scrub nurse, anesthetist, intern, etc.

SIDE-COACHING: *Show! Don't tell! Join as a definite character! Show Who through activity!*

POINTS OF OBSERVATION

1. Players are not to know ahead of time who the first player is or what he or she is doing.

2. Play this exercise until your students are entering into the problem with fun and excitement, just as they would in any game. This releases a flow of energy that results in group interaction and brings a natural quality in speech and movement. If this does not happen, you are not communicating the focus of the exercise. Players are not focused on

group activity but are simply ad-libbing or playwriting. Should this occur, have your first player start a game (ping pong, baseball, etc.) and encourage the others to join in.

WHO STARTED THE MOTION?[3]

▶ Play this traditional game as an introduction to MIRROR. Players stand in a large circle. One player is sent from the room, whereupon another is selected to start the motion, which everyone in the circle reflects. The big, full moves initiated by this player can be changed at any time and the whole group must reflect these motions. The outside player, having been called back to stand within the circle, is given three chances to say who started the motion. All others try to keep center player from identifying the mover. After a true call (or three miscalls), the mover leaves the room to become "it" and a new player is chosen to start the motion.

DIFFICULTY WITH SMALL OBJECTS

Use at intervals during training.

FOCUS: on having difficulty with a small object.

Part A

▶ Single player becomes involved with small object. For example: opening a bottle or a stuck purse, forcing a drawer open, tearing open a small package.

Part B

▶ Single player becomes involved with a piece of clothing. Examples: stuck zipper on back of dress, tight boots, a ripped lining in coat sleeve.

Part C

▶ Two or more players. This is the same as A and B except that more players are involved.

POINT OF OBSERVATION

Resistance to focus will show itself in a player who intellectualizes the problem. Instead of having a physical difficulty with an object, the player may

3. Ibid., p. 84.

for instance have a hole in a shoe and take a dollar bill out of a wallet to place in the shoe to cover up the hole. This is a "joke" and total avoidance of the problem presented.

HOW OLD AM I?

FOCUS: on showing the age chosen.

▶ Single players on two large teams. Teacher-director sets up a simple bus stop with benches or chairs facing the audience. Players can write down age on slip of paper and hand this to coach before going on stage, where they wait for bus, showing age.

For example: an adult player begins blowing bubbles with gum. She gets it stuck on her nose, cleans the sticky mess with tongue and finger. She fumbles in her pocket searching for something. Going quickly through all her pockets she pulls out a yo-yo and starts playing with it. The bus arrives; she puts yo-yo back into her pocket and anxiously fumbles around for bus fare. Another example, done by an eleven-year-old boy: a character comes on stage in a firm, aggressive manner, holding what seems to be a briefcase. He glances down the street, sees nothing coming, sits down on the bench, and opens his briefcase. He thumbs through a few of the sections, pulls out a paper, glances at it, takes a pen out of his inside coat pocket, makes a note on the paper, puts it back into the briefcase, zips it closed, looks down the street restlessly—still no bus.

SIDE-COACHING: *Put the age in the feet! The upper lip! The spine! The bus is half a block down! It's coming closer! It's here!* Sometimes adding, *It's held up in traffic!*

EVALUATION: How old was the player? Did he or she show us or tell us? Are age qualities always physical? Are age differences part of an attitude toward life? Did the player see the bus or just listen to coaching?

POINTS OF OBSERVATION

1. At this early stage a student-actor will usually give some bodily rhythms and a good deal of activity (business) to help clarify age. This is usually a form of "telling," not showing.

2. Discourage "acting" and/or "performing" during this exercise by repeating the focus: *Show us the age chosen!*

3. Coach *Held up in traffic!* only when you want to explore student's work further.

4. After playing this, play NO MOTION WARM-UP, p. 83, before going on with HOW OLD AM I? REPEAT.

HOW OLD AM I? REPEAT

F O C U S : on chosen age only, repeating the number frequently to oneself.

▶ Single players on two large teams. Team sits quietly on bench and players concentrate on age only; i.e., *the number* of years. When age emerges in the body, what is needed for the problem will come up for use.

S I D E - C O A C H I N G : *Focus on the exact age! Repeat the number to yourself! Send the message to the total organism!* When age appears: *Bus is a half a block away! Held up in traffic!*

P O I N T S   O F   O B S E R V A T I O N

It is difficult for the student-actor to believe that:

1. The blank mind (free of preconception) is what we are after. Adventuring!

2. If concentration is truly on age only, student-actors and audience alike will have a most inspirational experience as the bodies of players become older or younger spontaneously with little or no overt action or need for stage business.

3. This exercise will work only if the student-actor truly blanks the mind of any imagery relating to the chosen age (repeating this age over and over with the assist of the side-coaching will help in this).

4. Concentrating on the age alone serves to release body memory to such an extraordinary degree that the player shows us age with the minutest of body movements and gesture, subtleties that one would expect to see in only the most accomplished and experienced of actors. Again we see that to experience new adventures, we must trust the scheme and let the focus of the exercise do the work.

5. If the problem was solved, the student-actor should come from this exercise with more body grace evident because of some loss of rigidity, with muscular release and shiny eyes. New sources of energy and knowledge were truly released. "They showed age without doing anything!" is an excited comment often heard by student-actors.

6. To prepare for action, the player should concentrate on exhalation as in EXCURSIONS INTO THE INTUITIVE, p. 178.

OBJECT MOVING PLAYERS[4]

FOCUS: on the object that is moving them.

▶ Any number of players agree on object which is to move them simultaneously. They are to be an interrelated group. Examples: sailboat, car, merry-go-round, ferris wheel.

SIDE-COACHING: *Feel the object! Let the object move you! You're all in it together! Keep it in space! Out of the head!*

EVALUATION: To audience: Did they allow the object to move them, or did they initiate movement independent of the object? Did they move by watching the other players?

To actors: Did you make this a mirror game (reflection of others), or did you work on the focus?

POINTS OF OBSERVATION

1. See whether the players *feel* the object (space) between them. This sometimes occurs to an extraordinary degree when the students have played together many months or when they are concentrating deeply on the problem.

2. Many students will ask: "Should we watch the other players to know when to move?" This is the student asking the teacher "How do I do it?" which indicates a dependency. A simple "Let the object move you" repeated over and over again aids in breaking this dependency.

3. If focus is kept on the object (space), a group connection appears that is felt by the actors and is evident to the audience.

4. It may be that the players will finally "let go" and let the object move them only after constant coaching. Most of them will "let go" if the focus is understood and if the side-coaching reaches them; moreover, each team should be kept on stage until this does happen for most of them.

5. Repeat this exercise throughout the training.

4. See also USING OBJECTS TO EVOLVE SCENES, p. 194.

IT'S HEAVIER WHEN IT'S FULL[5]

FOCUS: on keeping the weight of an object in space and out of the head.

▸ Three or more players agree on an activity in which receptacles must be filled, emptied, and filled again, for example picking fruit, filling a box, carrying water.

Variation A

▸ Handling things of different weight, for example shovelling sand, pitching hay, lifting weights.

Variation B

▸ To be used after the beginning exercises in Where. The problem of varying weights is placed within the context of a Where/Who/What agreement.

SIDE-COACHING: *Feel the weight in your legs! Your back! Not only your arms. Feel weight with your whole body! Show! Don't tell.*

EVALUATION: Did the players show the difference in weight (bodily response) or tell (indicate, joke)? Players, do you agree?

PART OF A WHOLE RELATIONSHIP

FOCUS: on communicating Who (relationship) through an activity.

▸ One player goes on stage and starts an activity. Other players enter, one at a time. They know who they are as they enter the scene and the first player, who does not know who they are, must accept them and relate to them. For example: Man hanging drapes. Woman enters. Woman: "Now, dear, you know that's not the way I want them hung!" Man accepts that woman is playing his wife and he plays accordingly. Actors continue to enter, playing the couple's children, the next-door neighbor, the family minister, etc. All show relationship through joining the activity.

SIDE-COACHING: *Show! Don't tell! Stay with the activity!*

EVALUATION: Did she show us or tell us that she was the wife, neighbor, etc.? Did players all stay with the activity?

POINTS OF OBSERVATION

1. This game will show the primitive beginnings of a scene growing out of the focus as well as the first sign of relationship rather than mere simultaneous activity.

---

5. See also "Giving Reality (Substance) to Objects," pp. 269–70.

2. Let players enjoy this Orientation game even if the stage is somewhat chaotic because of the large group of "characters" in the scene, with everyone moving and talking at once as all very earnestly play the game. This childlike stage behavior releases pleasure and excitement and is essential to the social growth of the group (necessary to improvisational theater). Refrain, no matter how tempted, from trying to get an orderly scene. Subsequent exercises will slowly do this for the student. GIVE AND TAKE in particular (p. 149) will help.

PART OF A WHOLE[6]

FOCUS: on becoming part of a larger object.

▶ One player goes on stage and becomes part of a large animate or inanimate moving object. As soon as the nature of the object becomes clear to another, that player joins the player on stage and becomes another part of the whole. This continues until all the audience have participated and are working together to form the complete object. Players may assume any movement, sound, or position to help complete the whole. Examples include machines, abstract mechanisms, constellations in the universe. Others are statue groupings, a body cell, a flower, an animal.

SIDE-COACHING: *Use your whole body to show your part! Join in! Take a risk!*

POINTS OF OBSERVATION

1. This exercise generates a great deal of spontaneity and fun. Every age group responds to it with equal energy. You will notice that sound effects arise spontaneously when needed.

2. There is no need to give examples. If the game is presented clearly, players will come up with objects.

THREE CHANGES

Play this as the introduction to MIRROR, p. 61.

▶ Full group counts off in teams of two. Each player observes the opposite player and notes dress, hair, etc. Players then turn their backs on one an-

6. Many users call this "The Machine."

other and each player changes three things on his or her person—parts hair, folds cuff, unties lace, etc.

Players then face each other again and each player identifies what changes the opposite player has made. Ask players to switch partners and make four changes. Continue to change partners after each round of playing. Seven, eight, or even nine changes are possible.

POINT OF OBSERVATION

Do not let players know that you plan to increase the changes until after the first playing. Many are worried how to find three changes. Four or more will create a good deal of excitement. This is an excellent exercise for players, taxing their powers of making do (improvising) on a simple physical level. Players are forced to look at a "barren" land as it were and find things to use for the game their eye did not see at first glance. This has been called the Survival Game.

WHAT DO I DO FOR A LIVING?

FOCUS: on the chosen occupation.

▶ Establish a simple bus stop setting (chairs, a bench, etc.). Teams of five or more enter the area and wait, focused on occupation. Allow several minutes for the effects of the focus to become manifest. Players do not know one another and avoid dialogue.

SIDE-COACHING: *Feel the occupation in your whole body! Hands! Feet! Neck!* (When occupations begin to emerge:) *The bus is coming!*

EVALUATION: What were the occupations? Did players show or tell? Players, do you agree? Is it only through activity that we can show what we do for a living? Does the body structure alter in some professions? Is it an attitude that creates change? Is it the work environment?

POINTS OF OBSERVATION

1. Evaluation questions often provoke first insights into physicalizing character, but do not belabor this. Later games will allow further insights into playing character.

2. To prevent How, have players sit quietly concentrating on the profession each has chosen, nothing more. If focus is complete, what is needed for the problem will emerge.

MIRROR PENETRATION

Give this exercise throughout the training, especially before CONTRAPUN-
TAL ARGUMENT, p. 167, those games which follow it, and CHARACTER AGIL-
ITY, p. 248. This exercise is the first step toward PREOCCUPATION, p. 122.

FOCUS: on restructuring your face from the inside out to look like another.

▶ Players are paired with or choose partners with faces different from their
own in structure. Each team of two players decides on a simple relationship
(husband/wife, etc.) and chooses a topic for discussion or argument. Players sit facing each other and begin the conversation. When the side-coach
calls the name of a player, that player assumes the partner's facial structure while continuing the discussion, attempting to restructure the face to
look like the partner's. When partner's name is called, the first player re-
sumes his/her own facial structure. Players continue discussion as the
coach changes the "mirror" frequently.

SIDE-COACHING: *Rebuild your nose like your partner's! Jawbone! Forehead! Change the mirror! Focus on your partner's upper lip! Keep up the
discussion! Change the line of the chin! Exaggerate your partner's cheek-
bones! Sculpture your face to look like your partner's! From the inside out!
Share your voice!*

EVALUATION: Did you penetrate facial structure, or simply reflect expression and movement? Audience, do you agree with players?

POINTS OF OBSERVATION

1. Players are thrown into an explicit talking relationship; however, both
   partners must be so occupied with penetration and restructuring faces
   that the problem of dialogue is taken in stride.

2. At first, players will show very little physical change in faces. This game
   has value despite this modest response, since it forces a player to look
   at another and *see*.

3. Players must penetrate each other's faces in order to rebuild their own
   to look like the other. Superficial expressions are to be avoided. To relieve apprehension, coach players to *"Exaggerate the other's facial
   structure!"*

4. This exercise, like other MIRROR games, can be done by the entire
   group paired off, playing without an audience.

CONVERSATION WITH INVOLVEMENT

FOCUS: on continuing a conversation while eating a meal.

▶ Teams of two or more players agree on a simple topic of discussion and proceed to eat and drink a large meal while keeping up a continuous discussion.

SIDE-COACHING: *Keep up the conversation! Pass the salt! Try a sip of the water! Share your voice! Chew the food! Taste! Keep up the progress of the meal!*

EVALUATION: What kinds of food were the players eating? Players, do you agree? Did players show or tell? Where they able to eat the meal and keep up the conversation at the same time? Did objects appear?

POINTS OF OBSERVATION

1.   This is a two-part problem. Avoidance consists in doing one thing at a time, either chewing and swallowing *or* listening and talking but never both at once.

2.   Keep the players' focus on eating and conversing, lest they make a situation to be "performed" and resist working on the problem.

3.   Swallowing is crucial; it brings players into the moment. If players are pretending to eat food, side-coach *"Take time to swallow your food!"*

INVOLVEMENT WITH LARGE OBJECTS

FOCUS: on physical involvement with a large object in the space.

▶ Single player (or entire group of players all working individually) becomes involved with a large entangling object.

SIDE-COACHING: *Give life to the object! Use your whole body! Allow the object its place in space! Explore the object! Show! Don't tell! Feel the object with your back!*

EVALUATION: Was the object in space or was it in the players' heads? Did they show us the object or tell us?

POINT OF OBSERVATION

Be certain that the player's focus is on the *object* and not on emotional response to the involvement.

DRAWING OBJECTS GAME

FOCUS: on communication through an image.

▶ Prepare a list of objects with simple but outstanding characteristics (train, cow, cat, elephant, etc.). Divide the group into two teams. Each team gathers at an equal distance from the leader, who holds the list of objects. One player from each team goes up to the leader, who shows both players the same word simultaneously. For non-readers, the leader whispers the word. Players run back to their respective teams and communicate the word through drawing the object for their teammates to identify. The first team to identify and call out the object wins a point. Continue with a new word until each team member has had a chance to draw an object. A variation for advanced players is to use abstract words (joy, melancholy, triumph, generosity, etc.). Allow synonyms to count as correct identification.

SIDE-COACHING: *Draw as large as possible! Communicate!*

POINTS OF OBSERVATION

1. The ability to draw is unimportant since this is a game of spontaneous selectivity that allows players to quickly make a visual communication. Tell those who call out in advance of the communication, "This is not a guessing game."

2. The drawings can be made on smaller or larger sheets of paper with charcoal, markers, or even paintbrushes, or on blackboards with chalk. It helps to clip the paper onto a board.

3. The words can be images from a subject your class is involved with.

4. Words are represented by pictures in the writing of China, ancient Egypt, etc. Students playing this game are communicating pictographically.

5. All age groups love this game and almost always find that the score is unimportant.

TRAPPED

FOCUS: on escaping from the immediate environment.

▶ A single player chooses an immediate (close) environment from which to escape, such as a bear trap, tree trunk, elevator, etc.

SIDE-COACHING: *Show! Focus on the immediate environment. Keep the object* (when one appears) *in space!*

PHYSICALIZING AN OBJECT

FOCUS: on giving life or movement to the object.

▸ A single player selects an object, animate or inanimate, and handles and uses it, communicating the life and movement of this object. If, for example, the object is a bowling ball, the player must show what happens to the ball once it has left his or her hands. Other objects that can be physicalized: a fish, a pinball machine, a kite, a yo-yo.

SIDE-COACHING: *Let your whole body show the object's life! Keep the object in space! Out of the head! Show with your feet! Shoulder blades! Elbows!*

EVALUATION: Did they physicalize the object? Did they show or tell?

POINT OF OBSERVATION

The distinction between giving life to the object and manipulating the object is subtle. Be careful in presentation and side-coaching not to tell student-actors How.

MAINTAINING SURFACE HEIGHTS

FOCUS: on keeping the height of the surface stable and constant while setting various objects on it.

▸ A single player establishes a surface (table, counter top, etc.) on which he or she puts many small objects, setting them down with strong impact. The objects may be books, pencils, glasses, etc.

POINT OF OBSERVATION

Resistance to the focus will show itself by players piling objects one upon the other instead of placing them singly on the surface.

BEGIN-AND-END WITH OBJECTS

FOCUS: on the object.

▸ In this three-part exercise, a single player selects a small object such as a candy bar.

Part A

▸ Player performs a simple action with the object (e.g., taking off the paper wrapper and biting into it.)

Part B

▸ Player then repeats the action, this time calling out "Begin!" each time fresh contact is made with the object, and "End!" when each detail is completed. (See Point #1, below.)

Part C

▸ Player repeats the action again, this time doing it as fast as possible and without calling out "begin" and "end."

EVALUATION: To player: Was the first or the third action visible in the space for you? Audience, do you agree?

POINTS OF OBSERVATION

1. If Part B is done correctly, each detail will be like an individual no-motion frame within a strip of movie film. Coach the player to do *begin* and *end* with great bursts of energy. Example of Part B: Player touches candy bar: "Begin!" Grasps bar: "End!" Starts to tear the paper: "Begin!" Tears the paper: "End!" Begins to crumple paper: "Begin!" Crumples paper: "End!" Is ready to toss it away: "Begin!" Tosses it away: "End!"

2. Part C will be much clearer and sharper than Part A, played out of the head and into the space; thus visible.

3. BEGIN AND END, p. 125, involves the player in a simple Where, Who and What, bringing the scene to vivid life.

SPACE SUBSTANCE

SPACE WALK and SPACE SHAPING exercises (below) are ways of perceiving/sensing/experiencing the environment (space) around us as an actual dimension in which all can enter, communicate, live, and be free. Each player becomes a receiving/sending instrument capable of reaching out beyond the physical self and the immediate environment. As water supports and surrounds marine life, space substance surrounds and supports us. Objects made of space substance may be looked upon as thrusts/projections of the (invisible) inner self into the visible world, intuitively perceived/sensed as a manifest phenomenon, *real!* When the invisible (not yet emerged, inside, unknown) becomes visible—seen and perceived—theater magic! This is the fertile ground of the poet, the artist, the seeker.

SPACE WALK I (EXPLORATION)

FOCUS: on feeling space with the whole body.

▶ Players move around and physically investigate space as an unknown substance. Leader walks with players during side-coaching.

SIDE-COACHING: *Move through the substance and make contact with it. Use your whole body to make contact! Feel it against your cheeks! Your nose! Your knees! Your hips! Let it (space) feel you! Feel your body shape as you move through it!* (If players tend to use hands only, coach: *Let your hands be as one with the rest of your body! Move as a single mass!*) *Explore the substance! You never felt it before. Make a tunnel! Move back into the space your body has shaped. Shake it up! Make it fly! Make it ripple. Eyes open!*

SPACE WALK II (SUPPORT AND EFFORT)

FOCUS: on letting space support you or holding yourself together as side-coached.

▶ Players walk around, moving through the space substance, open to the side-coaching. After the players are responding to the support of space, coach them to support themselves. Then, coach players to go back to letting space support them. Calling out parts of the body helps to release muscle holds. Change back and forth until the difference between space support and holding self together is realized by players.

SIDE-COACHING: A: *As you walk, let the space substance support you! Rest on it! Lean into it! Let it support your head. Your chin. Your eyeballs. Your upper lip, etc.*

   B: *Now, you are your sole support! As you walk, you are holding yourself together! Your face! Your arms! Your whole skeleton! If you quit holding yourself together, you would fly into a thousand pieces! You are hanging onto your arms! Your mouth! Your forehead.* (calling out that which is held rigid) *Note what you feel when you are your sole support!*

C: *Now change! Walk through the space and let the space support you! Don't worry about what that means! Your body will understand! Let the space take over where you were holding! Note your body feeling! Let the space support you! Let space support your eyes! Your face. Your shoulders. Your upper lip. You go through the space and let the space go through you!* (Continue to change back and forth between support and effort until players experience the difference.)

EVALUATION: Players, how did you feel when space was supporting you? When you were your own support? Audience, did you perceive a difference between support and no support in the way players walked and looked?

POINT OF OBSERVATION

When players hold themselves together, are their own gravity line, so to speak, some shrink up, some seem to be afraid of falling, while others appear anxious or lonely and still others look aggressive. In fact, many "character qualities" appear. When, on the other hand, players lean on space, an expansiveness and fullness can be noted as they move through the environment. It is as if they know the environment will support them if they allow it to.

SPACE SUBSTANCE INTRODUCTION (FOR HANDS), p. 391, is the lead-in to the following games.

SPACE SHAPING/SINGLE

FOCUS: on allowing space substance to take shape as an object.

Part I

▶ Single players find any object they wish emerging out of the space substance.

SIDE-COACHING: *Play with the space substance! If an object begins to take shape, go with it! Feel the object! Stay with it!*

Part II

▶ Single players pull space substance around as though it cannot be separated from itself.

SIDE-COACHING: *Experiment! Move it about! Pull it! Let it pull you!*

POINT OF OBSERVATION

Most players can gather and handle the space substance as they would any other pliable mass, finding objects with confidence that show exactness and reality. Perhaps this is so because the player does not construct (invent) the object from the imagination but discovers (intuits) it as it comes up out of space.

SPACE SHAPING/ENSEMBLE

FOCUS: on allowing objects to take shape in the space substance between players.

Part I

▶ Two or more players allow an object, animate or inanimate, to appear out of the space substance and then keep it between them through play.

SIDE-COACHING: *Play with the space substance! Use full body energy! Go with it! Let it emerge! Keep it between you!*

Part II

▶ Coach players to pull the space substance about, keeping it attached in space, to swing on it, let it pull them, to wind it around each other, etc.

SIDE-COACHING: *Head to toe involvement! Follow the follower! Keep the space substance between you!*

TRANSFORMATION OF OBJECTS

FOCUS: on the use of full-body movement and energy to create change/transformation in a space object.

▶ Large teams of ten or more players stand in a circle. First player allows a space object to take shape and passes it to the next player, who plays with the object until it changes shape and then passes it on. For instance, if a player is handed a yo-yo and uses it, it might transform itself into a bird or an accordion, depending on how playing energy is heightened and used. If the object transforms itself, the transformation will come out of heightened, exaggerated playing with and handling of the object received. Player is not to change the object—it either transforms or they do nothing. Nor do associations count as transformations. If handed a comb, for instance, the player is not to make a mirror and use the comb. Objects are played with and exchanged between players all around the circle in turn.

SIDE-COACHING: *Keep the object in space! Use full body movement! Play with the object! Let your whole body respond! Heighten! Heighten! Pass it on!*

POINT OF OBSERVATION

If a player experiences the excitement felt when an object transforms itself, point out that this is exactly what focus will do, i.e., allow something to happen.

SPACE WALK III
(TOUCH & BE TOUCHED/SEE & BE SEEN)

FOCUS: on the side-coaching.

SIDE-COACHING: *Allow the space to flow through you and you flow through the space. Allow your mind to flow through your brain. Allow your sight to flow through your eye. Allow the space to flow through you and your fellow player. Take a ride on your own body and view the scenery around you. Touch an object in this room—a book, a cup, a piece of clothing, a chair. When you touch the object (feel it), allow it to touch (feel) you! Touch a fellow player and allow fellow player to touch you. Touch and touched! You flow through the space and allow the space to flow through you. See an object. The moment you do see it, allow the object to see you! See a fellow player. Allow the fellow player to see you! Then, occlude your fellow player: look full face but do not see or let yourself be seen. Change. See and be seen!*

Repeat several times. Vary players. Allow time between each side-coaching. Remember to keep players moving.

EVALUATION: Was it difficult to allow yourself to be touched? To be seen? Avoid analysis.

The following exercise is to be given just prior to HOW OLD AM I? REPEAT, p. 70, and to NO MOTION, p. 176. Because it also is to be given in conjunction with the Space Substance exercises, it is presented at this point in the text.

NO MOTION WARM-UP

FOCUS: on the still moments between the movement.

▸ Coach players to raise their arms up and down and to focus on No Motion while continuing to raise their arms up and down. Using the image of a flip-book, a series of stills, which when riffled create a moving picture, ask them to see the series of stills the raising of their arms has left in space. When they grasp this, go on to the same approach to walking, climbing stairs, ladders, etc. Properly executed, this exercise gives players a physical feeling and understanding of keeping out of their own way. By focusing on No Motion, hands, legs, etc. move effortlessly without conscious volition. This can be used as a physicalization to show how, with lack of interference, the focus can work for us. As one player said, "It is as if someone else is moving us about!" Another player said, "It's like being on a vacation."

POINTS OF OBSERVATION

1. Ask players if they remember as children pressing the backs of their hands hard against the insides of a doorway and then stepping forward, their arms lifting without effort, involuntarily. Players can have this experience at any time. It is like a feeling of "no-motion."

2. Homework for this exercise will accelerate workshop training. Ask students to take a few minutes out of each day to see a moving scene as a momentary still picture: a street view, an office, an ambulance racing past, a moment of themselves and another in an emotional situation.

    Ask students to "log" their daily experience, setting down just a word or two in a notebook at the very moment of some event. Each individual will know intuitively which moments to log.

    Like the focus in NO MOTION, this homework gives a sharp perception of the moving world about one. Brevity is necessary, for wordiness will take one beyond the moment of the event into subjectivity and introspection.

PENETRATION (SIGHT)

The following side-coaching might be used as a special warm-up during Orientation. It can also be integrated with certain of the Orientation sense exercises.

FOCUS: on penetrating the environment.

▸ Ask players to think of their sensory equipment as an extended tool, something that can move out, cut through, *penetrate*.

SIDE-COACHING: *Penetrate that color! Penetrate that taste! Let your ear penetrate the sound.*

ADD A PART

▶ A lead-in to this game is PART OF A WHOLE, p. 73.

FOCUS: on using part of a whole object in space.

▶ Teams of six to ten. First player uses or makes contact with a large object only he or she has in mind and then leaves the playing area. One by one, players contact other parts of the whole object until the whole object is left in space. For example, first player sits and uses a steering wheel, second wipes the windshield, third opens car door, etc.

SIDE-COACHING: *Let us see what you see! Give the part its place in space! Stay with the same whole object! Avoid planning! Let your part appear!*

EVALUATION: Audience, what was the complete object? Were the added parts in the space—or in the players' heads? Players, do you agree? First player, was that the object you had in mind?

ORIENTATION SUMMARY

Encourage student-actors to make a conscious integration of the physical world around them, to receive how things taste, feel, smell, sound, and look. Open consciousness of the world around is a necessary tool in the improvisational theater, the classroom, the home, and the arts.

If at any time during the workshops your players lose detail and generalize objects and relationships, it would be well to stop the class for a moment and play an Orientation exercise. These are almost all useful for awakening playing energy, at all times.

Throughout Orientation, pleasure and enthusiasm must set the tone. If players are apprehensive and anxious, constantly looking to see if they are doing "right," in your urgency you may be a pedant rather than a leader or guide of the group. You may be giving too many problems in one session, not allowing players to have the experience of flow as they would from a game.

Always try to begin sessions with a traditional game. See pp. 399–412.

You could follow this with FEELING SELF WITH SELF, p. 57, and a SPACE WALK, pp. 80–83. End if possible with an exercise which will give the players a non-verbal summation of the workshop's problems. PART OF A WHOLE ACTIVITY (WHAT), p. 64, PART OF A WHOLE, p. 73, and ADD A PART, p. 85, are just such exercises and will quickly show you to what extent the earlier exercises have been integrated by the students. If clowning, "acting," and exhibitionism persist, then it is obvious that involvement with or understanding of the process of Focus has not yet taken place.

Exercises involving single players may be played after the student-audience becomes "part of the game" through sharing focus and evaluation. This usually has occurred by the end of the second Orientation session. If not, delay singles.

CHAPTER IV

WHERE

INTRODUCTION

The Three Environments

Many actors find it difficult to "reach beyond their noses" and must be freed for a wider physical relationship with the environment. For purposes of clarification, three environments should always be kept in mind: immediate, general, larger.[1]

The *immediate* environment is that area close upon us—the table where we are eating, with its food, utensils, objects, etc. The *general* environment is the area in which the table is placed—the room, restaurant, etc., with its doors, windows, and other features. The *larger* environment is the area beyond—the space outside the window, the trees in the distance, the birds in the sky, etc.

All the exercises in environment (Where) are designed to awaken the players to all three areas and to help them move out, penetrate, and work comfortably.

Involvement with Where

The first Where exercise, EMERGING WHERE, p. 90, will provide players with the basic structure used in all subsequent game exercises. The Where is the "field" upon which they play; it brings them the full stage environment and shows them how to play within it and let the people, objects, and events met within this environment work for them.

Because of the importance of thoroughly familiarizing players especially interested in scene improvisation with the basic form, it is wise to spend a

1. See "Space Substance," p. 79.

great deal of time on this problem and the variations and additions suggested in the text. Understand, however, that many of the exercises in the latter part of this chapter are for advanced students, only to be returned to after exploring other parts of the book.

Used in formal theater, by placing the actor inside the stage set, Where exercises serve to provide an organic understanding of stage movement rather than an understanding based on memory.

EARLY WHERE SESSION

Establishing Focus on Where, Who, and What

Prior to presenting EMERGING WHERE, p. 90, hold a discussion with the group to establish focus on the primary Where and the secondary Who and What points of concentration.

Begin by discussing Where (relationships with physical objects).

How do you know where you are? If you get no response, try a different approach.

Is it true that you always know where you are? "Sometimes you don't know where you are."

True, you may be in an unfamiliar place. How do you know it's unfamiliar? How do you know when you are in a familiar place? How do you know where you are at any moment of the day? "You just know." "You can always tell." "There are signs."

How do you know when you are in the kitchen? "You can smell the cooking."

If there were nothing cooking, how would you know? "By where it is."

What do you mean? "By where it is in the house."

If every room in your house were moved around, would you still know which room was the kitchen? "Of course!"

How? "By the things in the room."

What things? "The stove. The refrigerator."

Would you know a kitchen if it had no stove or refrigerator in it? If it were in the jungle, for instance? "Yes."

How? "It would be a place where food is prepared."

And so, through discussion and the presentation of exacting questions, the student-actors conclude that "we know where we are by the physical objects around us." When this basic premise has been agreed upon, become more specific.

What is the difference between an office and a den? "An office has a desk and a telephone."

Isn't this also true of most dens? "Yes."

What might a den have that an office would not have? "Photographs, rugs, lamps."

Couldn't those be in an office?

On a large blackboard, set up two columns under the headings of den and office. Now ask the group to call out items which might be found in each place, listing them under the proper heading as they are mentioned. Eventually, it will become apparent that differences do exist; for, while both locations might have a desk, a water cooler and intercom system are more likely to be found in an office than in a den.

Continue along this same line. *How do you know the difference between a park and a garden?* The more detailed these discussions become, the more your students will realize that refined selection (capturing the essence) adds brilliance to the theater communication.

When the Where discussion has been completed, the Who and What points should be covered rather quickly.

In Who, we are interested in establishing human relationships—in encouraging the players to realize whom they are working with and to get some understanding of their mutual roles.

Do you usually know the person in the same room with you? Would you know a stranger from your brother? Your uncle from the corner grocer? "Of course!"

When riding on a bus, can you tell the difference between two school friends and a mother and child? Between two strangers and a husband and wife? "Yes."

How can you tell? "You can tell by the way they *act* together."

What do you mean, "by the way they act together"? The youngest actor replies, "Mothers are bossy ... sweethearts look silly ... husbands and wives argue." Sad commentary, indeed.

In discussing this further, the students will agree that people show us who they are through their behavior (as opposed to telling us). When they have arrived at this point, bring in the fact that actors, to communicate to the audience, must show Who through relationships with their fellow players.

When Who has been covered, move on to the last of the three points of concentration. What is the play of the players on stage?

Why do you usually go into a kitchen? "To make a meal." "To get a glass of water." "To wash the dishes."

Why do you go into a bedroom? "To sleep." "To change clothes."

The living room? "To read." "To watch TV."

As the questioning progresses, the students will agree that we usually have a need for being where we are and for doing what we do—for handling certain physical objects, for going into certain places or rooms. And so must the actor have his needs for handling certain props on stage, for being in a certain place, for acting in a certain way. When Where, Who, and What have been thoroughly covered, move into the WHERE EXERCISE.

EMERGING WHERE
Part I
FOCUS: on communicating/showing objects emerging in the Where.

▸ Teams of two to four players agree upon Where, Who, and What. One at a time, each player on a team enters the space and contacts (uses) an object found in the Where, such as a water cooler in an office or a towel rack in a bathroom. Player must *show* us the object, without *telling* (verbal communication).

SIDE-COACHING: *Share with the audience! Contact the object! Use the object!*

Part II
FOCUS: on contacting, using, showing each object that emerged for each player in Part I, and any other object that might emerge in the course of playing.

▶ Players go back and explore the Where, Who, and What, contacting every object that emerged in Part I as well as any other object that might emerge, relating to each other as Who and engaging in What (reason for being there; activity).

SIDE-COACHING: *Show Where! Don't tell! Each player must contact every object! Show Who! Follow the initiator! Show What!*

EVALUATION: Where were they? Who were they? What were they doing? Did each player contact each object? Did they walk through tables, etc?

POINTS OF OBSERVATION

1. Ideally, the object emerges for players when they enter the space. At first, many will think of an object, not yet trusting that one will emerge. Do not concern them with this at this point. Simply inform them that they are not to tell fellow players beforehand, but are to *show us.*

2. When finding objects one at a time, some players will try to complete an activity. When the object is apparent, simply call for another player.

3. As they are playing, side-coach them to show Who (relation) if necessary. Side-coach *"Follow the initiator!"* to help them see each other and the objects they are contacting.

4. This game can replace the WHERE EXERCISE WITH FLOORPLANS, p. 92. It is a later development.

WHERE/FLOORPLANS & STAGE DIRECTIONS

This simple demonstration combines relating to and preparation of floorplans with following and understanding stage directions. It is designed to be presented just before WHERE EXERCISE WITH FLOORPLANS, p. 92.

FOCUS: on following stage directions and relating to a floorplan.

▶ An end-stage space is established, open to audience view, with a chalkboard easily seen from both stage and audience positions. Outline the stage on the chalkboard and point out stage directions on the sketch (see Point 1 below). Full group then agrees on a Where (kitchen, schoolroom, etc.). Each player suggests an item for the Where which the leader adds to the floorplan using appropriate symbols (see diagram). When the floorplan is completed, call for individual players, one at a time, to take a specific position in the stage area, e.g., downstage right. Once in position, the player refers to the floorplan and names all the items around that stage position.

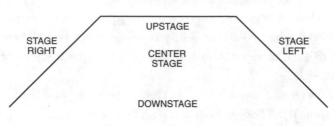

FIGURE 1. Stage directions

SIDE-COACHING: As required. For example: *Johnny, do you want the tele-vision upstage right? Do you all agree the Where is complete? Sally, go to center stage! Refer to the floor plan! What are you standing on? Point to the couch! Exit stage left!*

EVALUATION: (Questions will come up when players are in stage positions.) Do you see a chair there on the floor plan? Audience, do you agree?

POINTS OF OBSERVATION

1. Stage directions are always given from the on-stage player's point of view. Therefore, when a player exits "stage right," the direction refers to the actor's right when facing the audience from on stage. The five basic directions are diagrammed here to give specificity to the stage directions—"Go to upstage right," "Upstage left," "Downstage left," "Right of center," etc. (See Fig. 1.)

2. Common floorplan symbols are shown in the accompanying diagram. Feel free to simplify or add others needed by your group. (See Fig. 2.)

3. If time is limited, have many players on stage at one time.

WHERE EXERCISE WITH FLOORPLANS

FOCUS: on showing Where, Who, and What through use of all the objects in the Where.

▶ Count off in teams of two to four players. Each team agrees on Where, Who, and What and sketches a floorplan of Where on paper (see Fig. 3). As Where, Who, and What are played out, each player must make contact with (use) every object in the floorplan. Players place actual chairs needed in the playing area, tack the floorplan up for easy referral and call curtain

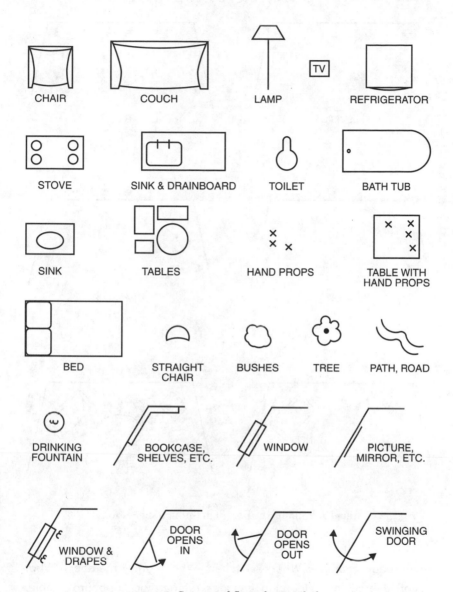

FIGURE 2. Suggested floorplan symbols

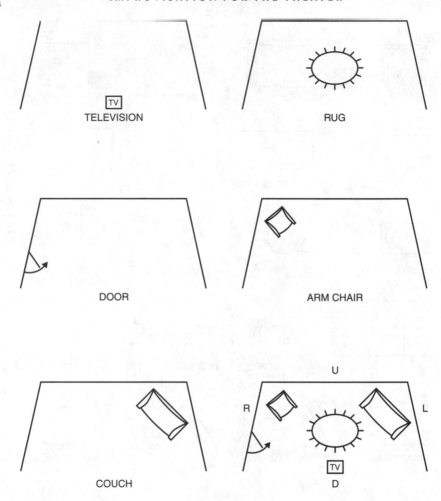

FIGURE 3. Building the floorplan through suggestions

when ready. Example: Where—kitchen, Who—family members, What —eating breakfast. Floorplan includes refrigerator, cupboards, table, sink, etc.

SIDE-COACHING: *Share with the audience! Show! Don't tell! Each player must contact every object on the floorplan! Refer to it if necessary! Keep objects in space and out of your heads! Refer to floorplan!*

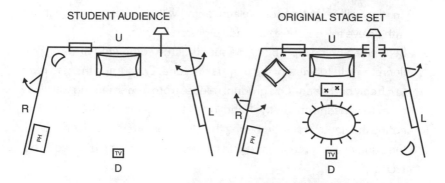

STUDENT AUDIENCE   ORIGINAL STAGE SET

FIGURE 4. Players' original floorplan compared to
audience's floorplan drawn from players' use of WHERE

EVALUATION: Did players use all objects on the floorplan? Audience, which
objects did players show us? Players, check them off against the actual
floorplan (see Fig. 4). Did players show Where, Who, and What? Or did
they tell? Were objects in space or in the players' heads? Players, did you
walk through tables? Did players integrate use of objects with Where, Who,
and What or did they sometimes use an object without a reason? Could
they have used their objects in a more interesting manner? Are hands the
only way of touching? Noses can be pressed against windows as easily as
hands can open them. Did they share what they were doing with us?

POINTS OF OBSERVATION

1. In developing floorplans, it is important that *each* team member have
   chalk or pencil and be encouraged to make use of it, for this allows even
   the most timid person to contribute at least one object to the floorplan.
   This is the organic beginning of group involvement.

2. Introduced here for the first time, the floorplan is a visualization of the
   actor's Where. It is important that the student-actor's initial floorplan
   be compiled correctly and purposefully. For this reason, the teacher-
   director would do well to wander from group to group during the first
   planning session, offering suggestions and encouragement wherever
   needed. At first, the student-actors will place their items haphazardly,
   some putting too many on the board and some too few. As time goes

on, they will become more selective and will choose and place items with an eye toward the total stage picture.

3. Before beginning a problem, be sure that the completed drawing of a floorplan is in full view of the players on stage. Encourage them to refer to it freely and often. This gradual release from remembering will allow them to concentrate on the handling of the objects themselves, eliminating the need for remembering their location on stage. Always check the audience's perceptions against the actual floorplan after each exercise.

4. Constantly remind the actors to show where they are by using all the physical objects on the stage. Through this coaching, a player's focus will become clear to him (or her).

5. When talking is mumbled or the actors hide in bunches outside the line of vision, side-coach: *Share the stage picture! Share your voice with your audience!* In almost every instance, students will respond.

6. These early scenes will almost certainly contain too much talking in the place of action—telling instead of showing. Relationships will be sketchy, object contact will be pedestrian, "sharing" will be negligible, concentration will be sporadic. This will all be remedied with time, discovery, and coaching.

7. To avoid early playwriting, do not allow the players to plan a situation. Observe the teams closely during preparation of the exercise. If How they will manipulate the set is discussed, if the scene is planned in advance, rather than What and Where being decided, then the exercise becomes an unspontaneous, rehearsed activity.[2] Keep What (play) a simple physical activity between players.

8. Have the student-actors add more and more detail to their floorplans each time the exercise is given. Pictures, candy dishes, cushions, radios—all should be included. As they move around the room, channeling their energies to solve the problem, self-blocking will appear, awareness of fellow players will emerge, and they will gain entrance into their full stage environment.

9. Be sure that contact is made by each player with all the objects during

2. See discussion of "Avoiding the How," p. 35.

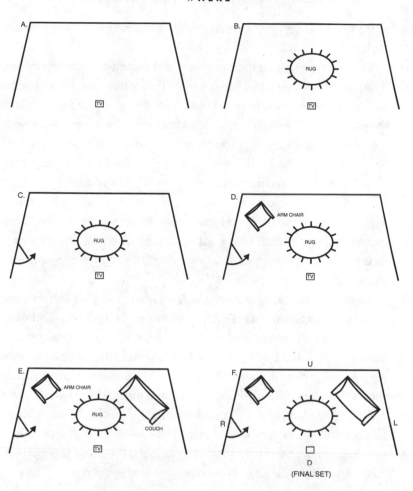

FIGURE 5. Additional information on floorplans

this early period. Later, they no longer need to touch every object on stage—indeed, it will interfere with their work. But the discovery of this freedom and subsequent leveling off rests entirely with the teacher's judgment.

10. The Where, Who, and What, focus of the exercise, and additional information as the scenes become more complex should be written at the bottom of each floorplan. A file of completed floorplans is useful for reference when planning a performance.

11. In the first few sessions of Where, have students use familiar interiors such as rooms in a house, offices, etc.

12. Players, being more on their own in these exercises than heretofore, may pull away from each other and work the focus separately although in the same situation. To avoid this, have the group show us Where through Who (relationship) and What (activity). If, for example, Where is a living-room and Who girl and boy friend, objects in the general environment might be used in many ways. The books in the bookcase might be taken to read poetry to the girl friend. The girl friend might use the chair by coming over and putting her arms around her boy friend who is sitting in the chair. It is the same problem of letting the focus move the players rather than imposing anything upon it. This is the only road to true scene improvisation, for it is only through relationship that stage action appears.

13. If players persist in using a built-in activity when doing Where, they are resisting focus and relationship. For instance, if a bedroom is chosen as the Where and the players are housecleaning, this then becomes a built-in or non-challenging use of Where. To avoid this, suggest a problem where the players use a What more or less unrelated to the objects within the Where. The bedroom could be a place where two students are studying. A machine shop, for instance, could have two players playing checkers on their lunch hour. These unrelated activities (What) then keep total absorption with the game, and the preoccupation (focus) on getting to the objects becomes the energy source.

THE WHERE GAME

FOCUS: on showing Where through objects within it.

▶ Teams of ten to twelve players. One player enters the stage space and shows Where through contacting physical objects. Any other player who knows Where the first player is may assume a Who, enter the Where, and develop a relationship both with the Where and with the first player through the objects in the Where. As Where becomes known, the rest of the players join in as related characters (Who) within the Where and the general activity (What).

SIDE-COACHING: *Show Where! Don't tell! Keep focus on Where! Relate to your fellow players! Show Who you are through use of objects in the Where! Focus on Where!*

EVALUATION: Did players show us or tell us? Were the objects in space or in the players' heads? Were players all in the same Where? Players, do you agree with audience?

POINTS OF OBSERVATION

1. This group interaction should create flow and energy. For example, if the first player establishes a counter, the second player could enter as a customer; the third, a cook; the fourth, a porter, etc. The focus remains on the Where, with Who a secondary focus.

2. The game ends when all are on stage in the same Where.

WHAT'S BEYOND? EXERCISES

The following WHAT'S BEYOND? exercises should be given in one session if possible. While the first handling of the exercise by new students will be primitive for the most part, repetition at intervals throughout the training period (e.g., after WORD GAME, during problems of Emotion) will bring added richness to the student-actor's work. When two more WHAT'S BE-YOND? exercises are given later (p. 121), repeat these early ones. These exercises heighten exits and entrances.

WHAT'S BEYOND?/WHERE

FOCUS: on showing (communicating) What room player has come from and what room player is going to.

▶ Single player moves through the playing area making an entrance and an exit, showing what room player has left and what room player is going to. No action takes place except that used to communicate *what's beyond?* For example, a player enters, yawning and stretching. While walking across the stage, player is slowly unbuttoning and easing out of what seems to be a loose-fitting garment; rubs tongue over teeth and exits.

SIDE-COACHING: *Explore and heighten! Reflect the room from which you have come! Stop mid-stage! Reflect the room you exit to!*

EVALUATION: Where did player come from? Where did player go to? Did player show us or tell us? Is it possible to show what's beyond without some on-stage activity?

POINTS OF OBSERVATION

1. After players have worked within this "room" situation, the exercise may be given again, with players entering or leaving a specific location (such as a forest clearing, a department store, etc.).

2. As in HOW OLD AM I? REPEAT and WHAT DO I DO FOR A LIVING?, try this exercise and the subsequent WHAT'S BEYOND? at a later date to see how much can be shown with the greatest of subtlety by "letting it happen."

WHAT'S BEYOND?/ACTIVITY

FOCUS: on communicating activity in a place just left or a place to be entered.

▶ Single player enters, walks through the playing area and exits, communicating without speech or unnecessary activity, what went on just before the entrance or what will take place after the exit.

SIDE-COACHING: *Show! Don't tell! Let your body reflect what just took place! Heighten it! Let your body reflect what activity will follow!*

EVALUATION: What happened off stage? Did player show or tell? What will happen? Did player show or tell?

POINT OF OBSERVATION

If this exercise is given early, tell players to keep activity simple (e.g., shoveling snow outside). When it is repeated later in the training, suggest that the off stage scene could be based on a relationship with other people (e.g., a quarrel with a sweetheart, a theft of a purse, a death scene, etc.).

FURTHER WHERE SESSIONS

WHERE WITH HELP

FOCUS: on physically helping fellow players make contact with every object in the Where.

▶ Teams of two players agree on Where, Who, and What and design a floorplan. Players help each other to make contact with all the objects in the floorplan without use of excessive dialogue. Exercise is over when all the objects have been contacted.

SIDE-COACHING: *Refer to the floorplan! Help each other make contact! Work on the problem! Keep focus on physically helping! Stay with the objects! Integrate your helping!*

EVALUATION: Did players make contact with objects through Who and What or was contact random? Did players physically help each other make contact? Or did they rely on dialogue alone?

POINT OF OBSERVATION

Tell players to use a great deal of detail in their floorplans but to keep their What (activity) very simple.

WHERE WITH OBSTACLES

FOCUS: on physically hindering each other from making contact with every object in the Where.

▶ Keep the same teams as in WHERE WITH HELP. Teams agree upon Where, Who, and What and prepare a floorplan as they did before. Players must contact every object, at the same time trying to physically hinder partner from making contact with objects. Activity must be integrated without using excessive dialogue.

SIDE-COACHING: *Hinder! Work on the problem! You must contact everything! Make an obstacle to your partner's move! Hinder! Avoid dialogue! Integrate that obstacle!*

EVALUATION: Which exercise gave Where more visibility? Which gave Who more reality? Did players integrate contact and obstacle?

POINTS OF OBSERVATION

1. Stress to players that their actions must come out of their relationship. Players must watch and involve themselves with each other most intently to solve this problem.

2. WHERE WITH HELP AND HINDER: This further variation, p. 397, ought to be played immediately following WHERE WITH OBSTACLES.

FINDING OBJECTS IN THE IMMEDIATE ENVIRONMENT

FOCUS: on receiving objects from the environment.

▶ Three or more players agree upon a simple stage relationship and a likely discussion which keeps everyone involved. This could be a committee meeting, family council, etc. During the course of this meeting, each player is to handle dozens of objects in the immediate environment. They do not plan ahead what these objects will be, but allow objects to appear.

SIDE-COACHING: *Take your time! Don't meddle, let the objects appear! Keep the discussion going! Work on the problem! Keep in contact with each other! Share your voice!*

EVALUATION: Did the actors invent objects or did they wait for them to appear? Did players see each other's objects and use them? Is it possible to do this exercise without being intent upon each other? Did they talk their objects or contact them? To actors: did objects come through association, or did they appear?

POINTS OF OBSERVATION

1. Suggest players select a gathering seated around a table.
2. This exercise is related to SPACE SUBSTANCE and belongs in the transformation group.
3. Resistance to working this problem will show itself in players using only the most obvious things and continuously pulling away from the environment and the other players. Inventing, they soon run out of things to handle. When the problem is solved, however, much to everyone's excitement, endless objects are the result: bread becomes crumbs, lint appears on a neighbor's coat, dust floats through the air, and pencils come from behind ears. Let your players discover this for themselves.
4. This is another of the two-way problems. The on-stage occupation, the meeting, must be continuous, while the preoccupation, focus, must be worked on at all times. Some players will keep the meeting going and neglect focus, others will work only on focus and neglect the meeting. Side-coach accordingly.

WHERE WITH UNRELATED ACTIVITY

FOCUS: on making physical contact with all the objects in the general environment while pursuing a mutual activity.

▶ Two players agree on Where and Who and make a detailed floorplan. The What is to be a mutual activity not dependent upon Where they are (e.g., a dancing lesson in the bedroom; building a boat in the living room).

SIDE-COACHING: *Keep focus on the problem! Contact all the objects!*

POINT OF OBSERVATION

This exercise helps players understand that it is through relationship (Who) and activity (What) that the environment (Where) can come to life for observers and players. The two-way problem gives players both occupation (activity) and preoccupation (focus), helping remove the censoring mechanisms that hold players to old frames of reference and stereotyped behavior.

WHAT TIME IS IT? A

FOCUS: on the time of day.

▶ Single player with no detailed Where. Player writes a time on a slip of paper and hands it to teacher before going on stage to show the time of day.

EXAMPLE I: Man enters and closes door with exaggerated quiet. He leans down and removes his shoes. Putting them under his arm, he stealthily and unsteadily crosses the stage. Accidentally bumping into a chair, he stands frozen and listens intently. Nothing happens. Silently hiccoughing, he moves with high steps toward an inside door, puts his head in very carefully, listens, and hears—with great satisfaction—a snore. He exits, still hiccoughing.

EXAMPLE II (done by a ten-year-old): Girl comes sleepily on stage, crosses, opens the refrigerator, and takes out what appears to be a bottle. Yawning, she takes a pan from a cupboard shelf and partially fills it with water from the sink faucet. She then places the bottle in the pan and lights the stove. As she stands watching it, her head nods sleepily in a doze. She picks up the bottle and shakes it on her forearm, yawningly puts it back in the pan, and again nods her head, heavy with sleep. Once more she picks up the bottle, shakes it on her forearm, seems satisfied, turns off the stove, and sleepily exits.

EXAMPLE III: A man enters and sets himself to work building something. After a time, he puts his tools aside, opens his lunch-pail, and proceeds to eat its contents. When he has finished eating, he returns to work.

EVALUATION: What time was it? Did the player show us or tell us? If audience says he was a drunken husband afraid of his wife, repeat: What time was it?

Is it possible to show time without an accompanying activity? Is lunchtime always noon? What about the night worker? Is it possible to show time without using our cultural frames of reference (i.e., in our 9-to-5 culture, we have set ways of showing 6 A.M., noon, 5 P.M., etc.)?

WHAT TIME IS IT? B

(To be given immediately after WHAT TIME IS IT? A.)

FOCUS: on feeling time with the whole body, muscularly and kinesthetically.

▶ Large group of players sit or stand on stage. Teacher-director gives same time to all of them. They are to sit quietly on stage, working separately. They may move only if they are pushed to do so by the focus; but they are not to bring in activity just to show time.

SIDE-COACHING: *Feel the time in your feet! In your spine! In your legs! No urgency! Feel time on your face! In your full body!*

EVALUATION: Is there bodily reaction to time? Is the drowsiness of late afternoon different from midnight drowsiness? Is there only sleep-time, work-time, hungry-time? Is clock-time a cultural pattern? Is it possible to communicate time without handling props, setting up Where, etc.?

POINTS OF OBSERVATION

1. Actors will vary considerably in feeling time. For instance, 2:00 A.M. will put some actors to sleep; but the night-owl in the group will become wide awake.
2. Time can now be added to the Where floorplan.
3. This exercise should be handled the same way as HOW OLD AM I? REPEAT and WHAT DO I DO FOR A LIVING?

WHAT TIME IS IT? C

FOCUS: on allowing time to determine the way the scene will develop.

▶ Three or more players agree upon Where, Who, What, and time of day. Evaluation and side-coaching follow the usual line.

WHO EXERCISES

WHO'S KNOCKING? A & B are natural warm-up exercises for the WHO GAME. See also SHOWING WHO THROUGH THE USE OF AN OBJECT, p. 129, ART GALLERY, p. 128, and WHO AM I?, p. 397.

WHO'S KNOCKING? A

FOCUS: on showing Who, Where, and What through knocking.

▶ Single player, out of audience's view, knocks on a door. Player is to communicate Who is knocking, Where, for What reason, time, weather, etc. For example: Police officer at night, telegram, rejected sweetheart, messenger from the palace, gangster entering a hideaway, spy, frightened neighbor.

SIDE-COACHING: *Share your knock! Try it again! Heighten it! Let the sound of the knock enter space! Put full body attention on the physical sound!*

EVALUATION: Who is knocking? At what door? What time of day? For what purpose?

POINTS OF OBSERVATION

1. In Evaluation, you will find many observers did not know the exact circumstances, the Where, Who, and What of a knock. Now that all know, ask the player to repeat the knocking. Observers will listen more intently and find communication clearer when they do not have to guess. Repeating the knock after Evaluation keeps audience players part of the game and involved in what other players are doing.

2. Some questions in Evaluation may be unanswerable, but asking them may bring new insights to the players.

WHO'S KNOCKING? B

FOCUS: on entering an event (scene) initiated by a knock.

▶ Single player, out of view, communicates Where, Who, and What by knocking. Any player may assume a Who and open a door if a communication is received. The out-of-view player may send the answering player back to the audience if the knock was not received as sent. Then the player knocks again. When the knock is answered correctly, other players may enter if moved to do so by Where, Who, and What.

SIDE-COACHING: *Share your knock! Put full body attention on the physical sound! If you know what is being communicated, take a Who and answer the knock!*

EVALUATION: None.

POINT OF OBSERVATION

This game is an example of how a simple warm-up exercise can trigger a scene. WHO'S KNOCKING? games can be used for composition. Ask students to write a sentence or paragraph on what is communicated by a knock.

WHO GAME

FOCUS: on allowing Who (relation) to reveal itself without telling a story.

▶ Two players, A and B. A is seated on stage. B enters. B has a definite, predetermined character relationship with A, but has not told A what it is. By the way B relates to A, A must discover who A is. For example, A (a girl) is seated on a bench. B (another girl) enters and says, "Hello, darling, how are you?" She fusses over A's hair. She walks around A looking her over; asks her to stand up, turns her around, saying "You look beautiful, darling, just beautiful." B then puts her arms around A, rocks her tenderly, wipes away a tear, fixes long skirt and headdress, until A knows that B is her mother and she is the daughter on her wedding day.

SIDE-COACHING: *No questions! Wait! No urgency! Let Who you are reveal itself!*

EVALUATION: Did B show the relationship or tell? Did A allow Who to be revealed? Or did A anticipate Who?

POINTS OF OBSERVATION

1. Use a bench rather than a chair, if possible.
2. After Evaluation, reverse positions and let A choose a relationship with B.
3. The game ends as soon as A realizes Who, but if time allows, continue if there is involvement between players.
4. This is one of the early steps in the direct handling of character relationship and can be repeated throughout the training.

WHO GAME/ADDING WHERE AND WHAT

FOCUS: for A, on allowing Who, Where, and What to reveal itself; for B, on communicating W.W.W. without telling a story.

▶ The game description is the same as in the preceding WHO GAME, with the addition of showing Where and What to B's communication with A.

SIDE-COACHING: *Show Where! Let Who reveal itself! No urgency! Show What! No questions! Don't tell!*

EVALUATION: A, did you allow Who/Where/What to reveal itself? Audience, do you agree? B, did you show Where/Who/What or did you tell a story? Audience, do you agree?

POINTS OF OBSERVATION

1. A variation would be to allow audience in on the preplanning from the known (B's) point of view, by asking B to write down Where/Who/What and pass it around for audience to read, or by sending A out of hearing and deciding Where/Who/What as a group.

2. Another variation is to have many Wheres, Whos and Whats on slips of paper; B selects one of each just prior to going on stage.

3. MIRROR PENETRATION, p. 75, played at this time will have value for your students. WHO AM I?, p. 397, is the final game in this series.

INVOLVEMENT WITH THE ENVIRONMENT

WEATHER EXERCISE #1

FOCUS: on chosen weather or climate.

▶ Two large teams each agree upon a type of weather or climate which is to be communicated to the other team as audience. Players, seated or standing in the playing area, show weather. Players are to work on the focus individually within the large team. When ready, team calls curtain.

SIDE-COACHING: *Feel the weather between your toes! Down your spine! At the end of your nose! Feel weather with your whole body! Head to toe! Keep focus on weather only! Not on your teammates! Show, don't tell! Everyone feel weather in your own way!*

EVALUATION: Audience, did weather envelop players? Did players use their whole bodies to show us weather? Players, do you agree? What was the weather you chose? Audience, did players communicate that weather to us?

POINT OF OBSERVATION

Be sure to coach players to focus on weather, thus avoiding character or situation. Repeat this exercise, now or at a later date.

WEATHER EXERCISE #2

FOCUS: on showing weather without the use of hands.

▶ Divide group into two large teams. Group sits or stands on stage. Players agree upon, or are given by fellow players or teacher-director, a type of weather or climate. They are to show audience the kind of weather they are experiencing, and they are to do it without using their hands.

SIDE-COACHING: *Feel weather with the whole body! Down your spine! At the end of your nose!*

EVALUATION: Players, did you feel weather differently without the use of your hands? Audience, was this a more interesting showing of weather?

POINT OF OBSERVATION

Give this exercise immediately after all the players have completed WEATHER EXERCISE #1 and its evaluation. Follow it with WEATHER EXERCISE #3.

WEATHER EXERCISE #3

FOCUS: on allowing weather or climate to move players through Where, Who, and What.

▶ Two or more players agree on a type of weather and Where, Who, and What. Players all focus on allowing weather to move them through Where, Who, and What.

SIDE-COACHING: *Feel the weather with your whole body! Focus on weather! Feel the weather with your back! Your toes! Your cheeks! No play-writing! Let the weather move you!*

EVALUATION: Did focus on weather affect players' interactions or was weather merely thrown in? Did weather help develop the Who, Where, and What? Did players use their whole bodies to show us?

POINT OF OBSERVATION

Climate can be added to group decisions from now on and mention of weather can be included in evaluations, since it can add interesting nuances to scenes.

EXPLORATION OF LARGER ENVIRONMENT

FOCUS: on relating to the larger, overall environment.

▶ Two or more players agree on a general large environment such as a forest, mountaintop, lake, etc., as Where. Players then agree on Who and What and explore the larger environment in space.

SIDE-COACHING: *What is above? Beneath? Beyond? Communicate with the larger environment beyond you! See the larger environment beyond! Let it fill all the space in the room. Let it go for miles around!*

EVALUATION: Audience, what was above players? Beneath players? Beyond? Did players show or tell? Players, do you agree?

POINT OF OBSERVATION

Some players have difficulty relating to environments other than those of home, school, or office. Side-coach players to see and communicate with what is beyond. The space where the audience sits may be included in the atmosphere of the larger environment.

QUICK SELECTION EXERCISE FOR WHERE

FOCUS: on indicating Where through one related object.

▶ Each student is to write down the names of three objects which most readily indicate each of the following places. The object is not to be part of the decor (such as sawdust on the floor) but should be one physical inanimate object (i.e., an altar would suggest a church, a movable bed would suggest a hospital, etc.). When individual lists have been completed, they are to be compared and discussed.

LIST OF PLACES

a jail	a church steeple
a dungeon	a tree house
a cellar	a cocktail lounge
a cave	a saloon
a boxcar	a greasy-spoon restaurant
a hospital room	a coffee shop
a child's bedroom	a dining room
a dormitory	a dentist's office
a mine	a library
an attic	a church
a tower	a drug store

EVALUATION: Did the object readily indicate the Where, or could the example have been more explicit? Can objects alone show Where? Is it attitude toward and use of objects that clarify Where?

POINTS OF OBSERVATION

1.   This exercise should give the student some understanding of how a selected detail will help make an interesting communication with an audience.

2.   This is *not* a game of association. It is an exercise in selectivity.

EXCHANGING WHERES

FOCUS: on communicating Where, Who, and What without forethought.

▶ Divide group into teams of two to four players in such a way that both sexes are equally distributed between all teams. For instance, each team might have one male and two females. Each team agrees on Where, Who, and What and draws a floorplan of the Where, noting on it Who and What, the time of day, weather, what's beyond, etc. Leader collects all floorplans and redistributes them, one by one, only when a team arrives in the playing area for its turn. No team is to get its own floorplan to work from. Players quickly look at the floorplan, decide quietly which players will be Who, and without further discussion, enter the event (scene) designated by the new floorplan, which they keep at hand. Leader must not tell players in advance that floorplans will be redistributed, but must let them work on them as if they themselves were going to play the scene.

SIDE-COACHING: *Check the floorplan as you play! Communicate Where! Take your time! Don't tell! Relate to each other through activity! Objects! Time of day! Show! Don't tell!*

EVALUATION: Did players follow the floorplan? Was the floorplan clear? Did players show or tell? Players, do you agree? Did you let the new floorplan move you? Or did you go back to your own team's first floorplan?

POINT OF OBSERVATION

This game alleviates the tendency to plan *how* in advance. Planning *how* leads to telling.

INVOLVEMENT WITH
THE IMMEDIATE ENVIRONMENT

FOCUS: on showing Where by continuously contacting objects in the immediate environment.

▶ Two players, preferably seated, agree on Where and Who. While involved in a discussion, players show Where they are by continuous involvement with small objects within arm's reach. For example, two players waiting for a bus find chipped paint, fallen leaves, specks of dirt, etc., while conversing.

SIDE-COACHING: *Keep focus on the objects you find around you! Show us Who you are through contacting the immediate environment! Keep the objects in space! Let the objects reveal themselves!*

EVALUATION: Did Where come to life through the objects? Did players show us or tell us? Did dialogue continue when objects were being handled? Did players allow objects to reveal themselves or were they invented by the players?

POINT OF OBSERVATION

Caution players not to perform a full activity such as eating a meal, but to be *occupied* with a conversation and *preoccupied* with the focus. When both appear simultaneously, extraordinary life and detail are apparent in the scene.

WHERE THROUGH THREE OBJECTS

FOCUS: on communicating Where through three objects.

▶ Single player goes into the playing area and shows Where using three objects. For example, player may select a lunch counter and use a jukebox, a napkin holder, and a cup of coffee.

SIDE-COACHING: *Keep focus on the objects! Let us see Where you are! Show! Don't tell!*

EVALUATION: Audience, did you see the Where? Did the use of the three objects communicate the Where or were they isolated objects, leaving us to assume (interpret) Where? Players, do you agree with audience?

POINTS OF OBSERVATION

1. If the focus is understood, an extraordinary sense of a total environ-

ment comes from the three objects and is communicated to the audience.

2. To accommodate the whole group, a time limit of one or two minutes
   may be necessary.
3. This is a valuable exercise as a step towards developing on-the-spot
   scenes from suggestions by the audience.
4. This exercise should be used after QUICK SELECTION EXERCISE FOR
   WHERE, p. 109. Repeat at regular intervals throughout training.

GIBBERISH

Developing Organic Response Through Gibberish

Gibberish is an extremely valuable exercise and should be used throughout the workshops. For the director of the formal play, gibberish is a great
aid in releasing players from the multitude of technical details surrounding the initial plunge into rehearsal and freeing them to move spontaneously and naturally within their roles.

Gibberish is, simply enough, the substitution of shaped sounds for recognizable words. It should not be confused with "double talk," where actual words are inverted or mispronounced in order to scramble the meaning. Gibberish is a vocal utterance *accompanying an action*, not the
translation of an English phrase. The meaning of a sound in gibberish
should not be understood unless the actor conveys it by action, expressions, or tone of voice; however, it is important that this be left for the
student-actor to discover.

A scene that cannot be understood in gibberish is usually nothing but
gags, story, plot, or ad-libbing. Gibberish develops the expressive physical
language vital to stage life, by removing the dependency on words alone
to express meaning. Because gibberish uses sounds of language minus the
symbols (words), this puts the problem of communication on a direct-
experiential level.

The actor showing the most resistance to gibberish is usually the person
who relies almost completely on words in place of experiencing and shows

great anxiety when these words are taken away. Since this player almost invariably fights contact in any form, everyday body movement is stiff; and isolation from fellow players is quite pronounced.

There will also be the student who will keep insisting that the teacher spell it out: "Should it be through action or gibberish that the communication is made?" The older and more anxious the student, the more he or she will prod you to answer this question. One anxiety-ridden student who finally received great insight remarked: "You are on your own when you speak gibberish!" When asked if that wasn't also true when she used words, she thought a moment and replied: "No, when you use words, people know the words you are saying. So you don't have to do anything yourself."

Let students find this out for themselves. Gibberish, if communicated properly, can only bring about total physical response. But if the teacher *tells* the student to do it through action, the player will then concentrate on action and will not have a personal experience. We want integration of sound with physical or organic response; and it must come spontaneously from the student.

Because sound without symbols—except in the case of pain, joy, fear, or astonishment—cannot be recognized without body functioning, gibberish forces the student-actor to show and not tell. Because the sounds are meaningless, the player has no way of escaping. Then physicalizing mood, problem, relation, and character becomes organic. Body holds are released, for players must listen and watch each other closely if they are to understand one another.

Scenes without sound, loosely called "pantomime" (see Chapter V), will not achieve the same results as gibberish; for we must not abstract sound (dialogue) from action. Dialogue and action are interdependent: dialogue creates action, and action creates dialogue. The players must be freed physically as they speak. The insecurity which can keep the flow and intonation of the dialogue static will disappear as the student-actors lessen their dependency on words.

Insight into useless dialogue (ad-lib) often appears at this time. Dialogue that is not part of the expressive physical language of the stage life, is, after all, only gibberish!

Introducing Gibberish

Developing fluency in "no symbol" speech brings with it a release from word patterns that may not come easily to some players. The coach must illustrate what gibberish is before using it as an exercise and one may have to practice one's own fluency before presenting gibberish to the group. An illustration might consist of initiating a simple communication by asking a player, in gibberish, to stand up—*Gallorusheo!*—accompanying the sound with gesture. If the player is slow to respond, strengthen the gesture and repeat the sound, or utter a new phrase in gibberish. You might ask other students to sit down (*Moolasay!*), move about (*Rallavo!*), or sing (*Plagee?*) for example. The following exercise may now be played by the entire group.

GIBBERISH/INTRODUCTION

FOCUS: on speaking in Gibberish.

▶ Ask the whole group to turn to neighbors and carry on conversations in gibberish as if speaking an unknown language, and converse as though making perfect sense.

SIDE-COACHING: *Use as many different sounds as possible! Exaggerate mouth movements! Vary the tone! Try gum-chewing movements! Keep your usual speech rhythm! Let the gibberish flow!*

EVALUATION: Was there variety in the gibberish? Did the gibberish flow?

POINTS OF OBSERVATION

1. Keep the conversation going until everyone participates.
2. Have those who are more fluent in gibberish converse with those who stick with a monotonous *dadeeda* sound.
3. While most of the group will be delighted at their ability to converse in gibberish, there may be one or two who are so tied to speech for communication that they will be almost paralysed, physically as well as vocally. Treat this casually and, in subsequent gibberish exercises, flow of sound and body expression should become one.

GIBBERISH/DEMONSTRATION

FOCUS: on communicating to an audience.

▶ Single player, speaking gibberish, sells or demonstrates something to the audience. When well begun ask the player to repeat, but this time *pitch* what is being sold or demonstrated. Allow one or two minutes clock time per player, calling time at the half-way point—"half-minute to go"—and at the end.

SIDE-COACHING: *Sell directly to us! See us! Sell to us! Share your gibberish! Now pitch it! Pitch it to us!*

EVALUATION: What was being sold or demonstrated? Was there variety in the gibberish? Did the player see us in the audience or stare at us? Was there a difference between selling it and pitching it?

POINTS OF OBSERVATION

1. Insist on direct contact. If players stare or look over the heads of the audience, asking them to *pitch* their sale should bring about actual seeing. *Pitching*, as practiced in carnivals or department stores, requires direct contact with others.

2. Both audience and player will experience the difference when staring becomes seeing. An added depth, a certain quiet, will come into the work when this happens.

GIBBERISH/PAST INCIDENT

FOCUS: on communicating without word structure.

▶ Two players, preferably sitting at a table. Using gibberish, A tells B of a past incident, such as a fight or a trip to the dentist. B then tells A something that happened, also using gibberish. To avoid preliminary discussion the two players could be picked at random just prior to going on.

SIDE-COACHING: *Communicate to your fellow player! Don't assume you know what is being said! Share your gibberish!*

EVALUATION: Ask A what B told. Then ask B what A told. Ask the audience what was communicated to them.

POINTS OF OBSERVATION

1. Neither player must *assume* what the other has related since B's assumptions will not help A make the necessary clear communication.

2. When this game is first played, students will act out (tell) their incident in great detail. If relating a trip to the dentist, they might hold their jaw, moan, poke at their teeth, etc. Later the integration of sound and physical expression will be more subtle. They will be able to show, not tell.

GIBBERISH/TEACHING

FOCUS: on communicating.

Teaching A

▸ Two players; each team decides on a Where, Who, and What that is a teaching/learning situation. Examples are learning how to take pictures; playing a guitar, etc. All speech is in gibberish.

Teaching B

▸ Teams of three to ten players agree on Where, Who, and What so that players are in a teaching/learning situation. Teacher and students play scene in gibberish. Examples: a reading class, an anatomy class, airline hostess class; the choices are many.

SIDE-COACHING: *Communicate to student! Student, work with teacher!*

EVALUATION: Did players communicate clearly to one another? Players, do you agree?

POINT OF OBSERVATION

Now is a good time to play GIBBERISH/ENGLISH, followed by GIBBERISH INTERPRETER, pp. 384–85.

GIBBERISH/THE WHERE GAME

FOCUS: on the gibberish while showing Where through objects within it.

▸ Teams of ten to twelve players speaking in gibberish play this exercise the same as THE WHERE GAME, p. 98. The first player sets up a Where, into which other players enter as Who, developing relationships and activity.

SIDE-COACHING: *Communicate to the other player! Show Where! Show Who you are through use of objects! Don't tell! Relate in gibberish!*

EVALUATION: Did players show us or tell us? Were objects in space or in players' heads? Was communication made in gibberish?

GIBBERISH/WHERE WITH GIBBERISH

FOCUS: on communicating to the other players.

▸ Teams of two to four players agree upon Where, Who, and What, preparing floorplans if desired. Scenes are first played in gibberish, then repeated in English.

SIDE-COACHING: During gibberish: *Communicate to the other players! Don't expect them to interpret! What are you telling them?*

EVALUATION: Was the meaning of the English dialogue close to or the same as the gibberish?

POINTS OF OBSERVATION

1. Repeating in English is done simply to determine how exact the communication had been when made in gibberish. During the English version, stop the action frequently to ask the players and audience, "Did he or she communicate that in gibberish?"

2. Unnecessary verbalizing comes sharply to the players' attention when there are no understandable words between them. The English version of the scene does not have to be completed once this point has been made.

GIBBERISH/FOREIGN LANGUAGE A

FOCUS: on communicating with those who do not speak the same language.

▶ Teams of four players divide into sub-team A and sub-team B. The players on each sub-team speak the same language; however, the opposite sub-team speaks a different language; and neither team understands the other team's language. All four players agree on Where, Who, and What. For example, two students abroad are seeking directions from two officials at a foreign border.

SIDE-COACHING: *Sub-teams, talk to each other! You understand each other! Sub-teams, communicate with the foreigners! Play the game!*

EVALUATION: Did players on the sub-teams understand each other? Did players communicate to "foreigners" (opposite sub-team)?

POINTS OF OBSERVATION

1. Note (if players are working on focus) the fluency of speech and gesture when partners share the same language and the labored gibberish and exaggerated gestures used to communicate in the "foreign" language.

2. Tell the players to avoid giving actual language rhythms to their gibberish (such as French, Swedish, etc.)

GIBBERISH/FOREIGN LANGUAGE B

FOCUS: on communicating with another who does not speak the same language.

▶ Two players; each speaks a language that the other does not understand. They agree upon Who, Where, and What and speak only in gibberish.

SIDE-COACHING: *Communicate to the other player! Make no assumptions! Communicate!*

POINT OF OBSERVATION

This exercise could be played as a lead-in to GIBBERISH/FOREIGN LANGUAGE A, as is done in *The Theater Game File.*

GIBBERISH/GIVE AND TAKE (TWO SCENES)

▶ Incorporate gibberish into GIVE AND TAKE/TWO SCENES, p. 149. The subteams must be alerted to the game's focus, and, since they are speaking gibberish, will be greatly involved in full stage action.

ADDITIONAL EXERCISES FOR

HEIGHTENING THE REALITY OF WHERE

Stop!

Before moving ahead into the following exercises, it is most important to go into WORD GAME, pp. 189–91. We may find students at a loss for fresh material. They become tired of the familiar living room or schoolroom; development slows down if they constantly assume characters of schoolteachers and an occasional storekeeper. This is particularly true of the young actor.

WORD GAME releases more "playing" and generates a good deal of excitement and fun. Because it allows each team to play two or three scenes, it brings a flow to their work; it further shows the teacher-director (similar to the run-through in directing a play) how far students have come and what their needs are.

It would also be advisable to do a few exercises from Chapters V and VII before coming back to the additional Where exercises.

VERBALIZING THE WHERE
Part A

FOCUS: on remaining in the Where, while verbalizing every involvement, observation, relation, etc. in it.

▶ Two or more players, having agreed on Who, Where, and What, sit quietly on stage. Without leaving their chairs, they go through the scene verbally, describing their actions in the Where and their relation to the other players. Players narrate only for themselves, not other players. When dialogue is necessary, it is spoken directly to the other player, interrupting the narration. All verbalization is in the present tense. For example:

Player 1: "I tie my red-and-white apron around my waist and reach for the cloth-covered cookbook on the table. I sit down at the table and open the book. I turn to the section on cookies and thumb through the smooth, shiny, white pages, looking for a recipe. *Hmmm, sugar cookie—that sounds pretty good.* I put the book down, get up and walk to a cupboard, looking for my large mixing bowl . . ."

Player 2: "I open the screen door and run into the kitchen. Darn it, I let the door slam again! *Hey Mom, I'm hungry. What's for dinner?* " (and so on).

SIDE-COACHING: *Keep it in present time! Verbalize the objects that show Where! Describe other players for us! Keep opinions out! See yourself in action! No playwriting! Keep objects in space! Use dialogue when it appears! Verbalize the way your hand feels on the chair! No opinions! What color is the sky?*

EVALUATION: Did player stay in the Where? Or was player in the head (giving background information—judgments, opinions, attitudes)? Players, do you agree? Was there more that could have been verbalized? Parts of the Where? Parts of the action?

Part B

FOCUS: on retaining physical reality from VERBALIZING THE WHERE, Part A.

▶ Players who have understood the focus of Part A (which has worked for them while seated) can now get up and actually play the event through. They no longer verbalize their actions as in Part A, but speak only when dialogue is necessary.

SIDE-COACHING: *Keep the physical sense of the Where—communicate it! Smells, colors, textures! Show! Don't tell!*

EVALUATION: Players, did verbalizing the scene help the on-stage situation in Part B? Did verbalizing make playing easier? Audience, was greater depth brought to the playing of the scene because of the verbalization? Was there more life than usual? More involvement and relation? Players, do you agree?

POINTS OF OBSERVATION

1. Part A can aid in breaking players of opinions and attitudes in their work. It makes evident the progress of players in learning to internalize/externalize the stage space. If players persist in rumination and emotional response to action or objects, return to simple space object games (PLAY BALL, p. 64, CONVERSATION WITH INVOLVEMENT, p. 76) and RELATING AN INCIDENT ADDING COLOR, p. 157.

2. Except for the practice of side-coaching some of the mirror and space exercises, the exercises up to this point have attempted to objectify student-actors, to make them a part of the group, the environment, and the exercise—to create a *loss of self*. In this exercise, we bring self back to the actor, who is made conscious of the self as a part of the environment. This is most important; for the actor, much like the player in a game, must always know where he or she is in relation to what is happening on stage.

3. Note the complete absence of playwriting in these scenes as true improvisation appears.

4. It is not necessary that every detail covered in the narration be a part of the playing of the scene. This exercise gives an enrichment in detail and underlining which will be accomplished even if the narration is not followed to the letter.

5. Take care that this exercise is given only to those students who have become truly objective in their work.

6. This exercise has been played successfully with as many as ten players in a scene.

7. The problem must be handled carefully to avoid playwriting. If narration deals with what the players are thinking rather than on the detail of *physical* realities around them, this exercise can become a series of "soap operas."

8. VERBALIZING THE WHERE is valuable to use during rehearsals of improvisational theater and during a run when details and reality are lost or become sloppy. It is also valuable for the formal theater rehearsal.

WHAT'S BEYOND?/UNKNOWN EVENT

FOCUS: on what's beyond.

▶ Two players agree upon a simple Where, Who, and What. A is on stage; B enters. A must find out where B has been and what B has done through B showing (not telling) A. For example: Where—dining room; Who—husband and wife; What—wife selecting food from a party buffet table. Scene opens with wife helping herself to a drink and some food. Husband enters with a very pleased look on his face. He lightly brushes off his jacket and smoothes his hair as he comes downstage to wife. Wife then starts action relating to where husband was and what he was doing before he entered; i.e., focus is on what's beyond.

SIDE-COACHING: *Involve yourself in the on-stage reality! Explore it! No questions!*

EVALUATION: Did A assume what was happening off stage or did B show it? Did situation move into scene or simply end when A knew what B had done? Did actors stay with focus or did they start acting?

POINT OF OBSERVATION

By expanding the off-stage reality, on-stage work is enriched. Growing subtlety of selection will occur if the exercise is repeated at intervals throughout the training.

WHAT'S BEYOND?/PAST OR FUTURE EVENT

FOCUS: on what has happened or will happen in the beyond.

▶ Two players agree upon Where, Who, and What and explore this What on stage. Either they have done something together before they entered or they are going to do something together when they leave. Holding what's beyond in focus between them, the players' total on-stage involvement is with Where, Who, and What. The game is over when what's beyond is brought out on stage. Examples include a wedding feast, a funeral, a birth.

SIDE-COACHING: *Hold what's beyond between you! Involve yourself in on-stage activity! Explore it! Heighten it!*

EVALUATION: What was beyond? Players, do you agree? Did you let the focus work through the on-stage activity alone?

POINTS OF OBSERVATION

1. This and the following game should not be attempted until using the

Where and relating to another player through an on-stage activity are second nature.

2. If what's beyond is brought on stage almost before the playing begins, simply stop the exercise and go on with another team or come back to the game at a later date.

3. Since what's beyond is between players, non-verbal communication will be markedly enhanced and there will be deeper personal relation apparent in the players' on-stage work.

WHAT'S BEYOND?/PRESENT EVENT

FOCUS: on what is taking place in the beyond.

▶ Two players agree upon Where, Who, and What. Players pursue on-stage activity while something that involves both of them is taking place in the beyond but is not discussed openly. For example: Where—office; Who—co-workers; What—putting out company newsletter; What's Beyond—meeting of the board of directors who are discussing reducing staff. The scene is over the minute what's beyond is revealed on stage.

SIDE-COACHING: *Stay with the on-stage activity! Keep the focus between you! Show! Don't tell!*

EVALUATION: What was beyond? Did the players hold the focus (what's beyond) between them?

POINTS OF OBSERVATION

1. Used too early in the training, what's beyond is revealed so fast that the exercise takes but a few moments. If done by advanced players, however, who have learned how focus works for them, the game can be kept going for a long time, with the audience totally absorbed.

2. This exercise is a superlative problem for developing scene improvisation.

PREOCCUPATION A

FOCUS: on total preoccupation with one's own thoughts, while using objects together in the immediate environment.

▶ Two players, preferably seated in the same immediate environment, are each totally preoccupied with their own train of thought. One player is verbal and garrulous about his or her preoccupation. The other is silent, presumably listening, while focused upon his or her own preoccupation. Both maintain their involvement with objects in the immediate environment.

For example: Where—restaurant; Who—two women friends; What—having lunch together. A is totally preoccupied with a problem she is having with her boyfriend and keeps up a continuous verbalization of her problem. B is preoccupied with some personal problem that need never be mentioned. While concerned with their preoccupations, both are eating, asking to have things passed, pouring tea, etc. B answers A only at the point where she actually hears what she is saying; however B never enters into or becomes part of what A is saying, keeping her own preoccupation at all times.

SIDE-COACHING: *Keep activity going between you! Keep relationship!*

EVALUATION: Players, did you maintain your preoccupations? Did you maintain the activity between yourselves? Audience, do you agree?

POINTS OF OBSERVATION

1. Involvement with each other takes place only at the moments a "bridge" is made between the players, at random moments when B hears A speaking or where the immediate environment brings them together.

2. Variation of the exercise: while A is talking, B is preoccupied with an *object*, instead of a personal thought.

3. Preoccupation is closely linked to CONTRAPUNTAL ARGUMENT, p. 167, and can be used in conjunction with this exercise.

SOME FURTHER THOUGHTS ON PREOCCUPATION

1. If preoccupation is total, the Where, Who, and What will come to total life and improvising is a fact. There will be no playwriting possible.

2. The scenes produced from this exercise will have incredible reality in detail. The audience will get to know everything about the characters and where they are without any telling. A fragment, with no beginning, middle, or end, this exercise produces an organic unfolding of the char-

acters, their relationship, their background, and their attitudes without benefit of exposition, information, facts, or story.

3. While it follows CONTRAPUNTAL ARGUMENT procedures (p. 167), this exercise does not necessarily call for simultaneous talking by the players. Sometimes they will talk at the same time, and other times one will talk while the other is busy thinking and working at the activity.

4. The players are not in any conflict. There is agreement on what they will talk about and agreement on activity. Their preoccupation merely results from their points of view, not from a basis for argument.

5. This exercise builds rich scenes and is therefore valuable in developing material.

6. If conflict appears, stop the scene and have the players restate their agreed subject. If the original statement implied conflict, have them restate it toward a point of view.

7. Watch to see that the preoccupation during the scene does not become the players' involvement with each other.

8. Be certain the players have an activity (What) going on stage that keeps them completely occupied in doing physical things together that have no relation to the point of view each one is pursuing.

9. A resistance to the focus of the exercise will show itself by the players using the on-stage activity or each other in such a way that it displaces the preoccupation. This point is difficult to understand, particularly by players who consistently resist the focus and rely on gags, jokes, and playwriting to make a scene. They do not "trust the scheme."

10. If student-actors cannot solve this problem, they need more work on their preliminary steps. All the WHAT'S BEYOND? exercises and CONTRAPUNTAL ARGUMENT should be solved first.

11. Players are not to answer one another unless it is a "jump" as in CONTRAPUNTAL ARGUMENT. Then such a response becomes a total organic one and not just intellectual and is very exciting to observe.

12. The moment the preoccupation replaces the activity (occupation) as the stage involvement, the scene is over, and in all cases this becomes an organic ending.

BEGIN AND END[3]
Part I
FOCUS: on Where, Who, and What.

▶ Single player sets up a very simple Where, Who, and What, then plays in the usual manner.

For example: player enters, looks around to make certain no one has seen entrance and is obviously about to do something one shouldn't. Looks around room. Spots dresser. Goes to dresser. Opens a couple of drawers and riffles the clothes. Runs back to door to make sure no one is coming. Returns to dresser. Goes through a couple more drawers, finally finding what is sought. Puts it into coat pocket. Takes quick look in mirror, checking appearance. Leaves through door.

Part II
FOCUS: on recognition of building each beat within activity (begin-and-end).

▶ Player must now break the little scene into a series of smaller scenes, or "beats." Each "beat" or smaller scene is to have its own beginning and end. Player is to call out "Begin!" at the beginning of each beat and "End!" when it ends. Player is to build or intensify each beat/scene one upon the other. Using the image of "walking up stairs" should clarify this point.

For example: Player enters (BEGIN), stands looking around to make sure no one is there and finally closes door (END). (BEGIN) Stands, looking around room, spots dresser and goes to it (END). (BEGIN) Opens a couple of drawers, riffles contents, thinks noise is heard, quickly closes drawers and goes back to door to listen (END). (BEGIN) Looks back at dresser, goes to it again (END). (BEGIN) Opens more drawers, finds object (END). (BEGIN) Looks at object in hand and puts it in coat pocket (END). (BEGIN) Looks in mirror, straightens coat, and walks out of room (END).

SIDE-COACHING: *Give the new beat more energy! Build the next beat higher! Hit the* BEGIN *(vocally) harder!*

---

3. This exercise speeds up Where and develops scene material for performances.

Part III

FOCUS: on playing the scene as fast as possible, and on keeping all the details of the scene.

▶ Player goes through scene as in Part I, without saying "Begin" and "End" but doing everything as fast as possible while keeping the details of the scene.

EVALUATION: For Part I and Part III only.

Player, which scene was most real for you? Audience, which scene came to life (existed in space) for you?

POINTS OF OBSERVATION

1. In almost every case, we will find that the final scene had life for both the actor and the audience. This is so because the first scene tended to be generalized, or the player was subjectively involved, using invention rather than creating. The "begin" and "end" forced the player into an outside (objective) detailing of the objects.[4] The speed-up scene, then, profited by the detail created by "begin" and "end" and by the fact that the player did not have time to recall the details "begin" and "end" had brought up, but had immediate contact with W. W. W., present to the present moment.

2. The "begin" and "end" might be one moment on stage, like putting the object in the pocket, or might be a series of activities, like closing the door, moving into the room, and walking to the dresser.

3. This is a very valuable exercise for those interested in direction, for it gives the director a detailed breakdown of what must come out of the total scene—it gives the single beats within the overall scene, giving knowledge of where one is going. It is equally valuable for the actors in improvisational theater, when scenes are being set for performance.

4. The process of speeding-up scenes without begin-and-end can be em-

---

4. As in BEGIN-AND-END WITH OBJECTS, p. 78, and NO MOTION, p. 176, the detail comes through because the static required in BEGIN-AND-END "holds time" momentarily so that we *see* an action.

ployed whenever the teacher-director wishes. It tends to remove the "generalizations" from a scene and brings the scene to more vivid life.

5. BEGIN AND END reveals an essence, without cerebral (left brain) interference.

RUMINATING

(For very advanced students. This exercise belongs in the group of advanced WHAT'S BEYOND? and PREOCCUPATION.)

FOCUS: on the past incident.

▶ Single player, as in WHAT'S BEYOND?, sets up a double Where, Who, and What. The first consists of the on-stage environment and activity; the second is the Where, Who, and What of a past incident in the player's life.

EXAMPLE

ON STAGE

Where: musty den

Who: old man of 75

What: working on his stamp collection

PAST INCIDENT

Where: at work

Who: fellow-employees

What: farewell party retiring him

SIDE-COACHING: This should help the player in sensory concentration on the past incident. *Concentrate on the objects in the past incident! See the Where! What are the people around you wearing? Keep your on-stage activity going! Don't tell us the past incident—let it come forth!*

POINTS OF OBSERVATION

1. When what player is ruminating about comes to full view of the audience, the scene is over. This problem produces the most subtle and exciting material and acting.

2. If the scene becomes emotional or takes the form of talking about the past incident, the exercise has been given too early. Go back to earlier exercises.

ADDITIONAL EXERCISES FOR
SOLVING PROBLEMS OF WHERE

The following exercises are extra problems to be given throughout the Where period of training. During these sessions, students could continue to draw floorplans.

THE SPECIALIZED WHERE

FOCUS: on showing specialized Where through the use of physical objects.

▶ Teams of two or more players are given the same general Where (e.g., a hotel room, an office, a schoolroom, etc.). They are each to develop the Where more specifically, having agreed upon Who and What. Examples of a more specific Where are a Paris hotel room, a hospital office, a jungle schoolroom.

EVALUATION: Were there specially picked objects that made the setting distinctive and recognizable, or did they have to tell us where they were through talking? Is it possible to show different variations on a Where through objects alone?

POINTS OF OBSERVATION

1. If solved, the problem will result in different rhythms, depending upon the type of specialized Where chosen. A stockbroker's office with constant ticker-tape bursts would be much different from the quiet rustle of a hospital office; a jungle schoolroom would be much different from a modern urban public-school classroom.

2. Encourage the actors to choose unusual, unrealistic settings (e.g., an office in Heaven, a hotel in the jungle). If they have had WORD GAME this will be no problem for them.

3. Use WHERE WITH HELP and WHERE WITH OBSTACLES whenever the playing needs an assist from the teacher.

ART GALLERY

FOCUS: on showing physical characteristics (tall, fat, midget).

▶ Where: art gallery or museum. Who: to be developed within exercise.

What: visiting the art gallery or museum. Game is played by teams of two players.

A is seated on stage. B makes entrance, walks around viewing exhibit. B decides what A looks like and must in some way show this to A. When A knows what he or she looks like, A gets up with the character qualities B has given, walks around the gallery, and exits.

POINTS OF OBSERVATION

1. This may be too difficult and will not be solved by many students in the early sessions. They will, however, find it most interesting. Most important, it creates an intense observation of each other.

2. The teacher might suggest that the players can get fanciful about the other character (e.g., ten feet tall, big feet, light as a balloon, etc.). But the teacher should not give students samples beforehand.

SHOWING WHO THROUGH THE USE OF AN OBJECT

FOCUS: on showing Who through the use of an object.

▶ Two players agree upon one object that will show Who they are. They use that object within an activity.

Example: Who—two physicists; Object—blackboard. A and B are sitting quietly looking at something a short distance in front of them. A gets up and walks to the object. He picks up a piece of chalk and writes down a series of numbers—obviously an equation—on it. B watches, mumbles some indistinct sounds, shakes head, mumbles some more. A looks inquiringly at B. B concentrates on blackboard and then gets up, moves toward it, and writes another equation on it. B turns to A inquiringly. A: "You're right. That's the solution!"

EVALUATION: Did they show us or tell us?

POINT OF OBSERVATION

Continue to caution: *Show, don't tell! Act, don't react!*

WHERE WITH SET PIECES

FOCUS: on letting the objects (set pieces) create the scene.

▶ Two or more players. All teams are given a list of identical props and furniture. Where, Who, and What agreed upon. Players do scene.

EXAMPLE: A typical list of furniture and props might be:

window to a fire escape

door to a clothes closet

door to a bathroom

door to the outside

window to the street

pull-down bed

small refrigerator

glasses, coffee pot, miscellaneous hand props

bookcase

dresser or chest

easy chair or two

photographs

EVALUATION: Did they write a scenario around the objects, or did the objects create a scene? How different were the scenes from one another? Did the fire escape bring up a new view, or was it just a prop?

POINTS OF OBSERVATION

1. Do not evaluate until all the teams have worked on the exercise.

2. This exercise should help the teacher-director to determine whether actors are beginning to understand the phrase "let the Where create the scene." If they imposed a scene upon the objects instead of letting the objects create the scene, then the way focus works is not yet fully understood.

WHERE HOMEWORK EXERCISE

FOCUS: on all dialogue and action coming out of contact with the physical objects.

▶ Each student fills out floorplan at home, concentrating on Where, and studies how it might be used by characters. The student plans for two characters, setting up about a three-minute scene, and then writes a script setting up characters and action in relation to Where. Students come to class with their floorplans and scripts, and members of the group follow these and go through the exercise.

EXAMPLE: Where—living room. Who—boy and girl. What—studying.

Boy (focusing on desk) sits at desk writing (uses desk, pen, etc.). Girl (focusing on door) knocks on door (handles door). Boy (focusing on door) goes to door and opens it (handles door). Etc.

EVALUATION: Did each action come out of Where, or was the action imposed upon it?

POINTS OF OBSERVATION

1. Player must focus on objects first. This focus will generate an action toward it.

2. This exercise can be done within a workshop session. Teams of two can first work it out on paper and then go on stage and do scene.

THE ABSTRACT WHERE A[5]

FOCUS: on allowing Where, Who, and What to emerge from a setting.

▶ Some of the students arrange the stage behind a closed curtain. The intent is to create a setting which is not a literal representation of any particular place. They may use stage blocks, pieces of cloth, strange props, and unusual lighting effects. When they have finished, the curtain is opened. Another player must go up into the setting and remain quietly within it, but not perform any activity until inspired by the setting to do so.

SIDE-COACHING: *Do not force! Take all the time you need! Remain quiet!*

EVALUATION: Did the setting generate the W. W. W., or did the actor impose the W. W. W.?

POINTS OF OBSERVATION

1. Genuine set pieces and lighting are essential to the success of this exercise, since they stimulate mood, perception, and action.

2. Urgency for activity often moves an actor into a scene before it emerges. Watch for this.

3. Another actor may be sent on stage after the scene begins to move, not to impose any outside mood on the scene, however, but simply to come on stage waiting for the initiator of the scene to show the way. The onstage player may call for other actors—within the mood of the scene, of course.

5. EXCURSIONS INTO THE INTUITIVE, p. 178, is a similar exercise.

THE ABSTRACT WHERE B

FOCUS: on the grouping of props and set pieces and on letting them work for the player.

▶ Player A sets up a grouping of furniture such as chairs, combination of chairs, tables, window frames, etc., that suggests some human activity. The student audience observes the set-up, and anyone then enters into a scene suggested by the groupings.

EVALUATION: Did the players allow the "set" to work for them or did they impose a story upon it? Did the one who set up the stage have a story in mind? A scene? A definite goal?

POINT OF OBSERVATION

This problem requires set pieces and props and lighting to be fully utilized. The one who sets up need not have a story in mind but can let the "life in the object" suggest ways of grouping.

SHOWING WHERE WITHOUT OBJECTS

FOCUS: on using sensory equipment and/or relationships to show Where.

▶ Two players must show Where by any one of the following:

1. by looking at something (seeing)
2. by hearing (listening)
3. by relationship (who you are)
4. by sound effects
5. by lighting effects
6. through an activity

EVALUATION: Did they use an object to show us? Did they just do an exercise in seeing, listening, or whatever (as in Orientation), or did they show us Where?

POINTS OF OBSERVATION

1. This exercise will help to remove the fearful student's "crutch": using physical objects only by handling to show Where.
2. While this may appear similar to the kind of exercise given in early Orientation, the focus here is on Where—a subtle difference, but an important one.

3. Do not use this exercise until SHOWING WHERE THROUGH WHO AND WHAT has been covered thoroughly and is automatic with students.

4. Character relationships grow in great intensity throughout this exercise.

5. Advanced students find this problem most challenging; and many sessions can be spent on it, using all the methods for showing Where.

SENDING SOMEONE ON STAGE

FOCUS: on developing and/or ending an event (scene).

▶ Two players agree upon Where, Who, and What and begin scene. Other players enter during the playing if their presence will help develop or end the scene.

SIDE-COACHING: *Explore that action! Heighten that feeling! Accept the new player! Enter only if needed! Enter to develop! Explore and heighten!*

EVALUATION: Did players who entered the scene help develop it? Did the player come in at a time of need? Other players, do you agree? Audience, do you agree?

POINTS OF OBSERVATION

1. This exercise is useful when a performing group is doing suggestions from the audience; it alerts all players to enter (when needed) to develop and/or end a scene that has become bogged do\   ᷅hough "one minute!" cannot be called out during performance, this serves the same purpose.

2. This exercise is similar to THE WHERE GAME but more advanced in that players who enter the scene do so only if they can help develop and/or end it.

3. Variation: New player or side-coach calls "Freeze!," whereupon on-stage players freeze and a new player bumps a player or enters as a new Who.

THE THUMBNAIL SKETCH

FOCUS: on showing Who and What through the use of the Where.

▶ Single player decides on Where, Who, and What and plays scene.

POINT OF OBSERVATION

A variation of this exercise adds a point of decision to the person's life. Examples: whether or not to go to poorhouse; whether or not to give up son; whether or not to commit suicide.

SHOWING WHERE THROUGH WHO AND WHAT

FOCUS: on showing Where through using Who and What.

▶ Two or more players. Where, Who, and What agreed upon.

For example: Where—an orphanage; Who—a little girl and a man; What—new parent picking up girl. In this case, the whole sense of the orphanage came through.

EVALUATION: Did trying to show Where through Who intensify relationship? Is it possible to show Where through Who?

POINTS OF OBSERVATION

1. The student-actor must never tell Where he or she is.
2. This exercise serves the purpose of intensifying relationships.

WHERE WITHOUT HANDS

▶ Played the same way as INVOLVEMENT WITHOUT HANDS, p. 66.

Watch to see which players are breaking dependency upon the teacher-director and without being told integrate using no hands. In a bedroom scene, for instance, the player may have fresh nail polish on her fingers, making it necessary to open and shut drawers and closets with feet, elbows and shoulders. A player enjoying a walk in the park might keep his hands in his pockets as he kicks rocks, lets trees brush his shoulders, and buries his face in a bed of flowers. Players who do not integrate use of no hands will keep focus on hands instead of using objects to show Where, which completely alters the problem. Let players discover this for themselves.

CHAPTER V

ACTING WITH THE WHOLE BODY

A player's knowledge that he or she is one unified organism arrives when the whole body, from head to toe, functions as one unit in a life response. (See p. 219.) The whole body is a vehicle of expression and must develop as a sensitive instrument for perceiving, making contact, and communicating. The side-coaching *"See it with your elbow!"* is a way of helping a player transcend the cerebral concept of a feeling and restore it where it belongs—within the total organism. We must, in fact, cry with our stomachs and digest with our eyes.

This chapter contains exercises which help the players to physicalize for themselves the side-coaching used throughout the workshop: *Feel your anger in the small of your back! Hear that sound in your fingertips! Taste the food all the way down to your toes!*

Ideally, however, all acting workshops should be implemented with regular bodywork by a specialist in the field. It is the avant-garde teachers who are sought, those who are also investigating the problems of movement as it relates to the environment. Those have come to realize that body release, not body control, is what is needed for natural grace to emerge, as opposed to artificial movement.

EXERCISES FOR PARTS OF THE BODY

FEET AND LEGS ALONE

These exercises are designed to develop more organic use of the feet and legs and to awaken the student to the realization that feet and legs are integral parts of the body.

A stage curtain is needed for these exercises, a curtain raised just high enough to show the feet and legs of the actors. If the stage curtain cannot be raised up and down, a cloth can easily be hung at knee-height. Just be certain the upper part of the body is concealed.

Part I

FOCUS: on showing Who and What and/or a state of being with the feet and legs.

▶ One at a time, each player shows, without speech, either Who, What, or a state of being (impatience, grief, etc.) using only feet and legs. Encourage players to work barefoot when possible. Knowing their feet are exposed, players will work with greater understanding.

SIDE-COACHING: *Show Who you are with your toes! Put all that energy into your feet! We cannot see your face! Put your feeling in your feet!*

EVALUATION: What state of being was communicated? What was the player doing? Did legs and feet show or tell? Could the expression have been stronger? More varied?

POINTS OF OBSERVATION

1. This exercise, like others isolating parts of the body, helps players physicalize the side-coaching used in many of these theater games: *"Feel the anger in the small of your back!" "Hear the sound with your fingertips!" "Taste the food all the way down to your toes!"*

2. The phrase *"See it with your toes!"*, for instance, helps players transcend cerebral concepts of a feeling and restore that feeling to the total organism.

Part II

FOCUS: on communicating with feet and legs alone.

▶ As above, only feet and legs are visible. Two players agree on Where, Who, and What. No dialogue is to be used. Feet and legs alone are to communicate relationships, feeling states, Where, etc. Examples: young lovers on a park bench; watching a movie; refusing a salesman at the door.

SIDE-COACHING: *Show through your feet! Heighten it!*

EVALUATION: Who were players? Where? How old? Was communication clear? Was there variety of movement?

POINTS OF OBSERVATION

1. After the problem is solved in twos, the number of players can be increased.

2. Note students' later work to see how much has been absorbed by them. Are their feet brought more into action? Are doors shut by feet? Are feet used more for contemplation, for anger, within a scene? Do the feet come alive? Do the actors show more head-to-toe energy in their work? Did the feet tell a story, or did the scene evolve?

HANDS ALONE

Many actors who do use their hands along with their faces and voices are oblivious to their full value. Others wave them about as if they were gunny sacks, gesture like French chefs, or use them only to hold cigarettes. And, of course, some immature actors use their hands to accent every word spoken—uninteresting usage of some very important energy. In the following exercise, the student-actor learns to show relationship through the use of hands.

In preparation for the exercise, the teacher-director must see that a small, puppet-like stage is available, a stage which hides the students' bodies from view. An oblong table, curtained off, might be used. A light may be needed to illuminate the miniature playing area. Hand props are useful but not essential.

FOCUS: on showing Where, Who, and What, by means of the hands alone.

▶ Teams of two. Players agree on Where, Who, and What. Speech is not to be used, nor are the players to use any part of their bodies except their hands and forearms.

EXAMPLE 1: At first we saw the hands of someone writing on a piece of paper. They laid the paper aside and made a gesture for someone off stage to come in and sit down on the other side of the desk. The second pair of hands entered. They were tense and seemed gnarled and twisted, as if they belonged to a paralytic. They tried to hide themselves, to become composed. The first hands smoothly reassured them and proferred the paper for the paralyzed hands to sign. They pushed over a pen, which the latter picked up with great difficulty. While the paralyzed ones struggled to sign the paper, the first ones made smoothing, confident, friendly gestures. The scene went on for some time; with all our attention focused on these hands alone, the scene became intensely emotional and exciting.

EXAMPLE II: Where—priest's study; Who—priest and criminal; What—criminal is confessing to the priest.

SIDE-COACHING: *Laugh with your fingers! Shrug your hands, not your shoulders! Remember, we can't see your face! Put all that energy into your fingertips!*

EVALUATION: See Evaluation used in EXERCISE FOR BACK. Emphasize, to audience: did they communicate relationship? To players: did you plan a story?

POINTS OF OBSERVATION

1. Exercise can also be done as FEET AND LEGS ALONE, with single players. They are to show: who they are; what they are doing; state of being such as grieving.

2. At first, students will have a strong tendency to use their faces or other parts of their bodies, which are, of course, invisible to the audience. If they solve the problem of showing Where, Who, and What with their hands, they will soon develop articulate fingers.

3. At all times avoid discussing over-use of hands. If students begin to think in terms of energy, using this terminology is useful, because instead of telling them *not* to use their hands, the teacher can suggest that their energy be shifted to a more suitable location. In most cases it need never be mentioned.

4. Finger exercises are useful for hand development.

5. The tendency to plan a story is strong in this exercise. Players may have to be reminded again to let the focus work for them.

EXERCISE FOR BACK

FOCUS: on using back to show inner action.

▶ Any number of players.

Through this exercise, student-actors should be made aware that "no backs to the audience" is merely employed as insurance against loss of communication with the audience. The actor learns to communicate without the aid of dialogue or facial expression—in short, to communicate with the body.

Preliminary Work: Ask two students to come up in front of the class. One is to face the audience, and the other is to stand with his or her back to them. Have the audience list the parts of each person's body which can be used for communication, having the student move the parts as mentioned.

FRONT VIEW

1.	Movable forehead	9.	Teeth
2.	Movable eyebrows	10.	Shoulders
3.	Movable eyes	11.	Expandable chest
4.	Pliable cheeks	12.	Hands and arms
5.	Wrinkling nose	13.	Movable stomach
6.	Movable mouth	14.	Knees
7.	Working jaw	15.	Ankles and feet
8.	Movable tongue	16.	Curling toes

BACK VIEW

1. Head (no moving parts)
2. Shoulders (same as front)
3. Torso (solid mass)
4. Arms and hands (limited movement)
5. Buttocks
6. Heels, ankles, and backs of legs (comparatively immobile)

Now have individual students sit as if at a piano with their backs to the audience. They are to show how they feel through their manner of playing. Let them find their own attitudes. Some examples of attitudes might be: practicing unwillingly, concertizing, playing with nostalgia.

Following this, students agree on Where, Who, and What. Scene must be played with their backs to audience. They must choose a setting where dialogue is not usable (e.g., a church, around a mine disaster, a place where strangers gather). Since the focus is on using their backs to show the audience their inner action—what they are feeling—they should take something which has a focus of interest (e.g., people watching a man threatening to jump from window ledge, people watching gang fight, people watching football game).

EXAMPLE I: Where—bare waiting room with benches; Who—refugees, doctors, nurses, etc.; What—flood; Time—four A.M.; Weather—thunder and lightning; Problem—trying to sleep and ease discomfort.

SIDE-COACHING: *Don't show it in your face, show it in your back!*

EXAMPLE II: A play in which an eight-year-old played a nasty little princess required her to shove her prime minister off the stage. In the side-coaching, she was asked to show her anger and nastiness in her shoulder blades. The resultant action was not only body-wide, but her voice rose to great rage; and interesting stage business appeared as she shoved the minister out of the room. She was told to keep the anger in her shoulder blades as she came prancing down to her desk. She literally filled the stage with her feeling and had no trouble solving the problem. It was understandable and amusing to her to be "mad with your shoulder blades."

EVALUATION: Did they show us with their backs? Could they have found more variety of movement? Did they diffuse or concentrate expression? How old were they?

POINTS OF OBSERVATION

1. Variations of this exercise can be done using single players.
2. Do not expect too much at first. Only the more naturally skilled will be able to give a complete expression in the beginning.
3. The teacher-director may have to use this exercise early in the work, when the "backs or no backs" argument first comes up.
4. This exercise is useful for the formal theater in rehearsal for such things as a crowd scene.

PARTS OF THE BODY: FULL SCENE

FOCUS: on the specific part of the body previously covered.

▶ After each individual exercise or series of exercises concentrating on parts of the body, divide the group into teams. Where, Who, and What agreed upon. Scene is done in regular way, with student-actors in full view of audience.

POINT OF OBSERVATION

Note that many mannerisms have disappeared. For instance, student-actors who previously relied on facial grimaces will in many cases have lost this crutch as a result of these exercises.

EXERCISES FOR TOTAL BODY INVOLVEMENT

TOTAL BODY INVOLVEMENT

FOCUS: on head-to-toe involvement.

▶ For advanced students. Two or more players agree upon Where, Who, and What, choosing a What which involves head-to-toe action. For example: revival meeting, pilgrims crawling to shrine, deep-sea divers hunting treasures underwater, removing boulder from mouth of a cave, non-gravity space ship, etc.

RHYTHMIC MOVEMENT[1]

FOCUS: on rhythmic movement of the body.

▶ Large team sits or stands in playing area.

Part I

▶ Coach calls out an object. Each player instantly, without reflection, makes some movement that the object suggests, and continues until movements become rhythmical and easy. Coach provides musical accompaniment, if possible.

SIDE-COACHING: *Feel your rhythm! Forget your objects!*

Part II

▶ When group is moving rhythmically, coach suggests a Where. Without stopping rhythmic movements, players develop Who and What within the Where. For example: a carnival with strongmen, sideshow, dancers, freaks, etc.

1. See also RANDOM WALK, p. 201.

SIDE-COACHING: *Keep your rhythm going! Let your movement suggest your character! Give and Take!*

EVALUATION: Did the rhythmic movement develop the character in the given situation? Did players share the stage picture? Did players give and take? Players, do you agree?

POINTS OF OBSERVATION

1. GIVE AND TAKE WARM-UP, p. 386, is a good preparation for this exercise.

2. If individual players have difficulty finding characters, the coach may move in the playing area to help. This must be done quickly, without stopping the rhythm.

TENSE MUSCLE

FOCUS: on tensing up some part of the body.

▶ Two or more players agree upon Where, Who, and What. Each is to tense up some part of the body and is to keep it tense throughout the scene. However, this is not to be a part of the scene—it is to be a purely personal thing. Although the tenseness will almost always be noticed by the audience, the actor should not attempt to show it to the audience or to justify it in any way. A player who takes a stiff leg, for example, is not to justify it by being lame but is to play the scene as if the stiffness did not exist.

SIDE-COACHING: *Keep your focus constant! Don't relate to tense area!*

EVALUATION: Did the actors try to justify their tenseness, or did they simply work with it? Did their concentration on tense muscle give more spontaneity to the actors' work? To actors: Did your concentration on tense muscle give you a freedom of response?

POINTS OF OBSERVATION

1. On the initial presentation of this exercise, note that many players will tense up what is already a personal muscular problem for them (i.e., the stiff-necked person will take a stiff neck; the student who over-uses mouth and face will concentrate on a facial muscle). Do not point this out to the student-actors until the full group has completed the exercise the first time. Then, after bringing this out into the open through an evaluation, have them re-do the scene, taking another tense muscle. Needless to say, this may necessitate two or more sessions.

2. The resistance to focus which comes up in all the exercises will be very evident here. Choosing to tense up what is already a tense muscle constitutes resistance to working on the problem.

3. This exercise keeps players intensely preoccupied as they move through the scene. In one case, a student-actor who resisted almost all the problems had a dramatic breakthrough on this one.

PUPPETS AND/OR AUTOMATION
Part I

FOCUS: on moving like puppets.

▶ Two or more players on a team agree upon Where, Who, and What. They are to play, moving limbs and whole bodies as if they were controlled like string puppets. W.W.W. need not be connected with puppetry in any way. For example: a boy meets a girl for a first date. If possible, teacher-director could bring a string puppet to class and demonstrate, discussing its movements with students.

SIDE-COACHING: *Move your jaw like a puppet! The elbows! Knees! Sit! Walk! Gesture like puppets!*

EVALUATION: Did players maintain puppet-like movements throughout? Players, do you agree?

Part II

FOCUS: on moving like puppets and toys.

▶ Two to ten players, with Where established as a toy shop for all teams. Each team, in turn, agrees on Who and What within the established Where. Players can become talking/walking dolls, robots, jack-in-the-boxes, wooden soldiers, dancing bears, wind-up toys, etc., or let Who include the humans that work in or come into the toy shop. The What can be toys coming to life after dark, toys being repaired, cleaned, sold, etc. Young children delight in this exercise.

EXAMPLES: One man, in power, manipulates a large group of people who respond as puppets. Or, a puppet-maker puts on a show.

SIDE-COACHING: *Maintain the mechanical movements! Show! Don't tell!* (Use only if confusion arises on stage:) *Give and take! Move like a toy from head to toe!*

EVALUATION: Did players maintain toy-like movements throughout? What toys were they playing? Did players hear and see one another? Did they give and take or was there more than one center of attention at a time?

Part III

FOCUS: on mechanical movement.

▶ Teams of two or more players agree on Where, Who, and What. Players are machines or humans who operate the mechanisms, for example: sailors in a penny arcade, scientists with robots, mathematician and computer, man fixing a grandfather clock.

SIDE-COACHING: *Use your whole body to show! Don't tell! Maintain mechanical movement!*

EVALUATION: Did players show or tell? Players, did you stay on focus? Or did you playwrite?

POINT OF OBSERVATION

These puppet and automation exercises are given to encourage total body involvement with movement.

CHAPTER VI

NON-DIRECTIONAL BLOCKING

FUNDAMENTALS

One of the marks of the seasoned player is natural purposeful stage movement. Stage movement, or blocking, must be understood for what it is. The director must not influence exactly where actors stand or how they get on and off the stage except where position strengthens or weakens relationships, mood, or characterization.

Blocking should facilitate movement, emphasize and heighten thought and action, and strengthen relationships. It can be used symbolically or visually to underline conflict, relationship, and mood. It is mass balancing mass, mass balancing action, mass balancing design. It is the actor inside the set moving within the color and background of set and costumes. *It is the integration of the stage picture.*

Blocking must be understood in this way. The actors must learn to consider the demands of the scene. Like lithe ballplayers, they must always be alerted to where the ball may land and as they move about the stage be aware of fellow players as well as of their place and parts within the total environment. Actors must become so sensitive to blocking that they keep the stage picture interesting and the sight lines clear in every moment of their work.

For the formal play, blocking should never intrude or appear to be a learned response. Players must not move from sofa to chair to door like awkward dancers who have learned their steps by count. Premature blocking arbitrarily put upon unseasoned actors not only creates this unpleasant rigidity but also renders the players unable to meet crises during performances. Those actors who have been trained in non-directional blocking greatly implement the work of the director as they move around the stage, always aware of their place within the total picture. Non-directional blocking achieves spontaneous selection and the ability to meet all crises.

For improvisational theater, the necessity to understand this point is apparent. And, as with other stage conventions, student-actors must absorb this awareness until it becomes intuitive or second nature to them. Spontaneous blocking appears to be carefully rehearsed when players are *truly* improvising.

Non-directional blocking gives the actor and director the same relationship that they must have when developing scenes for improvisational theater presentation. It is give and take between actor and director. Because the director has a different look-in and is seeing the canvas from the viewer's standpoint, he or she can (by observing what has been achieved spontaneously by the actor) take from the actor what is best needed for the scene and give it back. The director thus selects, rejects, or adds to what is being done on stage, plus the playwright's suggestions. In this way the actors and director work as one unit, strengthening the finished play with the totality of their individual creative energy.

The growing ability to see the stage from the audience's point of view while on stage gives the players awareness of action in relation to others and so becomes a great step towards self-identity, ridding them of the crippling effects of egocentricity and exhibitionism.

Stage Business

Stage business is closely tied in with blocking; and the two will grow hand in hand. The most skilled director or actor cannot always intellectually find interesting stage business. Like blocking, business should be unobtrusive and spontaneous in appearance. This can only happen when it grows out of the stage relationship. Stage business should not be an activity just to keep actors occupied. Aside from the obvious method of adopting the business suggested in the script itself, the director of formal plays will find that using the following acting exercises will create more business than the director or actor could find in many hours of work on the script.

Share with Your Audience

The phrases "Share with your audience" and "You're rocking the boat" will give the students a sensitivity towards the problem of blocking. The word "blocking" itself is deliberately avoided in the workshops, since it is a label. "Share with your audience" should become a personal problem to the student-actor. When it is thoroughly understood, then the word "blocking" can be introduced; although, even with professional actors, "Share with your audience" brings out a more natural response than a comment on their poor blocking, for sometimes professional actors need to be reminded that they are on stage for a reason.

Many interesting moments occur on stage when actors, in trying to share the stage picture, must move other actors. When the director coaches, "Share the stage picture," he or she should never call the name of any particular actor. *Every* actor on stage is responsible for everything that happens. If some actors are not aware of the stage picture, other actors must move them. If this cannot be done, then all must move into a new stage picture around the unaware actor. This awareness of each other creates continually flexible, moving stage. In a sense, whenever necessary each actor fills the role of director or prompter.

When actors work for the total scene, they can only be grateful for such help. For instance, the situation is an office. Howard is standing in front of the secretary, and so we cannot see her. Howard is oblivious to the fact that he is "blocking" and does not respond to the coaching: "Share the stage picture!" The secretary simply says, "Will you please be seated?" Or, "Would you please come here?" Or, if there is still no response, she may physically move him to a more satisfactory position; or, if this is not possible, she will re-block herself in relation to him.

STAGE PICTURE, p. 393, is the exercise to play.

EXERCISES

Following PREOCCUPATION A (p. 122) are many points of observation regarding both A and B versions of this game.

PREOCCUPATION B

FOCUS: on total preoccupation and verbalization of one's own point of view
while maintaining an interrelated activity with fellow player.

▶ Two advanced players agree upon Where, Who, and What. Players also
agree on a subject or point of view to be discussed during the activity. This
activity (What) must totally involve both players; for example, preparing for
a picnic, dressing to go out, etc., so that all through the scene they consistently need each other's help—as in the case of a picnic, the preparation
of food, helping each other find things, etc. Players keep a flow of dialogue
on their agreed preoccupation from separate points of view while relating
to each other with action and dialogue. They must have total occupation
(physical) together and total preoccupation (thought) at the same time
(see NO MOTION, p. 176).

SIDE-COACHING: *Keep your own point of view! Keep the activity going on
between you! Meet each other only because of the on-stage activity!*

EVALUATION: Audience, did players have total preoccupation with their
views? Did they work together on the activity? Did they use the Where continuously? Was preoccupation with players' points of view separate in that
they did not build on each other's? Did their preoccupations keep them
from each other on one level, while the Where, Who, and What kept them
fully involved and relating in the stage present? Did they verbalize regarding things in the immediate environment without displacing the preoccupation?

POINT OF OBSERVATION

Other examples: Where—lawn; Who—sweethearts; What—playing cro-
quet; Agreed subject—kissing in public. Where—bowling alley; Who—
husband and wife; What—scoring; Agreed subject—what to do with his
mother. When the second sample situation produced conflict in actual use,

it was stopped, discussed and restated. The restatement, "What to do about old people," was more appropriate and "What to do with mother" appeared out of it naturally.

GIVE AND TAKE/TWO SCENES

(GIVE AND TAKE WARM-UP, p. 386, is the lead-in to this exercise.)

This game, requiring give and take, is also closely related to problems of listening and speech and should be exploited for these purposes. The first four parts of this exercise, A through D, should be used in problems of listening and speech. Although subsequent exercises are directly related to self-blocking, A through D ought to precede them for clarification.

Without listening, a team can neither give nor take. And when a team is taking, the other team cannot give unless the voice cuts into their scene with sharpness, resonance, and clarity. For this reason give and take (players' choice) is especially valuable for speech resonance. The exercise can be played with both teams so attentive to giving and taking that dialogue comes through with depth and resonance. To give or take, a voice must, like an instrument, make its tone felt. Players can develop this ability to give and take so sharply that sometimes teams can give or take the scene with a single word. GIVE AND TAKE originated when it was noted that actors had difficulty relating when they were in a scene with four or more on stage at once and where there was more than one center of attention, such as a restaurant, a party scene, etc.

A. Give and Take (with direction)

FOCUS: on listening/hearing with partner to know when to give and take.

▶ Divide into teams of four. Teams sub-divide into teams of two. Set up two tables on stage, with a sub-team at each table. The members of each sub-team set up a relationship between themselves (e.g., sub-team A, a husband and wife deciding on a separation; sub-team B, two businessmen trying to agree on a contract). At no time during the exercise do the sub-teams have any interchange with one another. Each sub-team works as an independent scene.

Both sub-teams start their scenes at the same time. Once they've begun, the teacher-director steps in and calls upon one sub-team, say sub-team A, to *"Take!"* Sub-team B must then fade out of the focus and give the frame or focus to sub-team A. In other words, when sub-team A is called, their scene becomes the focus on stage (much like a camera closeup), and they must share their voices and their problem of relationship with the audience. At the same time, sub-team B must stop all visual and sound activity. Sub-team B is not to freeze, however, but is to continue relationship and problem even though they have moved out of focus. When the teacher-director calls sub-team B, they are to move back into focus and share their voices and problem with the audience, with sub-team A moving out of focus and stopping all sound and visual activity, while maintaining relationship.

For example, when sub-team A is called, sub-team B (the businessmen trying to agree on a contract) might, though stopping all sound and visual action, stay with their relationship by reading over the contract, leaning head on hand contemplatively, eyeing each other speculatively.

When sub-team B is called, sub-team A (husband and wife deciding on separation) might turn their backs on each other in anger, weep or mope, embrace.

These techniques serve to keep the sub-teams out of the focus and yet still relating to each other and their problem.

SIDE-COACHING: *Table A! Take! Table B! Give! Keep relationship within the fade! Table B! Take! Table A! Give! Do not freeze!*

POINTS OF OBSERVATION

1. If either of the sub-teams is obviously waiting for their "turn," if they freeze, then they have not solved the problem. Many student-actors find it difficult to maintain relationship and tension in stillness. They will manage to keep themselves in constant activity no matter how minute. If this becomes a problem with your group, give them the exercise called SILENT TENSION #1 (p. 175) along with the present one.

2. Watch for spontaneous breakthrough in players struggling with the problem of "giving" without freezing and without depending on the

teacher for examples. If this exercise is to be used for public performance, then verbalizing all possibilities of retiring from scene would be explored.

B. Give and Take: Using "Give!"

FOCUS: on *giving* focus to the other sub-team.

▶ Instead of the director calling on sub-teams to give, the sub-teams give the focus (frame) to each other, when and how they determine to do so.

SIDE-COACHING: *Give! Play the game! Give as one unit!*

C. Give and Take: Using "Take!"

FOCUS: on *taking* focus from the other sub-team.

▶ Sub-teams must now take the focus from each other. This will often turn into shouting and confusion, but keep with it. When spontaneous selection is forced up by the problems of the scenes, players will sing, jump on chairs, stand on their heads, etc. if such tactics are necessary to take the focus.

SIDE-COACHING: *Take! Take!* (until focus is taken).

D. Give and Take: Player's Choice

FOCUS: on *giving* and on *taking* without specific side-coaching.

▶ This time the sub-teams are to give and take from each other as the situations arise, giving focus back and forth without benefit of side-coaching.

EVALUATION: Players, was there a problem giving focus? The answer is usually "Yes." We couldn't hear the other sub-team so we didn't know when to give it. Players, when were you able to give focus? When the other team came in strong.

Did you have a problem taking the focus? Yes. Why? Because we couldn't come in strong enough to take it from them.

The evaluation will cause most of the actors to realize that whether they give or take, relationship is implicit in either one and must take place before a play can come into focus. The student-actor in improvisational theater must know when to give the focus and when to take the focus. In either case, the same result will be apparent: heightened stage energy and a clearer stage picture.

POINTS OF OBSERVATION

1. When stages get cluttered with everyone talking at once, side-coach *"Give and take!"* and actors will give or take as necessary.

2. This exercise should be repeated continuously throughout training. Frame can be used interchangeably with focus.

3. This exercise has value for the student director.

CONVERGE AND RE-DIVIDE

FOCUS: on giving and taking the focus of an event (scene).

▶ Teams of four, six or eight players agree on Where, Who, and What, then divide into sub-teams of two players who are in an immediate relationship. For example: Where—a party, Who—guests, What—eating, drinking, etc. During playing, sub-teams give and take focus from each other as in GIVE AND TAKE. At intervals, side-coach calls "Converge!" and all players come together and find a common action, for instance, getting food at a buffet table. When the side-coach calls "Re-divide!," sub-teams must split, and the players continue with new partners, again playing give and take. The coach calls "Converge!" and "Re-divide!" until players end in their original sub-team relationships.

SIDE-COACHING: *Give and take! When one team takes, other teams give! Give and take! Converge! All teams converge! Re-divide! New sub-teams! Give and take! Take and give! Converge!*

EVALUATION: If sub-team A had the focus, did B and C use interesting ways of fading out? Did players integrate converging and re-dividing with the overall event or scene? Did players give and take for the enrichment of the event or scene?

POINT OF OBSERVATION

It is recommended that all teams go through the example given to quicken understanding, converging at a buffet set up in the Where and re-dividing into the room. When "Converge!" is called, full group interaction results. It is then that new pairings-off are found.

LONE WOLF

FOCUS: on giving and taking the focus of a scene.

▶ This is a variation of CONVERGE AND RE-DIVIDE. However, one of the sub-teams of two players consists of only a single player. Thus, if there are five people in a group, the sub-teams will consist of two, two, and one; if there are three players, the sub-teams will consist of two and one.

All sub-teams agree on a Where which could be a group situation, such as a doctor's waiting room, a bus depot, hotel lobby, or library. The sub-teams then separately choose Who and What. For example: Where—newspaper office; Who—sub-team A, two reporters; Who—sub-team B, copy editor and photographer; and Who—sub-team C, copy boy.

Re-dividing will produce a new single player (Lone Wolf) whenever it is called, whose problem it is to gain the focus of the scene without having a player to work with. Side-coaching must be attentive to this, sensing when or if to call "Converge!" or "Re-divide!" and sensitive to what occurs through "Give and Take!"

SIDE-COACHING: *Give and take! Sub-teams, when one team takes, you give! Converge! All teams converge! Redivide! New sub-teams! Give and take! Play the game! Converge!*

POINT OF OBSERVATION

Until "Converge!" is called teams remain preoccupied with their own dialogue and relationships. During the converging, dialogue and action of all players intermingle. When they re-divide the teams relate to a new single player.

CHANGING PLACES

FOCUS: on connection with fellow players.

▶ Four to eight players per team agree on Where, Who, and What and divide into sub-teams of two. Players on sub-teams are numbered One or Two. After playing has started, when side-coach calls "*One!*" that player on each sub-team changes stage position and player Two goes to the place that One has just vacated. When "*Two!*" is called, players numbered Two initiate moves and Ones go to where Twos have been. Call changes until players are moving easily. After this either player may initiate movement that the partner must respond to. All action is integrated with Where, Who, and What.

SIDE-COACHING: *One, move! Two, move!* (Call changes until all are playing easily.) *You are on your own! Follow the initiator!*

EVALUATION: Audience, were movements integrated? Were movements non-pedestrian?

POINTS OF OBSERVATION

1. Players may or may not know each other within the situation. In a party scene, for instance, the characters are assumed to know one another, but this would not necessarily be true of a scene laid in a train station.

2. The concentration required in observing one's partner's movements, while at the same time initiating movement, brings an interesting sparkle to the stage as the players are alerted to each other.

3. Do not allow teams to select a "built-in" movement situation as in an art gallery. Remind student-actors to keep the problems challenging.

SIGHT-LINES
(TRANSFORMATION OF STAGE PICTURE)

▸ Sharing the stage picture will eventually become an organic process for the student-actor. However, this exercise is especially helpful in emphasizing the visual tie between the actor and the audience. It also has value in stimulating unusual design and movement within the stage picture.

Stage blocks, risers, and ramps are particularly useful in helping to find interesting and different uses of stage levels.

1. Using a blackboard, sketch out a diagram of the line of sight from the individual actor on stage to the individual in the audience.

2. To increase awareness of perspectives, have student place a hand a few inches in front of his or her face and note how the objects beyond the hand, although larger, are almost obliterated from view.

3. Discuss the uses of the blocks and risers in clearing sight lines and creating an interesting stage picture through the use of levels.

4. Have the teams do scenes in the usual way, keeping in mind the actor-to-audience sight-lines and utilizing the stage levels.

5. (a) Through a series of commands to "Change!" players continuously transform the stage picture; (b) players initiate change. In either case, there is to be no forethought as to the changes.

POINT OF OBSERVATION

Professional actors can use this exercise as a freshener and reminder that they, too, should strive for interesting and exciting stage pictures to share with the audience.

MOB SCENES

FOCUS: on participation.

▸ To give life and vitality to mob scenes, each individual within the mob must have a personal reality. Improvisations around such characters' lives prior to joining the scene can give substance to their mob participation. It is important in mob scenes that the sight-lines to individuals or groupings are kept clear. Mob scenes can often be very refreshing to the eye if broken lines are used. Use of backs creates broken lines (see Chapter V).

EXAMPLE: To create a mob scene in which many people hovered around a disaster area, improvisation was used in the following manner. Prior to going on stage, each family group or individual who was to be in the scene was put into a "house" of their own. Each group established a Where, Who, and What. A large room off stage was used for this, and about fifteen of these units were set up simultaneously. All were busy with their own private lives. Some visited others, some talked over the fence to their neighbors, etc. The director moved down the "street," calling "Focus!" at different houses. Each group called, then played its relationships. When the disaster whistle blew, bedlam broke loose, and there were some truly interesting scenes: dashing from house to house, collecting children who were playing, etc. Then, en masse, the players rushed to the scene of the disaster—to the stage. Thus the mob became a real lively excited group of people.

EVALUATION: This exercise has extra value, since the actors very often need to feel they are more than a mob—as indeed they are. By individualizing them and making them realize they are an essential part of the play, the stage gains depth.

POINT OF OBSERVATION

The director of formal plays should never have individuals in mobs make incoherent sounds. They should all speak and shout full meaningful remarks. To achieve this, the director can have each one speak a line individually. Then, like a conductor, he can bring up or lower individual voices to create the mob composition.

EXITS AND ENTRANCES

An actor must integrate not only entering the stage but also leaving it.[1] There must be a sharp focus on the player, if only for a fleeting moment. It is sharpness in framing details that gives stages clarity and brilliance.

FOCUS: on making exits or entrances which have the full involvement of fellow players.

▶ Teams of four, five, or six players agree on Where, Who, and What. Players each make as many exits and entrances as possible within Where, Who, and What, but each exit or entrance must be so framed that on-stage players are fully involved with the player's entrance or exit. Audience players are free to call out: "Come back!" or "Go back! You didn't make it!" if players barge in or out without the full attention and involvement of fellow players.

SIDE-COACHING: *Keep on-stage involvement! Don't plan your exits! Watch for the moment! Stay with the activity! Play the game! Let exits (entrances) come through Where, Who, and What!*

EVALUATION: Which exits and entrances truly had full involvement and which were only trying to get attention? Players, do you agree?

POINTS OF OBSERVATION

1. This exercise should organically clear the difference between getting attention (isolation) and getting involved (part-of-the-whole).

2. If on-stage players give attention and become involved in player's exit or entrance, no action is barred, no matter how fanciful it may be.

3. As a variation, reverse the emphasis. Now the other on-stage players must frame the actor as he or she exits or enters.

BEGIN AND END

▶ This is the time in workshop development to repeat BEGIN AND END from the Where sessions (p. 125).

1. Cf. WHAT'S BEYOND?/WHERE, p. 99.

CHAPTER VII

REFINING AWARENESS

Actors in improvisational theater must listen to fellow players and *hear* everything that they say if they are to improvise a scene. They must look and *see* everything that is going on. This is the only way players can play the same game together.

The exercises that follow serve as tools for actors in the formal theater as well. They will, if pursued, relieve players of rigidity and posed movements; for when an actor sees another actor and listens to another's dialogue rather than mouthing or sub-vocally reading the other's lines as memorized along with his or her own, work has a naturalness on stage. If actors in formal theater would see a fellow player opposite them, not a character, their work too would be free of "acting."

That exercises in verbal agility are necessary to the improvisational actor should be self-evident. Moreover, learning to communicate within silences can lead to heightened moments on stage.

Listening and Seeing games must be used throughout workshops. Some good ones are THROWING LIGHT GAME, p. 166, NUMBERS CHANGE, p. 407, SINGING SYLLABLES, p. 409, WHO STARTED THE MOTION?, p. 68. These are all traditional games from Neva Boyd's *Handbook of Recreational Games*.

LISTENING

RELATING AN INCIDENT ADDING COLOR
FOCUS: on seeing an incident in full color as it is being told.

▶ Two players. A tells B a simple story (an incident limited to five or six sentences). Then B retells the same story, putting all the color into it that B saw during A's telling.

For example, A narrates: "I walked down the street and saw an accident between a car and a truck in front of the school building." B retells: "I was walking down the grey street and saw an accident between a green car and a brown truck in front of the red brick school."

SIDE-COACHING: *See the other! Let the other see you! See the color as you hear the story! Talk directly to one another!*

EVALUATION: Players, did you add as much color as possible? Did you stick to what your partner said? Audience, do you agree?

POINTS OF OBSERVATION

1. Direct seeing of the other is stressed for players who turn away from the storyteller to concentrate on color.
2. Other qualities may be substituted for color (texture, odor, sounds, shapes), as may adverbs and adjectives.
3. This exercise can be a preliminary step to VERBALIZING THE WHERE, p. 118.

GIVE AND TAKE/TWO SCENES

▶ Repeat this exercise from the previous chapter (p. 149). It is invaluable for getting student-actors to hear one another.

BASIC BLIND

FOCUS: on moving in the space blindfolded, as if one can see.

▶ Teams of two or more. The playing must be done blindfolded, with real props and set pieces, including a telephone. Members must agree on Who, Where, and What and devise a What in which many things will be handed from one person to another—a tea party, for example. The blindfolded players are to move about the stage as if they can see. A scene in which "not seeing" is implicit (such as with a blind character or in a dark room) cannot be used. The coach has a bell with which to signal the ringing of the on-stage telephone.

SIDE-COACHING: *Integrate that groping! Follow through on that action! Find the chair you were looking for! Hang up your hat! Be adventurous!*

EVALUATION: Did they move naturally? Were all gropings and movements integrated by their Where, Who, and What? Was such integration interest-ing? (A player who was looking for a chair might use a swinging hand or rolling body motion as part of the character, to avoid what might otherwise be groping.) Were they adventurous?

POINTS OF OBSERVATION

1. Any groping while hunting for seats, props, etc. must be integrated through Who (a physical quality of the characters they are playing) or What (part of the activity of the scene). If, for any reason, players leave the playing area, they are to remain blindfolded until the end of the scene.

2. In the beginning, the loss of sight produces great anxiety in some play-ers. Often student-actors will not dare venture out into the exercise but will sit glued to a seat, hang onto another person, or stand immobile in one spot. Side-coaching and the use of the telephone will help. The telephone will move the frightened, clinging student away from his or her "straw." The teacher simply rings the bell and asks the student who answers to call the student who needs helping to the phone. It also has the opposite effect upon some. One student remarked after a blind session: "I feel so much freer doing blind." This showed the teacher that this student was still not part of the game and still fearful of expo-sure on stage. When one student articulates a feeling, it is certain he speaks for others as well.

3. Unless children younger than ten are doing this exercise, keep opposite sexes on separate teams. Because they are unable to see, fear of body contact keeps actors tense and not free to solve the problem. Contact such as handing things to each other is necessary to the success of this exercise.

4. If possible, do this exercise in a flat area where there is no danger of student-actors falling off the stage. This will remove a very real fear of doing so. Be sure to avoid using sharp, pointed, or breakable props.

5. Watch for players who might be peeking, so expertly do they move from place to place. Go on stage and alter a few things here and there and check that blindfolds are secure.[1]

---

1. See comments on the uncertain child, p. 266.

BLIND FOR ADVANCED STUDENTS A

▸ Students play BASIC BLIND in the regular way. However, they must state what they are going to do before following through with actions. For example, "I think I'll have some candy" must be stated; and then the candy must be sought. A group will have to be fairly skilled to do this.

BLIND FOR ADVANCED STUDENTS B

FOCUS: on using all the objects on the floorplan and on sharing with the audience.

▸ This exercise puts the audience back into the picture. Teams of two or more players agree on Where, Who, and What and provide the audience with a floorplan. This must be drawn large enough to be visible, using words instead of the usual symbols. Players are blindfolded and assemble on a bare stage without props. They must use all the objects on the plan and proceed as if they could see— and they must *share with the audience*. An actor who achieves close communion with the audience will know when he or she has lost the way.

SIDE-COACHING: *Share the stage picture! Share your face!*

Summary on Blind Exercise

By breaking the student-actor's dependency on the sense of sight, energy is released into new areas—the most important of which are hearing and listening. This exercise forces the student-actor to develop *physical* head-to-foot attentiveness to what is happening on stage and creates a total bodily awareness of objects and fellow players. Because of the total involvement with the focus of the game in this exercise, BLIND develops an awareness of space and sound in space and makes this space a living, palpable substance for the player.

Players must follow through on every action, utilizing contact and interchange between people. The character who offers tea to another must then locate that actor and present the teacup; the other actor must, in turn, find the teacup that is being handed out. Or, should an actor make an entrance into a scene as a guest and be greeted by the hostess, extended hands must be shaken and wraps received and hung up.

If the scene is a cocktail party, one of the actors may "get drunk" and integrate groping or bumping into things this way; however, if one preplans this before going into the scene, it will have lost its spontaneity and, therefore, its usefulness. For the student's development, it then becomes a rehearsed bit (performance) rather than a working on solving-the-problem during action.[2] Another actor, searching for the art-object the hostess is handing over, may take a few steps at a time as if viewing the art-object critically from a distance. This stopping and starting and continuing dialogue around the object will help to locate both the hostess and the object to be handled and will integrate the "searching." Or, an actor who is having trouble locating things may develop a physical (character) quality such as mincing steps or a rolling body and swinging arms.

Any failures to integrate connections to one another should be watched for. If A enters the scene saying "Hello!" and holding out her hand, B quite naturally will not see it. A must then follow through on her action—and must let B know that the hand is extended for a handshake; and B, in turn, if he fails to shake hands, must physicalize not seeing or accepting the extended hand immediately. An excess of real props and set pieces should be used; and players should wear lots of extra hats, bags, etc., to make the problem of handing things around more challenging.

SEEING AND NOT STARING

The following exercises emphasize visual involvement with fellow players. A student must not only look but must also see to "solve the problem." These exercises can be used throughout the workshops to precede exercises in relationships of a more complex nature. For the director of formal theater, they can be interjected throughout rehearsals, using the dialogue and actions of the script.

Staring is a curtain in front of the eyes as surely as though the eyes were closed. It is a mirror reflecting one back upon oneself. It is isolation.

2. For using BLIND during rehearsal of a formal play, see p. 326. Players who continue to grope with their hands have little or no body awareness. Repeat SPACE WALK and SPACE SHAPING exercises (pp. 80–83) as a warm-up for BLIND.

Student-actors who *stare* but do not *see* prevent themselves from directly experiencing their environment and entering into relationships.

Staring is easily detected by watching for certain physical characteristics: namely, a flat look to the eyes and a rigidity to the body. Gibberish will quickly show the teacher-director the degree to which this problem exists in student-actors. One adult player who consistently resisted the focus, avoiding contact with fellow players in every way by playing "characters," had a breakthrough on this problem.[3] When it was pointed out that he was working on a character and not on the problem of seeing, he replied, "How can I see if I am not a character?" "Well, how can you?" he was asked. He thought this through seriously and was most perplexed. A further question was asked: "What do you do when you see?" He could think of no answer but, "You just look." That was the answer. "That is all the problem is asking you to do, to see."

If you as teacher-director can induce a player to *see*, even momentarily, you will observe how the face and body become more pliant and more natural as muscle holds and fear of contact disappear. When an actor sees another, direct contact without attitudes is the result. Recognition of a fellow player gives one a compassionate glimpse of oneself as well.

By this time, students have learned to respond to the meaning of sharing with the audience. The audience has now lost the role of "judge" for them and has become part of the experience. However, there still may be a strong resistance to involvement on the part of some players, evidenced by the editing, judging, joking, and playwriting that persists in their work. In such a case, it may well be that the player is being his or her own audience in the most subtle sense. The following exercise will help eliminate this "last judge."

MIRROR/SUB-TEAMS REFLECT FEELINGS

FOCUS: on reflection of feelings.

▶ Teams of four divide into sub-teams A and B. The game is played exactly as MIRROR/SUB-TEAMS FOLLOW THE FOLLOWER, p. 67, which emphasized

---

3. See Chapter XII.

simple activity. Here, the sub-teams must strive to mirror the feelings of the other players. One sub-team begins initiating and the other reflecting; after a time, "Change!" is called and teams are playing follow-the-follower.

When teams confer over W. W. W., have them add a problem to give a scene of an intimate or personal nature between two people where there will not be too much moving around (e.g., sweethearts at a drive-in movie, husband and wife working on budget late at night). In this more complex observation of relationships, too much movement can defeat the focus of the exercise.

POINT OF OBSERVATION

After this exercise, there should be greater intensity and involvement with the total stage picture in players' work. If not, repeat the exercise at a later date.

GIBBERISH/DEMONSTRATION

▶ This exercise, outlined on p. 114 (selling or demonstrating something to audience) can be used very successfully to emphasize seeing and not staring. This exercise has probably already been done in the ninth or tenth session of Where.

For the director of formal theater whose actors are staring, this will be a great assist.

PITCH

FOCUS: on communicating with (showing) the audience.

▶ Single player must sell or demonstrate something to the audience. After going through the speech once, have player repeat it again, but this time, *pitch it!*

EVALUATION: Was there a difference between the two speeches? Did pitching it make the scene come to life? In order to pitch, must a player communicate with the audience? Audience, did the player involve you when the pitch was made?

EYE CONTACT #1

FOCUS: on making physical, prop, or eye contact with every member of the audience.

▶ Single player must sell, demonstrate or teach something to the audience and make physical, prop, or eye contact with every member of the audience during the course of the speech.

EVALUATION: Player, did you make physical as well as eye contact with the audience? Audience, was contact made with each one of you?

EYE CONTACT #2

FOCUS: on making direct eye contact with other players and on directing sight to the stage area to which one is referring.

▶ Two or more players agree upon Who, Where, and What and play with heightened focus on eye contact. In the course of playing they also must direct eyesight to any prop or area of the stage that they refer to.

EXAMPLE: Mary enters the room to visit John.

JOHN: "Hello, Mary" (eye contact to Mary). "Won't you come into the room?" (eye contact to room).

MARY: "Hello, John" (eye contact to John). "Here's the book I said I'd bring" (eye contact directly to book). "Do you want it?" (eye contact to John).

EVALUATION: Did they solve the problem? Was extra focus (energy) given at the time of eye contact?

POINT OF OBSERVATION

To get the heightened energy or extra focus, the teacher-director should suggest that their eyes take a closeup as with a camera. It is good to get this heightened focus at the time of eye contact, even though it may be exaggerated. In time, student-actors will learn to integrate eye contact with all their work (subtly). This exercise could follow CONTACT, p. 171, and be repeated at intervals throughout training.

SHADOWING[4]

This is a fairly advanced problem which can be given after group members have already shown some degree of breakthrough and insight into former problems, usually well into training.

4. See DUBBING, p. 211, and VERBALIZING THE WHERE, p. 118, for material to be used in conjunction with this exercise.

FOCUS: on Where, Who, and What.

▶ The game is played with a sub-team that shadows and makes continuous comments to the players they are shadowing. The shadow must stay close to the actor and speak quietly so that the other actor and shadow do not hear. Four players sub-divide and agree upon Where, Who, and What.

Sub-team A plays the scene and sub-team B shadows them. For example, a husband and wife are in a bedroom getting dressed to go out. As sub-team A goes through the scene, one member of sub-team B shadows the husband, and the other shadows the wife.

The husband's shadow says: *Why does she always hog the mirror? Do you see the brown flecks in her eyes?* The wife's shadow says: *Are you going to let him wear that tie? The picture of your mother on the wall is crooked.* The husband's shadow says: *Why don't you help her zip up her sequinned dress?*

POINTS OF OBSERVATION

1. Shadows are not to direct, to take over the action, but merely implement and strengthen the actor's physical reality.

2. Shadows can comment on inner action if desired. If scene becomes soap opera, however, stop the exercise and keep shadows commenting on the physical objects in the environment. It can be deliberately used this way, however, if a soap opera scene for performance is wanted.

SHADOWING THE SELF

FOCUS: on silently shadowing the self.

▶ Teams of any number agree on W. W. W. and play scene, maintaining dialogue with fellow players while silently shadowing the self. An obvious detachment is often reached.

OCCLUDING, p. 389, is a related exercise.

VERBAL AGILITY

The following exercises are designed to help the student-actors toss dialogue, as a ball, back and forth among themselves, so as to constantly keep building the scene. As the actor in improvisational theater must verbalize

on the run, so to speak, the following problems should facilitate verbal agility and the place of dialogue within a scene.

Dialogue must be used to further flow between players, not to impede it.
Building dialogue goes hand in hand with building action.

THROWING LIGHT GAME[5]

FOCUS: on non-verbalizing the topic of conversation.

▶ Whole group. Two players decide upon a secret topic of conversation. They
then begin discussing the topic in the presence of other players. They try to
mislead the others without making false statements.

The others may not ask questions or guess the topic aloud, but are to join
the conversation when they feel they know its subject. The first two may
challenge any newcomer, who must whisper what he or she thinks the topic
is to one of the two conversation leaders. If correct, player may stay in the
game; if not, player must go back.

A player may join in the conversation for some time without arising suspicion and being challenged. The game is played until all players are in, or
have made three wrong choices and are out of the game.

POINT OF OBSERVATION

THREE-WAY CONVERSATION, p. 394, and UNRELATED CONVERSATION, p.
395, can be played after this game.

BUILDING A STORY SERIES

See the exercises BUILDING A STORY, Parts I & II, p. 381, which are the
later evolutions of STORY-BUILDING. This is the time to play these important verbal group exercises.

STORY-BUILDING

Yarn

FOCUS: on continuing the story at the point where the last player left off.

5. Adapted from Neva L. Boyd, *Handbook of Recreational Games* (New York: Dover
Press, 1975).

▶ The first player on a team of four or more starts a story about anything. As the game progresses, the leader points out various players who must immediately continue the story from the point where the last player left off. This is continued until the story has been completed or until the leader calls a halt.

Rhyme

▶ First player gives one line, second player adds a line, and so on. All lines must rhyme. Leader can point out at random a player to supply the next line to add an extra challenge to the exercise. The game can also be played so that every player missing the rhyme drops out.

Song

▶ Using rhyme as a singing vehicle was charmingly done in Chicago during the Christmas holidays with the madrigal form. The audience was asked to name an object or an event. And this object or event was sung by each person in line and picked up in a tra-la-la chorus by the whole group. The cantata or oratorio form can be used similarly.

POETRY-BUILDING

▶ Teams of four or more. Each person in the group writes out the following on individual slips of paper: an adjective, a noun, a pronoun, a verb, an adverb.

Then the slips of paper are placed in separate piles according to their classification, and these piles are jumbled up. Each player must then pick up five slips and construct a poem from the five words chosen, adding prepositions and other parts of speech if necessary.

When ready, the groups compare their poems.

CONTRAPUNTAL ARGUMENT

Part I

FOCUS: on pursuing flights of thought using a specific subject as the springboard.

▶ Two players choose a subject of conversation such as travel, war and peace, habits, health, etc. A table between players may be used. On cue from the leader, both players begin speaking directly to each other, each developing thoughts from the subject without mentioning the name of the subject itself (or the pronoun "it" in place of subject). Each player is to earnestly pursue thoughts arising from the original subject, allowing each new thought to become the stepping-stone (or a higher rung on the ladder) to the next.

Points are given for hemming and hawing, saying "I," "you," or "it" in place of the subject, naming the subject, repeating partner's ideas, or responding in any way to partner. Time: one minute. Low score wins. Same team proceeds with Parts II and III at the same sitting.

SIDE-COACHING: *Talk directly to each other!* (This may have to be repeated many times.) *Let go of "I!" Let go of "You!" Keep talking! Share your voice! Avoid information! Avoid opinion! See each other! Go forth! You are together!*

EVALUATION: (on the scoring:) Did players allow the subject to springboard them into new ideas? Were players afraid to let go? Players, do you agree?

Part II

FOCUS: on pursuing thoughts that spring from a subject and trying to get partner to pick up from one's evolving flights of thought.

▶ Two players individually pursue the thoughts emerging from the original subject, speaking simultaneously. Each player attempts to get the other to pick up thoughts. Score one point each time a player draws from the thoughts of the other. Players are not to trick each other into picking up on their thought, but to simply allow their emerging thoughts to "win" for them. Same team proceeds immediately after playing this game, to Part III.

SIDE-COACHING: *Talk directly to each other! See each other! Maintain full involvement with each other! Avoid "I!" Share your voice! Avoid information!*

EVALUATION: How many times did Susan pick up on Richard? How many times did Richard pick up on Susan?

Part III

FOCUS: on pursuing flights of thought that spring from a subject, at the same time drawing from partner's evolving thoughts.

▶ Speaking simultaneously as in Parts I and II and continuing to expand their own emerging thoughts, players now hear, draw from, and build on each other's evolving thoughts and words as well. No time limit.

SIDE-COACHING: *Penetrate your partner's point of view! Expand your thought! You are together! Talk to one another! Share your voice! Explore and heighten your thought!*

EVALUATION: (On the dialogue:) Did players' thoughts transform? Did new insights emerge? Players, do you agree?

POINTS OF OBSERVATION

1. These exercises demand an extraordinary exchange of physical energy as players talk to each other and not *at* each other. By letting go of "I," "you" and "it," a springboard into new thoughts and insights is possible. When the exercise succeeds, players physicalize their speaking. The thought takes over the player from head to foot. The player is *there*, so to speak.

2. An intuitive jump can take place between players when they penetrate each other's thoughts and take what is needed to transcend their own.

3. When properly executed, CONTRAPUNTAL ARGUMENT can bring us to the beauty and economy of language.

WANDERING SPEECH A

FOCUS: on preventing fellow player from completing a desired activity through random speech.

▶ Both players agree upon Where, Who, and What. One player is delayed from completing an activity because of the chattiness of the other, who keeps talking, changing the subject, and digressing into different areas of conversation. Reverse so that both players have a chance at chatty role. They may change the W. W. W. at this time if they wish.

EXAMPLES: Who—chatty customer and salesman. Where—department store. What—customer has come to buy something for his wife's Christmas present. Customer is chatty. Salesman tries to make a sale, but customer keeps digressing.

Who—chatty nurse's aide and hospital visitor. Where—information desk in hospital. What—visitor needs admission card to get on elevator. Nurse's aide uses telephone, gives directions to others, etc., while visitor stands by trying to get card from her.

POINTS OF OBSERVATION

1. Hostility is *not* a part of this exercise. The chatty person is not to deliberately set up an obstacle. The digression is to be a purely innocent, friendly one.

2. If the focus is held, a great deal of humor will develop, and the result will be many charming vignettes. The exercise is very helpful for development of scene material.

WANDERING SPEECH B

FOCUS: For A, on equal response to both other players; for B and C, on exclusive relation to A.

▶ Three players agree upon Where, Who, and What. One player (A) is the center. The other two (B and C) are each absorbed with their own train of thought and/or activity. They come to the center player for comment, advice, etc., while completely ignoring each other. The center player (A) must be equally attentive to both B and C.

EXAMPLE: Where—living room. Who—hostess, two guests. What—visiting. Guest B is examining the family album and making comments and asking questions of the hostess A. Guest C is talking about the problems of a mutual friend.

POINT OF OBSERVATION

This can be played with many more players. Avoid situations where multiple demands for attention are built in and therefore not challenging (as teacher and pupils). Change around and allow each member of team to be the center player.

CONTACT

Contact can provoke many highly dramatic scenes. Since the actors cannot verbalize everything, they must stand and think. And so, the schism between expression and thought begins to dissolve, and the student-actors begin to find more economy in dialogue and movement.

While it is probably true that the fear of making physical contact may be tied up with psychological problems, it is not our role to deal with this. If we present only objective problems which are solvable, however, many subjective resistances such as these may be washed away.

The complex CONTACT exercise has been a dramatic turning point for many student-actors. It develops a closer communication and a deeper relationship with fellow actors because of the necessity of physical touch.

In CONTACT, the nature of the exercise makes an absolute necessity of staying with the focus, thus creating a great stage intensity. The players are put directly on their inner resources (X-area), and stage business is given infinite variety as more subtlety and nuances are brought into the work.

CONTACT also intensifies scenes for the written script and is extremely useful to the director rehearsing a formal play. It teaches the student-actor that one can be a part of a scene even if one is not the center of action. The overly verbal student-actor is forced to stop idle chatter in order to solve the problem: no contact, no dialogue.

CONTACT

FOCUS: on making a direct physical contact with each new thought or phrase of dialogue.

▶ Two or more players agree on Who, Where, and What. Each player must make direct, physical contact with (touch) his or her fellow player whenever verbal communication is made. With each new thought or change of dialogue, a different physical contact must be made. The player who initiates the dialogue is the one responsible for making contact. Non-verbal communication (nods, whistles, shrugs, etc.) is acceptable without contact. If contact cannot be made there is to be no dialogue. Tell players that when you side-coach "*Contact!*" they have spoken without physically touching the other player. Read the example of the exercise which follows Evaluation.

(As a surprise to players, add more challenging rules as in side-coaching for Parts II through IV).

SIDE-COACHING: *Contact!* (when players speak without touching) *Vary the contact! Use your full playing area! Be quiet if you cannot make contact! Play the game!*

The following variations increase the energy level and bring great variety to the playing:

CONTACT, PART II: *No contact twice in the same spot!*

CONTACT, PART III: *No hands! No contact with hand! Contact!*

CONTACT, PART IV: *No contact with feet!*

EVALUATION: Audience, was involvement between players greater because of contact? Was there variety in the contact? Did the contact come out of Who, or was it done mechanically? Players, did you keep focus on making contacts or were you more concerned with the activity and scene?

EXAMPLE: The doorbell rings, and John opens the door for his friend, Jim.

"Hello, Jim. Nice to see you" (contact by shaking hands).

That was one phrase, one whole thought. If John wants to say more, such as "Come in and sit down," he must make a fresh contact (e.g., he might put his arm around Jim and lead him to the chair).

"Nice shirt you're wearing" says Jim (contact by touching the chest or shoulders, not the shirt).

Jim sits down, and John goes to the table, half a stage away. It looks as if they are immersed in a great deal of concentration and thought. There is even a faint suggestion of some intense emotion in the air—actually, they are merely thinking of how to make the next contact.

Jim gets up from his chair, book in hand, and goes to John, poking him with his knee to make him turn around.

"Say, have you seen this story?"

John takes the book (this is not contact, unless the hands touch). He leafs through a few pages, and Jim walks back to chair. How can John answer Jim, who is on the other side of the stage, and still be a part of the reality of the scene? John continues to thumb the pages of the book as he works on the problem of contact. He gives himself over to the focus, looks up from the book, lets out a long whistle, and laughs and clicks his tongue as he communicates his response to the book Jim has given him, because he has no way of making physical contact.

Actors not yet adept at contact suddenly realize that a good fight would solve all their problems—as indeed it does. So, what they have now discovered as they throw each other around the stage, is that a conflict will strengthen any contact situation. However, a fight, like any huddle scene, is the easy way out.

Actors should work toward the less obvious ways of making contact.

POINTS OF OBSERVATION

1. Contact should be subtle and related to the character relationships, not to the dialogue alone. It should be natural and spontaneous, not forced.

2. Keep the problem challenging. Have the actors avoid scenes where they are all huddled together.

3. Let student-actors find their own ways of putting variety into their contact. Fingers can rumple hair, feet can kick, there can be jostling, bumping, pushing with the hips, falling into one another's arms, etc.

4. If the student-actors complain that they cannot find ways of making variety in contact, remind them that there are other ways of communicating besides dialogue (see Chapter V).

5. No contact is necessary if there is no dialogue, but do not allow actors to avoid the problem by doing a completely silent scene. Remind them (only if absolutely necessary) that they may communicate through singing, laughing, crying, coughing—in fact, any sound without making contact.

6. Keep student-actors from planning contact during preparation of scene ("When I tap you on the shoulder, you . . .").

7. Student-actors who resist contact usually have a personal fear of touching another person. Going back and doing more intense work in the earlier problems of relationships, body work, and space substance should help student-actors break through this fear. Such resistances show themselves in the following manner:

A. General irritation at having to find variety. They will continue to use hands and poke at each other for contact. This constitutes pushing others away from them, which is the exact opposite of what we are trying to achieve.

B. Trying to make contact through props.

C. Using only the most casual, socially restricted contact (tapping on shoulders, etc.).

8. A homework assignment is of definite value here. Ask student-actors to spend five minutes a day consciously making contact with whomever they may be with. They should not tell this person what they are doing. The class period following this assignment should devote some time to a discussion of what they observed.

9. If your players will not wait for the focus of the exercise to work for them and still feel urgent about making something happen themselves, they will fall into irrelevant ad-libbing, poke at each other instead of making real contact, and invent useless activity. When this happens, it is an indication that they are not ready for contact. Go to the next exercise, on silence, and return to contact at another time.

10. When student-actors can solve the contact problem by making their physical contact an integrated, organic part of the scene and not something "stuck on," their work will develop subtlety of relationship and will provide enriched content for the scene.

11. When the players work fully on the focus of CONTACT, laughter, crying, singing, coughing, etc., come into very unique use as means to solve the problem.

12. CONTACT is an excellent problem from which to observe your student-actors who are still resisting involvement and relationship. A warm-up game which may be helpful is EMOTION THROUGH CAMERA TECHNIQUES, p. 228, which often involves contact.

SILENCE

In the silence exercises the student-actor is not to substitute sub-vocal or unspoken words but is to concentrate on the silence itself and learn to communicate through it. True silence creates an openness between players and a flow of very evident energy, making it possible for them to reach into deeper personal resources. These exercises done with an advanced group of players often result in uncanny clarity on a non-verbal level of communication.

SILENT TENSION #1

FOCUS: on the silence between players.

▶ Two or more players (two preferred) agree on Where, Who, and What. Tension between players is so strong that they are unable to speak; there is to be no dialogue during the event (scene). Where, Who, and What must be communicated through the silence. Some examples: two sweethearts who have just broken their engagement; an elderly couple hearing a burglar downstairs; a miner's family waiting for news after a mineshaft disaster.

SIDE-COACHING: *Focus on the silence! Communicate through the silence! "No motion" on the inner dialogue! Look at one another! See one another!*

EVALUATION: Did we know who and where players were? Did they communicate through silence? Players, do you agree?

POINTS OF OBSERVATION

1. This exercise usually produces highly dramatic scenes, for it necessitates intensely close visual contact with fellow players.

2. Often these scenes end in a single scream, a laugh, or some sound. *Do not tell this* to students, however. If they solve the problem, it will come spontaneously. If an actor says, "I wanted to scream but thought you didn't want us to," he was working not on the problem but on the teacher for approval.

SILENT TENSION #2

FOCUS: on openness to one another.

▶ Two players at a real table. No W. W. W.

SIDE-COACHING: (gently) *Keep silence between you! Silence above, around, within!*

NO MOTION EXERCISES

The following NO MOTION exercises offer another means of stopping compulsive cerebral activity, expressed in questions and wordiness that keep players out of contact and relationship. No Motion is the static used dynamically to punctuate scenes and increase stage tension. It is a way of communicating process and suspense to actors and audience alike. It is the preoccupation that holds the energy content of a scene.

It should be preceded by a warm-up with SPACE SUBSTANCE (p. 391), dwelling upon the NO MOTION WARM-UP (p. 83) in particular. This will remind the players once again that out of concentrating on No Motion all necessary movement evolves.

NO MOTION #1

FOCUS: on sending a message of No Motion to the entire organism.

▶ Two players agree on an immediate environment, such as a restaurant, car, bed, etc., and decide on a Who in which relationship between them exists in two areas: the one on stage where we meet and see them, and another about which we (the audience) know nothing. The What, or stage occupation, is also planned. They then play the scene, using dialogue. As the action progresses, they send a message of No Motion to their total organism as in HOW OLD AM I? REPEAT and EXCURSIONS INTO THE INTUITIVE. They use No Motion to accent their communication and reveal their relationship. The audience will learn everything about them through this non-verbal communication.

POINTS OF OBSERVATION

1. No Motion is not a freeze. Its purpose is to create a resting or non-thinking area between people precisely when they are busy with on-stage dialogue and activity. If done with understanding, out of the resting or non-thinking area energy bursts through and expresses itself in unique use of props and dialogue, intensifies character relationship, and builds rising tensions within the on-stage scene.

2. Some players find the words "silence" or "quiet" or "wait" more useful to them in achieving the physical feeling necessary for the exercise.

3. As the purpose of the exercise is to stop conceptual thinking, and verbalization of the relationship, avoid over-presentation. Your players, who by now have had WHAT'S BEYOND?, and in some instances PREOCCUPATION, will know how to handle it. An experiment in using this exercise with a group who had little if any theater background and only six workshop sessions was tried. They had been given intense work on all aspects of SPACE SUBSTANCE, and repeated work on WHAT DO I DO FOR A LIVING? REPEAT, HOW OLD AM I? REPEAT, and MIRROR PENETRATION. They were asked simply to think No Motion or Rest. The result was astonishing. The objects in the immediate environment came to life to the minutest detail, whether it was reaching for an ash tray to drop an ash, or picking up and nibbling the crumbs from the table cloth. There were great stretches of true improvisation which is rare so early in training. Animation, excitement, and energy abounded in the workshop. At first the players found it difficult to look at each other and did a lot of giggling as well. In this instance, however, it constituted shyness rather than withdrawal, for contact and recognition had been made between them. It is interesting to note that when this problem was done with professional improvisational actors their "shyness" was also evident.

4. No Motion does not mean holding back or inhibiting an emotion or a verbalization, nor is it a censoring mechanism. This, then, would make every scene an "acting" scene. By keeping complete occupation on stage, the preoccupation of No Motion unfolds the scene step by step. The players are walking "the edge of the cliff" and student-audience and players alike are breathlessly involved in the problem. This element of suspense should exist in all two-way problems.

NO MOTION #2

FOCUS: on No Motion to thinking and deciding.

▶ Single player sets up W. W. W. Player is at a point of decision. Scene is played with No Motion on this.

NO MOTION #3

FOCUS: on No Motion to heighten relationship.

▶ Two players agree upon W. W. W. and play scene with No Motion on heightening of relationship.

NO MOTION #4

FOCUS: on No Motion to heighten relationship.

▶ Large group of players agree upon W. W. W. and put No Motion on heightening relationship, as in NO MOTION #3.

EXCURSIONS INTO THE INTUITIVE

An experiment in dramatic tension without benefit of content.

FOCUS: on exhalation through the mouth, from the back of the throat.

▶ Students sit on chairs. Instruct them to sit as if their legs grew straight down from their buttocks. This will give a released, straight line to the spine. Their shoulders should be free of tensions, and their hands should rest on their thighs. Everyone is to concentrate on a slight hissing sound on the exhalation.[6] Eyes open, they sit looking on the stage. They are to force nothing and to think of nothing. When and if anyone feels the urge to go up on stage and do something, he or she is to do so.

SIDE-COACHING: *Release your shoulders; Concentrate on exhalation! Look at the stage! Trust yourself! Stop thinking what to do!*

EXAMPLE: Player A goes on stage, walks around, looks over edge as if from on high. He grabs a chair, climbs onto it. Player B walks up to him: "Here, read the newspaper." Player A stops and looks at her: "Thanks." Player B waves as she leaves; player C enters and walks slowly back and forth as if in great contemplation. Player A mirrors him . . . etc.

POINTS OF OBSERVATION

1. With an advanced group, this exercise can be extraordinarily interesting, since it invariably leads to an avant-garde type of scene. There is often little dialogue as the stage, full of tensions, comes to life.

---

6. "In the expiratory phase lies renewal of vigor through some hidden form of muscular release"; Mabel Todd, *The Thinking Body*, p. 261.

2. Make it clear that students are not to think of something literal, nor should they "do something" just for the sake of doing something.

3. After a scene, it is interesting to read into it a literal thread or story which can be given to the random stage activity. Repeat some scene with the "story."

4. HOW OLD AM I? REPEAT and similar exercises are preliminary steps to this one.

5. This exercise should not be used until student-actors are a *group* and therefore will not feel "silly" (exposed).

Silence Before Scenes

If students are urgent, rushed, over-active, throwing themselves into scenes without thought, have them sit quietly on stage before they begin to play. They are to concentrate on exhalation, to blank out imagery, and are to sit quietly as long as necessary. The action will begin whenever one of the students gets up and starts it.

CHAPTER VIII

BROADCASTING
AND
TECHNICAL EFFECTS

RADIO AND TV

The radio and television exercises are intended not to train the actor specifically for radio or television but to focus energies within the limitations of each medium. The radio workshop is recommended at least once a month. However, it should not begin until after the students have handled enough improvisations to be able to use a focus as the acting problem demands.

Here the actor works on the problem of showing an audience only through the voice, and must be able to select those things which will allow the audience to see the story "through their ears."

In radio exercises, the scenes take place behind the curtain, since we are concerned with the voices alone. The focus of each exercise is to show the Where and Who by voice and sound alone, without telling in so many words. Each improvisation must have sound teams of one or two who do nothing but open and close doors, push back chairs, ring bells, howl like the wind, etc. Sound effects are not to be planned any more than dialogue.

For formal theater, using the microphone technique to clean up a problem of voice in a character is often useful. This brings focus to the problem without giving it undue *critical attention.*

Among materials useful for radio exercises are a tape recorder and a curtain to separate actors from the audience's vision. It is wise to rig up a sound table with bells, buzzers, a small wind machine, a rain box, a door, a box of broken glass, a turntable, a few recordings, newspaper, chalk, blackboard, etc.

For preliminary work, a short discussion on radio itself is advisable, so that students will be able to clarify what they are trying to do. The problem of showing rather than telling in this medium is most challenging.

When you listen to the radio, what happens? The answer will arrive eventually: "The listener *sees* the story."

Then, when you do a radio improvisation, what are you trying to do? "Let the audience see the story in their minds."

How can we show we are in a classroom by the use of sound and voice alone, without telling our audiences where we are? "By using physical objects over the microphone."

Give some examples of physical objects which make sounds appropriate to a classroom? "Chalk could squeak on the blackboard . . . some could use the pencil sharpener . . . a lot of chairs could be pushed back from desks as the lunch bell rang."

On the problem of relationships, which also arises in the radio scenes: *How can we show a mother and son?* "The boy could come in and say, 'Hello . . . I'm back from the store. Can I go out and play now?'"

A discussion held in the same way as questioning during Where sessions will stimulate actors to find for themselves many sounds especially pertinent to a classroom, a kitchen, or a living room.

FIRST RADIO EXERCISE

FOCUS: on showing Who (relation) through sound and voice.

▶ Teams of three or more players decide upon Who. Each player makes a list of the characteristics he or she is attempting to convey: age, weight, temperament, coloring, etc. They then begin their scene. As action progresses, audience players are to make their own list of characteristics through hearing just sound and voice. When playing is over, lists are compared.

Through the same procedure, the focus can be changed to showing Where.

EXAMPLE: Where—a country schoolhouse. Who—the teacher and her class; teacher is about forty-five and rather dislikes teaching! one boy in the fourth grade is "slow." After the inevitable commercial, the program opens.

TEACHER: Three times three equals?

CLASS: (in unison) Nine.

TEACHER: Three times four equals?

CLASS: Twelve.

TEACHER: Three time five equals?

CLASS: Fifteen.

TEACHER: Did you open your mouth, Johnny? Did you know the answer or didn't you? Speak up!

JOHNNY: No, ma'am.

TEACHER: You will kindly come up and write down every answer the class gives.

SOUND: Sound person pushes back chair and gets chalk ready for blackboard.

TEACHER: Again . . . where were we? Oh, yes. Three times six equals?

CLASS: Eighteen.

SOUND: Chalk on blackboard.

TEACHER: That's an awfully sloppy-looking eight. Three times seven?

CLASS: Twenty-one.

SOUND: Chalk on board.

TEACHER: Johnny! What do you have in your pocket?

SOUND: Sound person peeps like a little chick.

CLASS: Laughter.

TEACHER: Johnny! I asked you what you have in your pockets!

SOUND: Sound person peeps like a little chick.

CLASS: More laughter.

EVALUATION: After the improvisation, the student-audience compiles their impressions about each character to see how closely they coincide with the actor's lists.

How old was the teacher? What did she look like? How many students were in the class? How old were they? Was it a city or a country school? How did you know?

Did they show us Where and Who by sound and voice alone? Most often, some things are shown while others are told. How could they have made that point clear without telling us?

POINTS OF OBSERVATION

1. Try to avoid the omnipotent narrator. When students put their minds to solving Where and Who, there will be no need for narration.

2. The acting problems in WORD GAME or THEME-SCENE can also be used for radio improvisations; but the problems of Where and Who will more than likely keep a group busy for some time.

ANIMAL IMAGES

▶ See this exercise on p. 241.

Animal improvisations for building character can also help with speech. One boy with a high, thin voice was given the animal image of a hippo to help him with a character. By working on this visualization in his scenes, he was able to lower his voice tone considerably.

Children's Introduction to Radio

The seven-to-nine-year-olds will enjoy working at radio (using a tape recorder) and listening to playbacks of what has been recorded. This is the best way to work on speech with young children; for, since it is necessary for them to speak clearly in order to share with an audience, they learn to work on cleaning up their own speech. A "Roving Reporter" type of exercise is useful in introducing this age group to radio exercises, since it allows even the most timid child to speak and to hear his or her voice in playback.

ROVING REPORTER A

FOCUS: on speaking clearly in response to questions.

▶ An assistant could be the "roving reporter" in all these exercises, someone who is more skilled in drawing the children into a conversation than another child would be. For example, "Hello, Hello . . . and who are you, young person?" The child then gives name and address, etc.

ROVING REPORTER B

FOCUS: on showing Who (relation) through speaking.

▶ After the initial name-and-address interview, the assistant can suggest other characters, and the student must then respond.

Interviewer: "Well, here comes an old man. Hello, old man,"
Student then responds by replying as an old man.

ROVING REPORTER C

FOCUS: on animal speech rhythms.

▶ Now have the interviewer suggest animal images which the children must take on when they speak.

Interviewer: "Well, here comes a cat! Hello, cat! How are you this morning?" "Meow, meow . . . I'm fine."

Many children will respond initially in this stereotyped expression of an animal. Suggest that they speak with the sound of the real animal in mind. Have them try to recall the speech rhythm of the animal as they have heard it—i.e., the dog would be staccato, the cow would be long and heavy, etc.

For variation, have the child suggest the animal by altering his or her speech patterns. The interviewer must then guess what animal is being interviewed.

Interviewer: "Well, here comes someone! And how are you today?" Child: "Eeeeooowww . . . lllllllmmmmmmm . . . fiiiinnnneeeooww."

When the interviewer cannot identify the animal, then the children are forced to clarify their speech. It is interesting to watch the swift development of young students in terms of speech and uses of tone of voice when this exercise is given.

TELEVISION EXERCISE

FOCUS: on seeing and on being seen.

▶ Four or more players (a director, a cameraperson, and actors). The director casts actors and gives them a scene to enact. There should be a definite Where; scene should be simple (perhaps part of a larger scene), and should not be longer than three or four minutes.

A camera can be simulated with a large theater spotlight on wheels, a photographer's floodlight with long cord, or even a flashlight. The important thing is that light may be turned on and off. Microphone and earphone are not difficult to imitate with batteries and wires. They are not indispensable, although they add greatly to enjoyment of this exercise.

Cameraperson follows the scene with light, moving in for close-ups, back for long shots, etc. Student-audience can tell what shots have been taken only by where the light falls. The light is the camera's eye—the picture being taken.

Players go through a dry-run rehearsal without camera. Director makes a few changes here and there. Cameraperson moves in and out to warm up. Then the camera lights up, and they are on the air.

EXAMPLE: Dining-room scene. Family is eating dinner. The little girl does not want to eat her spinach. The parents plead, cajole, and threaten. Finally she eats the spinach. End of scene.

EVALUATION: Did the actors take directions from the director? Have a full discussion of this. All will get a chance to be director and will soon understand the necessity in theater for following direction. The youngest actors become easy to handle during rehearsal of a play after they have been "Director."

Did the cameraperson take the most interesting shots? First ask the cameraperson, and then the student-audience. Where might the cameraperson have made shots clearer and more interesting? How?

POINT OF OBSERVATION

Before beginning the exercises, a quick discussion on the basic camera shots (long shot, medium shot, close-up) is helpful.

TECHNICAL EFFECTS

It is most important that every student learn to improvise using the technical aspects of the theater.

In early workshop sessions, the teacher-director would do well to initiate a short demonstration of the workings of the sound and lighting equipment, with particular emphasis on the resulting effects and moods. Students should take turns handling the equipment and producing the effects until they are familiar with the set-up.

When a basic understanding has been achieved, then assign technical crew members to each team, alerting them to improvise any sound or lighting effect the scene might demand. Or have each group select one or two of its members to handle lights and sound.

In improvisational theater the necessity that technical skill be used in improvisations should be obvious. Lights, sound, music and dialogue must all become an organic part of the unfolding scene. This spontaneous selection of effects and placing them into a scene at the time of improvisation gives the student-actors an added alertness and sensitivity to what is going on. As in the exercise SENDING SOMEONE ON STAGE, the actors on stage must respond and act upon the new element introduced into the scene.

INTEGRATION OF ON-STAGE AND BACK-STAGE ACTION A

FOCUS: on integration of on-stage action with appropriate technical effects.

▶ Two or more players on stage. Two or more players back stage. Where, Who, and What agreed upon. Where should offer many opportunities for effects (a forest, desert, home, farm, etc.).

On-stage players must play scene and cue back-stage players for effects as they go along (''It's getting dark outside . . . do you think there'll be a storm? It's time for the rooster to crow . . . '') or through physicalization. Reverse teams.

POINTS OF OBSERVATION

1. This exercise can be done successfully with children as young as five years old. If the sound effects are simple to handle and a simple lighting set-up is available, any child can carry out the technical cues.

2. This exercise has an extraordinary maturing value for the very young actor, who suddenly can be found handling the outcome of a scene, in response to fellow players' needs.

3. Many other acting problems can be adapted or developed with this purpose in mind.

INTEGRATION OF ON-STAGE AND BACK-STAGE ACTION B

FOCUS: for players, on playing their scene according to the effects provided by the back-stage crew.

▶ Same as A, except that in this exercise the back-stage crew originates the lighting and sound effects and the on-stage players must then improvise around these effects.

CREATING MOODS ON STAGE

FOCUS: on creating the mood of the Where through technical effects and response of on-stage players.

▶ Three or more players on stage. Two or more players on back-stage crew.

Several Where's are written on slips of paper. Team selects a slip of paper and must then create the mood of this Where. Players agree on Who and What or may just enter stage letting Who and What evolve out of the effects.

Scene begins, with back-stage players providing sound and lighting effects to create the mood and the on-stage players adding to the mood.

Once mood has been achieved, scene may be stopped or played through, as the director wishes.

EVALUATION: Did the lighting and sound effects coincide to set the mood? Did the players add to the mood or distract from it?

POINTS OF OBSERVATION

1. This exercise quickly shows which players are able to let the effects carry them without manipulating them.

2. Similar to THE ABSTRACT WHERE (p. 131) and can be used in conjunction with it. As with EXCURSIONS INTO THE INTUITIVE (p. 178), a stage can be set up with lighting and props and story content added later.

VOCAL SOUND EFFECTS

FOCUS: on producing sounds vocally that are usually given by recording.

▶ After agreeing upon Who, Where, and What, two or more players, hidden from audience's view, use microphones to establish Where through vocal sound effects alone.

The sound effects—e.g., birds, wind, sirens, bells, etc.—are not to be mechanically reproduced but are all to be produced by vocalization alone.

EVALUATION: Were the vocal sounds as effective as recorded sounds?

POINTS OF OBSERVATION

1. Players should work with sounds as they would with other players.

2. Almost invariably, one or more students will delight in this exercise and will develop skills in sound effects to such an extent that mechanical aids will be almost unnecessary.

3. For homework, ask the students to listen to the sounds around them and to try to reproduce them.

4. Some examples of scenes where sound is inherent are railroad stations, jungles, and harbors.

5. Microphone essential to the success of this exercise.

6. As a warm-up, pass the microphone around and ask individual players to make any sound of their choosing. Their fellow players are to call out what was communicated (a rocket, an animal, horses running, starting a car, etc.).

7. Hidden teams agree on a Where to communicate to audience-players (a farm, a harbor, a jungle, etc.).

8. Use of easily available materials to create non-vocal sound effects can also be suggested after exploring VOCAL SOUND EFFECTS. Straws can bubble water, cellophane crackles, pencils can be hit against empty glasses, etc.

CHAPTER IX

DEVELOPING MATERIAL
FOR SITUATIONS

The exercises in this chapter can broaden an acting group's insight into finding fresh scene material. After a few experiments with WORD GAME (below), for instance, ideas may literally pour out as players transcend their everyday orbit. Those involved in community theater, interested in developing material around a certain event, should find WORD GAME B particularly useful.

To be effective, these exercises must be supplemented with lighting, music, sound, set pieces, and costume. In short, the full technical theater should be utilized.

Although these exercises are especially helpful in handling situational material—usable for performance—many other exercises in this handbook can do this. If the focus of an exercise is understood by the players, and they *keep* their focus on the problem (object) which the focus of the theater game presents, in a sense anyone and everyone can develop scenes.

BOX FULL OF HATS, p. 380, can be introduced here.

WORD GAME A[1]

FOCUS: on obscuring a word within a series of scenes.

▶ Two or more teams. Each team selects a word and divides it into syllables,

---

1. WORD GAME should be brought into workshops after the twelfth or thirteenth Where session.

then agrees on Where, Who, and What for each syllable. Each team casts for the situations and selects back-stage workers.

The team then acts out the syllables of the word. At no time is the word itself (or the syllable being acted out) to be mentioned verbally. Every effort should be made to hide the syllable (and subsequent word) within the involved stage action.

EXAMPLE: "Let's use the word 'industrial,' which we can divide into 'in-dust-trial.' " *What can we do with the syllable "in"?* "We could be walking in a door." *If there are four or five people on a team, would it be interesting if all of them simply walked through a door? What are some possibilities for a real scene with a Where, Who, and What?*

This might lead to the discussion of a situation in which a student had an "in" with a teacher or a salesman with a receptionist. Reminding students to disregard the spelling of the syllable and think only of the sound sense might prompt someone to suggest a scene at an "inn." Any one of these suggestions could facilitate a complete scene.

Help the teams to realize the scene implications of each syllable. The "inn" might be in the country at night, with a cast of characters ranging from the wayfaring stranger to the sleepy bellboy. There might be a reconciliation between the stranger and a long-lost brother, or perhaps a robbery when the thieves see the moneybelt around the stranger's waist. Action that will help disguise the syllable and make it more difficult for the audience to guess the word should be encouraged.

What can we do with "dust"? "We could come from a mining camp and be dusting off our clothes." *Could that be developed into a full scene with Who, Where, and What? What else does "dust" imply? What do we associate with dust?*

They might think of gold dust and of a potential gold miners' situation; the dust-bowl period of U.S. history; a clue in a mystery story. The variations are unlimited.

"Trial" is obvious, but student-actors should be reminded to think of a situation so that attention is taken away from the word itself.

EVALUATION: Before the class evaluation of the theater aspects of the scene, allow the student-audience to guess the word enacted. It is advisable that the teacher-director know the word in advance, so as to provide hints to shorten the guessing period.

Did they solve the problem? Were the syllables they acted out hidden? Did they put in a major distraction to obscure the word? (For example, a team that acted out the full word "parcel" had a delivery boy bring in a mechanical servant, acted out by one of the players; the scene developed around the mechanical servant, and the word itself was obscured.)

Did selection of the costume piece bring the character into sharp focus? Could more have been done with lights and sound?

WORD GAME B

FOCUS: on obscuring a word within a series of events (scenes).

▶ Two or more teams. This exercise usually produces much satirical material. The team selects a word, as in WORD GAME A. Instead of giving them free rein in creating their scenes, the teacher-director provides specific themes on which the scenes must be based. The themes might be as follows:

1.	religious	8.	blackout
2.	political	9.	automation
3.	sociological	10.	transformations
4.	scientific	11.	educational
5.	historical	12.	*specific* community or
6.	fantasy		school problems
7.	current events	13.	clownishness

It is not at all necessary to limit the teams to one theme per syllable. Indeed, teams wishing to work on more than one theme per syllable often excite great selectivity trying to find material for five or six different situations.

Where, Who, and What is then set up, technical crew stands by, costume pieces are selected, and the games begin!

EXAMPLE: Suppose the team chooses the word "monkey." For their purposes, it is broken into two syllables: monk-key. The players must create a scene around the first syllable, monk, using one of the above-mentioned themes. For instance, a religious scene using monk is obvious; or perhaps a sociological scene, portraying a monk in relation to the lay citizen; or a historical scene, showing a monk at the time of the Spanish Inquisition. The possibilities are endless.

The second syllable, key, is handled in the same way. Political: the mayor hands over the key to the city to a visiting dignitary; scientific: a research chemist finds the key to preventing a dread disease; fantasy: a magic key takes the bearer to Shangri-La; transformation: anyone keeping the key becomes transformed.

And for the whole word, "monkey," infinite possibilities exist.

POINTS OF OBSERVATION

1. Make it clear to the teams that the sound sense of the word can be used instead of the actual spelling. (E.g., "mistake" becomes miss-take or mist-ache; or, using greater poetic license, "petrified" might become pet-try-fried.) Since all are after flights of fancy, as much freedom with words as possible should be allowed, so long as the words are not completely distorted.

2. Have the student-audience suggest other situations around the syllables and words enacted. Prompt them into suggesting ideas of transcending possibilities. Let the student-actors learn to make their theater reality whatever they desire on the stage; if the group agrees, a scene can take place at the gates of heaven or in the bowels of the earth. Bring in unusual set pieces and costume pieces for them to choose from.

3. Two-syllable words are better than three-syllable words in a class situation because of the time limit. WORD GAME takes more time for preparation by the students than other acting problems; assignments of words and themes may be given to the groups earlier so that they may work out the Where, Who, and What before coming to class. Care should be taken, however, that they do not plan out the How.

4. This exercise has been developed into a most successful evening of entertainment for an audience. It is particularly valuable in a summer camp situation, where the time element prohibits workshops and more formal presentations and where the arts and crafts classes can help in making props, set pieces, etc.

5. It has been found that WORD GAME has little value for children under nine years of age. The meaning of words before this time is generally too literal and connotative for them to use words in an abstract sense.

6. Like the run-through of a formal show, when two or three scenes are done at one time as they are here, the weaknesses and strengths of the players are highlighted. This highlighting gives the teacher-director an excellent indication of where individuals need help and what kind of problems they should be given. If possible, it is most valuable to set aside extra time for WORD GAME *in addition* to regular workshop. If the student-actors show lack of involvement with objects, if they do not make contact and develop Where, Who, and What, if their stage pictures are cluttered and meaningless, it is time to retrace our steps and return to earlier exercises. And by now, the teacher will also know what exercises to give them.

7. The similarities between this and the old game of charades are evident, although here they have been adapted to meet our needs. The teacher-director should concentrate on heightening the students' selectivity and expanding their experience—not on producing charades experts.

8. It is probably clear at this point that the teacher or students have merely to peruse the dictionary now and again to find enough material to keep classes going for years. When students first play the game, the teacher should bring a list of words to class in case the students are at a loss. Let them bring the syllables to life. The simpler composite words are easier to use and make the WORD GAME more quickly understandable to students.

9. The student-actors should have worked on some technical problems before doing this exercise.

10. After WORD GAME has been played four or five times in workshop sessions, an awareness of the vastness and variety of choice of material possible for use in solving problems opens up for the student-actor.

11. If the situations develop into story and playwriting, suggest the team add an acting problem (of their own choice) to the syllable they are acting out.

ONCE UPON A TIME

▶ Here the exercise outlined on p. 284 should be used.

USING OBJECTS TO EVOLVE SCENES

This exercise should help the student-actor to increase his or her aware-ness of the simplest of objects, a starting point for developing scenes. It constitutes an early step in excursions into the intuitive.

FOCUS: on the object, which then sets the player in motion.

▶ One player. Coach whispers the name of an object to player seated on stage, who then waits quietly until focus on the object sets him (or her) into motion.

EVALUATION: To actor: did you sit quietly until something happened, or did you plan the use of the object before you went into motion?

To audience: was the object used in a pedestrian way? (Putting a log on the fire, or Satan rising from the fire?)

POINTS OF OBSERVATION

1. The player is to keep eyes open while quietly viewing the stage and con-centrating on the object. Closed eyes will withdraw the player from the immediate environment; and this is to be avoided.

2. Coach the actors not to feel urgent or hurried about allowing their ob-ject to put them into motion. Suggest they concentrate on exhalation.

3. Watch the growth from the known to the unknown. Was vegetation just someone watering a garden, or did it become a man-eating vine?

4. If concentration is complete on getting the object to move them, and not on an activity relating to the object, students may do some charm-ing fantasy or intensely dramatic scenes.

5. If actors remain tied down by uninteresting activity, stop the exercise and quickly go through the following exercises. When this has been done, then return to the single player's object-motion exercise.

DETAILING THE OBJECT (TRANSFORMATION)

FOCUS: total focus on, and exploration of, the agreed object.

▶ Two players (advanced students only) agree upon Where, Who, and What and an object upon which to focus. Players keep the object constantly in focus through handling it while playing the agreed-upon structure. Side-coaching is essential.

SIDE-COACHING: *Stay with the object! Penetrate the object! See it in detail! Set it in motion!*

POINTS OF OBSERVATION

1. Be certain that players stay within the immediacy of the stage environment and the object and do not pull away from the problem by giving history, information, or any free associations. Direct seeing!

2. Preoccupation with the object creates either a change of relationship, of character, or of the object itself. It is difficult to say exactly why this works as it does, but as in the CONTRAPUNTAL ARGUMENT and all the PREOCCUPATION exercises, an intuitive jump between players seems to take place through this total involvement with the single object. The object melts away, so to speak, and a transformation takes place, sometimes developing delightful fantasies, sometimes dramatic relationship changes. To achieve this, however, it is important to penetrate the object in every way possible. The solving of this exercise requires intense absorption with the immediate object in the immediate present together with another player. Side-coaching is essential.

3. If this exercise is done with students who are not too advanced it is, at best, a help in directing focus; only some activity will be generated around the object. This problem can be truly solved (and a transformation take place) only by the most advanced students. It shows quite clearly the potency of a focus when it is understood and properly handled.

HERO EXERCISE

FOCUS: on making the object the hero of the scene.

▶ Teams of two or more players come to a group decision on an object and on Where, Who, and What. The scene evolves from the situation surrounding the object. Many fairy tales use this form.

TRANSFORMING THE OBJECT[2]

FOCUS: on allowing the object between you to become the springboard to play.

2. See "Space Substance," p. 79, and TRANSFORMATION OF OBJECTS, p. 82.

▶ Full group of players (similar to STORY-BUILDING, p. 166). They stand in a circle, visible to each other.

First player creates an object out of space substance, plays with it, and passes it to second player. They "play the object" between them. In this way a miniature scene develops with each object in which it may transform. Second player passes the object to third player and both play with it until it changes (if it does). Third player then plays with fourth player, and so on, until object has gone through all the players.

A variant is to play the game with only two players. To help very young actors understand this problem, bring clay and have each student mold one object out of another.

TELEVISION SCREEN

F O C U S : on agility in changing character, costume, and content.

▶ A large shadow screen is set up in the playing area. It can be made of a cotton sheet, about 6' × 5', hung with rods slipped into the hems to make it taut). A spotlight is set up behind it, and a well-supplied costume rack and prop table are provided alongside it.

On each team will be two or more actors and two or more viewers. Actors go behind the screen while the viewers sit facing screen, where they have gathered for an evening of TV. Each viewer can call out a favorite show, then go to the screen and "turn on the set." At this moment, front room lights are dimmed, light behind the screen is brought up, and the actors play the show called for.

The viewers may "change the channel" or call for a new show at any time. The actors never know when they are going to be "shut off."

POINTS OF OBSERVATION

1. A variation is to cut a large opening in a cardboard carton for "talk shows" or to build an oversized TV frame for the actors to play behind, without a shadow screen in either case. A great variety of props and costumes may be used. Organize backstage set-up well so that TV actors can quickly obtain what they need.

2. The scenes, for the most part, will center on take-offs of current TV shows.

3. Viewers may be family members, friends, or any group gathered to watch TV. The concept of a family gathered in a "living room" is especially useful when working with children.

LEAVING SOMETHING ON STAGE

FOCUS: on whatever is to be left on stage.

▶ Two or more players (advanced students). Where, Who, and What agreed upon. A scene is played in which an object, a sound, a light, or a thought are left on stage at the final curtain. There are no actors on stage when the scene ends, just the thing left there.

EXAMPLE A *(done by adults):* Focus was the plague. Where—a room in a home. Who—a man and his servant. What—avoiding contact with the populace.

The scene developed showing that the characters, fearful of dying because of a plague, never left their home. When they exited from the stage to retire for the night, a curtain fluttering on an open window in the empty room was the "something" left on stage—the concept of the plague.

EXAMPLE B *(done by adults):* Focus was an execution. Where—office of the prison warden. Who—girl, social worker, warden, minister, prisoner. What—a marriage.

The scene look place in the warden's office of a prison. A girl was permitted to marry a prisoner before his execution in order to legitimize their child. After all had exited from the room, the empty stage had a momentary blackout—the moment of electrocution.

EXAMPLE C *(done by teenagers):* Focus was a searchlight. Where—inside the barbed wire fence of a concentration camp. Who—two prisoners. What—escaping.

Two characters were escaping from the camp, crawling and creeping along the ground trying to get through the barbed wire. A large searchlight kept sweeping the full theater and stage as the escapees flattened to the ground (this was a 1000-watt revolving spot in the rear of the studio-theater). When it appeared that the prisoners had finally escaped, a cry of "Halt!," a rattle of machine guns, and a scream were heard. The searchlight was left, revolving around the empty stage and through the theater.

EXAMPLE D (done by children): Focus was the sound of a baby crying. Where—bombed-out building. Who—women, children, old people. What—trying to escape falling bombs.

As this scene developed, the group of people had to leave the shelter because the bombs were coming close in. When all had left, and the bombing quieted down, a baby's cry was heard.

POINTS OF OBSERVATION

1. This exercise is extremely valuable for developing an understanding of building a scene and heightening theatrical response.

2. An equipped stage is necessary for this exercise, since lighting and sound usually play a great part in the scene's development. A studio theater with simple equipment and props makes it possible to set up these scenes within a short time; and as many as three or four such scenes have been done within one workshop period.

3. This exercise should not be given until the group has become technically adept and ingenious in setting up Where, Who, and What, with real props quickly and effectively.

4. The fluttering curtain in Example A was achieved by using an electric fan and focusing it on a window frame with hanging curtains.

SCENE-ON-SCENE

FOCUS: on when to "take" or "give" (fade), through intense involvement with on-stage activity.

▶ Teams of four or more advanced students (closely related to STORY-TELLING, p. 290).

Each team divides into two sub-teams. Sub-team A sets up a scene in the present and, in the course of the scene, through conversation, brings to mind another scene (e.g., flashback, a moment in history, speculation on the future, etc.). Sub-team B must then act out the suggested scene.

There may be any number of these interjected scenes, as B completes the scene and throws it back to A and the present. A then suggests another situation, B plays it out, and so on. A may break in with the present and take the scene away from B at any time.

SIDE-COACHING: Change! Change!

EXAMPLE: Two old ladies (sub-team A) are chatting over their teacups. One reminisces over her girlhood and that wonderful night when she and George took their first sleighride together. Sub-team A now fades out, and Sub-team B comes into focus and plays out the scene. When they've completed the scene, they fade out, and sub-team A—the two old ladies—take it back into the present. And so on.

POINTS OF OBSERVATION

1. Lights, sound, music, and props should all be used for this exercise.
2. This is a complex problem, for the sub-teams are working from their own point of view. This constant attentiveness as to when to enter the scene requires the most intense involvement with everything that is happening on stage.
3. Both sub-teams should have a chance to initiate and follow.
4. This exercise should only be given to advanced students.

THEME-SCENE

FOCUS: on constant repetition of theme.

▶ Two or more teams.

This exercise is recommended for students who have worked several months on the advanced acting problems. It involves a more complex use of experiential data and is valuable as a step toward suggestions from the audience. Like WORD GAME, it should utilize full technical resources.

In this exercise, a "theme" is some activating phrase, such as "Big fish eat little fish" or "Stinginess leads to remorse." A "scene" can be any place at all: rooftops, cave, cloud, on top of the Eiffel Tower, etc.

Half the group writes theme ideas on individual slips of paper, while the other half writes scene ideas on individual slips of paper. The themes are scrambled together in one hat, and the scenes are scrambled together in another. Each team blindly chooses a theme and a scene and then works out a theme-scene using Where, Who, and What. They proceed to play the theme-scene, focusing on constant repetition of theme.

EXAMPLE A: Love Is Where You Find It—Mountain Cabin

A married couple has gone to the mountains for the purpose of patching up their marriage. An escaped convict and his pal break into the cabin and hold the couple prisoners. The wife shows the gangsters how to get away, then returns to her husband. It was afterward suggested that the wife might (since the marriage is a failure) leave with the men, thus carrying out the theme more accurately.

EXAMPLE B: The World Owes Me a Living—Rooftop

Two sweethearts on a New York tenement roof during a hot summer night. They are tense over the problem of her pregnancy, for he is not willing to take the responsibility of marriage and parenthood. He feels himself to be an artist, and nothing will make him take a drudging nine-to-five job. He is "special" and feels indeed that "the world owes me a living." The girl commits suicide by jumping off the roof.

POINTS OF OBSERVATION

1. This exercise can be extended and varied indefinitely. Any combination of theme and scene will work. The variations in characterization when one theme is used in several different scenes is amazing.

2. THEME-SCENE tends to become a structure for a story line and therefore to lapse into group playwriting. What we seek is total preoccupation of the players with the theme so that it moves them (as object) instead of them manipulating it.

SUPPLICATION

FOCUS: on pleading, accusing, or determining success of supplication. Each part of the triangle has a different focus.

▶ Teams of three or more advanced students. Players are divided into three parts of a triangle: (1) Supplicant (who pleads for something); (2) Accuser (who makes a charge); (3) Judiciary (who makes the choice and determines whether supplicant is successful).

Either individuals or teams can play each corner of the triangle. For instance, in a trial scene there would be a Defendant, a Prosecutor, and a Judge (the audience would be the Jury, an extension of the Judge).

EXAMPLES: a Salem witch trial; an ordinary misdemeanor trial; a murder trial; an Indian pow-wow arguing some important point; deliberations with prisoners during a prison break.

POINT OF OBSERVATION

The Supplicant should be encouraged to work with the student audience (playing the jury, a mob, etc.).

ORCHESTRATION

FOCUS: on taking on the qualities of a musical instrument and playing as part of "the orchestra."

▶ Four or more players each decide what musical instrument they will be, and agree upon a Where, Who, and What in which to be these instruments. Rather than literally becoming their instruments, as in fantasy, they are to *play* as if they have taken on the qualities of their instruments—through voice quality, body movements, etc. At various times throughout the scene, the teacher-director must coach *"Orchestrate!"* All the players must then "play" together.

An example is a cocktail party where different "instruments" can play in harmony with each other.

SIDE-COACHING: *Orchestrate!*

POINT OF OBSERVATION

As an interesting variation, ask group to select a "conductor." In the preceding example, for instance, it could be the host, who must then, through the scene's progression, get the "instruments" (guests) to play together, as duets, solos, or full orchestra. This gives the actor playing the host a director's view while working inside the scene. This is a most advanced use of a similar technique used with young children in activizing them within a scene.

RANDOM WALK

▶ Any number of players. Requires a pianist capable of improvising.

Actors walk at random around stage, exiting and entering. The mood, rhythm, etc., are usually set by the playing of music. At intervals during the walk, activities of one sort or another are called out to players who move from the walk into the activity. This is a most exhilarating exercise; it creates a tremendous freedom, gaiety, and unusual spontaneity in the activities.

The end of the walk comes in a slowing down of the music and walk to a standstill.

RANDOM WALK has great value in connection with exercises in seeing. While players are walking to the piano rhythm, simply call out various things for them to look at—a tennis match, a bull fight, etc. This is to be done without interrupting the rhythm generated by the walk.

HIDDEN PROBLEM

FOCUS: on keeping the problem hidden.

▶ Teams of two or more advanced players set up Where, Who, and What as usual. They decide on a category or emotion but are never to bring it out in the open. Categories could be: teaching, fantasy, love, hate.

EXAMPLE A *(teaching):* Where—kitchen. Who—mother-in-law and daughter-in-law. What—a visit by the former to the latter. Hidden problem—to teach.

SIDE-COACHING: *Keep activity going between you!*

POINTS OF OBSERVATION

1. In the foregoing example the mother-in-law hid her teaching by helping, insinuations, suggestions, etc. It developed into an intensely interesting scene in which "to teach" never came up. See "Conflict," p. 229.

2. The Where, Who, and What are to be unrelated to the hidden problem. Teaching, for instance, is not to be placed in a schoolroom.

3. Variant: players act to alter opposite players' attitude.

EXAMPLE B *(fantasy):* The following example was a scene improvisation titled "The Orange Tree." Where—living-room, dining-room combination. Who—husband and wife. What—wife's birthday (husband brings her a miniature orange tree). Hidden problem—fantasy.

This scene developed into a charming, whimsical piece on the growth of this little tree in this simple home to an orange grove within the apartment building, and the couple retiring on the proceeds from orange-juice.

EXAMPLE C *(love):* Two players. Where, Who, and What agreed upon. A strong emotion is felt between these people but never expressed because for some reason it is impossible or inappropriate or unknown. The focus is to keep up mutual activity without ever mentioning the emotion. See NO MOTION, p. 176.

Where—old people's home. Who—man and woman in their eighties. What—gardening.

An interesting shift of the above could be to make a wide age difference between them. Young doctor and old woman or very old man and young nurse—any situation where the difference of age, race, class, etc. make consummation or declaration of love impossible. Again it could be love as in friendship, for example: Where—fishing wharf. Who—Civil War veteran and young boy. What—fishing.

EXAMPLE D *(hate):* Where—bedroom. Who—husband and wife. What—preparing for their fiftieth anniversary celebration.

SUGGESTIONS BY THE AUDIENCE[3]

▶ Taking suggestions by the audience can be a delightful part of an improvisational theater program and quickly makes the audience part of the game.

Organization for taking SUGGESTIONS BY THE AUDIENCE has many variations. Some improvisational theaters base their whole structure on this technique. This can be dangerous, however, for it may easily become a gimmick that can kill the art form. The following are a few ideas for structuring this form:

1. On-the-spot scenes developed without off-stage preparation.
2. Use of individual members of the audience as actors.
3. Off-stage preparation.
4. Use of one outside person who can take the position of a narrator or storyteller or just an extra player when the scene needs or requires one. See SENDING SOMEONE ON STAGE, p. 133.

Players should structure for an action or problem and not a story or joke,

---

3. SUGGESTIONS BY THE AUDIENCE, which has become the hallmark of improvisational theater throughout the world, was first created by the author in 1939, in Chicago, with children performing for children. *All* were involved in the excitement of playing.

otherwise many of the audience's suggestions fizzle as players struggle to be "funny." Sometimes the players will let the audience in on the problem, sometimes it is just used by the players as their focus while working out the suggestions. What category the audience suggests is up to the players. Where, Who, What, Objects, Events, Emotions, and Styles of Playing may be varied and combined. If Where is suggested, for instance, it can become WHERE WITH OBSTACLES or WHERE WITH HELP. If it is Objects, TRANSFORMATION OF OBJECTS, or OBJECT MOVING PLAYERS, or PHYSICALIZING AN OBJECT can become the acting problem used to put the audience suggestion into motion. The Object suggestions can be used within Where, Who, What or handled simply as Objects with either single or more players. Many combinations are possible.

Whether the audience knows or not, an acting problem is valuable to use when players structure scenes. If the audience is asked for a problem, then players supply the Where, Who, and What; if the audience is asked for Where, Who, and What, then players must supply the problem. Whether doing an on-the-spot improvisation or preparing one off stage (during intermission or while other plays are performing), ability to solve problems and quickly picking an exercise that will free all for playing will determine the quality of scenes. For even, as in workshops, if the scenes do not always quite come off as "story," the very act of playing is exciting to watch.

Agility and speed in getting a character, setting up Where, and selecting an acting problem are necessary to the success of this stage activity, and all such exercises in the book should be used continuously in the workshops. WHERE THROUGH THREE OBJECTS and all the exercises of character agility are especially useful. Many of the exercises in the book can be used exactly as they are done in workshops, with exhilarating results.

The following is an agility exercise in quickly thinking up problems that might generate stage action. With paper and pencil players write down as many answers to the following as they can within an agreed time limit. The teacher-director may add other categories.

1. getting rid of something
2. getting rid of someone
3. getting out of something

4. wanting the same thing someone else has

5. a moment of indecision

Audience's suggestion	Players' structure
Where: Underwater	Where: Use the WHERE THROUGH THREE OBJECTS exercise
Who: Divers	Who: Select a character by quickly selecting a rhythm image as played in CHARACTER AGILITY game.
What: Seeking treasure	What: This is the What acting problem to use (i.e., "jump emotion," "unknown problem," "teaching," etc.)

In this way the actors place their own organization within the structure given by the audience and go ahead solving the audience suggestion exactly as they would any workshop problem. When theater games become "flesh on bones," no acting problems as such are necessary, for stage actions will be spontaneously selected during the playing.

See "Developing Scenes from Audience Suggestions," p. 215.

CHAPTER X

SPEECH AND
ROUNDING-OUT EXERCISES

SPEECH

Spolin was interested in acquainting players with what she termed the "physiological structure of language" and devised the exercises EX-TENDED SOUND and VOWELS & CONSONANTS, p. 396, which she said "bring a respite from subjective thought and interpretation." Other speech exercises new to this edition are ECHO, p. 383, MIRROR SOUND, p. 387, MIRROR SPEECH, p. 388, and GIBBERISH INTERPRETER A, B & C, p. 385. Along with VOWELS AND CONSONANTS, p. 396, they are to be found in the appendix. All have value both for work upon the scripted play as well as for improvisational theater. SINGING DIALOGUE, p. 207, will be heightened by playing a round of EXTENDED SOUND, which follows. Playing EXTENDED SOUND during rehearsals of scripted work, sending dialogue into space and letting it land, can have surprising results, even with amateurs.

EXTENDED SOUND

FOCUS: on keeping the sound in space between players and letting it land in fellow player.

Part A

▸ All players stand in the space at a distance from each other. One player sends a sound (not a word) to another player and lets it land; this other player then also sends a sound to a fellow player. All players send sounds in turn, attentive to the side coaching until each has contacted all or most of the others.

SIDE-COACHING: *No words! Keep the sound between you! Keep the body* *upright! Send forth the souuuund! Keep the sound in the space! Let the sound land! Extend the sound! Send the sound in slooooow motion! Speed up the sound! Speed it up as fast as you can! Normal speed! Keep the space between you! Extend the souuund! Give and take!*

Part B

▶ Players are coached to focus on the sound as above, but this time to send a *word* and to let it land on a fellow player.

Part C

▶ Players now send a sentence, keeping the focus.

EVALUATION: Players, did you keep the sound in the space between you? Did the sound land? Players, did you physically extend the sound? Did you give and take?

POINT OF OBSERVATION

This game shows that sound (dialogue) occupies space. Extending sound into space and letting it land in a fellow player brings about communication in the theater.

SINGING DIALOGUE[1]

FOCUS: on extending dialogue to fellow player through singing.

▶ Two or more players agree upon Where, Who, and What and sing all dialogue. Singing must be addressed to the fellow player(s).

SIDE-COACHING: *Sing out your words! Sing with your whole body! Heighten it!*

EVALUATION: Did players explore all the areas into which singing dialogue could lead? Players, do you agree?

POINTS OF OBSERVATION

1. Good singing voices are not necessary as this is an exercise in the extension of sound. Singing permits elongation of the word. Singing also permits repetition.

2. The flow of sound created between players integrates players and audience. The flow of sounds is a bridge to the intuition.

1. See also madrigal and cantata for improvised singing, p. 167.

2. Melodic structure must come naturally through the playing of the game and not be imposed by the coach.

4. Players who recite words dramatically (*recitativo*) can be coached to jump to melody.

Students should not be made overly conscious of their speech variances. As they move alone into their stage problems, their speech will be cleaned up organically, and this clarity will usually carry over into their daily speech patterns. To quote Marguerite Hermann, co-author with her husband Lewis of manuals on dialect, "Unless a student has basic speech problems, no great change in pronunciation should be forced upon him. A 'cleaning up' and 'toning up' should be all that is necessary."

CALLING-OUT EXERCISE

FOCUS: on making vocal contact at long distance.

▶ Two or more players. Where, Who, and What agreed upon. Where should be a setting in which the players must, of necessity, call to each other across a wide distance.

EXAMPLE: Where—cave; Who—guide and tourists; What—tourists are separated from guides. Where—mountain top; Who—mountain climbers; What—climbers, connected by a long rope, are scaling mountain.

EVALUATION: Was the vocal contact realistic within the situation?

POINT OF OBSERVATION

See that students give a reality to the alleged distance through the use of their voices.

STAGE WHISPER WARM-UP

▶ This warm-up to the following exercise is to be found on p. 394.

STAGE WHISPER

FOCUS: on stage whispering; on whispering with full projection and open throat.

▶ Teams of two or more players agree on Where, Who, and What in which the players are forced to whisper to each other, such as a schoolroom, thieves in a closet, lovers quarreling in church, etc. Focus is on stage whispering.

SIDE-COACHING: *Open your throat! Use your whole body! Whisper from the bottom of your feet on up! Share your stage whisper with the audience! Stage whisper!*

EVALUATION: Audience, did they talk low or did they use a stage whisper?

POINT OF OBSERVATION

The great physical energy released in solving this problem brings alive, exciting stage situations; almost instant vignettes. Coach players back to the focus—"*Stage Whisper!*"—whenever they get caught cerebrally.

CHORAL READING

FOCUS: on following cues given by fellow players. Conductor, chorus, and players all play "follow the follower."

▶ Two large teams agree upon Who, Where, and What. Each team consists of two players, a large choral group, and a conductor. Choral group can sit or stand on stage right and left, perhaps on risers. The two players play scene center stage while the chorus repeats phrases, and supplies music and sound effects. The chorus is cued by the conductor, who is cued by the players. All play "follow the follower."

GREEK CHORUS

▶ Two large teams. (This exercise is used primarily with very young actors.)
Same set-up as CHORAL READING. Choose a children's game and have the chorus sing the verses as the actors act them out. Chorus can also do sound effects, such as wind, birds, etc.

EXAMPLES: Thorne Rosa. All Around the Mulberry Bush.

POINT OF OBSERVATION

Useful for public performance.

A variation: Set up a structure in the usual way using a Greek Chorus for underlining (through chanting) the stage action—similar to SHADOWING and STORY-TELLING.

WHISPER-SHOUT EXERCISE

FOCUS: on released throat.

▶ Two or more players. Where, Who, and What agreed upon. Players do same scene three times. The first time, they *whisper*; the second time, they *shout*; and the third time, they speak in their normal voices. A variation is to have the team choose a setting where whispering, shouting, and normal speech can be integrated into one scene.

EXAMPLE: Where—jail cell. Who—prisoners. What—planning a break. This scene had ample room for all three voice ranges and was a highly effective, dramatic presentation.

EVALUATION: Follow the usual lines of evaluation. Include the question: was the voice more resonant in normal speech after whisper-shout?

POINTS OF OBSERVATION

1. The need to be heard in the whispering sequence helps the student-actors realize that the total body is involved in speech. If they whisper properly, with full projection, voices will be resonant and free from throat sounds. The teacher should listen carefully for tensed throats—this tension means the problem has not been solved.

2. To shout with released throat, the student-actor will have to keep tones full, round, and extended. Instead of a clipped "Hello there," "Heel-llooo theeerrrrre" is usually the result. A player who just yells is using throat tension and has not solved the problem.

3. When the players do the third scene, using normal speech, have the audience listen carefully to determine whether or not the group members are maintaining released throats.

4. The three scenes should take no more than a total of fifteen minutes. To insure this, give time warnings.

PHYSICALIZATION

DEAF AUDIENCE[2]

FOCUS: on communicating a scene to a deaf audience.

▶ Two or more players. Who, Where, and What agreed upon. Members of the

---

2. This is closely related to, and can be used in conjunction with, GIBBERISH exercises.

audience are to plug up their ears while watching the scene. Players are to go through scene as they normally would using both dialogue and action.

EVALUATION: Did the scene have animation? Did you know what was going on, even though you could not hear them? Where could they have physicalized the scene?

POINTS OF OBSERVATION

1. This brings to the student-actors (by being audience) a realization of the necessity for showing, not telling.

2. The lifelessness of a scene when actors talk instead of playing becomes evident to the most resistant.

3. This is a particularly good exercise to use to freshen up improvisational actors who are performing and rely on jokes and ad-libbing to carry their scenes.

4. Variant: have audience close eyes instead of plugging ears.

DUBBING

FOCUS: on following the follower, with the voice of one player and the body of another player becoming as one whole single player.

▶ Teams of four players decide Where, Who, and What and also decide which two will play bodies on stage (Sub-team A) and which two will provide their voices (Sub-team B). The voice players can sit facing the playing area so that their view is clear, and their voices are heard as they reflect the onstage activity through dialogue. The body players move their lips as if they are speaking, but are silent. Both sub-teams follow the follower in voice and action. See MIRROR/FOLLOW THE FOLLOWER, p. 62. After a time, have the voice and body players exchange places and continue the same Where, Who, and What or choose a new one.

SIDE-COACHING: *Follow each other! Avoid anticipating what will be said! Reflect only what you hear! Reflect only what you see! Move your lips! Become one voice! One body!*

EVALUATION: Did voice and body become as one? Audience, do you agree?

POINTS OF OBSERVATION

1. Allow ten minutes of playing time before reversing teams. At first, play-

ers will become one body/one voice only in flashes, but when the connection is made players are united in true relation. If this does not take place and the voice simply follows the body's moves or vice versa, play more Mirror and Space games until players experience what happens when they don't initiate, but follow the initiator, who is also following.

2. Side-coaching comes out of what is emerging, and explores and heightens what is seen, rather than being a demand.

3. When voice becomes one with on-stage player's actions, on-stage players get a sense of having actually spoken the words. Voice players must allow time for on-stage activity to emerge. The use of microphones adds pleasure to the exercise, but is not really necessary.

SLOW MOTION

When your players first begin to move in slow motion, most will simply move slowly with jerky, stop-and-start movements. Use side-coaching phrases to help players bring their whole bodies into slow motion: *"Blink in slow motion!" "Breathe in slow motion!" "Chew your gum in slow motion!"* In time and in playing, players will organically realize the body is in fluid motion as in a slow-motion film.

EXPLOSION TAG, p. 383, is the great lead-in to SLOW MOTION/ FREEZE TAG.

SLOW MOTION/FREEZE TAG

FOCUS: on moving in complete slow motion.

▶ If there is time, allow half the group to be audience to the other half's playing. Many can play. After a short warm-up of EXPLOSION TAG, p. 383, play freeze tag in very slow motion within even smaller boundaries. Appoint the first "It." All players run, breathe, duck, look, etc. in very slooow mootion. On tagging another player, "It" must freeze in the exact tagging position. The new "It" proceeds in slow motion and freezes in position as another player is tagged, who becomes "It." All untagged players must stay within boundaries and move in slow motion between and around frozen players (as around trees in a forest). Game continues until all are frozen.

SIDE-COACHING: *Run in sloow mootion! Breathe in sloow mootion! Duck away from "It" in slow motion! Tag in slow motion! Lift your feet in slow motion! Stay within bounds in verrry sloooooow motion!*

EVALUATION: Is there a difference between moving slowly and moving in slow motion? Audience, did you see a difference between moving slowly (start, stop, start, stop) and moving in slow motion?

POINTS OF OBSERVATION

1. Restrict the boundaries of the playing area or the game can become too time-consuming. If the group is too large, appoint two taggers and at the end, coach *Taggers, tag each other!*

2. In true slow motion there is fluidity of movement.

3. This is a variation of the traditional game, King of the Mountain.

SLOW/FAST/NORMAL

Part I

FOCUS: on exploring the Who, What, and Where at different rates of speed.

▶ Two or more players agree upon Where, Who, and What and play a few minutes of the W.W.W. in normal speed.

SIDE-COACHING: *Use your Where! Connect with each other!*

Part II

FOCUS: on repeating the scene in slow motion.

▶ Players go through the scene again, this time in Slow Motion.

SIDE-COACHING: *Sloowww Mootionnn! The Space is moving in Slow Motion! See each other in Slow Motion! Think in Slow Motion!*

Part III

FOCUS: on repeating scene in fast time.

▶ Players re-do the action as fast as they can.

SIDE-COACHING: *Fast! As fast as you can! Faster, Faster! Keep Going!*

Part IV

FOCUS: on repeating scene in normal time.

▶ Players go back and replay the action, with no side-coaching.

EVALUATION: Was there a difference between the first and last playing? Was there more depth or defined relationships between the players? Players, do you agree?

POINTS OF OBSERVATION

1. Keep the playing time fairly short. Give players just enough time to be in relation to one another and the Where.

2. As this exercise allows players to be in a state of play, it is not necessary to be concerned with repeating the action and dialogue exactly each time.

3. The players will intuitively edit elements that are not essential to the playing and go forward with the action and dialogue.

4. This is a self-editing exercise.

5. Watch for players who are "acting out" slow motion, rather than being in a "state" of slow motion.

SEEING

CAMERA

FOCUS: on putting full focus and energy on the other player.

▶ Two or more players agree upon Who, Where, and What. Director calls out the name of one player at a time who becomes the subject of head-to-toe focus by the other players. Action and dialogue are to continue through these changes, as the side-coach calls upon players to put all their focus— *Camera!*—on a certain player.

SIDE-COACHING: *Camera on Mary! Full body attention! See with the back of your head! Your forehead! Your shoulders! Camera on Jason! See unlabelled! No Camera! See in Slow Motion! Camera on Emily!*

EVALUATION: Did players give full body attention? Did they see a fellow player or were they staring? Did stage activity continue?

POINTS OF OBSERVATION

1. In explaining the focus, use the image of becoming a camera, or suggest that the player is one large eye or lens (head to foot) to help in players' focusing their energies on one another. During other games, calling "Camera!" can help a player to *see* a fellow player.

2. Staring is detected by a flat look and a rigidity to the body, a curtain in front of the eyes.

SEEING THE WORD[3]

FOCUS: on the side-coaching received.

▶ Single player goes on stage and describes an experience, such as taking a trip, watching a football game, or visiting someone. Without stopping, player is to accept focus provided by the side-coaching, and to continue narrating the scene.

SIDE-COACHING: *Focus on the colors in the scene! Focus on sounds! Is the wind blowing? Is the sky sunny or gray? Share your voice! Focus on the way you feel about the game you are describing! See yourself there! See yourself! Heighten the color! Heighten the smells! Heighten all sensory stimuli!*

EVALUATION: Do you know at what point you left the word and went into the experience? Audience, do you agree?

POINTS OF OBSERVATION

1. As greater perception is awakened in the player by the side-coaching, notice at what moment the player leaves the word and relates to the experience. When the player no longer hides behind words, but focuses on the environment, the voice will become natural, the body will relax, and words will flow.

2. Do not play this game often, for it deliberately uses recall and must therefore be carefully handled.

3. For the formal theater, SEEING THE WORD is useful to players with long speeches.

DEVELOPING SCENES

FROM AUDIENCE SUGGESTIONS

The following exercise trains players in developing immediate response to audience suggestions. It is one of the preliminary steps toward actual im-

---

3. This exercise is helpful in training the student-actors to use words with more dimension. It stimulates scenes in full sense perceptions and is also a great asset in correcting artificial reading habits for the formal theater. See the remarks on dialogue and words in Chapter II.

provisation of audience suggestions at public performances. See SUGGES-
TIONS BY THE AUDIENCE, p. 203, for further discussion of this important area.

ON THE SPOT

FOCUS: on responding to audience suggestion by improvising a scene.

▶ Teams of two or more. Players ask the audience Who they are to play (the relationship), Where they are (their setting) and What they are doing (their activity). They can ask for Weather, Time, etc. Players will play one of the many theater games they are experienced in and explain its focus to the audience before moving quickly into their improvisation.

EVALUATION: Could audience have cast more effectively? Did the team work as a cooperating unit in playing? Did they give and take (build upon each other's material) effectively? Did team improvise a scene or write a script? Was play true to the theater game and its focus?

POINT OF OBSERVATION

Scenes must be set up quickly and quietly. Do not allow cleverness and gags to replace discipline and integrity.

VALUABLE MIRROR EXERCISES

MIRROR exercises continue to be valuable and exciting tools in getting players to work closely with one another. They can also be done in performance, when audience gives suggestions for Who, Where, and What.

MIRROR/THREE-WAY

FOCUS: on following the follower.

▶ Four or more players, who are to use a three-way mirror, agree on Who, Where, and What. For example: man trying on clothes.

MIRROR/COMBINATION

FOCUS: on reflection of fellow players.

▶ Five or more players agree upon Who, Where, and What. Three players are mirrors and two play the scene, or one is the player and four are mirrors, or whatever combination is desired.

MIRROR/DISTORTING

FOCUS: on distorted mirror reflection.

▶ Many players agree upon Who, Where, and What, using whatever mirror/player combinations they wish. The "mirrors" distort as in an amusement park.

MIRROR/GROUP FOLLOW THE FOLLOWER

FOCUS: on follow the follower.

▶ Many players play mirror or look into mirrors, allowing mirror roles to change back and forth, playing follow the follower.

AUDIENCE PLAYERS SIDE-COACH

AUDIENCE DIRECTS (SIDE-COACHES)

FOCUS: on the playing.

▶ Teams of two or more players agree on Where, Who, and What. Each team in turn acts as group side-coach to another team's event (scene). As a scene is played out, side-coach team players call out focus, depending on what on-stage players need, such as "Contact!", "Gibberish!", "Slow Motion!", "Extended movement!", "Explore and heighten!", etc. On-stage players hold a focus until another problem replaces it.

SIDE-COACHING: *"Side-coaches, keep the players playing!"*

EVALUATION: On-stage players, was the side-coaching helpful? Side-coach players, did you focus on the playing and coach to keep players playing? Or did your coaching impose on the playing?

POINTS OF OBSERVATION

1. Side-coaching develops directing skills in everyone. If too many side-coaches create confusion, try having one chosen by quick consultation of teammates.

2. Side-coaching must emerge from playing needs and be part of the whole.

EXPLORE AND HEIGHTEN

FOCUS: on being open to exploring, heightening, and expansion of on-stage playing.

▶ Teams of two players agree on Where, Who, and What and play the scene, alert to side-coaching. The initial side-coach must be the teacher-director. Those who have played the game, however, can side-coach the next team. Two, three, or four student side-coaches can select moments, objects, ideas, attitudes, whatever, to explore and heighten.

SIDE-COACHING: *Explore that idea! Explore and heighten that object! That involvement! Heighten it! Explore the silence! Explore that sound! That beat! Explore that object* (name it)*! Heighten it!*

EVALUATION: Players, did anything happen when you were coached to explore and heighten? Players, did side-coaching come out of what was happening or was it imposed?

POINTS OF OBSERVATION

1. EXPLORE AND HEIGHTEN calls for transformation of the beat and helps players recognize and act upon the varied formations arising out of their playing. From the formations (plays, as in a game) come beats, and from the heightening of the beats emerges a scene. It is best played after CONTRAPUNTAL ARGUMENT, Part III, p. 168, (transformation of the point of view) and TRANSFORMATION OF RELATIONSHIP, p. 250, have been understood and solved.

2. *"Explore and heighten!"* can be used as side-coaching in any game. It is supportive, increases the energy level, and defeats the tendency to "playwrite" or invent, which bogs down a scene.

3. A side-coach must be totally attentive, watching and listening for sounds, movements, ideas, pauses, etc., which ordinarily might slip by unnoticed. The simplest gesture is explorable, alerting everyone to the possibilities for an inspired stage life.

4. In side-coaching, attempt to be specific: *"Explore the sound of the waves!"* or *"Explore the spider-bite!"* Give focus to events as they arise.

CHAPTER XI

EMOTION

From the beginning student to the performing artist, great argument ensues as to how to get emotion or feeling for a particular scene.[1] The problem of clarifying what is meant by emotion is far from simple, but if emotion is to be handled as a direct acting problem in the training, a position must be formulated. One thing is certain. We must not use personal and/or subjective (what we use in daily living) emotion for the stage. It is a private matter (like feeling and believing) and not for public viewing. At best "real" emotion put on stage can be classified as psycho-drama no matter how skillfully it is written or played, and it does not constitute a theatrical communication.

The emotion we need for the theater can only come out of a fresh experience; for in such experiencing rests the stirring of our total selves—organic motion—which when combined with the theater reality spontaneously brings forth energy and motion (stage) for actors and audience alike. This prevents the use of old emotion from past experiences being used in a fresh moment of experience. It could well be the same formula that created the original personal emotions to begin with, and if this is so, all the emotion we use in daily living should evolve out of organic motion—out of the Where, Who, What, the involvements and relationships of our personal lives.

---

1. While one book on acting may say that "joy is expressed by raising the hands over the head in a figure eight," student-actors will learn that joy can also be shown by wriggling the toes ecstatically.

In this way—creating our own structure (reality in the theater) and playing it instead of living out old emotions—a whole process is set going which manufactures its own energy and motion (emotion) then and there. This prevents psycho-drama from appearing on either side of the stage, for psycho-drama is a vehicle specially designed for therapeutic reasons to abstract old emotions from the participating members and put them into a dramatic situation to examine them and so release the individual from personal problems. This dramatic structure then, is the only resemblance to the play. In theater training, emotion can easily be provoked by many devices, and great care must be taken not to misuse individual emotion or allow the players to do so.

When psycho-drama is confused with a play or scene—is in fact considered to be the scene—it leads players to exploit their emotions instead of experiencing total organic motion. What can psycho-drama do but abstract the tears that should come out of our personal grief alone, thus making artistic detachment impossible? Emotion newly generated on stage, however, remains detached because it is usable only within the structure of agreed reality.

When exercises in the workshops are used for emotional release they must be stopped; for the players are working out of and on their personal feelings alone. However, as the focus of the game is understood and used, subjective emotion becomes a thing of the past, where it truly belongs.

By taking the whole problem of emotion, then, and physicalizing it, we move it out of its abstracted use and place it within the total organism, making organic motion possible. For it is the physical manifestation of emotion, whether it is a quiet widening of the eyes or a violent throwing of a cup, that we can see and communicate.[2]

Therefore we must not bring students to the exercises of emotion too early if we wish to avoid exhibitionism, psycho-drama, and general bad taste. The student-actor must not withdraw into a subjective world and "emote," nor should one intellectualize about "feeling," which can only

---

2. There are many ways to heighten emotion on stage for the audience's enjoyment through music, lighting, props, etc. Here we are dealing with the student-actor alone.

limit the expression of it. An audience should not be interested in the personal grief, joy, and frustration of the performing actor. It is the skill of the actor playing the grief, joy, and frustration of the character portrayed that holds us captive.

PHYSICALIZATION

SILENT SCREAM

FOCUS: on feeling emotion (inner action) physically.

▶ Full group.

To help the student-actors feel emotion physically (inner action), ask the seated group to scream without making a sound. Coach them: *Scream with your toes! Your eyes! Your back! Your stomach! Your legs! Your whole body!*

When they are responding physically and muscularly as they would for a vocal scream—and this will be very evident—call: *Scream out loud!* The sound should be deafening.

This exercise not only gives students a direct experience to remember but is very useful for rehearsing mob scenes. Watch for students tensing, rather than releasing muscular rigidity in the act of screaming with parts of the body.

INABILITY TO MOVE A

FOCUS: on being physically immobilized in the face of outside danger.

▶ Single player goes on stage and presents situation in which he or she is physically immobilized and is being threatened by an outside danger. Player focuses on the inability to move, using inner action to show W. W. W.

INABILITY TO MOVE B

FOCUS: on physical immobility caused by outside danger.

▶ Two or more players agree on Where, Who, and What. They represent a group of people in a situation whereby it is impossible for them to move because of some outside danger. For example, soldiers stranded in a minefield, robbers hiding in a closet.

POINTS OF OBSERVATION

1. Only now will the introduction and discussion of activity and inner action be meaningful for students. Action does not necessarily mean activity, nor does activity always mean action. For our purposes, the word "activity" is used to denote outward stage movement, and the words "inner action" to explain internal movement. The term "inner action" means physicalization of feeling and replaces the term "emotion" whenever necessary.

2. To help students acquire this new awareness, bring up a discussion of the two terms. They must understand which comes first—activity/dialogue or inner action. Does the actor, like the White Queen in *Alice in Wonderland,* cry out before the pin has stuck the finger? All have probably seen the roughness and lack of reality in the scene where the actor reads, "It's cold in here," and then proceeds to shiver; for although the two might in some cases occur simultaneously, inner action generally precedes activity/dialogue:

    1. Inner Action: Hunger—Physical response: Salivary glands work, etc.
    2. Activity: Go to refrigerator
    3. Dialogue: "What's there to eat?"

3. An infant acts with the whole body (internally and externally), laughs or cries from head to toe. However, as we grow older, we muscularly *hold* many manifestations of feeling. As a result of cultural pattern, we are forced to hold our tears and stifle our laughter. An emotion may work in our stomach, tingle along our spines, or give us cold chills, but outwardly, we have become conditioned to show this emotion physically only in isolated areas. We grit our teeth, clench our fist, and keep a stiff upper lip. It is essential to release these holds for full natural movement.

4. From now on use side-coaching to remind the student-actors: *More inner action, please! Physicalize that feeling! Feel it in your toes!* This focus will enable players to really *show* how they feel instead of merely talking or pursuing meaningless activity.

CHANGING EMOTION

When student-actors thoroughly understand inner action (physicalizing), show them how it can shift and change, even though the activity remains the same.

FOCUS: on physicalizing emotion or feeling states through the use of space objects.

▶ Single player. In this exercise, the player completes an activity. Then, for some reason, the activity must be undone after it is completed, using the same objects the second time, but in reverse and with a different inner action.

   EXAMPLE: Activity—a girl is making up and dressing for a dance. First inner action—*pleasure,* caused by her feelings about the event. Second inner action—*disappointment,* caused by learning that the dance has been canceled.

   As one part of the activity, while influenced by the first inner action the girl might have taken the dress from the closet and held it against herself as she danced dreamily around the room. After learning that the dance had been canceled, she might have held the dress against herself and then rolled it up and thrown it back into the closet—thereby reversing motions in the same activity and responding to the second inner action.

SIDE-COACHING: *More inner action, please! Physicalize that thought! Explore and heighten that object!*

EVALUATION: Was the activity identical before and after the turning point? Was the inner action communicated to the audience through body changes? What does pleasure do to one physically? What does disappointment create kinesthetically? (See remarks on showing inner action through the use of objects, p. 226.)

POINTS OF OBSERVATION

1. The same activity must be carried out both times. As in the example, if the girl applied her make-up and then took the dress from the closet, she would put the dress back and remove the make-up after the turning point.

2. When the first inner action is well set, the teacher-director can ring the

phone or send another student on stage to provide the necessary information to change the inner action, if necessary.

3. It would be well to note that the students can communicate their feelings very effectively by their handling of objects (as shown by the girl's handling of her dress before and after the turning point).[3]

4. If changing inner action is shown only through facial mannerisms, students are "acting" (performing) and have not understood the meaning of physicalization. Go back to early exercises of involvement with objects.

CHANGING INTENSITY OF INNER ACTION

FOCUS: on changing the emotion from one level to the next.

▶ Two or more advanced students. Where, Who, and What agreed upon. Emotion must start at one point and then become progressively stronger. For instance, the sequence might run: from affection to love to adoration; from suspicion to fear to terror; from irritation to anger to rage.

The inner action can also run in a circle, concluding back at the original emotion (e.g., affection to love to adoration to love to affection). However, this can only be accomplished through side-coaching by the teacher.

EXAMPLE: Where—a camp scene. Who—a group of teen-age girls. What—they think their counselor has deserted them for another group. *Changing inner action*—loss to sadness to grief.

In this scene, the inner action was carried through a full cycle by side-coaching. When they arrived at grief, the coaching began; and they responded emotionally in the following order:

1.	self-pity	7.	affection
2.	anger	8.	love
3.	hostility	9.	self-responsibility
4.	guilt	10.	understanding
5.	grief	11.	self-respect
6.	sadness	12.	admiration for each other

EVALUATION: Were they acting (emoting) or showing inner action (physicalizing)?

3. See PHYSICALIZING AN OBJECT, p. 78.

1. In this exercise, you must work very closely with the players, taking your cue from them as they pick up their cues from you. Follow the follower.

2. If the group is ready, these scenes can produce very exciting energy. However, if the scenes end up in mere chit-chat, the exercise has been presented too soon and the students need more foundation work.

JUMP EMOTION

FOCUS: on changing from one emotion (inner action) to the next.

▶ Two or more players agree upon Where, Who, and What. Each player chooses some radical change of inner action, for example, fear to heroism, love to pity, etc. The Where could be carefully planned, particularly if players are getting sloppy about stage set-ups.

EXAMPLE: Where—foxhole. Who—two soldiers. What—a dangerous mission. Jump changes of inner action—#1, anger to understanding; #2, fear to heroism.

Soldier #1 was angered at the cowardice shown by soldier #2, a shy sensitive boy whose seeming cowardice was a revulsion against killing another person. During the scene, a bullet struck soldier #1, wounding him; and soldier #2 bravely undertook the mission, although it was not his duty to do so. As the players kept their concentration on trying to make their shifts of emotion during the action, the scene developed to unusual dramatic height.

EVALUATION: Was emotion shown physically? Players, do you agree?

POINT OF OBSERVATION

To make a game of this exercise, designate examples of changing emotions on some slips of paper, put Where suggestions on others, and then let the players draw from each pile, as in the THEME-SCENE exercise (p. 199).

SHOWING EMOTION THROUGH OBJECTS
Part I

FOCUS: on using an object, selected spontaneously at the moment one needs it, to show a feeling or relationship.

▶ Two or more players agree upon Where, Who, and What. A variety of real objects are on a table which is easily accessible to all players on stage without disturbing their stage movement or their Where. Examples below describe players showing emotion through objects.

SAMPLE LIST OF REAL OBJECTS NEEDED

(other items may be substituted or added as desired)

balloon	bell
sandbag	feathers
ball	egg beater
chains	rubber band
triangle	jumping rope
bean bag	party toys
horn	trapeze (or swinging rope)
	ladder

EXAMPLE A: Where—bedroom. Who—three sisters, two older and one younger. What—two older sisters are dressing to go out; younger sister wishes she could go along with them.

While dressing, the two older sisters discussed their anticipation of the evening's fun. They threw balloons, blew feathers, and jumped rope. The younger sister, sadly bewailing the fact that she could not go with them, walked around the bedroom weighted down with a sandbag, which she sometimes put on her shoulders and sometimes dragged along on the floor.

EXAMPLE B (for formal theater): A love scene between a bashful couple could make use of a ball rolled back and forth between their feet.

EXAMPLE C: A scene where someone was trying to "pass the buck" could be physicalized by tossing a bean bag back and forth among the two or three players involved.

EVALUATION: Did the objects follow the action?

POINT OF OBSERVATION

This exercise is especially helpful for the director of formal theater. It can give unusual nuances to actors, even those with small amounts of training.

Part II

FOCUS: on retaining the feeling of the objects without using them.

▶ Players repeat the same scene as in Part I, attempting to retain the emotion shown through the objects without using them.

EVALUATION: Did they retain the quality of the scene when they worked without the objects?

POINT OF OBSERVATION

The second time the scene is done, keep reminding the players (through side-coaching) of the objects that were used for the first scene.

EMOTION GAME

FOCUS: on inner action.

▶ One player starts game, which is open to participation of other players (as in PART OF A WHOLE and WHERE games). Player communicates Where and Who. What happens must be around a disaster, accidents—events which cause hysteria, grief, etc. Other players enter the scene as definite characters, set up relationships with Where and Who, and play the scene.

EXAMPLE A: Where—street corner. Who—elderly man. What—car hits man as he crosses street.

The old man tentatively steps into the street. He is hit by a car and falls screaming to the ground. Other players enter as driver of car, cops, friends, passersby, ambulance driver, doctor, etc.

EXAMPLE B: Where—hospital room. Who—woman. What—seated at bedside of dying relative.

Player moves around room showing hospital environment. She shows us her relationship with the patient in the bed and her grief at his state of health. Other players enter scene as relatives, doctor, nurses, priest, another patient, etc.

POINTS OF OBSERVATION

1. If the teacher-director observes that the players are not entering into the game with enthusiasm, energy, and excitement, then it has not been presented properly, and steps should be retraced.

2. This game may be scattered throughout training or presented at the time emotion is introduced to the group. It is very useful when working on crowd scenes.

REJECTION

FOCUS: on effective rejection.

▶ Two or more players. Where, Who, and What agreed upon. Players must reject other players, adopting one of the following patterns:

1. One group rejects another group.
2. A group rejects an individual.
3. An individual rejects a group.
4. An individual rejects an individual.

EXAMPLES: New person in neighborhood is rejected. Someone is rejected because of race, color, or creed. Substitute teacher is rejected by the class.

EVALUATION: Did they solve the problem? What was the weather? Did they show us the time?

POINT OF OBSERVATION

By now, all the scenes should have a definite theatrical life. Evaluation is a way to remind players they might be getting careless in setting up the details of a scene.

EMOTION THROUGH CAMERA TECHNIQUES

FOCUS: on focusing intense body energy on the actor being framed.

▶ Two or more players. Where, Who, and What agreed upon. Players begin scene. From time to time during the action, the teacher-director calls out to "frame" different actors. Each time, the other actors on stage become "cameras" and focus on the one framed. The actor thus framed continues to play the scene normally; but he or she now has the intense attention of all the surrounding players. The scene continues to play with all actors remaining in their characters, whether cameras or subject. The framing is simply a way of heightening the scene.

EXAMPLE: Where—throne room of a palace. Who—king, courtiers, a courier. What—waiting for news. The courier, badly beaten, comes into the palace with bad news. The court must decide what to do.

SIDE-COACHING: *Full focus on Rachel! Head to toe focus on Polly!*

EVALUATION: Was the full body energy used to focus on the framed actor? Did they show us where they were? How old was the king (or whoever was in the scene)?

POINTS OF OBSERVATION

1. The interchange of the word "light" with "frame" will aid in evoking the intensity needed. Side-coaching should shift the camera as necessary.

2. Exercises like this one when used during rehearsals of a formal play, where actual lights can be brought in simultaneously with the players' framing, can put much heightened stage energy into the players' performance.

3. This exercise is particularly good for student-directors, since they can easily take over the side-coaching.

4. This exercise is similar to GIVE AND TAKE (p. 149).

CONFLICT

Conflict should not be given to students-actors until they thoroughly understand holding the focus (object) to create relationships. If conflict conditions are given too early, involvement will take place between the players themselves, thus creating subjective emotional scenes or verbal battles between them. This is an important point and one difficult to understand. In fact, this writer used conflict extensively in the early years of her work as part of the Where exercise. It seemed useful, for it invariably created some stage energy (when it wasn't on a "you-did-and-I-didn't" level). This was because by creating involvement with each other directly, it stirred up personal feelings and tension in the players and in many instances was close to psycho-drama. This gave the players the feeling of "acting." As we are working in an art form, the personal emotions of players must be distilled and objectified through the form in which they are working—an art form insists upon this objectivity. In spite of this obvious fact, however, conflict seemed to bring "life" into the Where exercise and was a definite step towards contact, and so was retained as one of the problems given during the early stage of Where.

In time, it became apparent that unless the players used the *physical objects* in Where, for instance, to show conflict, many aspects of subjectivity (such as emotionalism or verbal battles) were bound to result. Further, very little if any scene progression took place. It was important to note that despite the unpleasant aspects, tension and release freeing energy (physical action) were always generated between players. Only after the author came to Chicago to direct workshops and discussed this many times with Paul Sills (original director of Second City) was the question of conflict finally resolved. The same tension and release generated through conflict can be accomplished with the student-actor who is kept on the problem as presented by the focus of a theater game and not allowed to wander off into story-telling or playwriting.

It became evident that the players' involvement with each other (as produced by conflict) instead of involvement with the focus was for the most part a mutual pushing around (which is confused in our minds as dramatic action) to get to one's goal and in no sense a process out of which scene improvisation could develop. This would seem so because conflict remained in the area of the emotional and could therefore never make the spring into the intuitive, which consistently happens when we allow the focus to work for us. On the other hand, relation between players created by involvement with the object made objective tension and release (physical action) possible and at the same time produced scene improvisations.

If players are simply absorbed with content, conflict is necessary. Without conflict, the scene gets bogged down, and little or no action can possibly take place. At best, however, it is titillation and imposed action and for the most part produces psycho-drama. However, when process is understood, and, further, that content is the residue of process, dramatic action is the result, for energy and stage-action are generated by the simple process of playing. By constantly stopping student-actors from playwriting and continuously clarifying the whole point of process *versus* content, the teacher found that conflict was no longer needed to generate stage-action, and so this exercise with its emotionalism and verbal battles fell into disuse.

Now conflict takes its place along with the later exercises. It is useful; it can be fun to do. A teacher-director may be tempted to use it earlier than advisable, when there are difficulties in understanding process and playing, to "stir up" some action. If you do this, however, you must know that it is a device — and because of the personal emotions it stirs up, it constitutes a "bribe." Its use in this way may be permitted us when it becomes most important to hold a student's interest until process and therefore playing are understood.

To summarize. Players working with content alone need a conflict to generate energy and stage-action. When they understand playing (process), however, tension and release freeing energy are clearly seen as an integral part of playing—in fact this *is* playing.

CONFLICT EXERCISE

Preliminary

▶ To give the communication of conflict being tension between two people, have student-actors go on stage in twos and have a tug-of-war with a real rope. Discussion on the tug-of-war should be around the physical tension in each one of them as they strive to pull their opponent over the center line. Further discussion should be on the outcome of the tug-of-war: when one pulled the other over, both fell over, or a stalemate was reached.

FOCUS: on the conflict (rope) between them.

▶ Two or more players. Where, Who, and What agreed upon. Add a conflict.

SIDE-COACHING: *Pull the rope! Stay with the focus!*

EVALUATION: Did they stay with the focus? Did each individual actor hang on to his or her end of the rope?

POINT OF OBSERVATION

In preparing the scene, listen to groups carefully to see that the conflict will be such that it will permit physical action and not just an argument. Conflict and/or rope are used interchangeably to help physicalize the conflict for the players.

HIDDEN CONFLICT

FOCUS: on never verbalizing the problem (conflict).

▶ Two or more players. Where, Who, and What agreed upon. Each player takes a conflict and states it to himself or herself in the first person without letting the other know what it is.

EXAMPLE: Where—kitchen. Who—husband and wife. What—breakfast.

Hidden conflict: Husband—I am not going to work. Wife—I want him to leave. I'm expecting a visitor.

POINTS OF OBSERVATION

1. Let audience know each player's hidden conflict.

2. When the hidden conflict is stated, the scene is over.

3. Variation of this is to write a series of hidden conflicts on slips of paper and let actors pick after they have decided on Where, Who, and What.

4. HIDDEN CONFLICT forces use of objects and was one of the early exercises that started the semantic shift from "conflict" to "problem," thus opening up new doors of inquiry.

WHAT TO DO WITH THE OBJECT

FOCUS: on *what* to do with the (space) object.

▶ Two players. Players agree on object between them. Object is to be set in motion in some agreed way such as: selling it, destroying it, building it, hiding it.

POINT OF OBSERVATION

This is similar to the Involvement exercises in the orientation session. It takes the players further, however, for it can be used to set up emotions directly involving players through the object. While the focus of an exercise in the earlier games was on the object between the players, the present point of concentration is on what is happening to the object. It therefore sets up a different relationship between the players. If a story is imposed on the object and players "act," limit them to a simple activity. Return to this exercise at a later date when the group has learned how to let the focus work for them.

CONFLICT GAME

▶ Full group. Played as in Orientation and Where games. Two players go on stage. They agree upon a conflict that can allow for many others to take part. Other members of workshop decide Who and enter scene to take sides.

EXAMPLES: Where—a street corner. Who—a police officer and a soapbox orator. What—an arrest. Conflict—policeman arresting orator because of the content of the speech. Players entering scene can be workers, bums, housewives, more police, etc.

Where—playground. Who—two boys. What—playing. Conflict—one boy is a bully. Those entering scene can become other children, teachers, parents, etc.

CHAPTER XII

CHARACTER

Character is presented as the last large problem in the handbook. It should not be given as a direct exercise until the student-actors have solved the earlier workshop problems and have learned to work with focus. Although it may be tempting to present and discuss character exercises in earlier workshops, it is best to wait until students appear to be fully in contact with each other and fully involved with the acting problem (see Chapter XI).

Character is intrinsic in everything we do on stage. From the very first acting class, this thread has crossed and re-crossed the fabric of our work. Character can grow only out of personal integration with the total stage life. If the actor is truly to play a role, character must not be given as an intellectual exercise independent of this involvement.

Premature attention to character on a verbal level may throw the student-actor into role-playing, preventing involvement with focus and relation with fellow players. Instead of reaching out into the stage environment, he or she will withdraw further behind self-protecting walls. It will be acting out private needs and feelings; it will be a mirroring of himself or herself; it will be an interpretation of character, an intellectual exercise.

In the unskilled student this will be quickly uncovered, but it is far more difficult to catch in the more clever and skilled actor. Character must be used as further theatrical communication, *not as withdrawal*. To insure this, do not work on character until students are playing. Always keep them from "acting" (performing) in their early work, by stopping an exercise if necessary. Avoid discussing character except in the most casual way, on a simple Who basis (relationship). Remember, since most students know that character is the essence of theater, this absence of direct character discussion may be very confusing to them until they begin to see character emerge out of the stage life and realize that "acting" is a wall between players.

When they learn to be involved with the focus of the exercise, relate to each other, and solve the group problem, they will "trust the scheme" and be ready for direct exercises in developing physical qualities for a character. An actor must see and relate to a fellow actor, not a "character." We play football with other human beings, not with the uniforms they are wearing. This simply means that both players know the other is playing and go along with the game.

DEVELOPING A CHARACTER

When student-actors plan W.W.W. around an acting problem, what is it that determines who among them shall play the grandmother and who the maiden aunt? This is all implicit in what is known as characterization.

In Orientation, the students—by simply observing whether others are comfortable or uncomfortable—are able to catch mannerisms. PART OF A WHOLE ACTIVITY, HOW OLD AM I? and WHAT DO I DO FOR A LIVING? all introduce character without calling attention to it. In Where we ask: "How do you know what people are to each other?"; and the youngest student answers, "By the way they act together." And every early Who exercise handles the problem of character.

In Evaluation we raise such questions as: "How old was he?" "Did he show us he was a man who farmed for a living?" "Did the miser look as if he loved gold more than people?" If we question carefully, even the youngest child will be able to express the differences between people—whether the distinguishing quality is in mannerism, tone of voice, or tempo of movement.

After many years, our usual facial expressions, posture, and movements become muscular reflections of our inner state. Emotion can be expressed only through character. In *The Thinking Body*, Mabel Elsworth Todd states:

Emotion constantly finds expression in bodily position; if not in the furrowed brow or set mouth, then in limited breathing, in the tight held neck muscles, or in the slumped body of listlessness and discouragement.

It could be said that, in time, one might well become a portrait of oneself—for a person becomes the physical expression of an attitude (a life attitude). How many of us can pick out a doctor, a public relations professional, a schoolteacher, or an actor in a crowd and be 85 percent correct?

Simple involvement with objects can come to life only through character. In developing material for scenes (Chapter IX), character development is handled more directly as the "play" is set up and the need for definite characters arises. GIBBERISH, CONTACT, BLIND, and other exercises insist upon strong stage relations which create definite character attitudes and actions.

What is acting with the whole body (Chapter V) but a way of showing a player how the body can be an expressive instrument? And for what purpose? To communicate with an audience more comprehensively. To communicate what? A character within a play.

Experiment with a group. Tell them that they will be given a quick command. When the teacher-director claps hands, they are to carry out the command instantly without thought.

"*Portray an old man!*" is called. Invariably, almost 90 percent of the students will lean forward, hand on hip, as if resting on a cane. Discuss their generalization (cliché) with them. Do all old men necessarily lean forward? There are millions of old men—some are straight and tall. What makes a person old?

The generalization (cliché) is not necessarily untrue, merely abstracted and thus limited. To the student-actor, the old man may well be a person who leans on a cane, has white hair, and moves slowly, and this economy of selection is important to keep.

Old age is, after all, recognizable. The students, in selecting the characteristics which would instantly communicate an old man, chose the simplest of them all, infirmity. And that was what they gave in answer to the command. It is from this kind of simple recognition that the actor develops a characterization.

What will finally emerge as they gain perception is that an old man can show his age and his feelings in his feet, his elbows, and his voice, as well as in his white hair and cane.

Developing a character is the ability to intuit an essence from the welter of the complex whole person. This ability to show the essence rather than a description of the detailed whole springs spontaneously from within. See HOW OLD AM I? REPEAT, p. 70.

The actor's skill depends upon this response and ability to communicate it. *All* can respond: the immature will do the obvious (leaning on a cane); an artist who trusts in intuition accepts what emerges with certainty (arthritic hand, cataract-blinded eye, thickened tongue, etc.).[1] But no matter what is used, simple or profound, and whatever the age or experience of the player, when one responds to stage life at the same time character appears; for characterization grows out of the total stage life as well as intuitive recognition of a fellow human being.

The actor is surrounded by a circle of characteristics—voice, mannerisms, physical movement—all of which are given life by his or her energy. The player will develop *himself* or *herself* as an alert, perceiving, free person, capable of reaching beyond day-to-day life, able to "play" a role. This player will be alive, human, interdependent, working with fellow players—playing the game of the character he or she has chosen to communicate.

How much better to think of players this way, as human beings working within an art form, than as schizophrenics who have changed their own personalities for the sake of a role in a play!

Physicalizing

A student can dissect, analyze, intellectualize, and develop a valuable case history of a character; however, if one cannot communicate this physically, it is useless within the theater form. Reaching the intuitive, on which the

1. The player need not "become" the old man. Rather, he presents the old man to us for purposes of communication.

insight into a role rests, does not come from a logical, intellectual knowledge of our character.

The following group of exercises deals with the problem of character on a physical structural basis, from which a character may emerge. The question arises as to whether an actor should assume outward physical qualities to get a feeling of a character or work on feeling to get the physical qualities. Sometimes a physical attitude or expression will give us an intuitive jump. In these exercises we play the game every way. (See also Chapters X and XI.)

WHO GAMES FOR CHARACTER DEVELOPMENT

Absorb the following exercises carefully so as to be able to present them to student-actors at the time when they will most effectively act as a series of simple steps toward character development. They can be used as warm-ups or developed into full exercises.[2]

WHO GAME/FACIAL EMOTION

FOCUS: on showing as many facial qualities as possible while playing scene.

▶ Two or more players. Who, Where, and What agreed upon. (Players should choose a simple relationship and activity, such as husband and wife watching TV.)

Have each player write on individual slips of paper a list of facial features and then descriptions of those features. The descriptions should be emotional rather than structural. Players should make out slips for each facial feature. For instance:

> lower lip—sad
> upper lip—petulant
> tip of nose—sharp
> nostrils—annoyed
> eyes—beady
> eyebrows—serene

2. Some of the Who games are presented in Chapter IV.

forehead—overhanging

chin—belligerent

shape of face—saucy

When the slips have been completed, separate them by features and put the slips into piles. Let each player pick one slip from each pile. The players are to take on as many of the descriptions as they wish and retain them while playing their scene.

EVALUATION: To actors: Did holding these physical aspects make you feel mechanical? Did you gain any new insights?

To audience: did any of the actors show a new character quality? Did the facial qualities seem integrated with the scene?

POINT OF OBSERVATION

Mirrors for the players when they first try to take on their physical characteristics can be helpful.

WHO GAME/BODY ATTITUDE

FOCUS: on showing feeling through body attitudes.

▸ Two or more players choose Where, Who, and What. Instead of choosing facial qualities, players list emotions with which to show the attitudes of the parts of their bodies during the scene. For instance, shoulders—sad, stomach—angry, chest—joyous, legs—suspicious. As in the game above, slips are placed in piles and each player takes one from each pile before entering scene.

POINTS OF OBSERVATION

1. Listing physical instead of emotional attitudes may be done instead in either of these WHO GAMES. Just substitute descriptions (e.g., stiff upper lip, harp nose, bowed legs, etc.).

2. Both games are useful in formal theater direction.

WHO GAME/ADDING CONFLICT

FOCUS: on allowing Who to reveal itself.

▸ Two players, A and B. A waits on stage; B enters, having a preplanned relationship with A, as in the WHO GAME, p. 106, but also having preplanned the *state* (conflict or tension) of the on-stage player. For example, B pre-plans that A is a mean, taciturn parent, while she herself is a teenager. Where is a living room and What is her late return from a dance.

POINTS OF OBSERVATION

1. This exercise can usually be continued beyond the solving of the problem, for tension between the two players comes up automatically.

2. Again, letting the audience in on the reverse point of view is intensely interesting.

PHYSICALIZING ATTITUDES

As a lead-in to the following exercises, present the SPACE WALK/ATTITUDE exercise, p. 392.

HOLD IT! A

FOCUS: on holding facial and bodily expression through a series of Wheres, Whos, and Whats.

▸ Teams of four or more players (even gender division desirable). Either players themselves or audience suggests for each a short statement of attitude, such as "Nobody loves me." "I never met a man I didn't like." "I never have any fun." "I know it all." "Tomorrow will be better." They move in the space, working for a full facial and bodily expression of their phrase. When achieved, and body expression takes over, side-coach "*Hold it!*" Players are then side-coached through a series of Wheres, Whos, and Whats, for example: nursery school playground, grammar school graduation, double date, office party, high school reunion, old people's home—the events of a lifetime.

SIDE-COACHING: *Let the attitude affect your chin, eyes, shoulders, mouth, hands, and feet! Hold it!*

EVALUATION: Were the basic expressions (attitudes) maintained, even if somewhat altered in each event? Did these attitudes affect relationships? Manner of speaking?

POINTS OF OBSERVATION

1. If a phrase does not evoke an attitude, suggest that the player take on an exact physical expression (e.g., belligerent chin, petulant mouth, overhanging forehead, wide-open eyes, etc.).

2. Do not use this exercise with young students. Players should be at least in their teens.

3. HOLD IT! can be given around the eighth or ninth Where workshop session and repeated at later dates.

4. One student, on completion of HOLD IT! said: "I feel as if I've gone through a lifetime!"

HOLD IT! B

FOCUS: on maintaining a physical expression of bodily quality throughout Where, Who, and What.

▶ Two or more players agree on Where, Who, and What after each has achieved a physical expression and has been coached to "Hold it!" Some examples are: hunched shoulders, pigeon toes, firm aggressive step, pulled-in chin, flabby stomach muscles, etc.

SIDE-COACHING: *Hold it! Hold it! Share with the audience! Hold it!*

EVALUATION: Did the players' chosen physical characteristics influence players' activities within Where, Who, and What? Players, do you agree?

POINT OF OBSERVATION

HOLD IT! exercises suggest to players that subjective emotional attitudes and their physical expression are often one.

PHYSICAL VISUALIZATION

The use of images in getting a character quality is an old and tried technique and can sometimes bring a totally new dimension to an actor's role. Images can be based on pictures or any object, animate or inanimate, that the actor chooses. However, getting character in this way is at best a device.

In the formal play, such images should be used only when the character development has not evolved from the total stage relationship. Actors who have had some experience with this way of working are eager to begin work on the character immediately and sometimes set about taking some image privately without letting the director know. This becomes a serious handicap, for the director and actor may be at odds with one another. The director may be working to get rid of the very mannerisms the actor is hanging on to because of the image he or she has created privately.

It is, however, useful in emergencies. Once, for example, a girl was asked to step into a small part on a few hours' notice, because of the sudden illness of the regular actor. She was playing in another one-act play on the same bill. In rehearsal, it was soon evident that she could not easily shake the characteristics of the other role. Her regular part was that of a shy, frightened girl; but the new one was a portrayal of a perky, talkative woman. By suggesting that she take an animal image, specifically a turkey, the director enabled her to project the necessary qualities for the role almost immediately.

In improvisational theater, when suggestions by the audience are part of a program, images can give the actor an instant character quality which adds to his or her versatility.

ANIMAL IMAGES

This exercise, attributed to Maria Ouspenskaya of the Moscow Art Theater, was adapted by Viola Spolin into a true theater game.

If at all possible, take the workshop group to a zoo or barnyard to observe the movement, rhythm, and actual physical characteristics of animals—the bone and facial structures are as important as the more obvious movement. In this way, players will have an actual impression to recapture, not simply a picture in a book. Generalization is to be avoided if the exercise is to have any value.

FOCUS: on integrating the sound and body movements of an animal.

▶ Four or more players each decide on an animal to portray. Each player is to take on the exact physical qualities of the animal and is then to move around the stage space as the animal, assisted by side-coaching.

SIDE-COACHING: *Re-shape your forehead! The nose! The jaw! Concentrate on the spine! Concentrate on the tail! The back legs!*

▶ When players have released their total selves into the animal qualities and have captured new body rhythms, coach them to make the sounds of the animals. Continue coaching until resistances are gone and sound and body movements are integrated.

SIDE-COACHING: *Give the sound of your animal! Integrate the sound and movement of your animal!*

▶ Now, coach the players to become human again, to stand upright and move about the stage, absorbing the animal characteristics and sound into their human actions and speech. Moving about the stage at random as before, they are to keep the rhythm of the animals in their bodies and the sound of the animals in the words they are mouthing.

SIDE-COACHING: *Become human! Stand upright! Keep your animal qualities! Keep your animal rhythms! Sound like your animal! Use a human voice with the animal sound!*

▶ To avoid breaking the flow generated by this exercise, ask for audience suggestions as players are now moving about the stage. By close observation of body attitudes, rhythm, and the voice qualities that appear when they are "human," a situation will spontaneously suggest itself. Quickly, having given the acting group a Where, Who, and What, based on audience suggestion, ask the players to move directly into the situation.

EXAMPLE: In a workshop of twelve- to fourteen-year-olds, four players were given for their individual visualizations a parrot, a cat, a hippopotamus, and an owl. In solving the problem, the parrot became a shrewish, talkative person, the cat lithe and shy, the hippo heavy-voiced, lumbering, and sullen, and the owl a wide-eyed and naive young girl. The combination suggested a school office, where childrens' difficulties would be settled by an assistant principal, parents, and children. A table, chair, and bench were swiftly set up. Windows and doors, drinking fountains, etc., were pointed out to define Where. The players were reminded to keep focus on integrating the sound and body movements of the animal each had taken on.

The parrot was the assistant principal, who decided which person could gain admittance to the inner office. Her staccato, repetitive phrasing lent itself well to this. The others were parents and children waiting to see the principal.

PARROT (ASST. PRINCIPAL): All right, all right . . . who's next? Who's next, I said? Who's next? I haven't all day, you know.

HIPPO (FATHER): (Moving slowly, rubbing his hands on his legs.) It's me, I guess. . . .

PARROT: Hurry up! Hurry up! Hurry up! I haven't all day you know. Just look at all the people we have to see today. Dear, dear, dear!

HIPPO: (Head forward, shoulders hunched, slow heavy voice.) It's about my daughter.

PARROT: (Voice rising.) Did you hear that? Did you hear that? (Cackles.) Of course! Of course! That's what you are here for. Your daughter is right there. I know her well. (Looks at owl who is on the verge of tears.) And this young man!

CAT (BOY): (Turns his head and body away from her sharp scrutiny and slides down to the edge of the bench.)

PARROT: Well, well, what are we going to do about these children?

HIPPO: I dunno . . . she said she didn't mean to do nothin'. (To Owl.) Didn't you?

OWL (DAUGHTER): (Wide-eyed, lips pursed, tearful.) Ooooooh . . . Oooooooooo . . . Oooooooooh!

PARROT: (To Cat.) Now you! You there! You! Where are your parents? They were to be here! You know that!

CAT: They c-c-couldn't beeeoooooowwww here!

POINTS OF OBSERVATION

1. If the actors lose their animal rhythms of body and voice when they stand upright, have them go back on all fours again to the original animal image. This should restore the qualities they are using.

2. When the actors speak as humans, they must sound like humans with the added animal quality; not like an animal talking.

STATUES

FOCUS: on body position and response to fellow players according to Where, Who, and What.

▶ Two or more players, one back-stage worker (optional). (This is based on the common children's game.)

▶ An outside person swings the players around and then lets them go so that each one falls into some random position. Players must then hold these positions until each position suggests to its player one of the following: a Where, a character (Who), an emotion, an activity, or a relationship. The players then make contact with one another and develop a structure using one or all of the above categories.

EVALUATION: Did the actors fall into position naturally when swung around, or did they set a position for themselves (thereby controlling or playwriting)? Did the action evolve spontaneously between them?

To actors: did you individually decide Where, Who, etc., or did it spring from the group contact? Did back-stage effects implement stage action or impose upon it?

POINTS OF OBSERVATION

1. Watch for the playwriters. They will try to maneuver the others into what they decide is the way the scene should go. .

2. Each category can be given singly in place of offering a choice. For instance, if Who (character) is the category, then the Where, What, Involvement, etc. must take place spontaneously out of Who.

3. Because many immature actors feel uncomfortable in long silences (see SILENT TENSION, p. 175), side-coaching on the focus of the game during the pre-scene quiet period will help relieve students of the urgency to premature activity.

4. A variation of this exercise is to instruct the players to end the exercise by returning to their original positions.

PHYSICAL ATTRIBUTES

PHYSICAL EXAGGERATION[3]

FOCUS: on exaggeration of a physical quality.

▶ Two or more players. Where, Who, and What agreed upon. Each player is to take on some exaggerated physical quality, and is to retain it throughout the scene.

3. See also Chapter V.

EXAMPLES: 10 feet tall, 2 feet tall, weighing 500 pounds, wearing size 20 shoes, a large chest, foot-long index fingers, legs and feet are pogo sticks, legs and feet are springs, legs and feet are round balls. This exercise can be done with full group. Players walk around stage and take on exaggerated qualities as coached.

COSTUME PIECE

FOCUS: on retaining the character qualities (attitudes) suggested by a costume piece.

▶ Two or more players each select a costume piece (cane, derby hat, scarf, umbrella, etc.). The player is to assume character qualities suggested by the costume piece. Players agree on Where, Who, and What.

EVALUATION: Did player impose character on the costume piece, or did player let the costume piece determine character?

POINT OF OBSERVATION

See BOX FULL OF HATS, p. 380.

PHYSICAL IRRITATION A

FOCUS: on integrating all attempts to relieve irritation with on-going activity.

▶ Teams of four or more players are seated on a platform waiting to make a speech. In turn, each player when speaking copes with a physical irritation which is tormenting and which cannot be easily remedied under scrutiny of the audience: a tight collar, sunburn, itch between shoulder blades. Speaking player masks all attempts to relieve the irritation, integrating the relieving through on-stage activity.

SIDE-COACHING: *Integrate your irritation! Share your voice!*

EVALUATION: Did players integrate their physical irritation with what they were doing?

POINTS OF OBSERVATION

1. Although this exercise often produces very humorous scenes, the teacher should stress that it is not being given for its "gag" value.
2. The student who solves the problem will be the one who most subtly tends to an irritation. However, the teacher-director should not tell the students that subtlety is looked for. Leave this for self-discovery.

3. This exercise is a great measure in determining the students' development.

PHYSICAL IRRITATION B

FOCUS: on integrating concealment of a physical irritation or blemish within Where, Who, and What.

▶ Teams of two players, A and B, agree on Where, Who, and What in which A is under close scrutiny by the other and must cover up a physical irritation or embarrassing blemish. All attempts to remedy or conceal must be integrated within Where, Who, and What. For example, A is being interviewed for a job by B and has garlic breath, or A is a school-girl on a blind date with a rip in her dress.

SIDE-COACHING: *Integrate your hiding! Integrate your remedy! Show! Don't tell! Share with the audience!*

EVALUATION: Did player make the physical irritation part of the whole or isolate it? Did player show concealment of a blemish or tell?

POINT OF OBSERVATION

If players are too overt in "hiding" the physical irritation, have players focus on the physical irritation alone until it moves player instead of player trying to manipulate it.

NERVOUS HABITS OR TICS

FOCUS: on physically adopting a nervous habit or tic.

▶ Two or more players. Where, Who, and What are agreed upon. Each player is to adopt a nervous habit or a tic. They should choose these from actual experience—recalling someone they have met who was actually afflicted with such a habit.

Action should be handled just as in PHYSICAL IRRITATION. Teacher-director should stress at the outset that the player is not to poke fun at this affliction but is to understand it and work with it.

EVALUATION: All players agree that people with nervous habits do not want them, nor do they necessarily have them at all times.

Do you think that a nervous habit is caused by something, or that it belongs to a person from birth? While we may not know the clinical reasons why a person has a nervous habit, let us never forget that it is the physical manifestation of some inner action.

In the case of stuttering, for example: *What do you think might be causing that? How many of you have ever stuttered?* It is surprising to see the show of hands. Most people have stuttered at one time or another.

Can anyone remember what caused them to stutter? What made it difficult for the words to come out? In almost every instance the reply is: "I was afraid." "I didn't know the answer." "Someone scared me." "I was asked to say something too fast." It seems, on this level, most stuttering is related to fear or sudden shock.

If we agree, then, that stuttering is the result of fear or shock, what does this do to us physically? Have students remember a moment of personal fear or shock. Note they almost invariably make a sharp breathing sound and then hold their breath when they have remembered something.

Have students go on stage as refugees from a war zone. Explain that when they hear a loud sharp noise, they are to treat it as bombs falling. *What happened in almost every case of reaction to the bombs?* "We stopped dead," they recalled. "We fell to the ground and stiffened out."

It is obvious to them that fear and shock brought a physical tension—not only to speech but to their bodies as well. They held their breath from head to toe. It well could be that physical manifestation of this sort in people are moments of past fear retained in a present environment.

POINTS OF OBSERVATION

1. Whatever the exact cause of an affliction, the student should be aware of some personal as well as physical problems of the sufferer. The exercise is not to be treated as a bit of comic business.

2. This exercise is useful because it clearly shows a student-actor that emotion and the physical expression (character) of that emotion are one.

DEVELOPING CHARACTER AGILITY

The following exercises are obviously valuable for the actor in the improvisational theater. They are equally valuable for the actor in the formal theater, in that they expedite the search for character attitudes.

CHARACTER AGILITY A

FOCUS: on the first impressions of character.

▶ Teacher-director supplies pencils and paper to all players and gives them the following categories, which they write down. Additional categories can be used. Time limit for each.

1. animal
2. image
3. rhythm
4. props
5. costume pieces
6. color

Teacher-director now reads off a list of characters one at a time. Players must write down whatever comes to them regarding each character for each of the categories. Possible characters might be:

Professor	Schoolteacher
Old Man	Astronaut
Psychoanalyst	Father
Little Boy	Aunt
Banker	Grandmother

EXAMPLE:

Character: Professor

1. animal: owl
2. image: rock
3. rhythm: staccato
4. prop: pointer
5. costume pieces: muffler, overshoes
6. color: purple

CHARACTER AGILITY B

FOCUS: on communicating character qualities.

▶ Instead of giving a variation of categories, name only one specific category. The players must then write as much about the character in this one specific category as they can within a one-minute time limit.

Or, the teacher-director might supply varied and seemingly unrelated categories, which the players must then fill in, also within a limited amount of time.

EXAMPLES: Single category—image. Varied categories—physical details; foods, tastes; background, friends.[4]

CHARACTER AGILITY C

FOCUS: on allowing random thoughts to take over without intellectual selection.

▶ Two players enter playing area and accept audience suggestions for character of each (e.g., schoolteacher and grocery clerk). Players then wait quietly as in EXCURSIONS INTO THE INTUITIVE, p. 178, and, when ready, move into a Where which emerges in the space.

EVALUATION: To players: did you allow random ideas to appear, or did you categorize your thoughts? Did your character come to life? Did you *play* the character?

To audience: was there a difference in the characters between random and categorized associations? Did this problem excite the actors into new aspects? Were there many body changes?

CHARACTER AGILITY D

FOCUS: on selecting Who according to qualities suggested.

▶ Teacher-director supplies pencils and paper, gives the image, mood, rhythm, etc., and has student-actors quickly write the character suggested.

CHARACTER AGILITY E

This is played by the full group as a warm-up. It is similar to the game BEAST, BIRD, OR FISH, p. 402.

FOCUS: on swift response to category or character given.

▶ Players sit in a circle with one in the center, who points to one of the players,

4. The varied categories can be used as "biography" for a certain character in a formal play.

and gives either a particular character category (image, mood, taste, rhythm, color, etc.) or calls a character, and then counts to ten.

The player must respond before the center player stops counting. If an image, mood, rhythm, etc., is used by the center player, a specific character must be named. If a character is called by the center player, then an image (tall, sad, slow, burgundy, etc.) must be given by the count of ten.

TRANSFORMATION OF RELATIONSHIP

FOCUS: on follow the follower relation between players within a series of changing relationships.

▶ Two players begin with a relationship (Who) and, while playing, allow Who to transform into new relationships, one after the other. The moment that a new scene emerges is also the moment of transformation. For example, a doctor examining a patient with a stethoscope (which is the object between the players) may find the stethoscope changing into a snake or a bedsheet, and both players emerge into a new Where, Who, and What, which in turn transforms. TRANSFORMATION OF RELATIONSHIP requires a great deal of body movement and interaction for the transformation to emerge. Often in playing, sounds will appear in the rising energy that accompanies body movement—howls, gurgles, and shouts. This is sound as physical energy rather than dialogue, which deals with ideas and can stop the transformation. Side-coach players to minimize dialogue and focus on head-to-toe body movement and interaction.

Players are not to initiate (invent) change, but "follow the follower." In the course of changing relationships, players may become people, animals, plants, objects, machines and enter any and every space and time.

SIDE-COACHING: *Don't initiate the change! Follow the follower! Follow fully! Go with the sound! That movement! That look! Explore that object between you! Use your whole body! Heighten that action! Change! Move! Change!*

EVALUATION: Players, did you invent or let it happen? Were you able to keep focus on relation or were you trapped in the event or scene or the relationship? Audience, do you agree?

POINTS OF OBSERVATION

1. As lead-ins to this exercise, play MIRROR/FOLLOW THE FOLLOWER, p. 62, and repeat Space Substance exercises, pp. 80–83.

2. When players are trapped in an event and are role-playing, side-coach *"Mirror each other!"* to help re-establish the relation between players and thus get back on focus.

3. In every scene the changing relationships reveal an event (scene) in microcosm before it shifts. The tendency is to stay with the new event, but the moment it emerges is also the moment of transformation. When the problem is understood, however, extraordinary breakthroughs occur as players enter into an endless succession of characters and relationships.

4. When used for public performance in Chicago, the audience suggested first and last characters. Another version of the exercise is for two to begin a series of transformations and for fellow players to enter one at a time until an entire group is on stage. Side-coach might ask for a relationship for players to begin with and to end with, but do not let this hold players to role-playing or stop the physical process of transformation, allowing change only to come through word association. Stop play that is not solving the problem. Return to physical energy, body movement, and focus on relation between players.

5. As in TRANSFORMATION OF OBJECTS, p. 82, change must not be made by invention or association, but by playing the game. After success with this theater game, bring students back to CONTRAPUNTAL ARGUMENT, Part III, p. 168 (transformation of point of view), and they will move more readily into transforming a thought.

CREATING A STAGE PICTURE[5]

FOCUS: on group communication.

▶ Any number of players agree on Where, Who, and What, as well as age. When scene begins, they appear in the stage space, posed as in a still pic-

5. Also see STAGE PICTURE, p. 393.

ture, In the Where they have decided upon. As in HOW OLD AM I? REPEAT, they wait quietly, with a blank mind. When inspiration comes to one of them, he or she moves into the scene. This is a sort of combination of EXCURSIONS INTO THE INTUITIVE and NO MOTION WARM-UP. Players are to come back into original "picture."

CHILDREN AND THE THEATER

CHAPTER XIII

UNDERSTANDING THE CHILD

Children nine years old and up can follow the steps set up in the first part of this handbook with exhilarating results. In fact, the non-verbal system of problems and rehearsal was developed *with* and *for* children. While many of the earlier exercises can be altered for the younger student-actor, just as some of the following exercises can be used for the older student, this chapter is geared to the particular needs of the six-to-eight-year-olds. Many of the special exercises in listening, seeing, and give and take have also been used successfully with the six-to-eight-year-olds when given to a well-established group. It is suggested, of course, that the Reminders and Pointers from Chapter II be read carefully before presenting this material, as well as the section on Directing the Child Actor in Chapter XVIII.

For ten or more years, summer workshops were held at the Young Actors Company in Hollywood for children from nine to fourteen years of age. The program consisted of a total of thirty hours per week, plus extra time for those children who wished for more activity in the technical aspects of the theater. With the exception of active games and folk dancing, every hour was spent on theater activity. There was never a moment's lag in interest. One summer the six-to-eight-year-olds participated in the program. They absorbed a good eight hours of work and wanted more. In fact, the combination of the theater games, body work, and rehearsal of plays made their eight hours almost too few.

THE TEACHER'S ATTITUDE

Children can make an honest and exciting contribution to the theater if allowed the personal freedom to experience. They will understand and accept responsibility for the theater communication, will become involved, develop relationships, create reality, and learn to improvise and evolve theatrically valid scenes as do their adult counterparts.

Harold Hillebrand, in his book *The Child Actors*, propounds the question: "Must we suppose that acting by children is a lost art, like Venetian glass making?" Mr. Hillebrand has obviously seen an average production with child actors. And yet, the uninteresting, precocious, often exhibitionistic level of most children's performances does not stem from inability to understand and learn theater on the part of the child. Rather, it reveals the absence of a method of teaching which presents material to the child that will permit creative potential within the medium.

There are few places outside their own play where children can contribute to the world in which they find themselves, a world dominated by adults who tell them what to do and when to do it—benevolent tyrants who dispense gifts to "good" subjects and punishment to "bad" ones, who are amused at the "cleverness" of children and annoyed by their "stupidities." So often the child is teeter-tottered between dictatorship and license and over-indulgence, and in either case no community responsibility is given. The child deserves and like the adult actor must get equal freedom, respect, and responsibility in the community of the workshop.

The problem of teaching the child is the same as that of teaching the adult. The difference is one of presentation. The need to intellectualize on the part of the teacher-director may well be the cause of resistance in work with younger age groups. We must recognize a great difference in life-experiences, and the phrasing of questions and introductions to exercises depends on this recognition.

Treating children as peers is not the same as treating them as adults; and this fine delineation must be recognized if you are to successfully guide your group. It is suggested that you again read the remarks on approval/disapproval in Chapter I.

The effects of relaxing adult tyranny are sometimes remarkable. A group of boys and girls once did an improvised play in which the children lived in a world where adults no longer existed. These young actors were tenement boys and girls who because of the struggle of their daily lives tended to do much yelling and fighting. The unfolding of the scene was quite a revelation. Never were boys and girls more charming, more courteous to one another. They were gentle and tender, they spoke in soft tones, they were concerned with each other's simplest problems—they loved one another! Watching the scene, one questioned, "Could it be that the adult is the enemy of the child after all?"

If permitted to do so, theater workshop will allow personal freedom and equality to flower. For when individuals of any age know that what they are doing is contribution and service to a project and not imposed authoritarianism pushing them about, they are free to release their humanness and make contact with those about them.

It is a thrilling moment, indeed, when the child accepts us, the adults, as peers within the activity!

THE INDIVIDUAL AND THE GROUP

The theater experience, like the game, is a group experience allowing students of differing abilities to express themselves simultaneously while developing individual skills and creativity (see Chapter I). The teacher-director should see to it that each individual participates in some facet of the activity at every moment, even if this means nothing more than "standing by for curtain." It is not only the over-aggressive child who is destructive to the group effort; the passive child may be equally harmful, for both refuse to give up their egocentricity. Group-work procedures should be followed at all times when working with the child-actor so as to release spontaneity and thus allow personal freedom of individual expression to emerge.

THE CHILD ACTOR'S THEATER ENVIRONMENT

The physical environment for this age group should stimulate, excite, and inspire. There should be at least two areas of work, if possible: a place for games and dance and a place for the theater set-up. In the theater area, it is important to have as many theatrical props as is possible to collect. On a very simple level, this would include a working curtain, a full costume rack, a prop shelf, set pieces, or large blocks, some lighting equipment, a place for sound effects, and of course a section for the audience. This should all be scaled to size, so that the children can do their own back-stage work. With a little effort and ingenuity, almost any room or corner can be fitted up for just such a little theater; and even if the results are not suitable for a public performance, the area will be suitable for workshops. Older children can shape their props and set (Where) out of space as adult-actors do.

When working with young children, it is advisable to have one or two assistants who can help the teams organize their improvisations and story-acting, assist in setting up stages, help the children into costumes, and watch for non-participants. These assistants are not to meddle, however, and tell the children what to do; they are simply to assist them in carrying out the group's decisions.

GAMES

The playing of games should be prominent in the teaching process for children. It is possible for the teacher-director to derive positive insight into each child actor's attitudes, reality, and behavior through this playing.

The competitive, the insecure, the apprehensive, are all quickly revealed, as are those more fortunate ones free of the need to do "right." A young girl responded to the early workshops with such a degree of apathy that she was thought to be of low intelligence. While playing the NUM-BERS CHANGE game, however, she showed an extraordinary degree of alertness. Her apathy, then, was easily recognized for what it really was—a protective cover for hidden fear. This early discovery helped the teacher-director to free the child for the creative experience more readily than would have otherwise been possible.

Carefully selected games also serve as a valuable tool in the training for the theater reality for this group. Thorne Rosa is not only a charming version of Sleeping Beauty in song and movement but also has definite "characters" as part of the game. Mulberry Bush, with its daily chores to perform, has the very young child actor doing exactly what the older actors do when working on object involvement and sensory problems. As Neva L. Boyd writes: "Like good drama, the game eliminates irrelevancies and brings events into close sequence in such concentrated and simplified form as to condense in both time and space the essence of a complex and long drawn-out typical life-experience. In this way, and because of the varied content of games, the child gets both more and different experiences from play than is otherwise possible in the process of everyday life." Again, "the vitality of the game lies in the creative process of playing it."

There are sense games and dramatic games, muscle-freeing games and intellectual games, and many other game categories from which to choose. (See Appendix II: Traditional Games, p. 399.) The teacher-director should make a special effort to choose the game pertinent to the problem of the moment and avoid the "gag" game, the game with no other object than to get a laugh at someone's expense.

It is also desirable to give diversified activities to child actors: rhythms, folk dances, extended movement, etc. All are essential in developing self and should be given a definite place in the workshop program. If it is not possible to have specialists in these fields work with students, then the teacher can work with them on the simpler activities in these areas. Any type of group participation with movement, rhythm, and sound is helpful (see Chapter V).

Games can be made up out of many of the sensory exercises: "What am I listening to?" "What am I looking at?" "What am I holding?" "What am I eating?"

The teacher-director can select and use many seemingly complicated acting exercises found throughout the handbook by presenting them in "game" manner. WHO'S KNOCKING? (p. 105) is extremely valuable. Combined with RANDOM WALK (p. 201), games were used as part of public performances by the Playmakers at Childrens Theater and were most successful.

ATTENTION AND ENERGY

There seems to be a definite relationship between the attention-span and the energy level of the very young child. Whether it be the child who evidences an over abundance of energy, the child with average energy, or the child whose energy level is below par, all — if given interesting problems to solve — will stay with an activity for a long period of time. If we think of attention-span in terms of the energy level of our group, we will know exactly when it is necessary to introduce an activity designed to stimulate child actors to new levels of vitality and perception, experience and learning.

Such stimulation may be provided through the simple expedient of changing areas of activity, having diversified activities, bringing in challenging acting exercises, using scenery and costume parts and props. To further extend the child actor's attention-span in the beginning workshop sessions, it might be advisable to divide each session into three sections: games, creative movement, and theater. Anything that will heighten awareness of the activity, color, music, etc., should be used. In this way, the young actors are re-awakened to the theatrical adventure and can move more easily away from the dramatic play of their early years into the theater experience.

DRAMATIC PLAY

Like their adult counterparts, children spend many hours of the day in subjective dramatic play. While the adult version usually consists of telling stories, day-dreaming, role-playing, wishful thinking, identifying with TV characters, etc., children have, in addition to these, the pretending and dramatizing of characters and events in their experiences from "the wild west" to parents and teachers.

In workshops with the younger children, moving from dramatic play (subjective) into the stage reality (objective) goes more slowly than with older students. In most cases, the child actors are not yet mature enough to cope with Evaluation in its fullest sense; and there is a greater dependency upon the teacher — a dependency which cannot be broken abruptly.

By separating dramatic play from, and then bringing it to, the theater reality, young actors learn to differentiate between pretend (illusion) and reality within the realm of their own world. However, this separation is not implicit in dramatic play. Dramatic play and real life are often confused for the young and, alas, for many adults as well.

A good example of the confusion between illusion and reality was evidenced in a young boy brought into the actor's workshop. Johnny was enrolled in the theater workshop because "he was lying too much." At the beginning sessions, he excited everyone with his "acting." Copious tears poured out of him when his stage sisters would not take him with them. And when they pushed him off stage "out of their room," he was found sobbing uncontrollably in the wings because "they wouldn't let me come along!" If he was banished from a scene, even as the Pirate King, he carried his rejection with him for a long time afterward. In short, Johnny had illusion and reality mixed up. In time, he learned to understand the difference. He became a frequent participant in the big theater shows and reports from home were that he no longer "lied."

All student-actors, young and old alike, must learn that the stage is the stage and not an extension of life. It has its own reality, and the players agree to it and then play it. On the stage we can be witches and sea captains, fairies and elephants. Playing, we can pop up to the moon or live in beautiful castles.

Improvising a situation on stage has, like the game, its own kind of organization. After a group of six- and seven-year-olds experienced the fun of playing house on stage, the following discussion took place.

Were you playing house or doing a play? "We were doing a play."

What is the difference between playing house in your backyard and playing house here? "You have a stage here."

Do you call it playing house here? "No, you call it a play."

What else do you have here besides a stage? "An audience."

Why does an audience come to see a play? "They like to—it's fun."

Did you make the playing house you just did fun for an audience? "No."

Why not? "We didn't share our voices and didn't make it more interesting for them."

What could you do to make it more interesting? "We could be naughty or all want to watch TV at the same time or something."

I'd like to ask you again. Were you playing house just now, or were you doing a play about a house? "We were playing house."

Do you think you could go back on stage and instead of playing house, like in your backyard, do a play about a family in a house and show us Where you are and Who you are and What you are doing there? "Yes."

The scene was done again, retaining all the fun of the first playing while adding the actors' real effort to "make it more interesting for the audience." The spontaneity of the backyard playing was retained along with the added reality achieved in trying to share their experience with their audience.

The child, too, can learn not to pretend but to "make it real," and can learn the theater magic of "pulling a rabbit out of a hat." A group of eight-to-eleven-year-olds were questioned as to why they needed to make things real for the audience and not pretend. "If you pretend, it isn't real, and the audience can't see."

NATURAL ACTING

The problem of bringing forth and then retaining a young actor's naturalness within the art form is a challenging one. The natural child is not necessarily the natural actor; indeed, the generality that "children are natural actors" is equally true or false as it is for the older actor. In either case, personal freedom to move out into the environment and experience it determines the extent of "naturalness" to begin with.

In many instances, unfortunately, whether child or adult, naturalness must be restored. Even young children come to workshop full of already learned mannerisms with physical tensions, held muscles, fear of contact, and natural body-grace distorted; ego-centricity and exhibitionism have already taken their toll. However, because the child's past life span is of fewer years than that of the adult and because he or she is, after all, a child, the breakthrough to an "original free state" comes about more quickly.

Again, the actor on stage must create reality. He or she must have energy, must communicate to an audience, be able to develop character and relate to fellow actors, have a sense of pace and timing, etc.

Although we may be highly successful in restoring and/or keeping the student-actor "natural," we may find that this is not enough. It does not follow that naturalness alone presents an interesting communication from stage to audience. So, we have a twofold problem: first, to release the vitality and beauty of the individual child and, second, to take this naturalness and restructure it to meet the demands of the art form (true for the older actor also).

What must be done, then, is to keep the child in spontaneous play and transform this playing into communicable stage behavior. There must be no intrusion of "techniques." As with an adult counterpart, the acting problems the student-actor is to solve must be presented in such a way that this stage behavior comes by itself "from the very core of the child and appears as if by accident."[1] As we know, whether child or adult, anyone who freely plays, totally involved with solving the workshop problem (focus of the exercise) achieves (or keeps) natural spontaneous behavior at the same time he or she is making the necessary heightened theater communication.

THE FIGHT FOR CREATIVITY

The teacher-director who forces set patterns of thinking and behavior (a "right" or "wrong" way of doing things) on child actors is restricting them most severely; and both the individual and the art form will suffer. When the child is forced into molds, taught by formula, or given a diluted, adult concept of theater, the performance can only be static and unpleasant, relieved only by the personal charm that most very young children still possess. If we will remember that rote teaching, formulas, and concepts are summaries of another's findings (see the discussion of approval/disapproval in Chapter I), our students can then grow and unfold in a free atmosphere.

Today more than ever before we are faced with the need for developing creative and original thought—in the sciences as well as in the arts. Children, who are our future, are talked at so much that a great many adult formulations are either lost to them entirely or swallowed whole, undigested

1. See Chapter II.

and unquestioned. Many times one hears a newcomer to the theater (as young as six years old) say "You mustn't turn your back to the audience."[2] Questioning will reveal that an individual in some position of authority in the child's life taught this. Here, on the very threshold of learning, a door is shut and obviously by one who doesn't have the faintest idea of what he or she is saying, who is simply passing on something heard or thought to be so. In how many areas must this go on, hour after hour, in a child's life? It is this type of authoritarian teaching that dulls our children and shuts off their centers of inspiration and creativity. Many years are wasted until children become adults, and then they may or may not rise above the hurdles that were put in their way during their growing years.

Creativity is often thought to be merely a less formal way of presenting or using the same material, in a more ingenious or inventive way perhaps—a different arrangement of the same blocks. Creativity is not just building or making something, not just variations of form. *Creativity is an attitude, a way of looking at something, a way of questioning, perhaps a way of life—it may well be found on paths we have not yet traveled.* Creativity is curiosity, joy, and communion. It is process-transformation-process.[3]

DISCIPLINE IS INVOLVEMENT

We are afraid of leaving the bounds of conventional patterns of thought and action. We feel more comfortable, more in control perhaps, and the thought of a free atmosphere in which free students abound conjures up a picture of bedlam in our minds. Is it possible that we confuse license with freedom?

Creative freedom does not mean doing away with discipline. It is implicit in true creativity that a free person, working in an art form, must be highly disciplined.

Let us examine the whole premise of discipline and ask a few questions. Just what do we mean when we speak of this problem with children? Do

2. See EXERCISE FOR BACK, p. 138.
3. See Chapter IV.

we mean keeping them quiet? Is it wanting an order given and carried out? Do some think of it as self-control by an individual? Or do we mean conformity? How many hide behind the word when they really mean either imposing their will upon, or suppression of, another? How many children are sent to bed because mother is tired?

A "good" boy or girl may not be a disciplined child at all but may simply be intent upon getting reward instead of punishment, approval instead of disapproval, seeking survival by appeasement. The so-called undisciplined child is seeking survival also; however, in rebellion against authoritarianism and restrictions not understood. His or her energy when not channeled into creative action often comes out as delinquent or undisciplined behavior. Again, rebellion often shows itself in a refusal to learn the daily lesson, and so we think many of these children are not quite "bright." It well may be that our "rebellious ones" are the most free, the questioners our most creative children, but they are lost to us if their freedom (because of their bewilderment) becomes a destructive force.

Many years ago around a settlement-house neighborhood, a gang of "bad" boys were bedeviling the neighborhood with their stealing and aggressive acts of all kinds. These boys were invited to an improvised play done by other neighborhood children about keeping alleys clean. After the show, they all promptly ran down the alleys and systematically spilled every garbage can they found, and in the meantime it was discovered that they had also rifled a few purses around the theater.

A meeting was called of the workshop members (ten to fourteen years old) to discuss what had happened. It was from the children that the teacher-director learned two important truths. The essence of what the children said was that the "garbage play" was a "scolding play," for all its theatrical effects. It was only a "costumed lecture" after all and as such had no reality. It did not create audience involvement, without which no insight into the problem was possible. At best it said, "Let's all be 'good' little boys and girls and keep our alleys clean." Since this group of boys were busy being "bad" little boys, they could only act as they did.

The children went on to say: "If we could get them into the theater, not to show them 'crime-doesn't-pay' plays but to have them act in the workshops, then they would find out that workshops are more fun than stealing, and they wouldn't *have* to be bad boys anymore."

Discipline imposed from above simply produces inhibited or rebellious action within the student; it is negative, and nothing is learned. For when the "cage"is lowered, all is as before and sometimes worse. On the other hand, when the problem of discipline is not an emotional tug-of-war for position but is freely chosen for the sake of the activity, it then becomes responsible action—creative action.[4] It takes dedication for group members to be self-disciplined. As in a game, when the dynamics are understood and not superimposed, the rules are abided by. "It is more fun that way."

If the workshop maintains the game-like structure, the child joyously enters the experience and in trying to solve the problem of the activity will self-impose these necessary disciplines. For any child who chooses to play will become involved and abide by the rules (group agreement) and accept the penalties and restrictions crucial to the game. In so doing, more human potential will be released as his or her social sense and individual talents develop.

Intensity of involvement should be the gauge of children's capacities and potential. Children with the lowest grades in school may be the most creative. Their involvement, unfortunately, is not stimulated by what is at hand. This writer's passion for play was so great that she neglected her school work and got through school by the skin of her teeth. She did not make the high-school drama group, because her grades were too low.

THE UNCERTAIN CHILD

The teacher-director will often be confronted with an apprehensive child actor who looks to see what the others are doing and follows their lead instead of working on an acting problem as an individual member of the group. When this occurs, we may wish to stop what the group is doing and have them play MIRROR (p. 61). This will often help the fearful child to

---

4. See "Approval/Disapproval," Chapter I.

realize that imitation is not wrong but that it belongs only to certain games, not to all. Once the MIRROR game has been played, the child will find it much easier to break away from imitation of others during workshop, especially if reminded that "You're playing the mirror game now instead of the game we are playing."

Another habit of the uncertain child is "cheating"—peeking during blindfold games, etc.—because of a drive to be best. For instance, if the game is WHAT AM I KNOCKING ON? (where the children are required to keep their eyes closed while guessing what is being knocked on), this child will openly peek at the object. When this occurs, the teacher-director need only utter a simple, "If you open your eyes, you are playing a different game. We are playing a *hearing* game, not a *seeing* game." In this way, without lecture or indictment, the child quickly realizes that if one is to "play," it is more fun to play the game the whole group plays. Soon the need to be first, best, right, etc. is replaced by the fun of playing.

CHAPTER XIV

FUNDAMENTALS
FOR
THE CHILD ACTOR

IMPROVISING WITH
SIX-TO-EIGHT-YEAR-OLDS

Inner Action

The concept behind inner action can easily be made clear to child actors, but it is best not to introduce it until the children have had a good deal of improvisation, story-telling, and even some microphone work (see "Radio and TV," p. 180). Here is an example of handling the concept of inner action when the workshop group is ready.

Do you know what your mother is feeling when you come home from school? If you want to go out and play and you have to ask permission, can you tell if your mother is feeling pleasant? The smallest child nods, remembering.

How can you tell? "By the way she looks . . . the way she acts."

Would someone like to go on stage and be a mother who is in a pleasant mood? Although young children rarely work onstage alone, it is occasionally an excellent experience for them. Choose one of the volunteers.

The young actor chosen goes on stage and becomes the "pleasant mother." When he or she has finished, either discuss the presentation with the group or have others go up individually and work on this single problem. The student audience will pay close attention to the child on stage.

Now have the children sit quietly and think about seeing their families. *Can you usually tell when someone in your home is worried?* "Yes." Ask them to *show us.*

One child at the Young Actors Company showed her father worrying by placing her head on her knees and putting her hands over her ears in the typical comic-opera worrier position. Later, when her mother came to pick her up, the incident was mentioned to her. She laughed and said: "I know it seems exaggerated, but her father does just that."

When it is clear that the group understands that people tend to *show* what they feel, then explain the acting problem as follows:

We are going to play a what-are-you-thinking-about game—and you will show us. Each of you will go on stage by yourself. You are to be somewhere, waiting for someone. While you are waiting, you are thinking about something. When you are through thinking, we in the audience will see whether we can know what you were thinking about. You may be waiting for someone who is late. You may be alone in a strange neighborhood and slightly afraid. You may be waiting for someone who is going to take you to a wonderful party. Everyone will pick an inside thought, and we will see whether you show us.

After they have completed their individual thinking and have communicated to the audience, then put all the children together, in a waiting room of a train station, for example. Here they are to work on thinking the same thing they thought about earlier when they were alone awhile ago.

If this work is presented so that the children are able to understand in terms of their own experience, some interesting inner action will result. Encourage the children to play a game of seeing "how people feel inside" outside of class. They will enjoy watching family and friends and knowing what they are thinking about.

Giving Reality (Substance) to Objects[1]

One afternoon, during an improvisation of a farm, a child actor went to the well to draw water, filled her bucket, and carried it away as easily as if she had not filled it. After the scene, it was suggested that everybody take a turn filling the bucket and carrying it back. Only one child out of ten showed that the bucket was full.

There was an outside water faucet in the patio of the theater. The children took the bucket out there, and each, in turn, filled it with real water, walked a few feet, and then emptied it out.

After all had had their turns, they were asked: *Was there any difference in the bucket before it was filled with water and after it was filled?* A thoughtful

---

1. See PHYSICALIZING AN OBJECT, p. 78.

pause filled the air. Then the youngest child, who had stayed on the periphery of the activity until now, spoke up and said, "It's heavier when it's full." This was indeed an exciting observation; and they all agreed immediately.

Why is it necessary for the actor to know that it's heavier when it's full?

Again the same silence. Finally a seven-year-old boy spoke up. "Because there is no real water on stage."

Yes! There's no real water on stage. A well on stage can only be made of wood or paper.

The children then went on stage and played a game called IT'S HEAVIER WHEN IT'S FULL (see p. 72). They set up their Once Upon A Time (Where, Who, and What) and "filled" their baskets and buckets with milk, apples, and treasures and then staggered around the stage under the great weights they had piled up for themselves.

How simply they had learned an important theater truth. How many of us have seen adults—lay actors and professionals alike—who sometimes forget that receptacles are "heavier when they're full"? This awareness of creating reality is easily transferable to other objects.

The Telephone Prop

The telephone is probably one of the most delightful and useful props for child actors. If at all possible, get a real phone from the telephone company. If not, have a full-sized (not toy-sized) phone built.

The telephone is particularly useful with the young actor who is slow to respond. The teacher just rings the phone (vocally) from wherever he or she is sitting. The most active child will make a bee-line for the prop. When he or she answers, ask for the child who is doing very little.

MILDRED: (answering) Hello!

TEACHER: May I please speak to Edith (the child who has just been sitting passively in the scene)?

MILDRED: Edith, it's for you.

EDITH: (walks to stage phone) Hello (soft voice).

TEACHER: Hello, hello, is this Edith?

EDITH: (faraway voice) Yes.

TEACHER: Strange, I can't seem to hear you very well. Perhaps we have a bad connection. Would you mind speaking a little louder?

EDITH: (Full voice.) O.K.

To give another example, a mother is sitting in her kitchen, apron right, waiting for her children to come back from their picnic. The children are having their picnic on the full stage. The scene has hit an impasse with both mother and children just sitting. The teacher-director rings the telephone.

MOTHER: Hello.

TEACHER: Why, hello, how are you?

MOTHER: Fine.

TEACHER: What are you doing today?

MOTHER: I'm waiting for my children. They went on a picnic.

TEACHER: My goodness, aren't they home yet?

MOTHER: No, they're not.

TEACHER: It's beginning to get dark, and it's raining outside (the light man goes to work). Don't you think you'd better go look for them and bring them home? It's close to their bedtime.

MOTHER: I certainly better.

And the mother is immediately spurred into action as she runs to get her children. When they return, ring again (if necessary).

TEACHER: Hello. Did you get your children home all right?

MOTHER: Yes, they're home now.

Complete or Incomplete Concentration

Give youngsters the concept of concentration in terms of energy. Send someone on stage to lift a large rock or push a stalled car. This would be the same thing as focus with the older actors. If their concentration is to be complete, they quickly see they must put "all their strength" on the stage problem.

Becoming Audience

"Becoming audience" is a phrase used to reinforce concentration.

A child, mirroring, may watch himself or herself on stage. This child may be a non-participating spectator to the actions of the other players and may look out into the house to see whether the teacher approves. Handle this problem simply: *We have a special place for the audience, and if you would rather be there than in the play, come down and watch. It's perfectly fine if you want to watch, but then you belong in the audience.*

The children will quickly realize that the stage is the place for actors and that they cannot be actors and audience at the same time. It is important that they understand this separation thoroughly, for this is one of the keys to the stage reality. They may have to be reminded from time to time through side-coaching: *The place for the audience is down here! We go where your eyes go! We see what you see!*

Rocking the Boat

"Rocking the boat" encourages self-blocking and is a phrase developed to evaluate the stage picture. It is a visualization which can be grasped by every child. Simply describe the stage as a boat—a rowboat or canoe. Now ask the students to think what would happen to a boat if everyone sat on one side. Just as the boat would become unbalanced and tip, so will the stage picture become unbalanced and upset the scene.

Once this phrase is understood, you have only to call out *You're rocking the boat!* during work on an acting problem to see them spread out into a more interesting stage picture. Without losing concentration, they will recognize the need for sharing voices, actions, and feelings with every member of the audience.

When rocking the boat has been discussed, ask students to go on stage. First, have them deliberately rock the boat. Begin by asking: *Do we ever want to rock the boat? When?* Have them do a scene where they deliberately rock the boat (as in a fire, mob scene, etc.). After discussion, have them do another scene, this time with the focus on *avoiding* rocking the boat.

Share with the Audience

This is used in the same way as with the adult group. Have actors play directly with the audience, as in a meeting.

Showing—Not Telling

The problem of showing and not telling can best be introduced to your child-actors in the evaluation following a scene: Did they show us they were playing in the snow, or tell us the snow was cold? How could he show us that he was the father? How could he show that he hurt his finger? Did we see the glass in her hand?

EVALUATION

There is no one as dogmatic as the six- or seven-year-old who "knows" the answer. He or she is already reflecting the opinions of the world at large. He or she is right, and they are wrong! It seems almost impossible at first to eradicate these judgmental and thus limiting words from the vocabulary of these very young children.

"He's wrong!" a child will say. *What do you mean by "wrong"?*

"He didn't do it right." *What do you mean by "right"?*

"Like this!" The child then proceeds to demonstrate the "right" way to jump rope or eat cereal. *But what if Johnny wants to do it his own way?* "He's wrong."

Did you see Johnny eat his cereal? "Yes." *Why was it wrong?* "He ate it too fast."

You mean he didn't eat his cereal the way you eat it? "You have to eat cereal slowly."

Who told you that? "My mother."

Well, if your mother wants you to eat cereal slowly, that is the rule in your house. Maybe the rule in Johnny's house is different. Did you see him eat his cereal? "Yes."

If the teacher keeps at it, individual differences are finally accepted and the words "right" and "wrong" will give way to:

"I couldn't see what he was doing."

"She didn't move like a doll all the time."

"He didn't share his voice with us."

"They had no Once Upon A Time."

"He became audience."

After the work on stage has been completed by a team of players, Evaluation is handled the same as with the older actors.

To the student audience: was concentration complete or incomplete? Did they solve the problem? Did they have a Once Upon A Time?

When student-actors are skillfully questioned, after a while they begin to say: "I walked through a wall"; "I became audience"; "I didn't share my voice." This sort of questioning and response has many more times the value in developing reality, personal awareness, and perception in children than do the limited and subjective phrases, "They were good," "They were bad."

The fallacy in thinking that there are prescribed ways of behavior came home quite forcibly one day. The student-actors did a family scene. Mother, father, and grandfather were sitting on a couch, having a tea party. The player showed us he was the grandfather by occasionally saying "By cracky!" Then in typical six-year-old fashion, he would climb up and around the couch (made of blocks).

In the Evaluation, Johnny was told that he certainly showed us that he was the grandfather. He was then asked by the teacher-director if he thought older men climb around the couch that way. Johnny was startled to hear that he had. Because of the way the questioning was put, Johnny shaped his thinking to meet the teacher-director's frame of reference and then and there accepted her authority and decided, too, that grandfathers *do not* climb on couches. Suddenly from the audience a young voice spoke up.

"My grandfather does!"

He does?

"Sure, every time he's drunk."

How a teacher-director questions the students during Evaluation must always be carefully watched, so as not to put our ideas or words into the minds and mouths of the students. And while it may be true that only one grandfather out of twenty thousand will climb around couches as does a six-year-old boy, it is a reality that is possible and therefore the student-actor has the right to explore it.

POINTS TO REMEMBER[2]

1. Maintaining the structure of the acting problem and group Evaluation does much of the work for the teacher.

2. Strive constantly to ask the questions during Evaluation that will meet the experience levels of the children and stimulate their learning.

3. Avoid trying to make the children fit subjective concepts of right or wrong stage behavior. Remember, there need not be any set ways of doing anything as long as communication lines are clear.

4. Noise that occurs around the organization and setting up of a scene must be understood as order and not disorder. The teacher can always hear when the sounds are undisciplined. Organizing a scene cannot be done quietly, since the very energy and excitement released can only be ex-

2. See also the section on directing children, p. 346.

pressed noisily. The children will learn to set up quietly when a curtain is used. This discipline will come most naturally to them in time. Do not stifle the spirit of play by concern for "order."

5. Until all the young actors are able to take the initiative in the workshop, place the children who are natural catalysts in positions where they can help spark the activity. Watch that they do not take over, however. In time, each and every child will develop leadership ability.

6. Do not be patronizing to children. Neither expect too much nor allow them to get away with too little.

7. As in a game, the theater workshop allows each player to take from it according to his or her own level of development and encourages individual choice.

8. Self-discipline will develop in students when their involvement in the activity is complete.

9. This age group, too, can learn to create a stage reality out of a group agreement equal to the adults.

10. As with the older actors, we strive for spontaneity, not invention, in our students.

11. Public performance, when children are ready, will raise their whole level of understanding and skills. However, do not hasten this prematurely. Be certain they have integrated their workshop training and will share their play. They must understand that the audience is "part of the game" and not merely exhibit themselves. For this age, too, can learn to handle the tools of the theater with sensitivity and intuitiveness; they can learn to work with a director together with their fellow actors and to perform in public showings, unaffectedly, and be a delight to behold!

In a play where a doll shop had a prominent role, six-year-olds were cast as dolls. Some research was done on the characters by the young actors. A couple of dolls were brought to class, and the children found that they moved only at the joints. In movement class, they worked on solving the problem of doing everything as dolls. They played "doll shop" for weeks prior to rehearsing with the full cast of older children (eleven to fifteen). By the time they (the children cast as dolls) were brought to rehearsals, they seemed like veteran actors. The only thing they had to adjust to was working with the older actors.

Stands were built for the dolls on which the children could sit during performance if they so desired. They were told that if a pin was sticking them, they should remove it. They could brush the hair out of their eyes, sneeze if necessary, or cough. There was only one point of concentration: *they were to move as dolls no matter what happened.*

Some of the most charming moments of the show thus occurred when they were least expected—when a nose had to be scratched or when a hat fell off. Many adults were amazed at the relaxed quality of the children, at their lack of affectation and their doll-like movements. They were surprised at the "acting" of these "babies."

The important thing was that these children had the full pleasure of performance without anxieties. They kept their complete energies on the physical problem of moving like dolls, and this focus gave them sureness and kept them "in character."

After one performance, the little talking doll (six years old) was besieged by children from the audience. Even a few adults clustered around her, crooning: "Isn't she darling! Isn't she the little actress!" The fuss would have been enough to turn the head of many an older person, but the little girl merely thanked the group and, turning to another actor, asked, "Did you think my concentration was complete?"

CHAPTER XV

WORKSHOP FOR
SIX-TO-EIGHT-YEAR-OLDS

PLANNING THE SESSIONS

The exercises set down in this chapter are those which are slanted directly to the six-to-eight-year-old. By no means should they be considered the only exercises suitable for this age group. They appear here for the sake of emphasis.

As was mentioned earlier, many of the exercises appearing in the earlier section of the handbook can easily be adapted for use by six-to-eight-year-olds. For example, the following groups of exercises have been given in six-to-eight-year-old workshops with exciting results: simple involvement exercises (p. 65); simple sensory exercises (pp. 77–78); broadcasting exercises (p. 181); technical effects exercises (p. 186).

As teacher-director you must use your own discretion in choosing, altering, and presenting suitable exercises. Once the introductory ONCE UPON A TIME has been given and absorbed, you will have an excellent understanding of students' needs and levels. Armed with this knowledge, you should then be able to plan workshop sessions most profitably from the wealth of exercises presented in the body of this handbook.

FIRST WORKSHOP SESSION

Six-to-eight-year-olds should not be given the EXPOSURE EXERCISE. EMERGING WHERE or WHERE WITH FLOOR PLANS are both too abstract for this age group, since they should be given real physical props, costumes, etc. as quickly as possible.

Accordingly, the Where for six-to-eight-year-olds is called ONCE UPON

A TIME. It may be done with or without an equipped stage. If no real theater is available, just be certain to designate from the start which areas in the room are to be used as the stage, back stage, wings, and audience. If a real stage is available, it is highly desirable to show the child actors around, pointing out various items to them.

The following versions of ONCE UPON A TIME are for beginning the first workshop session with child actors. One version requires no stage facilities. The other allows for stage facilities, and it is to be preferred.

Preliminary Work

Do you enjoy reading or having stories read to you? "Yes!"

What do you do while someone is reading you a story? "We listen . . . we hear it."

What do you hear? "You hear the story."

What do you mean "you hear the story"? Just what do you hear? "You hear what is happening in the story."

Let's suppose your mother was reading you the story of The Three Bears. *What do you hear in that story?* "You hear about the bears and the porridge. . . ."

How do you know you are hearing about the three bears? "Because the words tell you you are."

Now comes the most important question of all: *How do you know what the words tell you?* "You can see."

What do you see? The words? "No!" With much laughter, they tell you, "You see the three bears, of course!"

Continue the discussion of "seeing" the words. Tell them a story: *Once upon a time, there was a little boy and a little girl and they lived in a bright yellow house on top of a green hill. Every morning a little pink cloud floated by the house and. . . .*

Ask the children what they saw. Keep it a group discussion. Every child will see the story in his or her own personal terms. Have them describe the color they visualized for the girl's dress, what kind of roof the little house had, etc. Keep up with this discussion as long as the interest level is high, then go on to the next point.

What is the first thing your mother does when she is going to read you a story? "She comes into my bedroom . . . she sits down . . . she says, 'For five minutes, dear' . . ."

Then what does she do? "She reads the story."

How does she do that? "She reads it from the book!" By now the young actors are certain that they have a "silly" teacher who doesn't know the simplest things.

Now, think hard. What is the first thing she does before she starts reading, after she has sat down, after she has come into the bedroom? "She opens the book."

Of course! She opens the book! Would it be possible to read the story if your mother didn't open the book? "Of course not!"

In theater, too, we have a story. And, we too must open the book before we begin. Only, on stage, we open the curtain. (Curtain in this case can be lights. Or it can be the mere calling out of the phrase "Curtain!" to indicate the beginning of a scene if you have no actual curtain.)

How does the story usually begin? "Once upon a time, there was . . ."

You mean it starts in a place, somewhere? "Yes."

Are there usually people in the story? "Yes, people and animals."

The people in the story of Goldilocks and the Three Bears *are called characters when we take them on stage. Now, just as your mother opens the book and begins with "Once upon a time . . . ," we are going to show the bears and the house. Instead of seeing them in your head as when you are read to, you are going to see them on the stage.*

When your mother reads you a story, does she whisper so you cannot hear her? Does she read from another room in the house? "Of course not! She reads the story so that the children can hear it."

Because if you couldn't hear it, you couldn't enjoy it. Right? When they have expressed their desire to enjoy the story, go on with the discussion. They will articulate if the questions are clear to them.

The theater has people who are just like you when you're listening to your mother. The theater has an audience. They are our guests. The audience wants to enjoy the story they are seeing and hearing on stage. And, just as your mother shares with you the Once Upon A Time (Where) and the charac-ters (Who) in the book and what is happening to them (What), so the actors must share the story they are playing on stage with the audience. And show them everything: where they are, who they are, and what they are doing.

Does the audience sit and only listen the way you do when you hear a story? "No, an audience looks, like watching TV . . ."

Yes, an audience looks at what you are doing and sees the characters move around and do things and talk to each other. So, the way to help the audience enjoy themselves is to show them as much as you can and to share with them everything you do on stage.

The foregoing kind of discussion gives the teacher-director an opportu-nity to bring "share" and "showing" (not telling) into the workshop. How-ever, immediate results will not be achieved by any means. It will take time before learning to share and communicate with an audience becomes or-ganic with this age group.

After completing the initial discussion, go right into:

ONCE UPON A TIME, MINIMUM EQUIPMENT

▶ The first step is to set up the Where, Who, and What.

Where

Where would you like to be? Students will suggest many places, one of which will most likely be a schoolroom. If, however, the workshop itself is in a schoolroom program, shift to a living-room scene using the same pro-cedure.

Who

Who do you want in the schoolroom? For the most part teacher and pu-pils will be suggested.

What

What is everyone doing there? One of the suggestions will probably be learning arithmetic or reading. *What grade do you want? Kindergarten, first, second, high school?*

When the group has selected their grade, have them set up the stage. Have appropriate props available. As you and perhaps an assistant move the props among them, players should be reminded of the boundaries of the stage area (all props must be within it). Keep reminding them: *You must share your story. Do you think the desk in that position will do it?* Stop for a group conference if necessary. Although at this time the actual audience will only be teacher and assistant, keep the actors aware of their audience responsibility.

When the stage is set up, there will be many things missing from the schoolroom. Ask your students to close their eyes and try to *see* a schoolroom they are familiar with. Quietly coach them to see the floors, the walls, the color of the ceiling. Do not intrude on their visualization; simply give them some direction.

What was in your schoolroom which is missing on stage? "A pencil sharpener." *How many saw a pencil sharpener?* In this way can be compiled a whole list of extra objects which the children should then place on the stage, whether actual or created by the players.

It is best that the teacher-director cast the children during the first few sessions. In later meetings, they will be able to do this themselves.

When all the props are in place, have the children go on stage. Call "Places!" The teacher in the scene will go to her desk and the students to theirs. "Curtain!" is now called.

As this first scene unfolds, voice projection and movement will be at a low level (this is particularly true of five- and six-year-olds). Most of the children will sit and stare at the few who may be writing on the blackboard. There will be much giggling and looking out front. If the young actress playing teacher asks one of her students a question, she may or may not get an answer. A few alert children may take over the scene while the others sit as audience for the active ones.

At this point, the teacher-director's assistant has enormous value: to be sent into the play as a definite character (in a schoolroom scene, the principal is a logical activiser). The principal comes in to see what is happening and as the principal, presents activity to all the children and sees that it is followed up: she or he can quiet children who are taking over the situation and see that the shyer ones participate. This can all be accomplished through the character of the principal.[1]

---

1. This same technique is useful when inviting children from the audience to work in a scene from SUGGESTIONS BY THE AUDIENCE (p. 203).

PRINCIPAL: Good morning, Miss X. Isn't it a lovely morning? (She waits for a reply. If the child who plays the teacher responds in a faint, faraway voice, the principal repeats the question.)

I'm sorry, Miss X, but I didn't hear what you said. Don't you think it is a lovely morning? (The chances are that this will produce a projected response. If it still fails, the assistant takes a different tack.)

You know, Miss X, I'm certain the children would like to hear what you are saying. Isn't it a lovely morning? (The third question will bring a more lively tone, if only for that bit of dialogue. Even if the child sinks back into herself for the rest of the "play," whenever the "principal" talks to her, she will answer.)

Good morning, children. How are all of you this morning?

PUPILS: Fine . . . oh, we're fine . . . (etc.).

PRINCIPAL: (to a little girl) And what subjects are you studying today?

GIRL: (faint voice) Reading.

PRINCIPAL: I'm sorry, Mary, but I seem to have something the matter with my hearing this morning. Would you mind repeating what you just said?

GIRL: (firmer voice) Reading.

PRINCIPAL: How nice. (Turns to a boy who has sat without moving from the start.) Well, little boy, do you like reading?

BOY: (No answer.)

GIRL: (shouting) I like reading!

PRINCIPAL: (to energetic little girl) That's nice. (Back to boy.) Would you mind nodding yes if you like reading?

BOY: (Nods yes.)

PRINCIPAL: By the way, what is your name?

BOY: (in a whisper) Johnny.

PRINCIPAL: What a nice name! Now, which one of you students would like to lead the group in singing?

And so it goes until every child has participated in the "play," even if that participation is as slight as nodding the head. If the assistant can bring forth more action, fine; if not, then be satisfied with any bit of response. After a few sessions, many of the children will be able to play the principal and activate the others similarly. In time, all the children will be on their own, needing nothing but the problem to spur them on.

One six-year-old girl had an amazingly natural theater sense and quickly integrated all she learned. In fact, her energy on stage was so great that it was only with the greatest difficulty that she could be subdued to let the others work. If she was the mother, she rarely allowed her children to slip in a single word. She was told repeatedly: *Let all the characters share in the play.*

The problem was brought up during Evaluation. When her failure to share was mentioned, the girl replied: "But, if I don't do something, everybody just sits, and it isn't interesting."

How can you help the others? She thought she might tell them what to do.

But how can you "tell them" and still be showing us a "play" instead of telling a story? "I could whisper in their ears."

What could you do that would help the others on stage show the audience that they are part of the family? She thought a while and said, "I could give them things to do and ask them questions they could answer."

"Would you please take the papers out of your desk and bring them over to me?" was a question that occurred to her. Previously this child would have gone over and taken the papers herself.

Do not be surprised at the frequency with which this group will repeat a play situation. The schoolroom or the living-room scene may be done a dozen times or more. But with each playing, something new will be added, and the children will switch parts among themselves. Variations on the same scene might include: a new student entering the class, the last day of school, parents' visiting day, and even schoolrooms in other countries. Weather and time can be introduced. Because of students' repeated delight in such "plays," many acting problems can be solved by changing the focus within the same familiar Where.

EXERCISES

ONCE UPON A TIME, FULL EQUIPMENT

▶ This exercise was first created to meet the problem of giving a short-term theater experience to large groups of children such as Brownies, Scouts, etc. Its freshness and the excitement it generates were such that it was then used with six-to-eight-year-old actors with equal success. It was presented as a public performance of the Playmakers, the author's children's theater in Chicago, where it delighted hundreds of children and adults. However, in this case the audience simply called out the props they wanted, and the actors on stage produced them.

The success of this version of ONCE UPON A TIME is completely dependent upon an equipped stage. When done effectively, it transmits the total theater experience so suddenly and with such strong impact that participating players are pummeled into an active role before they can catch their breath. It would well be worth a teacher-director's time and effort to get a simple stage set-up so as to use this version of ONCE UPON A TIME.

To save time, it is necessary that the teacher have the Where prepared in advance for the first five or six presentations. This preparation should consist of seeing that the prop shelf has been appropriately stocked, that the costume rack is hung with enticing pieces, that recordings are ready in the sound booth, and that the lighting board (with dimmers) is working.

Since a living-room setting is usually the most familiar to the actors and is conducive to a large number of stage effects, it is excellent for first choice. Because so much will be happening to the stage itself for this first session, it is not necessary to use costumes. They can be brought in for later sessions.

Starting the session is simple enough. Ask the actors. *What is the first thing you do when you sit down to read a story?* When they answer, "Open the book," have an assistant open the curtain. We see an empty stage.[2]

As they sit looking at the empty stage, ask them to try to visualize their living rooms. Help them along as they concentrate: *See the walls. Look at the furniture. What's on the floor? Concentrate on colors.*

Tell them that each one of them will be asked to place something on stage that is part of a living room. They may choose anything that belongs in the living room they visualize. And, one by one, ask each of them what they would like to put in the room. The first actor who is asked to go on stage and get a couch, or whatever, may seem a bit hesitant, since the

2. Some of the material used in the preliminary discussion at the beginning of this chapter could be used here.

stage is empty. Tell the player to go back stage and see whether a couch can be found. All the audience watches with suppressed excitement: what will be found back there?

Assistance is needed here, since the children must know where their objects can be found when they go back stage to search for them. More advanced students are helpful; and to help is most useful for them, since it heightens their own learning.

If large blocks are among the props, a couch is made quickly; if not, substitute something else that will suggest a couch. The assistant and the student come out carrying the couch. *Where do you want it placed?* The player shows us and, with the assistant, places the couch. The student-actors sitting in the audience are eager to get into the adventure. The next student might ask for "a lamp," and so it goes down the line. Each student asks for a prop, goes back stage to find it, and then places it on the stage.

When a piano is asked for, everyone is aghast at so daring a request. This prop is great fun for the scene, and a small spinet piano that weighs but a few pounds can easily be built as part of your equipment (if not, a simple stage block will do).[3] Soon a radio, a TV set, a bookcase with painted books, and window frames with neat cottage curtains appear (these can be made so that they can be hung on wires stretched across the stage). A fireplace is a must; pictures, flowers, bric-a-brac, coffee tables, a bird-cage—in fact, every conceivable possibility for a living room should be available.

While the students are setting up, the teacher and assistants move around, helping and suggesting placements that will make it a pleasant living room. When it is finished, have the students come back into the audience and close the curtains immediately. For the sake of the first impact, the back-stage crew will now dress the set to help the final effect (such as placing a bulb and gelatin in the fireplace, giving area lighting to the lamps, putting flowers on mantelpiece, etc.). Now call, "*Curtain!*"

As the curtain slowly opens on the living room, with the fire in the fire-

---

3. When ONCE UPON A TIME was done as part of the performances, a block 2' × 3'6" was used as the piano.

place softly glowing, the lamps casting warm lights throughout the room, soft music floating through the air, and the bird chirping merrily away, there will be a tremendous sigh and "oh-h-h-h-h" from the audience. The aesthetic, artistic excitement that rises in the student-actors is thrilling to watch. Here is a stage that they put together, and they are awed by what they see. Each one had a part in creating it! This is the first impact of the reality that can be achieved on stage. This is the magic of theater!

Now the time comes to show how the theater reality is man-made, after all. Go on stage and call for work lights. Immediately the stage is altered: the music stops playing, the fireplace is cold and dead, the lamps are out. Walk to the piano and show that it's nothing but wood and cardboard (or a block of wood); pick up the lampshade and reveal that bulb and cord are missing; the radio is an empty shell; the TV set a piece of cardboard; the fire in the fireplace a bulb and some colored gelatin with a few sticks of wood.

How did the magic work? Move to the piano (cue the sound person with a line such as, "I think I'll practice the piano."). As you begin to move your fingers over the keyboard, a lovely nocturne drifts out into the audience. Another line of dialogue, and then you switch on a "lamp," bringing a brighter spot to the stage. And so you move around the set, lighting lights, turning on the radio to listen to a bit of news, striking a match and lighting the fireplace, and even turning on the TV where a program is already in progress (a couple of enthusiastic young actors from another group might go through a little TV show for your enjoyment). Continue until everything has been made to work, until the stage is restored to the original magic it held when the curtain first opened.

The audience is entranced. How does it happen that so many things that were nothing but cardboard and empty frames worked? Some of the answers will be quite amazing and far from reality. But soon out of the "mystery" will emerge the realization that "somebody" was doing it. Who? The technical crew, of course! The crew is called on stage so the students can meet them.

Now take all the students back stage and show them where the sound comes from, the lighting board, etc. "How does the back-stage crew know when to do all the things they must do?" *We tell them.* "But how?" The students learn that "telling them" is "cuing" and that unless they keep the back-stage crew aware of what they want and when they want it, the props will not work for them.

Have each student go on stage individually and cue the back-stage crew for something. He or she will learn that dialogue is tied up with back-stage response and that the back-stage crew cannot respond unless they hear what the actor wants. The shyest, most timid student, eager to get something to work on stage, will rise above his or her fear, and within one session, the teacher will have accomplished what might otherwise have taken many weeks to achieve.

During the performance, the actors are always alerted to the effects expected and can meet any crisis. In a production with six-to-fourteen-year-olds, a howling wind was to precede some dialogue relating to the wind. When the time came, no wind. The actors on stage kept up a clever run of dialogue; still no wind. This continued for a full three to four minutes until the sound effect was finally given. After the show, the cast descended upon the twelve-year-old sound person—What had happened? He had been visiting with the prop person and was not standing by for his cue. You may be sure that he never left his stand after that! And, also important, the audience was never aware that anything had gone awry.

When the students are completely familiar with their stage, it is then time to bring life into the setting: Who.

Who is usually in a living room? This is quickly settled by the group: it's simple to understand that mothers and fathers, children, and sometimes guests populate a living room. It is equally simple to understand that these people are called *characters* on the stage.

What are these characters doing in the living room? brings a rush of story material. A teacher might be coming to talk to the parents, the children might have to practice the piano, etc.

Should the audience know what the characters are doing? "Of course."
Why? "So they can enjoy the play."

Teams are quickly selected. The student audience will watch to see if the actors: (1) let the back-stage crew know what they need; (2) share what they are doing with the audience.

And so the workshop experience begins! Within this short hour or hour-and-a-half, the students learn the necessity for interaction, relationship, and communication if they are to have fun.

When the ONCE UPON A TIME without equipment is used, it is best to keep children six-to-eight as one group. When they are ready and the roles of the audience and actor are more defined, then they can be divided into teams. In ONCE UPON A TIME with equipment, however, note that breaking up into teams can take place from the very first session. As the full group creates the ONCE UPON A TIME together, their interest as an audience is held as they watch each separate team make different uses of the same Where. It is advisable, however, to end every workshop session with full group participation. Just as in the early workshops for the older actor, PART OF A WHOLE and similar group games are used to end each workshop.

When the actors become used to their stage and its conventions and after a few weeks of using different sets for each session, student-actors become capable of setting up their own stages, discussing effects with the back-stage crews, and entering into creative evaluation of each other's work with all the aplomb of veteran actors.

In organizing material for each succeeding session, it is wise to make a breakdown of what will be required in each category:

FOREST SCENE

Lighting	Sound	Set Pieces	Costumes
moonlight	night sounds	cave	bearskin
night	morning	rocks	rabbit's ears
dawn	sounds	stream	butterfly wings
lightning	thunder	trees	dog's tail and
(storm)	crashes		head
	animal roars		
	wind blowing		

Be prepared for anything a student-actor asks for. If the exact prop is not on hand, one can be suggested: a cave from arrangements of blocks or chairs; trees out of curtains wound together at various intervals; bushes from parts of actual bushes, with artificial flowers tied on; a waterfall out of blue lights on silver lamé cloth. As the workshop goes along, everyone's ingenuity will be stimulated to meet the needs of the moment, and spontaneous selectivity of appropriate set pieces will take place at a high rate of speed.

STORY-TELLING

This method follows the structure of improvisation in which the story-teller and the actors work together simultaneously. It is more inventive than spontaneous, for all must stay with the story as prescribed by the story and the story-teller. It is of value, however, to the story-teller, since it gives the embryonic director even as young as six to eight the total view of the medium and an understanding of the problems of integrating a scene. (See the remarks on spontaneity in Chapter I.)

FOCUS: on the story.

▶ The story-teller, who has been given the task a week before, comes to workshop with a narrative or poem that he or she has either chosen or made up. The story-teller then assigns the roles of the characters in the story to players in the group. A technical crew (to control lights and sound, props and furniture) is also selected. It is assumed that the story-teller is a member of the group, but if the story-teller is a guest, then the side-coach should assign roles. As a stimulus to organizing material, the story-teller may have been asked to draw pictures of characters, sets, costumes, and props. These drawings, while perhaps not too useful for visual reference, can be shared with the cast and crew. The story-teller now supervises the costuming of the show and setting of the stage, assigns backstage duties (stage manager, lights, sound, etc.), and directs the stage manager to call "Places!" The story-teller takes a place beside the stage (or at the microphone if there is a sound booth).

The story-teller then relates the story to the players on stage and they enact it. The narration provided by the story-teller must allow freedom of lines and action to the cast. For instance, "Then the mother told the little boy she loved him and he was happy again" gives more leeway than "Then the mother said 'I love you, Jack,' and the little boy hugged her," which would merely allow actors to stand around and parrot the story-teller. Once this point is understood, story-tellers will give players room to improvise their own dialogue and action and story-telling will be more exciting.

SIDE-COACHING: *Follow the follower! See the word! Share with the audience!*

EVALUATION: Audience, what parts of the story did you like best? Which seemed most real? Why? Did the characters do what you expected them to do? Players, when did you feel closest to the characters? Story-teller, did the actors surprise you by doing or saying things you hadn't imagined? Players, would you like changes in the story? Where? Audience, do you agree with the plot changes the players are recommending? How would you rewrite the story?

POINTS OF OBSERVATION

1. During a story-telling of Jack and the Beanstalk, the giant was a boy of six who sat by most passively while Jack stole all his things. The story-teller, wishing to get some activity out of the giant, said, "The giant was very angry when he woke up and found his eggs gone." The little boy on stage merely opened his eyes wider and looked about. This did not satisfy the story-teller, so she tried again. "And the giant was very angry, and he jumped up and down." Our giant tried to do this but without pleasing the narrator, for she continued, "The giant was real angry. He was never so mad before, and he jumped and hollered and said all kinds of nasty things."

    Then, to the satisfaction of all present, the six-year-old giant roared out, "Goddamnit, who stole my eggs!"

2. The side-coach or assistant must sit close to the story-teller to aid in keeping the whole cast and back-stage crew working. Delightful effects can come from the "technical" department. One story-teller said "It was night and the wind began to blow and frightened the little children." The light man (all of seven) promptly dimmed down the stage and made a howling sound through the microphone, while the actors huddled in fright.

3. Sometimes, after a story-telling period, it is valuable to pick out a few points to work on and choose some specific exercises for the actors to do. See also such related games as CHORAL READING, p. 209, and BUILDING A STORY, p. 381.

4. With older children and adults, actors and story-teller may improvise together (GIVE AND TAKE). The story-teller becomes the "guide," re-

lieving the players of concern as to where the story is going, helping the players explore the emerging beats (EXPLORE AND HEIGHTEN).

CREATING SCENES WITH COSTUMES

▶ Two methods may be suggested for creating scenes with costumes. Either players agree on Where, Who, and What and then pick costume pieces to fit scene; or players pick costume pieces at random and then choose Where, Who, and What based on their costumes.

At first, the student-actors will love the idea of costumes and will put them on indiscriminately, whether a scene requires them or not, odd piece by odd piece. After a few months, however, this attitude has gradually changed, and they are choosing only costumes that fit their specific scene.

A typical scene built around costume pieces was done in the following manner. The children looked over the rack filled with colorful costumes (if costumes are too large, pins and ties will make them fit).[4] One boy picked out a high silk hat and a feathered cap and hood which had been used for a bird costume in a play. Three girls took fancy dresses and crowns from the hat box. Another lad took a beard and a tropical helmet. A girl took a modern dress, hat, and veil. Another girl put on a dog's tail and ears.

After they had put on their costumes, they were asked whether they wished to choose their own characters or to have the group choose for them. They elected to choose their own. They stood before the mirror to see what they looked like.

In this case, the first boy decided quite logically to be a bird, and with the silk hat on, he further decided to be a rich bird. The three girls became a queen, a princess, and a friend of the princess. The beard and helmet naturally created an explorer, and the dog ears and tail made a dog. But the last girl, in the modern dress, had a problem. What should she be? The boy playing the rich bird who had been quite enamored of her had a suggestion: she could be a "bird-lover." The girl very coyly agreed.

---

4. Old neckties can be used as belts and make it possible to use any size dress or coat by simply pulling up extra length etc. to be held by the belt. Wire coathangers can quickly be bent to form many costume effects.

Here, then, was the cast for their scene:

Rich Bird	Princess
Bird-Lover	Friend
Explorer	Dog
Queen	

The scene went as follows:

The Explorer was in the jungle with his Dog, hunting for rare birds. He was in the employ of a lady Bird-Lover who was building a collection. The Explorer caught a rare specimen of a Rich Bird, brought it back, and the Bird-Lover decided to take it to show the Queen, the Princess, and her Friend. The Dog came along, too.

Was something missing from this situation? Perhaps. But both the children on stage and the audience loved it. And this sort of scene can be done with only partial costumes and small props, all of which can be readily collected.

See also BOX FULL OF HATS, p. 380.

FORMAL THEATER
AND
IMPROVISATIONAL THEATER

CHAPTER XVI

PREPARATION

THE DIRECTOR

This chapter is primarily for the community-theater director of the formal play. The director of improvisational theater will find that by the time you have passed through the handbook, putting on a performance will grow out of the exercises. However, there are some pointers in this chapter on directing which might prove useful.

The director is the eye and ear of the audience to come, whose energies must, at all times, be concentrated on finding deeper insights and perspectives for both actors and technical crew that will further enrich the theater communication.

If you are fortunate enough to have highly gifted and experienced actors and technicians, your work will be greatly implemented. However, from the first choice of the play (or selection of scene material for improvisational theater) to the approval of its lighting plot, what is finally selected is the result of the sensitivity, awareness level, and good taste of the director, who is the catalytic agent, seeking to channel the energies of many people into one unified action.

For improvisational theater, your part in the theater action is to see and select the scene or story as it emerges out of the actors' playing (while solving a problem). The director must always see the process going on (or set it in motion when the players have lost their way) out of which a scene can possibly evolve.

The Director's Focus

When directing production for performance (formal or improvised play) the teacher-director takes on a role different from the role in the workshop.

As teacher, you focus on the individual and what problems to give to help each player in experiencing. As director, you focus on the play and the problems to use to bring it to life. (An additional point for the director of improvisational theater is what problems to give the actors to find scene material.) Sometimes the roles are totally separate; sometimes and when necessary, whether in workshops or in rehearsals, they work together.

Rehearsals (playing) require an environment in which both actor's and director's intuitions can emerge and work in union, for it is only in this way that life can be brought to the director, the actor, the play, and the stage. This is why problem-solving techniques are used for rehearsing the play. They have been experimented with over the years, especially with children and lay actors, and, as in workshop, if the intent of the problem is understood by the director when presented to the players and if solved by them, a vitality and a high level of response both in acting and development of scene material is the result. It works!

This chapter suggests ways and means to help the director remain constantly focused on finding the play's *reality*. You must know what problems to give your players so as to have the play grow into a meaningful, harmonious, unified production.

Long before casting, you will have read the play through many, many times. You will have digested it and be familiar with it and the playwright. You may even have seen it done somewhere.

Then, you must discard your "dream" play and as much of the remembered one as possible. (The director of improvisational theater will not have this problem in quite the same way, although scenes may have been selected that have come up in workshop which need to be explored more fully. This would bring you to about this same point with the director of formal plays.)

The problem of bridging one's ideal of the play to its actual production on the boards is no small task. But, since a production is nourished by the skills, creativity, and energies of many, it is necessary that the director realize that we cannot push actors and technicians into preconceived patterns and still hope to have an alive performance. No solo flights for director or actors.

If, for instance, the actors are hung up on words, with little if any blocking or stage business appearing, the director may decide to use GIB-BERISH or perhaps extended movement or games to set the scene in action. The selection would be dependent upon a diagnosis as to what is causing the problem to begin with. If the intent of a scene is not clear, BEGIN AND END will sharpen the meaning for actor and director alike. For improvisational theater needing scene material, PREOCCUPATION, WHAT'S BEYOND?/UNKNOWN EVENT, EXPLORE AND HEIGHTEN, and other special exercises in this area can be selected.

Out of this playing, then, the play itself, its story, its life, will emerge for the director to see. Working this way continues group agreement and finding the solution to the stage problems through group solving of problems. Nor is the single actor negated, for if for any reason work on individual character development must take place or more understanding of relation to an individual role is necessary, there are many exercises to use.

For the improvisational director, this is the only way you can work. The substance of the scene itself must be evolved along with everything else, and this is the way it will come about.

THEME

The theme is the moving thread that weaves itself into every beat of the play or scene. It intertwines and shows itself within the simplest gesture of the actor and in the last bit of trimming on the costume. It is both the bridge from scene (beat) to scene (beat) and the scene (beat) itself.

In the theater as in all art forms, it is difficult to define theme exactly. Look for it to grow out of the parts of the very play that is being done, for within a well-built play or scene the theme awaits. As a comet is static unless shot out by the energy that propels it, so is the play until it is moved forward by the energy extracted from each second of its progression. The source of this energy must be found in the objective reality of each scene. This will give the play its momentum as each scene is fused into life. Paradoxically, the theme gives the play its life and finds its life from the play itself.

The improvisational theater is so structured that its energy source is reached at the same time that the scenes evolve, for every scene grows from an objective reality (agreement). This is why in the improvisational theater a theme can be stated and the scenes built around it.

In simple terms, then, the director should think of theme as the thread that links all the separate parts together—a means for keeping costumes, set design, play, technicians, director, and actors together, working under one banner. Sometimes, watching, listening, it is a single word or phrase that sparks us; sometimes it is simply a non-verbal "feeling" that develops. The director may find the theme before rehearsals begin, or may be well into rehearsals before it appears. In some cases it never shows itself. The director must be careful, however, not to be rigid about finding a theme and in desperation impose one upon the play. Such rigidity can produce a dead end rather than an open path for all.

CHOOSING THE PLAY

It is difficult to set down a blueprint for choosing a play. However, there are a few specific questions which the director should ask before making a final decision:

1. Who will my audience be?
2. How skillful are my actors?
3. Do I have a technical staff that can handle the effects the play will need?
4. Is it a play *I* can handle?
5. Is this merely a costumed lecture (moralizing)?[1]
6. Will the play respond to my work on it?
7. Is the play worth doing?
8. Is the play theatrical?
9. Will it be a creative experience for all?
10. Can I and the actors add touches?
11. Will it be fun to do? Will it play?
12. Does it have life (reality)? or is it psycho-drama?

1. See the remarks on involvement as discipline, p. 264.

13. Is it in good taste?
14. Will it give a fresh experience, provoke individual thought for the audience and thereby insight?
15. Are the parts (beats and/or scenes) within the play constructed so they can be brought back to life?

In considering a play, the director should think about whether each rehearsal period could be organized around an acting problem which when solved would stimulate a worthwhile performance. Break the play (or selected improvised scene) into many minute scenes or beats, small parts of the whole, and thoroughly absorb them (never losing sight of the *whole* play). Throughout rehearsal periods, observe each beat in action. Constantly question.

For the formal play:

1. How can the playwright's intent be clarified?
2. Are individual mannerisms getting in the way?
3. Should the scene be heightened visually with more meaningful blocking and business, unusual props or effects?
4. Are crowd or party scenes handled ineffectually?
5. Should we play more?

For the improvised scene or play:

1. How can the intent of the scene be clarified?
2. Can richer content be given the scene?
3. Is the scene contrived? Are the actors ad-libbing, making jokes, etc., instead of improvising?
4. Is it in good taste?
5. Should we play more?

From this referral point, then, the director prepares problems for the actors to solve. You give them the problem to play with and then take from them what they have to give while solving it. In order to enrich the scene, the players take what you have to give them in the way of bits and pieces, your own additions, which you spontaneously select while watching them work on the problem.

It is exactly this organic way, this spontaneous selection, between people, this give and take from the points of view of both the players and the director, that is used during the development of scenes for improvisational theater and that is equally useful for the written play. It keeps the integrity of both director and actor and gives each a shared part in the experience. It brings out scene material in the improvisational theater. For the formal theater it develops total action out of which the meaning of the play arrives.

SEEKING THE SCENE

One word to the director of improvisational theater in the search for scene material for performance. Unless a group has been working together for a very long time and understands the difference between ad-lib and improvisation, avoid going directly for a scene. This will invariably become a "story conference" while moving around stage instead of an improvisation. If the group is clever, such material may be very topical, ingenious, imaginative, even funny, and certainly usable for performances; if the group is not too clever, the material that will come out of their "story conference" will be uninteresting. In either case there will not be the rich textured fabric of both character and scene which comes out of true improvisation.

If the director is engaged in a community project specifically to dramatize a particular topical or local theme, you must give actors a problem and suggest the situation or structure or have them work around the theme. Just be certain they do not work on the *story*. For instance, if a community wishes to poke a bit of fun and decides to use suburbia as the theme, simply have players (when setting up a problem) place their Where, Who, and What in a situation that might bring a usable scene out, such as trying to get baby-sitters, or fighting off door-to-door salespeople, or the election of the local council. With this, use an acting problem that is particularly useful for scene-making as suggested in Chapter IX.

If the director decides, for example, to bring the problem WHERE WITH OBSTACLES to the cast and they decide to use a door-to-door salesman, a very amusing scene of a housewife trying to get something done may easily arrive out of the obstacle problem. Keeping the same situation of the salesman, the cast can run it through a variety of problems, or they can do the reverse, which would be keeping one problem and running it through a variety of situations. In either case, players will be working on the problem and not the story. It will be in process, not static. The actor who works with the set story is forced to ad-lib and cannot improvise; that is exactly why the director is always needed, whose role in this most democratic of groupings is to select material (whether fragment or play) which emerges from the playing, relieving the actors' concern about getting a scene. This further helps the players to "keep playing."

It is the sharing (union), this give and take, of each and everyone's excitement, experience, and intuitive energy that produces the improvised scene. This is why, after improvisational training, even people with little stage experience can produce stage-worthy scenes and are *never* at a loss for appropriate material.[2]

CASTING

The method of casting depends on the particular formation of the group of people who have come together for the play. Are they coming for the first time? Are they experienced or inexperienced? Children or adults?

If a play is done paralleling the workshop, it is simple to cast directly from the classes. Posing situations that will utilize the characters and the problems well in advance of the announcement of the play is easy on all con-

2. "As does all improvisational theater, Playmakers requires a special breed of actors. In this instance they are all students in . . . acting workshops, guided by Viola Spolin. It is often amazing to outsiders that these actors develop such skills and spontaneity despite the fact that they are not professionals. Their talents at improvisation result directly from workshop training. . . . Lawyers, lab technicians, secretaries, writers, salesmen, housewives and children all come to learn about improvisational theater. . . . The workshops teach more than just acting techniques. They teach the more vital part of improvisation which is the art of selecting and developing scene material."—*Chicago Scene*, March 15, 1962, following a Playmakers production.

cerned; and the student-actors, having no idea they are being cast, will give the director a clear picture for observation.

The try-out is, of course, the more common way of casting. It is fiercely competitive, however, and the severe tension does not always show people in a good light. Some actors are clever at first reading but never move much beyond that, while a poor first reader may be discarded who may even be potentially superior to the actor chosen. The director must have infinite insight, for we are, after all, looking not for a finished piece of work when we cast, but for a tone of voice, a sense of reality, a bodily quality—that indefinable "something" which is only sensed initially. You must consider the amount of work each person will take to develop. You may see someone who has the character qualities wanted but so little background or so many set patterns and mannerisms that it may not be possible to get what is needed during the rehearsal period.

Another method of casting is to utilize a combination of the try-out and the improvisation. This can be done quite successfully with new people. It tends to relax the actors; and, in a tension-free atmosphere, the director is more likely to see everyone's possibilities clearly. Give those trying out a quick verbal resumé of the scene: the Where, the problem, and a quick run-down of the kind of character. Then let them improvise it. Or, give a scene around a problem which is similar to, but not the same as, the play. After the improvised scene, they can then read for the play.

A fourth method—if the group has been together for a time—is to run through GIBBERISH (see p. 114).

In some cases, the director reads the full play to the assembled group prior to casting. If this is done, the director should take care to read with as little character quality as possible, to avoid subsequent imitation by the actors. Sometimes scenes are read. More often, actors are simply given "sides" to read with little if any comment by the director.

Whatever procedure is chosen, it is best that the director's anxieties be well concealed. Casting is a tense period, for much depends on your choice. It is certain that the seed of the character must exist within an actor when you finally cast a role.

Casting for improvisational theater is quite different. Many of the scenes the group will be doing have evolved out of the group playing; for the most part the actors, as in workshop, *cast themselves.*

THE ACTING SIDE

Now the play is cast and ready for rehearsals. What about scripts? Some directors use full scripts; others prefer "sides," which consist of one or two words of the cue and the subsequent full speech of the individual actor, usually with stage directions typed in. The side can be creatively stimulating and is to be preferred.

It should be typed on 8½ × 11 paper and folded horizontally so that it may be held easily. The addition of the action cue along with the word cue will eliminate much of the problem of slow pickups. The action cue is the word or combination of words which sets the next actor in motion or alerts him or her to answer.

Cue: quiet...*hear me?*

LINE: All right, if you feel that way.

Cue: Get out...*Get out!*

LINE: I will, and don't expect me back! (Exit)

In the first cue and speech, "quiet" is the action cue, and "hear me" (coming some words later) is the word cue. In the second cue and speech, the first "get out" is the action cue, and the second is the word cue. The inner action (bodily response) of the actor hearing the lines begins at the action cue; and he or she is ready for action and response on hearing the word cue.

If "action cue" is not clear to the actors, an explanation should be given at the time the sides are introduced: *Do we begin to answer another person while he or she is still speaking, or do we start thinking about our answer after he or she has finished?* "While he or she is speaking."

The director should carry on a conversation with the actors to point up the problem: *Do we always wait until the other person has stopped speaking*

. . . action—the actors are already answering . . . *or do we sometimes break into their conversation?* Some have already broken into the above speech and have answered, "We don't always wait."

The director should point out how they were able to anticipate the outcome of the discussion. You could suggest that they observe people as they converse, to determine which are the action cues and which are the word cues. Sometimes, of course, both cues will be identical (as in a cry for help).

The acting side prevents an actor from reading the others' lines subvocally and eliminates any mouthing. Mouthing is a common failing in unseasoned actors. They follow the other actors' lines by reading them rather than listening to them; and very often their lips actually move as the other actors speak. This mouthing is a serious mechanical reading habit and is often difficult to eradicate.

Sides prevent sub-vocal readings or mouthing, since the lack of a complete script involves players from the first moment and forces them to be part of what is going on. They must *listen* and watch fellow actors to follow the action and know when to come in. Unable to memorize the other actors' lines, they are forced to act upon the spoken word.

Sides are small and can easily be held in one hand. This frees the actor to pick up props, make contact, etc. Sides also help eliminate some of the problems of mechanical reading, particularly in children. It is possible this is true because the sides cannot be clutched in both hands, a position which may be associated with schoolroom reading.

Only stage directions which lead to action or dialogue (entrances, exits, etc.) should be included on the sides. Even if the director feels a security in keeping them, it is best to avoid many of the playwright's directions (such as "speaks happily," "heaves a heart-rending sigh," or "winks knowingly"). The director should let the physical actions and facial expressions come from the actors' own inner action and from the dialogue itself. There will be plenty of opportunity in the second section of rehearsal, when actors are free of all restrictions, for the director to bring in the playwright's stage directions to further the action.

CHAPTER XVII

REHEARSAL
AND
PERFORMANCE

ORGANIZING THE REHEARSAL TIME

The over-all rehearsal schedule can be broken down into three sections. Briefly, the first section is for warming up the actors and the director, for laying the groundwork in relationships and attitudes to the play and to each other. The second section is the spontaneous, creative period—the digging sessions, where all energies are channeled toward full artistic potential. The third section is for polishing and integrating all production facets into a unity.

The amount of time spent in rehearsal depends upon the actors' availability. Professional actors, of course, have no other commitments. But with lay actors in community theater groups, the opposite is true; and the number of hours they have free to rehearse is limited.

To rehearse a show within these limited hours becomes a real problem. But by utilizing the three rehearsal sections and by extending the over-all rehearsal schedule over a two- or three-month period, the director will have a picture of where they are going. When the daily hours of rehearsal are limited, this long time-span between casting and showtime is uniquely valuable; for it is in this period that seasoning takes place.

Not one minute of rehearsal should be wasted. The schedule should be carefully planned to be certain that every actor present is working at every possible moment. It is advisable to think in terms of two kinds of time: clock-time and energy-time. Energy-time is the more valuable, for the director can get as much from the players in two hours of inspired, excited rehearsal as in six hours of boredom and fatigue.

While it is unavoidable that all actors be present at run-throughs, it is wise not to keep them around at other times just on the chance that they may be needed. Some directors are more secure having the actors at their beck and call, and some feel that the actors should be around to see where the play is going; but proper organization of rehearsals will give the director a very good picture of the play at every moment without inconveniencing the actors. The psychological as well as the obvious benefits of such careful scheduling are considerable. The actors are always fresh, always excited and eager to work. They are pleased by the consideration shown them and respond, in return, with maximum results.

Whether it is a vignette, a one-act play, or a three-act play—whether the clock-time is eight hours or sixty—the rehearsal time can be figured by noting what must be covered in each session. If the group meets only three times a week and each session can have only a maximum of two hours, the director must schedule work accordingly. When the time arrives for costume parades, dress rehearsal, etc., you will, of course, have to find extra hours for these time-consuming activities.

Atmosphere During Rehearsals

If the rehearsal period is one of tensions, anxieties, competitiveness, and bad temper, this will be absorbed by the actors along with their parts and will be a shadow over the finished work. If, on the other hand, the atmosphere is relaxed, social, and joyous with the excitement of the work at hand and the anticipation of the show to come, this too will be evident in the final production. A nuance, perhaps, but an important one; for when actors are free and enjoying their roles, then the audience is relaxed, and an extra note of pleasure is added to their viewing.

Lay actors often come to rehearsals at a point where energy levels are low: after school, tired from a day's work or from putting the children to bed, etc. Outside problems may be carried into the rehearsal, whether they be a child's poor report card or an adult's quarrel with the boss. In either case, making their transition from one place to another a pleasant one is well worth the trouble. A refreshment break will often enhance the social aspect of rehearsal and also relieve fatigue.

The Director's Ability to Inspire

"Inspiration" is often a vague term. We know, however, that behind it something exists and that, in the case of a director, its presence or absence can be readily noted by observing those around him.

The most apparent characteristic of inspiration could probably be termed "reaching beyond one's self" or deeper "into one's self." People who are inspired may pace the floor or talk animatedly. Eyes sparkle, ideas pour forth, and the body releases its holds. If many people are inspired simultaneously, then the very air around them seems to sparkle and dance with excitement.

Inspiration in the theater situation can best be described as energy. "Energy" does not mean leaping wildly about the stage (although this might help at times). It is the intensity of the director's attention to what the actors are doing, plus the use of every skill you can call up, which subsequently prods the actors into extending themselves, into "reaching beyond." Sometimes the director must literally *pour* this energy into a cast as one might pour water into a glass; and, in most instances, the cast will respond and will be able to pour it right back. An actor once made the comment that "playing to you is like playing to a full house at the Opera!" This is the kind of energy the director must give to actors.

Never for one moment should the director show tiredness or boredom, for a director who loses energy is doing more harm to the play than can be imagined. If this tiredness should occur, it is far better to stop rehearsals completely and have the stage manager take over for a sit-down line rehearsal, or go into voice exercises or an improvisation, than it is to continue with a lifeless rehearsal.

An actor without energy is worthless, without contact with what he or she is doing. The same holds true for the director. The director must not make "inspiring the actors" a mere phrase. Indeed, when a lag in rehearsals does occur, you would do well to look to yourself.

Am I giving enough energy? Am I staying overlong on mechanics? Which actors need individual attention? Do they need more improvisations? Are rehearsals too drawn out? Am I nagging at the actors? Am I attacking the actors? Are the actors working at odds with me? Is the problem physical or psychological? Am I just being a traffic manager? Is it necessary to stimulate more spontaneity? Am I using the actors as puppets? Am I over-anxious? Am I asking them for more than they can give me at this time?

If the director searches for and handles the problem honestly, it will be solved. The only initiative needed is the knowledge that when necessary one's ingenuity, spontaneity, and energy can give inspiration to the actors.

Blocking the Show

Natural-looking blocking is possible with any age group or experience level. Neither the child actor nor the lay actor need move around the stage awkwardly, clinging to props and furniture, spreading fear and discomfort through the audience. Exercises in non-directional blocking should be given the cast if they have not had workshop training (see Chapter VI).

As long as the lay actor is constantly directed in the mechanics of stage movement and does not understand that stage movement can only grow out of involvement and relationships, he or she can, at best, only remember the conventions and will therefore be unable to move naturally.

To test this theory, the following experiment was carried out by actors with little or no theater experience and only minimal workshop training. They were given two different scenes.

For the first scene, the actors were given full scripts which contained the lines for all the characters plus the stage business and blocking as set down by the playwright. During the first rehearsal, they were constantly stopped for blocking by the director. Then they were asked to take their lines home and memorize them.

For the second scene, the same actors were given acting sides only. The action cues and word cues of the other actors were all they had to work with. There were no stage directions given. During the first rehearsal, they were occasionally coached by the director to share the stage picture. They did not take their lines home to memorize.

At the next rehearsal, the difference was remarkable. During the first scene, set rigidly from the outside, the actors neither saw their stage nor heard their fellow actors as they struggled to remember cues, lines, and stage directions. Their concentration was so intent upon remembering, and their fears of not performing well produced such physical tensions, that they were rigid. Their bodies could not move freely. The stage movements of these unskilled actors under such imposed conditions could only be stiff and awkward — what is commonly called "amateurish."

The second scene, though more complicated in its demands, did not trouble the actors; for, intent upon each other and with nothing to remember (no performing) other than "sharing," they were free to solve the problems that came up during the actual rehearsal. This experience was similar to the improvisation, where the problem must be solved during the playing of the scene and not away from it. It is in this way that actors achieve spontaneity.

In another experiment, lay actors with many months of workshop training behind them were given the full script (as in the first scene with the new actors). In their case, they were able to take the directions given by the playwright and the director and translate them into the necessary stage relationships. But lay actors who in play after play are directed rigidly, step by step, with every movement plotted for them, cannot hope to discover natural stage movements (blocking) by themselves. Fear and tensions stemming from their first rehearsals and all subsequent work have been memorized along with lines and stage directions and keep players in memorization (the past) rather than in process (the present).

The director who wraps the actors up in yards of imposed movement and inflections until they cannot walk is the same director who places the burden of "stupidity" or "no talent" on them when they cannot function on their own. We bemoan their inability to loose the ties that bind them, but it is we, in reality, who have secured the knots. Rigid actors are often the product of rigid directors.

Integration in Blocking

Integration is being present to the moment that is present. Integration is an organic response to the stage life. While it is sometimes necessary for an instruction to be given to the actor, he or she must translate it into an organic or integrated experience. The following dialogue was with a ten-year-old player.

Why did you go upstage just then? "Because you told me to."

Isn't that mechanical? "Yes."

Why do you think you were directed to go upstage? "I went upstage to wait for Tom to enter."

Why couldn't you wait for him where you were? "I wasn't part of the scene going on at the moment. I have to be out of the scene, but I can't leave the stage."

What can you do standing where you are, out of the scene, and still be part of the stage picture? "I'll put my focus on listening for Tom to come in."

Stage Business

It must be realized that the most skilled director or actor cannot always intellectually find interesting stage business. It is the director who must often stimulate stage business when neither the actor nor the script are helpful. There are many ways to accomplish this. Sometimes the director will receive inspiration from the actors at the moment it becomes necessary and will then spontaneously select from this what is appropriate for the actor and scene. Using the acting exercises (see Time Chart, p. 341) will bring up more business than the director or actor could find in many hours of work on the script.

Both the director and the actor must understand that stage business is not just a random activity to keep actors occupied. Like blocking, it should be interesting and non-obtrusive and should appear spontaneous.

General Improvisations Around the Play

In the first rehearsal section, keep all improvisations close to the Where and the problem of the actual play; but in the second section, when it becomes necessary to provoke the actor beyond the exact lines and to bring a greater reality to relationships, general improvisation is most helpful. General improvisations will seem to have no direct relation to the written play. They are presented, however, to give the actor insight into the character he or she is playing.

In a production of *The Emperor's New Clothes*, establishing the relationship between the minister (who was the villain, browbeating and cheating the weavers) and the weavers became a problem. It was solved by stopping rehearsals and doing an improvisation around Nazis coming to a village during the war. The weavers took the parts of villagers; and the minister and his entourage played the Nazi soldiers. The Nazis marched in, billeted themselves, herded people together, established authority, and used physical violence against those who protested. The villagers wept, fought, and shouted. All the emotional conflicts necessary for the play they were working on came forth and were heightened. It was never necessary to rehearse these relationships again in this play by Charlotte Chorpenning.

Once the quality needed for a scene is captured, it remains (with rare exceptions). In the foregoing example, the reality of the Nazi scene had to be shaped into the structure of the play; but the intensity was never lost. Audiences were moved by the strength of these scenes and were astonished that "mere children" (who were playing the roles) could give such amazing portrayals.

General improvisations often give actors an insight beyond their words by helping them to "see the word" and achieve a reality for the scene. In effect, they resemble WHAT'S BEYOND? for improvisational theater. Sometimes improvisations are not necessary; but when used, they will invariably enrich the work.

The Non-Stop Run-Through

The non-stop run-through is especially valuable to the director with a limited amount of rehearsal time. It is, simply, a complete run-through of the play *without stops of any kind*. It should be held sacred; under no circumstances should a director break in for any reason. Notes for spot rehearsals, pointers for individual actors, and places in the individual acts that need more work can all be jotted down by the director and cleaned up at a later rehearsal.

These non-stop run-throughs strengthen the whole basic structure of the production, for the flow and continuity that they generate give the actors a sense of the movement and rhythm of the total play which can only help them with the details of their scenes.

The mechanical problems which the director has in getting the cast and play together during the first rehearsal section are so time consuming that a non-stop run-through would be impossible during this time. Indeed, setting just one act of a three-act play usually takes most of the daily rehearsal period at this early stage. But in the second rehearsal section, when blocking, relationships, character, motivation, etc., have already been roughed in, the non-stop run-through should be scheduled as often as possible.

The Relaxed Rehearsal

The Relaxed Rehearsal, falling within the second rehearsal section, gives perspective to the actors.[1] By this time, they should be off their lines. The actors lie on the floor, shut their eyes, and breathe slowly with strong accent on the exhale. The director walks around from time to time, lifting a foot or a hand to make sure muscular release is complete.

The actors then go through the lines of the play as they lie there with their eyes closed. They are to concentrate on visualizing the stage, the persons with them, and themselves in the scenes.

The director should continue to insist on complete release. The actors' voices should be quiet and almost sleepy. In spite of the past work, old reading patterns and anxieties will often show up in rehearsal, particularly on a first play. Actors might be tense and worried about the mechanics of their action, memorization, cues, movement, etc. This relaxed rehearsal, coupled with the visualization of the stage, usually dissipates that sort of fear.

During the relaxed rehearsal, the director should quietly remind the actors that they are not to mouth the other actors' words but must try to hear them. They must concentrate intensely on seeing the stage in their

---

1. VERBALIZING THE WHERE, p. 118, could be combined with "Relaxed Rehearsal."

own minds. The director quietly asks them what colors they are seeing and how far away the other actors seem. Perhaps you can even give them the image of a stereoscopic camera. They should try to see the stage in full dimension, color, and movement, to be hyper-conscious of everything that takes place.

If properly handled and prepared for, this time will be enjoyable to all. The actors will be able to extract bits and pieces from their former work and add them to their conceptions of their roles. The last vestiges of anxiety will usually disappear; and this still weeks before the opening!

Spot Rehearsals

As a rule, it is best to schedule spot rehearsals in the third section, when the play has definite shape and flow. The spot rehearsal is utilized to give special time to working over a scene which has been troubling the director and/or the actors and which has not developed within the general rehearsals. It might be a simple entrance or an involved emotional scene. It might be a problem of achieving a more effective mob scene or helping a single actor to underline and heighten a long speech. In improvisational theater, playing a problem is often the way to evolve a scene.

This type of rehearsal will often intensify a scene which has previously been weak. Spot rehearsals pull the actor and the director away from the generality of the overall play and focus on the minute details of a scene. They create quiet concentration and an intimacy between the actor and director which result in deeper insights for both. While the director may spend hours on a scene that takes but a few moments on stage, such intensive work on selected bits and pieces enriches the actor's role and brings added depth to the total play.

SEASONING THE ACTOR

We speak of an actor as being "seasoned" who stands in good relationship to the part, the play, and the other actors, who has ease of movement and flow of speech, and is, above all, aware of responsibility to the audience.

One of the most common weaknesses of the lay theater is the awkward, rough level of performance given by most of its actors. While much of this roughness can be attributed to inadequate experience and training, other factors are also involved.

How often are most lay actors on stage? Their work, for the most part, is directed toward one date—one production—and when that moment has passed, the experience ends. This abrupt breakdown in group expression thwarts creativity just when it should be blossoming forth. It stops the growth, the seasoning process.

For the group interested in developing a repertory company, the seasoning that takes place during performance is especially valuable. But, between the problems of rehearsal time and the technical and mechanical difficulties which most community theaters face, there is little opportunity for gaining insights into the play and accomplishing the desired seasoning.

No director can expect to get fully seasoned actors in a short period of time. However, the following suggestions, if carried out, will round off many of the rough, uneven edges:

1. Plan a long time-span for rehearsing.
2. Use acting exercises during rehearsals.
3. Do not allow actors to take their lines home too early.
4. Use non-directional blocking whenever possible.
5. Create a tension-free pleasurable atmosphere during rehearsals.
6. Bring in costume pieces and props early in the rehearsals to assure ease and comfort at the time of performance.
7. Work to have actors meet every crisis and adjust to sudden changes.
8. Break dependency upon words.
9. Have a weekly run-through of the full show throughout the second rehearsal section.
10. Schedule as many performances as possible; show to many different audiences; show in other places, if possible.

Memorization

In community theater, memorizing lines is usually considered the most important single factor in working on a role in a play. In truth, it is only one of many factors in rehearsing a play and must be handled carefully to keep it from becoming a serious stumbling block to the actor. For those trained in improvisational techniques, memorization is not a boogey-man!

The director should not allow the actors to take their sides home after rehearsal. This may be confusing to them, for many feel that line-memorization should be done immediately and gotten out of the way so that the actual direction can begin. However, it is important to realize that dialogue should grow out of the involvement and relationships between players; and premature memorization creates rigid patterns of speech and manner which are often very difficult (and sometimes impossible) to change.

The director should stop to think just who may be waiting in the home to "help." What well-meaning friends or relatives who fancy themselves a good judge of talent and cannot resist the chance to find the "right" way for the actor? And how many mirrors reflect the image of the actor busily emoting in front of them as he or she learns lines? The time between rehearsals should be a fallow period as far as the play is concerned—it should lie quietly.

Memorizing the lines too early brings many anxieties; for the fear of forgetting them is great. These anxieties remain as a shadow over every performance. If for some reason early memorization is unavoidable, the director should show the actors how to accomplish it in a relaxed manner.[2]

Actors may feel a bit concerned when they are not allowed to take their scripts or sides home during the early rehearsals; for even the youngest actor has tied up working on a part with learning words (memorization). Because of this, they are often quite fearful that they may not be able to memorize in time. It is the director's job to reassure them.

All the elements of production should be organically memorized simultaneously. It is only during rehearsals with the cast that relationships are worked out and understood. It is during rehearsals that the actors are freed from the words they are seeking to memorize. When this freedom becomes evident, it is safe to let them take lines home. For when the director

2. See p. 348, points 5 and 6, in "Removing Amateur Qualities," Chapter XVIII.

sees that actors are integrated and relating to all the aspects of theater communication, then are they ready to memorize — in fact, for most of them the job has already been done. They will find that they need only to go over a difficult speech here and there. In fact, sometimes all that is needed is to take the sides from their hands during rehearsals; and, much to their surprise, they will know their lines!

If the groundwork has been laid and the Time Chart (p. 341) has been followed, the director will probably find all the actors off their lines before the start of the second rehearsal section. This method of working is particularly valuable for child actors, where the fear of reading and of not being able to memorize lines becomes a serious obstacle in their work and keeps many of them from developing as actors.

A director from a community theater once visited the Young Actors Company at a dress rehearsal. She was surprised to see the director down at the mouth because of the usual "dress rehearsal." "You should feel elated," she said. "Your young actors are all off their lines!" This is indeed a sad state of affairs when the bogey of knowing the lines determines the whole quality of the performance.

Reading Lines Naturally

The student-actor is often quite fearful around words—particularly the child actor, whose anxiety grows out of past experiences with reading. As he or she struggles to pronounce the words "correctly," discomfort is continuously in the foreground. In the unseasoned actor, the inability to read lines naturally is often evident. Lines become words "in place of" dialogue—a substitute for action and relationship between players.

The first step in helping student-actors to lose this preoccupation with the lines is to preoccupy them elsewhere. Avoid any direct reference to the cause of their anxiety. Give them an acting problem that will remove focus from the words and solve the matter for them.

Gibberish, extended movement, dance movement, singing dialogue, contact, and postponement of memorizing words are all designed to help the actors in this way. If they are to lose their fear of line-reading, actors must come to sense that lines grow out of dynamic action and involvement. For those who read haltingly, give gibberish or ad-lib lines until relationships form. It works. Try it!

Another way to "lose" words is to focus on the shape of the words—the vowels and consonants—independent of meaning, concentrating on the visual appearance of the vowels and consonants, their physical shape and design as written or printed. In a sit-down reading, have the cast concentrate first on only the vowels, then on only the consonants. In reading, they are to heighten these *vowels and consonants* in any way they wish—sound, body movement, etc. Try to keep the reading at a normal pace. Stop at an appropriate time and resume the normal reading of the lines. Have the cast think of words as sound which they shape or design into word patterns.

VOWELS AND CONSONANTS, p. 396, is a full version of the exercise. SPELLING, p. 392, is another rehearsal refresher, as is GIVE AND TAKE FOR READING, p. 386.

Timing[3]

As much as actors would like, timing cannot be developed intellectually. Such skill can only be learned through experiencing. That is why rigid blocking and the mechanical following of directions must be done away with. An actor's sense of timing must come from the innermost self.

Timing is generally believed to exist in only the most seasoned actors. However, if "seasoned" is understood to mean that actor who has both self-awareness and the ability to attune to the needs of the scene, the other actors, and responsibility to the audience, then every student-actor can develop timing to some degree.

If problems are solved, the cumulative effect of all the acting exercises in the workshops will develop timing in the actor; for each problem insists on really playing, and in this rests selectivity and attunement to multiple stimuli. The player who has developed timing will then know when a play is dragging, when cues are dropped, and when stage action is not alive—in short, when "guests" are not enjoying themselves.

3. See also "Timing," Chapter II.

If actors are without workshop training, try to find a problem to be solved in each separate scene within the written script. Then have actors focus on problems exactly as they would in workshop. This will send them out into the stage environment and help objectify their work, which is the essence of timing.

Picking Up Cues

Slow cues cause a serious lag in a scene. If the director is still having trouble with slow cue pickups in the third rehearsal section, the actors have not completely solved the problem of involvement and relationship. Other devices must then be used.

The director might snap fingers simultaneously with all cues. Shadowing might be used to encourage quicker uptake. Or tossing a ball back and forth between actors; the moment the ball is caught, an actor must begin speaking. Or, the director might have the slower actor deliberately top the other's lines, cutting off the last few words.

The actors should be cautioned that picking up cues does not mean faster speech. If a speech has a slow tempo, then tempo remains slow, even though the cue itself is picked up rapidly.

Laughter in Rehearsals

During the second rehearsal section, actors are usually quite free from early tensions, social aspects are high, movements are fairly sure, and the actors can begin to have more fun. Fun, however, must be understood as the pleasure of working within the play and with the other actors. Uncontrolled laughter and wisecracking during rehearsals should be seen by the director for what it is.

When laughter is moderate and enjoyable, it is useful. It most often denotes a breakthrough. It will help, not impede the work. When it has elements of hysteria in it, however, it will prove destructive and must be carefully handled by the director. In time, the director will listen to laughter and know what it means, much as a mother is able to tell what each separate cry of her child means.

Although actors will assure the director that they "will never laugh on stage," one might be permitted a moment of doubt. It might help to tell them the Soup Story:

A wife tried to get her husband to stop making noises when he drank soup, since they were soon to have company for dinner. "Don't worry," he said. "As long as we're by ourselves, I can make all the noise I want. But when company comes, I will drink my soup quietly."

The next time they had company for dinner, the man was very careful not to make noise; and for the first few spoonfuls all went well. He did so well, in fact, that he completely relaxed. The longer the soup course went on, the more he enjoyed himself; and the more he enjoyed himself, the louder he slurped. To the embarrassment of the guests, he ended up making more noise than he had before his wife warned him.

Sometimes, when laughter breaks out among the cast in rehearsal, the director can let them release it by actually helping them to laugh and joining in on the joke. However, if the laughter is uncontrollable, one should recognize the danger sign, stop the scene, and go on to another.

Young actors and older lay actors will often say, "He makes me laugh!" But it is important to point out to them that "he" never makes them laugh. It is their own lack of focus, for whatever reason, that causes the trouble. Laughter sometimes is a means of pulling away from the stage environment and becoming a judging audience. They are playing a role and suddenly see their friends instead of the other characters. Or they see themselves doing something, expressing some emotion out of the ordinary.

Laughter is energy; and players can learn that its physical impact on the body can be re-channeled into another emotion. As in workshop, student-actors learn to "use their laughter." Laughter can readily be turned to tears, tantrums, "play" laughter, physical action, etc.

Growing Stale

There are two points at which actors may grow stale: one is during rehearsals, the other is during a run of performances. When this happens, it is a sign of grave danger, for when actors become mechanical and lifeless, something has gone wrong.

Sometimes this is because of a serious weakness in the basic structure of the production; at other times, it may be just a temporary setback. Sometimes the choice of material is poor, and the director can work only with such superficiality that the material responds only slightly. Sometimes actors have ceased to "play," and spontaneity and creativity have been replaced by the actors simply repeating themselves. Or the actors may have lost focus and begun to generalize their environment, their relationship (Who), and their settings (Where), so that no reality exists for them. Rehearsals, like the play itself, should have a growing developmental theme and climax. Staleness may be a sign that the director has neglected to carefully plan rehearsal time to build maximum inspiration and excitement for the actors (see the Time Chart, p. 341).

Several factors may account for the cast going stale during rehearsals:

1. Director has set the play too definitely from the outside, giving every movement, every piece of business, every voice inflection to the actors.

2. Actors have memorized lines and business too early. Characters, blocking, etc., were set before relationship and involvement developed.

3. Actors have been isolated too long from the other aspects of production and need a "lift." The director should bring in a handsome set piece, a costume part, or a prop and space this so maximum effect will be derived. You must heighten the theatrical atmosphere as you move to the third rehearsal section. This opens up new vistas for the actors and builds greater vitality for the production.

4. Actors need more fun or play. This can be handled through re-channeling the director's attitude or by using games. This is particularly true of children and lay actors, where it may take months of workshop before their involvement with the theater problems generates enough energy to hold their interest without outside stimuli. Traditional games (pp. 399–412) are excellent for any rehearsing group.

5. Actors with limited backgrounds are certain they have reached their goal and achieved characters—they want the performance to begin. Sometimes only one or two actors may be having difficulties. It may be that they do not like their parts, or they may feel they should have had larger ones.

Other faults that usually lead to staleness during performance:

1. Imitating previous performances.

2. Seduced by audience reaction.

3. Never varied performance. (Actors can vary performances endlessly, respecting the limitations of the play's structure.)

4. Giving "solo performances."

5. Actors getting lazy and sloppy.

6. Actors losing detail and generalizing objects and stage relationships. (Use VERBALIZING THE WHERE, p. 118, when this occurs.)

7. Actors need director's guardianship.

8. Play needs pickup rehearsals.

An interesting problem arose with an actor who was playing in his first performance. It was at a settlement house; and he was a neighborhood man who did a brilliant piece of work when he stood up to the villain of the play. After the first performance he received a thunderous applause. The next performance there was *no* applause. He was perplexed and wanted to know what had happened.

The first time you played, you were really angry, and we all knew it. The second show, you were only remembering the applause. He thought for a moment, nodded his head, and as he rolled up his sleeves and flexed his arms, he said: "Wait till I get him tonight!"

ACTING EXERCISES DURING REHEARSALS

Interjecting an acting exercise in a rehearsal that is going nowhere brings refreshment to both the actors and the director. For the most part, the director should select the exercises that help solve the problems of the play, as mentioned earlier in this chapter. Sometimes, however, exercises independent of the play are useful for generating energy in the actors and are an aid in the maturing or seasoning process.

Every early rehearsal should make use of at least one acting exercise. The Time Chart (p. 341) suggests many methods for doing this; but at best it is only a general plan, and each director will learn to add or subtract from it as individual problems appear.

Gibberish

Because gibberish (see p. 112) requires total body response to make a communication, it provides excellent exercises to use throughout the three sections of rehearsal. Gibberish quickly opens up the actors and helps the director to see the individual potentials of the group. Because it physicalizes the relationships and involvements, it has extraordinary value in developing spontaneous business and blocking and gives many clues for procedure to the director.

If employed early in rehearsals, gibberish produces remarkable acceleration in every aspect of production. In an experiment with a one-act play that had only eight hours of rehearsal time (using actors with limited backgrounds), gibberish was used four times, consuming two and one-half hours, or one-fourth of the rehearsals. The resulting performance had unusual vitality; and the cast handled their play with the ease of experienced actors.

When using gibberish during rehearsals, take the actors who have not had workshop training through the GIBBERISH exercises on pp. 114–18. After that, work on the problem of the play using gibberish. A scene that will not "play" in gibberish is a scene without reality, therefore without life. Theater communication cannot be made through words; the actor must truly *show*.

Where

Where exercises (see p. 87) can be used at the very beginning of rehearsals. During the second sit-down reading of the play, draw a floorplan of the set (if it is too early for specifics, approximate it) and place this in front of the group so that they can refer to it. As they are reading, have them think themselves around the stage within the set. Ask them to concentrate on colors, on the weather, on the style of clothing. (This should only be used by actors who have had workshop Where.)

Divide the cast into small groups and have them solve Where (making physical contact with all the objects on stage). This is to be done on an empty stage with only the blackboard for referral. The playing may or may not relate to the problem in the scene; but the floorplan on the blackboard will be for the play they will be doing.

THE SPECIALIZED WHERE (see p. 128), with real props, is very valuable and should be given after a few walk-throughs. If the play calls for a window to a fire escape, a door to a closet, a door to a bathroom, a pull-down bed, a telephone, and a wall safe, have the cast (separated into small teams) use exactly these set pieces for improvisation. They are to do a scene around them independent of the action of the play, although they must take similar characters (the old man in the play can be the old man in the improvisation, etc.). In specialized Where exercises, they must let the set pieces suggest the situation.

If all or some of the foregoing Where suggestions are used, the first walk-around rehearsals with lines will find the actors moving quite easily about the stage area.

Contact

We sometimes see plays where actors stay in their own little areas, afraid to touch, look directly at, or listen to each other. Strong contact between actors, where a hand really holds another's arm or an eye looks into an eye, makes productions more alive, more solid. An audience is able to sense when a real contact has been made. And the director should remind actors of this throughout rehearsals.

Contact may be made either through direct physical touch, the passing of props, or eye focus (see SPACE WALK III, p. 83). A cast that has not had workshop training can gain much by taking time out to do a scene from the play as a contact exercise.

Objects to Show Inner Action

Exercises in using objects to show inner action are *continuously* useful during rehearsal and should be used whenever physicalization is needed (see p. 225).

Space or Extended Movement

Using space or extended movement during rehearsals helps to integrate the total stage movement (see p. 79). Such exercises break the static isolation many actors still cling to in spite of work on other acting problems. While especially useful for fantasy, movement exercises also do much for realistic drawing-room plays. Then try the opposite NO MOTION. Exercises in using space substance (p. 79) parallel the use of dance or extended movement and can be applied during rehearsals with satisfactory results.

This type of rehearsal helps players, young and old alike, to realize that, like a dancer, an actor is never to "wait his or her turn" while working on stage. The whole body, even when still, must always be ready to spring into stage action. This gives an interesting energy to the stage, and often a choreographed quality appears.

Blind

As it did in workshop, the exercise called BLIND (see p. 158) will force listening and help actors to move firmly within the stage environment, as they feel the space around them and develop a sense of "each other." During rehearsals, BLIND is best given to actors after they are off lines and are quite familiar with their stage.

Working on a darkened stage can contribute to rehearsals, although of course the director cannot see the actors. It does, however, help a director hear the actors and the actors to hear one another. This is similar to the technique of "listening to your actors" discussed next. If it is impractical to move your actors about, similar to the relaxed rehearsal, have them just sit on a darkened stage reading lines to one another.

Listening to the Actors

At various intervals during rehearsal the director should turn away from the actors and listen to them. This listening without seeing them in action often points up weaknesses in relationship, uncovers lack of "seeing the word," reveals falseness of characterization, and shows up "acting."

In the improvisational theater useless dialogue is quickly recognized.

Seeing the Word

Exercises in visualizing words as shapes come in handy for spot rehearsals (see p. 215). They help to underline and enrich many lines and moods. Add inner action to an exercise if sensory awareness alone does not work.

For instance, a student-actor who had a serious problem of monotone speech was given the special exercise of describing a flood he had witnessed. Coaching him to see color, concentrate on motion, sound, etc., had little effect on his speech. But, when asked how he felt "inside" when he saw the water, he replied that he had a funny feeling in his stomach. The "funny feeling" then became the basis for side-coaching during his talk, and the changes were immediate. As he concentrated on fear of drowning, animation came into his speech.

In the case of this young boy, he would have been unable to recognize the fact that he had "fear." Asking him for an "emotion" would have provoked no response. But asking him how he felt "inside" (physically) enabled him to concentrate on his physical feeling and made it understandable to him.

Shadowing

Shadowing (see p. 164) should not be used until the third, or polishing, section. Then the director must get on the stage with the actors and follow them around. Prior to doing this, the director should explain that they are not to lose their focus no matter what he or she might do; for if they are amused or disturbed by the shadowing, then the point of the action will be lost.

Shadowing will help the actors to understand their own inner action, to visualize, to make contact, to move. It will also give the actors' point of view and may clarify a few things for the director, who must talk to the actor being shadowed. Close proximity allows one to speak quietly without disturbing the others and to pick up the reactions of that actor as well as the others.

Why does he look at you like that? . . . Doesn't that irritate you? . . . What right has he to do that? . . . Do you think he's going to talk to you? . . . What makes him look out the window that way? . . . Why don't you force him to look at you? . . .

This gives the actors an extra burst of energy from the director; in a sense, it exposes them, some weeks before the opening, to the most scrutinizing of audience reactions, for shadowing is like the closeup of a camera. If they get rattled when being shadowed, they are not secure in their parts and need more work on spots.

This particular technique should not be used until the actors have been with their roles long enough for some seasoning to have taken place.

Use of Games

Like dance or space exercises, games release spontaneity and create flow as they remove static body movements and bring the actors together physically. Games are especially valuable in cleaning up scenes requiring sharp timing.

A difficult problem arose in a cocktail-party scene where six or seven players had to mill around and socialize while surreptitiously watching for the high-sign from their leader to break loose and create bedlam. When the scene was rehearsed, the results were static and unspontaneous. The problem was finally solved through the game WHO STARTED THE MOTION? (p. 68).

After WHO STARTED THE MOTION? was played four or five times, the cocktail-party scene came off, and the needed "looking without looking" quality emerged very sharply. The excitement released by the game was retained by the players throughout their performances.

A park scene with passersby crossing and recrossing the stage (requiring continuous entering and exiting) created a serious problem of timing for the actors. It was impossible to "set" the crosses through cues, since there had to be random crossing but never too many at one time. The game OB-JECT RELAY (p. 407) solved this problem for the actors.

After OBJECT RELAY had been played once, it was repeated, but this time the actors walked instead of running to the goal and back. This solved the problem on stage for the actors from then on; and as one or two exited, the others entered with no lag or static.

The director would do well to have a few good game books on hand at all times and to be familiar with their contents for that moment when a stage problem may be solved by playing a game.

This edition of *Improvisation for the Theater* contains an appendix with many of the traditional games that are commonly played in association with Spolin theater games as warm-ups or energy enhancers. Most of the games printed here are taken directly or adapted from Neva Boyd's *Handbook of Recreational Games* (Chicago: H. T. FitzSimons Co., 1945; New York: Dover Publications, Inc., 1975).

Biographies

Toward the end of the second period of rehearsal, ask the actors for biographies of their characters. It is a device for getting them to think of character in dimension and occasionally brings some insights. Within this material the director, too, may find something that is usable to help the actor who seems to be getting nowhere with a part.

The biography is everything about the character being played. Write out as fully as possible: schooling, parents, grandparents, favorite foods, main ambitions, loves, hates, what entertains, how evenings are spent, etc. Add the reasons which brought this character to the immediate stage situation.

This should not be done until the character is settling into the actor. Done too early, it is harmful and creates quite the opposite effect, for it keeps the character in "the head" of the player.[4] Some biographies may be

---

4. Because of this, it is avoided in training for improvisational theater, and exercises on character agility are used instead.

sketchy, irrelevant, and superficial. There should be no discussion about them. Simply accept them as they are and use them for reference material if and when the need arises. In a well-written play, an actor need only do the scene, for the character we meet holds his or her past within.

A biography written by a fourteen-year-old girl who was playing in a fantasy stated that she and the villain had gone to school together as children and that she had loved him very much. While logically this would have been impossible in the social structure of the play, it gave her relationship with the villain another dimension. She was able to give a sense of former love for the character she now detested. The audience, of course, was never aware of this "story," but it brought much greater depth to her work. (When these two players grew up, they married each other.)

SUGGESTIONS FOR THE FIRST REHEARSAL SECTION

1. You must trust your casting. Great fear will sometimes arise in the early rehearsals that you have erred in your choice of actors. If this is really so, you must re-cast quickly, for your attitude will affect everyone.

2. Without telling the cast, select two actors for barometers: one whose response is high and one whose response is low. This way you will always know if you are giving too much or too little in your rehearsals.

3. Do not allow actors to keep their eyes glued to sides when other actors are reading. Watch for this even at sit-down readings and remind them to watch the other players and to listen to them whenever necessary.

4. Avoid artificial reading habits from the first moment. Use special exercises if necessary.

5. Handle cue pickups naturally by having the actors work on action cues. *Do not handle this mechanically.* If it becomes necessary to work on word cues, wait until the latter part of the second or early part of the third rehearsal section.

6. Avoid setting character, lines, business, or blocking too early. A "rough-in" is all that is necessary. There is plenty of time.

7. Details are unimportant in the first period. *Do not nag the actors.* Once the character and relationships are set, it will be simple to bring in details. So, the life of each scene within the play must be found.

SUGGESTIONS FOR THE
SECOND REHEARSAL SECTION

This is the digging period. Players are now ready for fuller utilization of their creativity. As they bring up actions through the exercises or in the reading of the script, the director picks them up, enlarges them, and adds something more, if necessary. The play is more or less blocked; and almost everyone is completely off lines. Relationships are clear.

1. The beginning of self-discipline. No chitchat in the wings or in the theater. At this time, stage attitudes and stage behavior off the stage as well as on are to be established.

2. If the groundwork has been well laid, the director can move directly to stage action with no danger of intruding on the actor's creativity or a static quality appearing. You can cajole, shout, plead, and give exact steps without developing anxieties or stopping spontaneity. There will be no danger of this hampering the stage work.

3. Some first-section exercises can be continued here if necessary. Gibberish exercises are particularly good for digging up more stage business.

4. Director's energy must be high and apparent to the actors.

5. Watch for signs of growing stale and correct them quickly.

6. Work for more heightened characterization. Nuances of blocking and business are important to note also.

7. Spot rehearsals, when done, must be thoroughly pursued, going over a scene again and again until full realization, full climax, is achieved.

8. Use acting problems from workshop in spot rehearsals when needed.

9. If the full cast can meet only three times weekly, the director should be working *daily* in spot rehearsals.

10. Director should begin to build scenes one upon the other. Each scene has its own beginning and ending and its own climax. Every subse-

quent scene must be above the one before it—like a series of steps, each a bit higher than the last—as they build to the play's climax.

11. After the big climax, the subsequent scenes gentle off into the end of the play.

12. Work outdoors whenever possible during this period. The need to rise above the outdoors distractions seasons the actors.

13. Have actors rehearse barefooted and in shorts (climate permitting). You can then watch full body actions and tell quickly whether an actor is mouthing words or physicalizing the stage situation.

14. Listen to the actors as well as watching them. Turn away from the stage and concentrate on dialogue alone. Superficial readings, sloppy speech, etc., will then appear very quickly to the director's ear.

15. You must not allow a sense of urgency to cause you to stop run-throughs. Just keep notes on action that can be gone over again when the single act or spots are done. Remember, there is plenty of time.

16. If actors seem to be working at odds with you, then you would do well to check the overall theme. Is there one? Are the cast and director treading the same path?

17. Third acts have a way of taking care of themselves. Give most of the work and spot rehearsals to the first and second. If relationships and characters are well established, the third act will need only the resolving of the play.

18. Some scenes may have to be gone over dozens of times to move them smoothly. Others may need very little work other than the regular rehearsals. Any scene that has special effects must not appear awkward in performance, even if it means hours of work.

SUGGESTIONS FOR THE
THIRD REHEARSAL SECTION

This is the polishing period. The jewel has been cut and evaluated, and now it must be put into its setting. Discipline must be at its highest. Lateness to rehearsals and failure to read the call-board or check in with the stage manager must be sternly dealt with. The director is preparing players for a performance in which a late actor or a misplaced prop could throw the whole show.

The organization of back-stage work must begin as early as work on the stage; and the rules must be observed. In most little theaters, the technical crews are also composed of lay people. Prop, sound and lighting people must all be just as attentive to time and responsibility as the actors; and their responsibility must be built up rehearsal after rehearsal. Any ten-year-old can handle the light cues efficiently if respect is given both to the child and to the job at hand.

Spot Rehearsals

In the third rehearsal section, the director will find many fine points which have to be covered. By this time, the run-throughs should have a certain smoothness; the seasoning process has borne fruit; the characterizations exist. Can the director go further than this with non-professional actors? Are the problems of pace and timing and the finer distinctions of character beyond reach? Pace, timing, and finer character detail develop out of the essential life of a scene.

This is where the spot rehearsal is of inestimable value, for finding this reality often happens here. The director should schedule as many spot rehearsals as possible during this period. If actors can only come individually three times a week, you can still schedule daily spot rehearsals.

The Director's Re-Evaluation

The director must now re-read the play in a quiet place, free from the tensions of the theater. By now the play will be more than a projection of your own ideal. You will be meeting the playwright again, and, like a doctor observing patients' symptoms, you will probably see very clearly what has been a problem within the show—and this while you still have time to work on it.

Re-reading will aid you in holding the reality and theme, observing the action of the play and discovering where it is going. You will see the actors in motion and will be able to see extra nuances of character that can be added, bits of business here and there, ways of strengthening the mood, building climax, etc. All of this will come rushing out of the script.

For the first time, perhaps, you will be able to coordinate the confused images of rehearsal into a definite picture and will visualize the stage in dimension and color and action. This will tend to relieve your anxiety in much the same way that the Relaxed Rehearsal freed the actors. You will, in all probability, *see the show.*

Seeing the Show

"Seeing the show" is simply the director's insight into the production— the moment when all aspects can suddenly be seen integrated. There will suddenly be rhythm, pace, characterization, fluidity, and a definite unity to all of it. Many scenes will be rough, sets will be far from finished, costumes will still be in the "talking" stages, and a few actors will be moping around; but it will seem, on the whole, a unified piece of work.

The director may see this unified show for an instant and then not see it again for a number of rehearsals. But this is no cause for concern—it was there, and it will come again. You must now clean up rough spots, strengthen relationships, intensify involvement, and make alterations here and there.

Once you have "seen the show," you must accept it even if you feel it should have been different. This is most important. There are few directors who are completely satisfied with their productions. To work with young people and unseasoned adults, the director must be aware of their capacities. If you are not satisfied with the production because of the limitation of the actors, you must nevertheless realize that at this stage of growth it is all one can expect from them. If there is integrity, playing, life, and joy in performance, it will be well worth viewing.

Stage Fright in the Director

If you do not accept your show at this late date, you will intrude your own emotional problems on the actors. By now, you are getting stage fright and are concerned with whether the audience will accept and like "your" presentation. This feeling must be hidden from the actors. The very process of doing a show has a great deal of natural excitement. If you add your own feeling of hysteria to this, the actors will catch it from you. During this period, you may be short-tempered. Explain this to the actors, warning them that you may be gruff during the integration of the technical aspects. They will respond to you sympathetically.

A director who worries actors until the last minute, hoping to squeeze a little more out of them, will not help the play in any way. One way to prevent this stage fright is to give the production over to the technical aspects of the play in the last hours of rehearsal.

Makeup and the Actor

This is a good time to have character makeup sessions, especially if the play is fantasy which requires unusual makeup. Time spent on applying makeup and allowing actors to experiment with their own characters will aid their work on stage. Just as lines must come as a part of the actor, so must makeup. It is far better that players develop their own makeup, with an assist from more experienced people, than to have it applied for them.

Whenever possible, encourage research on characters. During rehearsals for The Clown Who Ran Away, Bobby Kay, a clown from the Clyde Beatty Circus, came to the Young Actors Company to tell the cast about clowns and clown makeup. He so entranced the young actors with his stories of the traditions behind clown performances and the dignity with which each clown "puts his mark upon his face" that when the time came for them to create their own clown characters, not one of them made just a "funny face." Each struggled to place his or her "mark" upon his or her face with all the individuality of a real clown creating a character.

It is advisable, after a session or two, to have all players make charts of their own makeup and keep it for reference. If makeup is handled as a developing factor in the total fabric of the theater experience, children as young as six can learn. (It was not an unusual sight at the Young Actors Company to see a seven-year-old helping a five-year-old to apply his makeup; although it was our guess that, at home, the seven-year-old couldn't even comb her hair properly.) Makeup, like a costume, must be worn easily and with conviction. It should not be used for the first time on the day of the opening performance.

Makeup must not totally mask the players, giving them a facade to hide behind. It should be recognized for what it is—an extension of a character, not the basis for it. Eliminating makeup, particularly with young actors playing older roles, can often provide a valuable experience for both actors and audience. This, of course, is particularly true for improvisational theater, where a hat or a scarf or a beard on a string is all the costume or makeup an actor ever wears as he or she changes from role to role.

This keeps the actors as "players." As such, they personally are always visible to the audience and so help create the "artistic detachment" essential to objective viewing and thus keep the audience "part of the game."

The Costume Parade

It is advisable to run the costume parade together with a makeup rehearsal. Briefly, the parade is just that: a grouping of the actors, completely dressed and made up, so that the director can see how they look under the lights. Changes can be made quickly, if necessary; and everything will be looked at for fit, comfort, etc. If there is no time for a costume parade alone, it may be combined with a rehearsal.

A costume parade can be tedious or fun, depending upon its organization. If possible, the director should schedule it at a time when the actors will be fresh and free from other commitments. It can help to make the last week a joyous, relaxed time, instead of an anxiety-ridden one. This time should not be squeezed in. The director may need a good number of hours to complete the dress parade, depending upon the type of play and the number in the cast.

The First Dress Rehearsal

There is an old theater superstition that "a bad dress rehearsal means a good performance." This is nothing more than an obvious attempt to keep everyone from becoming discouraged. A first dress rehearsal should be kept as free from tension and hysteria as possible, despite all the confusion which it will bring. It may, indeed, seem a bit lifeless; but this partial let-down is far better than a rehearsal in which chaos is come again.

Under no circumstances should the first dress rehearsal be stopped once the curtain has gone up. As with the run-throughs, the director should take notes as the acts progress and should have a meeting with the cast after each act to cover sight-lines, roughness, etc. You must only bring up those things which can be altered without disturbing past work.

If you do not have a "show" at the first dress rehearsal, you will not get one by overworking actors during the last hours. You must have faith in yourself and in your actors. The first dress rehearsal for any play is usually discouraging, but a second dress will follow — as well as the preview before an invited audience — to pull the show together.

The Special Run-Through

There are no "mistakes" onstage as far as the audience is concerned, for they do not know the script or the action of the play. And so, an actor need never let the audience know when he or she has gone astray. *The audience knows only what the actors show them.*

The special run-through puts the cast completely on their own. Developed for child actors, it works equally well with adults. It goes as follows:

At a regularly scheduled run-through of the play (just prior to dress rehearsal), tell the cast that in the event of a break of any kind (laughter, lost lines, etc.) by one of the actors, all — the *full cast* — must cover up and keep the scene going. If they fail to do so, they will have to go back to the beginning of the act. For instance, if an actor breaks at the very end of the second act and no one has covered for this, the director quietly calls: "Begin the second act, please!"; and the actors must go back over the ground they have just covered.

After a few "begin again's," the director will find the cast descending upon the culprit who made the break. If this should occur, remind them that all of them are equally responsible for keeping the play going and they must cover for their fellow actors in case of trouble.[5]

This is the fullest expression of the group experience at work.[6] It puts a severe discipline upon the individual player, who is now directly responsible to the group (the play). At the same time, it gives the player a deep sense of security to know that no matter what happens on stage and in whatever crises or danger one finds oneself, the group will come to one's aid for the sake of the play.[7]

The special run-through is very exciting for the actors and keeps them all on their toes, alerted for that moment when it may become necessary for them to cover up for a fellow player. After one or two such rehearsals, the show will go on even if the very roof should fall in.

THE PERFORMANCE

The audience is the last spoke which completes the wheel, and its relation not only to the play but to the playing is most important. The performance is certainly not the end of the line. It brings the whole creative process of doing a play to its fruition; and the audience must be involved in this process.

No one can use an audience for self-glorification or exhibitionistic reasons. If this is done, everything the director and actors have worked for will be destroyed. If, on the other hand, the whole concept of sharing with the audience is understood, the actors will have exciting performances. They will get the feel and rhythm of the audience, just as the audience gets the feel and the rhythm of the actors and the production. The mark of the fine actor is this response to audience. That is why it is desirable to give as many

5. See also the remarks on self-blocking, p. 145.

6. The intent of the director is not to harass or punish, but to simply function as a part of the group. This is the last salient point—the special run-through cuts the actors *away* from the director, and they are in truth "on their own."

7. Constant adaptability and resourcefulness are of course basic to improvisational theater, and so the special run-through is never needed prior to performance.

performances as possible—to allow this response to be developed in the actors.

Freedom and creativity must never go beyond the limitations imposed by the play itself. Laughter from the audience often causes an actor to lose his or her head (and focus). This distorts the actor's relation to the whole, as each performance is worked to achieve the laughter again. Here is an actor working only for applause, for personal gratification. If this persists then the director has somehow failed this actor.

It is difficult to state all the problems which will arise during performance. Often the director is forced to work with insufficiently trained actors or with people who hold fast to preconceived ideas of what an actor's role should be. The director's own experience and temperament will have to be allowed for. You must remember to strive for audience appreciation of the play as a whole and not of just one or two of the actors or the set or the lighting. The audience's response to the production can help you, the director, to evaluate your work.

RANDOM POINTERS

1. Stay away from the back-stage area during the show. Everything should be so well organized that it will run smoothly. Messages can always be sent back stage, if necessary.

2. Be certain that costumes are always well buttoned and sitting right. A runner who is worried about whether his shorts will hold up is not free to run.

3. Be easy and pleasant around the cast if you should drop into the dressing rooms.

4. Have one run-through between performances if possible—unless they are nightly. If this is not possible, a short talk after each performance will help to eliminate the few bits of roughness or sloppiness that may be appearing here and there.

5. A short pickup talk prior to performances may be necessary from time to time.

6. Rehearsals during the run of the show help actors keep focus on the

problems in the play and keep them from getting lazy and generalizing. They also bring greater clarification of random flaws and more intensification of what already exists.

7. Actors should learn to allow the audience full laughter. Begin to train early with the simple rule of allowing laughter to reach its peak and then quieting it by a movement before beginning the next speech.

8. Back-stage discipline must be observed strictly at all times.

9. The actors will grow in stature during the performances if all factors allow them to do so. The stage is the X-ray picture, where everything structural shows up. If the play is presented shabbily, if its "bones" are weak, this will be seen, just as any alien objects show up in the X-ray. False and dishonest characterizations and relationships come through. This can be understood and stressed for the actors whenever necessary.[8]

10. Working through the rehearsal plan outlined in this chapter may not produce a fully seasoned actor in the first show, but he or she will be well on the way.

11. If, toward the end of the run, the actors decide to "cut up," remind them that their last performance is the audience's first. Enjoyment must come from the performing itself, not from cheap tricks on fellow actors.

---

8. In improvisational theater this point would relate to scene structure as well. If a scene is structured simply for making jokes and imposing cleverness upon an audience, this would be clearly X-rayed.

CHAPTER XVIII

POST-MORTEM
AND
SPECIAL PROBLEMS

Every play and every group is different and has individual problems peculiar to it; but the need for growth and creative expression must be recognized in all. Remember that the techniques needed to rehearse the play have grown out of the acting workshops.

Recognize *growth* as against forcing, *organic* direction as against mechanical direction. Remember that mechanics are mere devices and that while snapping the finger to achieve a fast cue may work, using shadowing, tossing a ball, etc., will give organic response to picking up cues.

THE TIME CHART FOR REHEARSALS

The following chart outlines the plan that was followed most successfully by the author over her career in working with unseasoned actors. It has produced remarkable results, but of course it may be modified as the individual director sees fit.

Time Chart for First Rehearsal Section

DIRECTION	PURPOSE
Children begin here. Tell story of play. Gibberish. Give stage set in mind.	Helps cast. Orients actor to stage locale. Early work on relationships.
Reading of play aloud by director, then casting. Or casting and then reading play aloud.	

Time Chart for First Rehearsal Section, continued

DIRECTION	PURPOSE
More gibberish. Add Where with blackboards of stage locale. Characters as cast.	Familiarizes actors with stage space. Thinking on cluttered stage pictures started.
Adults begin here after casting.	
Sit-down reading, stopping for pronunciation, typographical errors on sides.	Eases into use of sides and familiarizes with content.
Second sit-down reading.	
(a) Reading, focusing on seeing the word: VOWELS AND CONSONANTS, p. 396.	(a) Brings words into dimension.
(b) Concentrate on color, other actors, weather.	(b) Helps understanding of words.
(c) Concentrate on visualizing stage set.	(c) Relates spoken words to stage environment.
Walk-through with sides, first act.	Non-directional blocking—general blocking may be added if necessary, setting reality.
General stage-plan given.	
(a) SPECIALIZED WHERE, p. 128.	(a) Gives flexibility in use of set, especially in fantasy.
(b) Walk-through with sides, second and third acts.	(b) Non-directional blocking— director keeps notes of business which emerges.
(a) Extended movement following movement necessary to play. SINGING DIALOGUE, p. 207, use of games.	(a) For business, ease of movement unusual blocking comes up). Develops character, pace, timing, and total group action.
(b) Walk-through with sides (actors almost off lines).	(b) Keep as much of the new action that comes up as possible.

Time Chart for First Rehearsal Section, continued

DIRECTION	PURPOSE
(a) Walk-through three acts. (b) Stop to clarify relationship, when necessary.	The first step in giving the player a sense of the unity of the full performance.
CONTACT, p. 171. Sides now taken home for *difficult* readings only.	Forces player to see another and strengthens relationships, and extra stage business emerges.
	Shows how to use the techniques of the Relaxed Rehearsal while reading at home.
(a) BLIND (actors off lines).	(a) Develops "sixth" sense, timing, strengthens stage environment and places actor solidly within it by giving space substance.
(b) Sit-down reading. Concentrate on the words.	(b) Cleans up speech with no danger of rigidity.
(c) Concentrate on action cues.	(c) Picks up cues.
(d) EXTENDED SOUND, p. 206.	(d) Develops organic voice projection.
(a) Calling over long (Where) distances.	
(b) Rehearse outdoors if possible.	
(c) Director moves a far distance from stage, calling "share voices!" when necessary.	
(d) Singing dialogue.	

EXPLORE AND HEIGHTEN, p. 217 (transformation of the beat), should be used throughout all rehearsal sections. It fosters exploration of content and relationship.

Time Chart for Second Rehearsal Section

DIRECTION	PURPOSE
Relaxed Rehearsal	Removes anxieties. Helps actors visualize the total stage movement and environment (including himself or herself).
	Shows dialogue to be an organic part of play.
Complete non-stop run-through once a week from here on.	Continuity of play established. Speeds seasoning process.
Wear different costume parts.	
No interruptions (keep notes).	
(a) Rehearsals of individual acts. Stop and start.	(a) Heightens all facets of play.
(b) Stage movement—*did you integrate that?*	(b) Gives direction for action.
(a) Improvisations around problems (conflict) in play.	Strengthens individual characterization and group relationships; helpful in mass scenes.
(b) Improvisations away from the play. WHAT'S BEYOND?	Bring life and group agreement to on-stage scenes.
Gibberish. Spot rehearsals.	Freshens meaning of, and action behind, words. Creates new stage business.
NO MOTION.	Excites new energy from deeper sources.
Wearing costume parts, handling difficult props; check biographies. Barefoot rehearsals.	Gives further clues to help actor with character.
Acting problems based on situations in the play—reverse parts.	Helps develop insight into characters, play as a whole.
Spot rehearsals on business. Whenever show has difficult scenes, try them in a different way; play games, use space exercises.	Removes awkwardness, smoothes way for complex business. Gives new insights.

Time Chart for Third Rehearsal Section

DIRECTION	PURPOSE
Director re-reads play. Complete non-stop run-throughs more often. Makeup rehearsals.	Implements seasoning and learning process. Gives flow to play.
(a) Stop and start rehearsals of individual acts. Bring in interesting set-pieces.	(a) Heightens all aspects of play.
(b) SHADOWING. EXITS AND ENTRANCES. BEGIN AND END.	(b) Helps physicalizing, gives extra inspiration, creates extra stage business and heightens stage energy.
(c) Work on picking up cues, heightening speech and reactions.	(c) Pace and timing strengthened.
Spot rehearsals. Stage movement.	Gives actor insight into the role. Heightens moments in playing. Supportive.
Special run-through.	Group functions as one unit. Actors will meet every crisis during performances—will be able to assist each other.
Last week of rehearsal. Technical run-through, costume parade, makeup rehearsal.	Integrates technical aspects of production.
First Dress Rehearsal.	Integrates complete show.
Second Dress Rehearsal.	
Preview Performance.	Working for response with sympathetic audience.
Day of rest.	Relieves tensions of final week.
First Public Performance.	Full creative expression.

DIRECTING THE CHILD ACTOR[1]

Most of the non-authoritarian techniques for training and directing the actor for performance used in this handbook were originally developed for the sole purpose of retaining the joy of playing for children from six to sixteen at the moment of dedicating them to service in a great art form. Our boys and girls can learn to be players on stage and not exhibitionists. A great and overwhelming love for the theater can be instilled in them so that their performances have reality, exuberance, and a vitality that is exciting and refreshing to behold.

Children can and should be players in plays for children. The average viewer, unfortunately, has a deplorably low standard for child performers, and a clever imitation of adult clichés, blatant exhibitionism, or cuteness is often called talent. There is no need or excuse for distorting the child by imitation of the adult, nor, in trying to avoid this problem, is it necessary to limit the theater experience to dressed up dramatic-play.

A twelve-year-old may not be able to play a villain with the same psychological insight of an adult, nor would it be in good taste to do so. However, a child can keep the rhythm and line of a character and give it full energy. Like the adult, the child can develop the ability to select a few physical characteristics which are heightened in a role and brought sharply to the attention of the audience (See Chapter XII).[2]

Naturally there are plays with adult characters that are inappropriate for child actors, and such roles could well be distorting to the child. But, this same child can play adult characters that many fanciful plays call for.

As far as back-stage work is concerned, an eleven-year-old prop person can check a list like an adult. A twelve-year-old can follow a cue sheet and handle as many light cues as the play demands. The assistant stage man-

---

1. See also Chapters XIII–XV.

2. By changing the word "child" to "non-professional actor" and the word "adult" to "professional actor" in the context of the foregoing paragraphs, we can see that this same problem exists for the older lay actor as well.

ager (the stage manager should be an adult) can perform duties and exact discipline from actors who will respect his or her role.

For ten years, the Young Actors Company in Los Angeles, using no one but child actors from six to sixteen, played to city-wide audiences and received constant review on the drama pages of the metropolitan newspapers. The young actors were respected for the quality of their work and for the refreshment received by the audience from their plays. As actors, children can be as exciting and refreshing to view as adults, and they can learn to meet every crisis as it arises. At the Young Actors Company, and later at the Playmakers in Chicago, the ability to step into another's role (as a result of improvisational training) with little or no rehearsal was such that rarely indeed were there understudies for any part. Any message sent back stage, whether it was to get something off stage or to end a scene (improvisational theater), was handled effortlessly and ingeniously by the young actors within the action of the play.

One of the most difficult problems in rehearsing a show with children is adult regulation of their lives. Children cannot give all their time and attention to the activity and can rarely, for instance, say definitely that they will be at rehearsal, since parents may decide they must be somewhere else. They cannot be kept overtime, since the average child has an extremely active program of extracurricular events.

A few extra reminders when working on a play with children up to fifteen years old:

1. Do not be the "teacher" in the theater situation. There is only the director and the actors.

2. Always have an adult back stage to be in charge; this is usually an assistant or stage manager. Neither parents nor the director are ever allowed back stage during performance. At the Young Actors Company, there were always the strictest orders to keep the director out of back stage during the show. And the boys and girls knew they were allowed to enforce it.

3. For the children as well as the adults, have a call-board which they are to use.

4. All back-stage organization mentioned in this chapter is suitable for children.

5. All recommended rehearsal suggestions are to be followed by children as well as adults.

6. If children come to the theater after school, be certain there is some food for them. An energy drop often results just from being hungry.

7. Remind children repeatedly that "an audience does not know what the play is about" and thus that any mishaps can be turned into part of the play.

REMOVING AMATEUR QUALITIES

Many of us have sat through shows cast with children or non-professional adults where, aside from an occasional glimmering of natural charm or a moment of spontaneity, there was little or nothing to redeem the performance. The actors might, indeed, have been "expressing themselves," but they were doing so at the expense of the audience and the theater reality.

This section sets down some of the so-called "amateurish" qualities in young and inexperienced actors. It does so not only to aid the director in recognizing them but also to show their causes and refer to the exercises which will help free actors from crippling limitations.

The Amateur Actor

1. Has intense stage fright.
2. Does not know what to do with hands.
3. Has awkward stage movement—shifts back and forth, moves aimlessly about stage.
4. Must sit down on stage.
5. Reads lines stiffly, mechanically; forgets lines.
6. Has poor enunciation, rushes speeches.
7. Usually repeats a line he or she has misread.
8. Mouths the words of fellow actors as they are playing.
9. Creates no theater "business."
10. Has no sense of timing.
11. Drops cues, is insensitive to pace.

12. Wears costume awkwardly; makeup has a stuck-on look.
13. "Emotes" lines rather than talks to fellow actors.
14. Is exhibitionistic.
15. Has no feeling for characterization.
16. "Breaks" on stage.
17. Has a fear of touching others.
18. Does not project voice or emotions.
19. Cannot take direction.
20. Has slight relationships to other actors or the play.
21. Hangs on to furniture or props.
22. Becomes his or her own audience.
23. Never listens to other actors.
24. Has no relationship to the audience.
25. Casts eyes downward (does not look at fellow players).

This is a horrendous list, but the majority of child and adult lay actors possess at least ten, if not more, of these characteristics.

Causes and Cures

1. Stage fright is fear of judgment. The actor is afraid of criticism, of being ridiculous, of forgetting the lines, etc. When it occurs in a trained actor, it is usually the result of rigid authoritarian training. It can be overcome by a dynamic understanding of the phrases "share with the audience" and "showing, not telling."

2. Most immature actors use only the mouth and hands. When students learn to act with the whole body (physicalize), the problem of what to do with the hands disappears. In fact, it will never arise after student-actors understand the idea of the focus of an exercise, for they will always have a strong objective focus while on stage.

3. Awkward stage movement is usually the result of imposed stage direction. An actor who is trying to remember, instead of allowing stage movement to evolve out of the stage reality, cannot help but move awkwardly. Any object-involvement exercise will help here.

4. Some immature actors feel they must sit down on stage, or shift from

foot to foot because they are trying to "hide" from the audience. They lack focus and integration. WHERE WITH OBSTACLES, p. 101, will help here.

5. Mechanical reading is the result of not creating reality. Recitation of the words has become more important to the actor than an understanding of their meaning and relationships. They have remained "words" instead of "dialogue." See "Dialogue" (p. 358); SEEING THE WORD (p. 215); "Gibberish" (p. 112); "The Relaxed Rehearsal" (p. 314); and VERBALIZING THE WHERE (p. 118).

6. Poor enunciation and rushed speeches usually result from a lack of understanding on the actor's part that the audience is an integral element of theater. Poor enunciation also stems from the same source as mechanical reading. In the event that a real physical defect exists in the actor's speech, therapeutic exercises may be necessary. See Chapter X and EXTENDED SOUND, p. 206.

7. Lines misread and then repeated word for word are examples of rote memorization taking its deadly toll on spontaneity. Training by rote is also the cause of many other amateurish qualities. Meeting a crisis on stage should become second nature to even the youngest actor, who through training can learn to improvise through any problem of lost or misread dialogue (see Chapter I).

8. Mouthing of each other's words is caused by premature memorization and often by allowing young actors to take scripts home, where they memorize everything on the page.

9. The ability to create interesting stage business and blocking can come only from a real understanding of group relationships and involvement (see Chapter VI).

10. The sense of theater timing can be taught. Timing is recognition of others in the theater reality.

11. Dropped cues and failure to sense pace (like timing) occur when an actor is insensitive to an audience and fellow actors. *All exercises are geared to develop this sensitivity.*

12. The awkward appearance of an actor in costume and makeup may result from the failure to comprehend all the elements of the play (set

theme, fellow actors, relationships, etc.) as an integral whole. Or the player may have been given difficult costuming too late in the rehearsal period.

13. Declamatory acting or "emoting" results from isolation and using the stage subjectively. It is egocentric and exhibitionistic, for the actor is unable to relate the words to fellow actors and thus to the inner feelings which have caused them (see Chapter XI).

14. The exhibitionist, the "cute" child, the "ham"—these types result from approval/disapproval orientation and thus lack a sense of self (see Chapter I).

15. Everyone has a natural feeling for characterization in varying degrees (see Chapter XII).

16. When actors "break" or fall out of character on stage, they have lost sight of the internal relationships of the play and their focus as well.

17. This is resistance and fear of involvement. CONTACT and GIVE AND TAKE exercises do specifically what growing security in the training will do naturally (see pp. 171, 149).

18. Inadequate projection is caused by fear or neglect of the audience as fellow players.

19. The inability to take direction often stems from a lack of objectivity or inadequate communication between actor and director. The actor may not be free enough yet to meet his or her responsibility to the group. TELEVISION EXERCISE (p. 184) gives the student a look-in at the director's problems.

20. The actor with little or no relationship to fellow actors and the play stands on the ground floor of theater training. Playing games and using all the acting exercises of group involvement should help.

21. The actor who moves hesitantly about the stage, clinging from chair to chair, or moves aimlessly about the stage, is showing fear of being exposed to the audience, the central problem of non-professional theater. Stressing exercises of group interaction and sharing with the audience will help.

22. When actors move outside the play and become audience, they are seeking approval. Their focus is on themselves.

23. Failure to listen to other actors is a vital problem. It means the whole skein of stage relationships has been broken or never understood. BLIND (p. 158) is an especially valuable exercise specifically devoted to eliminating non-listening.

24. An audience's response comes to the seasoned actor (see p. 147). Be aware that the phrase "share with the audience" is the first and most important step.

25. The actor pulls everything into the immediate environment, making his or her world the size of a postage stamp. The exercises WHAT'S BEYOND? (p. 99), SPACE WALK and SPACE SHAPING (pp. 80–83), and CALLING-OUT EXERCISE (p. 208) should help break the fear of moving out into the larger environment. CONTACT and EYE CONTACT (pp. 171, 163) will alleviate fear of looking at another player.

The exercises in this book are not uniformly scaled to eliminate *single* problems. The exercises are cumulative and if used *simultaneously* will solve the above problems almost before they arise. In a short while students will all function organically, and when this occurs, the skills, techniques, and spontaneity needed in the theater will fast and forever *become their own*.

DEFINITIONS

DEFINITION OF TERMS

Teaching is necessarily repetitious, so as to make the material the students' own. The following terms are defined with this in mind in the hope that they will act as a further teaching tool. If they seem over-defined, it is because they attempt to fit as many readers' frames of reference as possible, so as to spark insights and thus clarify the intent of theater games.

ACT: To make something happen; to move out into the environment; to act upon.

ACTING: Avoiding (resisting) focus by hiding behind a character; subjective manipulation of the art form; using character or emotion to avoid contact with the theater reality; mirroring one's self; a wall between players.

ACTING PROBLEM: Solving the focus; a problem when solved results in an organic knowledge of the theater technique; a problem which prefigures a solution; developing theater techniques; theater games.

ACTION: The energy released in working a problem; the play between actors; playing.

ACTIVITY: Movement on stage.

AD-LIB: Not to be confused with improvisation; ad-lib is individual cleverness, not evolved dialogue.

ADVANCED STUDENT: A player who becomes involved in the focus of a game and lets it work for him or her; one who accepts the rules of the game and works to solve the problem; one who keeps the agreed reality alive; one who plays.

ASSUMPTION: Not communicating; letting fellow actors or audience detail a generality; letting others do actor's work; filling in for another player; *Show what you mean! Say what you mean!*

AUDIENCE (INDIVIDUALS): Our guests; the most revered members of the theater; part of the game, not the "lonely looker-inners"; a most important part of theater.

AUTHORITARIANISM: Imposing one's own experiences, frames of reference, and behavior patterns upon another; denial of self-experience to another.

AWARENESS: Sensory involvement with the environment; moving out into the environment.

BEAT: A measure; the time between crises; a series of scenes within a scene; can be one moment or ten minutes; "begin and end."

BECOMING AUDIENCE: Tendency to lose objective reality and begin to judge oneself as one plays a scene; looking out to audience to see if they "like" one's work; watching fellow actors or one's self instead of participating in the scene.

BELIEVING: Something personal to the actor and not necessary to creating stage reality.

BIOGRAPHIES: Information, statistics, background, etc., written about a character in a play in order to provide given categories to assist the actor in playing a role; sometimes useful in formal theater to help the director to gain insight into the actors; should be avoided in improvisational theater, for it prevents spontaneous selection of material and keeps players from an intuitive experience; "No biographies!"

BLOCKING: Integration of the players, set pieces, sound and light for the stage picture; clarity of movement for communication; emphasizing character relationship; physicalizing stage life.

BREAKTHROUGH: The point at which a student's spontaneity arises to meet a crisis on stage; the moment of "letting go" resistances and static frames of reference; a moment of seeing things from a different point of view; a moment of insight into the focus; trusting the scheme; the moment of growth.

BODILY AWARENESS: Total physical attentiveness to what is happening on stage and in the audience; skill in using all parts of the body (doors can be shut with feet, and a hip can move an object); physicalizing.

BODY MEMORY: Memory retained in the body at the point of past experiences; physical memory as opposed to mind or intellectual retention of past experience; sensory retention of past experiences; muscular attitudes; "Let your body remember!"

CHARACTER: People; human beings; real people; the physical expression of a person; speaks for himself or herself.

CHARACTER AGILITY: The ability to spontaneously select physical qualities of a chosen character while improvising; ability to use image, color, sound, mood, etc., to locate character qualities.

CHARACTERIZATION: Selecting certain physical mannerisms, tones of voice, rhythm, etc., in order to play a specific character or type of character; giving life to the character through the stage reality.

COMMUNICATION: Experiencing; the skill of the player in sharing stage reality so the audience can understand; direct experience as opposed to interpretation or assumption.

CONFLICT: A tug-of-war with one's self or between players calling for some decision; persuasion or goal to be reached; lack of agreement; a device for generating stage energy; an imposed tension and release as opposed to problem (organic).

CONTACT: Sensory impact; physical and visual involvement with the theater environment (Where, Who, audience, etc.); to touch, see, smell, hear, and look; to know what you touch; communication.

COSTUME PIECES: Partial costume bits which can be used in creating character; character costume suggestions as opposed to full-dress costumes (a box full of hats).

CREATION: Create (limited) plus intuit (unlimited) equals creation.

CRISIS: A heightened moment ready to change form; theater (playing) is a series of crises; alternative; the peak or breaking point of a static moment or situation where many eventualities are possible; a moment of tension in which the outcome is unknown; the player must be primed to meet any change, simple or extraordinary, the crisis may bring.

DETAIL: Every object, minute or massive, animate or inanimate, that exists within the stage environment.

DETACHMENT: Involvement with Who, Where and What (a direct experience); an optimum position; distancing oneself for better viewing (focus). Separation from our ego-centered self allows a relation free of emotional involvement.

DIAGNOSIS: The teacher-director's skill in finding out what problems are needed to solve problems.

DIALOGUE: Words actors use in talking to one another to implement and build the reality they have created on stage; a vocalization of the physical expression of the scene; verbal extension of the involvement and relationship between players; verbalization growing organically out of the life of a scene.

DIGNITY: Being one's self at any age; the acceptance of a person without trying to alter him or her.

DIRECT EXPERIENCE: A space where individual equipment is awake and alive to what is going on; your whole self attentive; a space for intuition to emerge to assist in the ongoing event.

DRAMATIC PLAY: Acting out and/or living through old (or someone else's) real-life situations to find out how to fit within them; common play among nursery school children attempting to become that which they fear, admire, or don't understand; identifying with characters in film, stage, and literature; living the character; not usable for the stage.

EGOCENTRIC: Fear of no support from others or from the environment; mistaken self-protection.

EMERGE: Appearing from the invisible; becoming visible; to come forth; revelation.

EMOTE: Imposing self on audience; role-playing instead of playing a role.

EMOTION: Organic motion created by the playing; subjective emotion carried to the stage is not communication.

ENERGY: Level of intensity with which one approaches the problem; the inspiration released when a problem is solved; the power held bound in resistance to solving a problem; the power released in "explosion" (spontaneity); diagnostic action; the result of process (playing); contact.

ENVIRONMENT: The conditioned stage life agreed upon by members of the group; all the animate and inanimate objects within the theater, including self and the audience; an explorable place.

EQUALITY: Not to be confused with sameness; the right of everyone of any age or background to become part of the theater community, enter into its activities, view its problems, work on them; the right to gain knowledge; the right to knock on any door.

EVALUATION: Method of criticism through involvement with the problem rather than each other.

EXPOSURE: Seeing or being seen directly, not as others would like you or themselves to be.

FEELING: Private to the actor; not for public viewing; feeling between players on stage must become the object between them; belongs to sensory equipment.

FLOORPLAN: A drawing or a plan (on paper or on a blackboard) of the structure for an acting-problem Where (the objects), Who (the actors), What (the activity), focus (the problem); a layout of the Where agreed upon and drawn up by a group of players; the "field" upon which the "game" will be played; a map of the territory the players must enter into and explore; groundplan.

FOCUS: Directing and concentrating attention on a specific person, object, or event within the stage reality; to frame a person, object, or event on stage; it is the anchor (the static) which makes movement possible. The point of concentration of a theater game that keeps players in process.

FRAME OF REFERENCE: A referral point on which judgments are made; a referral point from which one views the world; a reference conditioned (framed) by cultural, familial, and educational patterns.

GAME: An accepted group activity which is limited by rules and group agreement; fun, spontaneity, enthusiasm, and joy accompany games; parallels the theater experience; a set of rules that keeps a player playing.

GENERALIZATION: Occluded sensory perception; refusal to "give life to the object"; assuming others know what you are trying to communicate.

GHOSTLY VOICES: The past; emotional dependency on rules of behavior subtly woven into our own voices, psyche, and gestures by parents, teachers, spouses, institutions, employers, dictators, and culture.

GIBBERISH: Meaningless sounds substituted for recognizable words so as to force the players to communicate by physicalizing (showing); an acting exercise.

GOOD TASTE: Allowing something its own character without imposing anything alien upon it; adding nothing to detract from itself; a sense of the inherent nature of an object, scene, or character; it is one's recognition of the nature of something.

GROUP: A community of interests; individuals freely gathering around a project to explore, build, use, or alter it.

GROUP AGREEMENT: Group decision; agreed reality between players; agreed reality between players and audience; acceptance of the rules of the game; group agreement on focus; we cannot "play" without group agreement; breaks tie to teacher-director.

HEIGHTENING: Intensifying a relationship, a character, or a scene on stage; creating a high level of reality; giving a greater dimension to life reality; underlining life; enlargement of character or event for clarity in communicating to audience; to make a point through heightening; using anything or everything (acting, technical, or verbal) to make an impact.

HOW: Pre-planning How keeps the intuitive from working by plotting of a situation as opposed to meeting whatever comes up at the moment of playing; preparing one's self for every move as opposed to waiting to see what will happen; fear of venturing out into the unknown; giving examples of ways of solving the problem; performing.

ILLUSION: The theater is not illusion; it is a reality agreed upon by the group and understood by the audience; subjective projection.

IMAGINATION: Subjective; inventive; creating one's own ideas of how things should be; playing in the theater requires *group* creation as opposed to individually creating one's own idea of how things should be; belonging to the intellect as opposed to coming from the intuitive.

IMPROVISATION: Playing the game; setting out to solve a problem with no preconception as to how you will do it; permitting everything in the environment (animate or inanimate) to work for you in solving the problem; it is not the scene, it is the way to the scene; a predominate function of the intuitive; playing the game brings opportunity to learn theater to a cross-section of people; "playing it by ear"; process as opposed to result; not ad-lib or "originality" or "making it up by yourself"; a form, if understood, possible to any age group; setting object in motion between players as in a game; solving of problems together; the ability to allow the acting problem to evolve the scene; a moment in the lives of people without needing a plot or story line for the communication; an art form; transformation; brings forth details and relationships as organic whole; living process.

IMPROVISED PLAY: A scene or play developed from improvisation used for performance; group-created material; a scene or play developed from situation or scenario; play or scene evolving out of the group playing; not a "story conference."

INNER ACTION: Recognizing an emotion through sensory response; use of inner action allows player the privacy of personal feelings (emotion); using emotion as an object, "Physicalize that feeling!"

INSIGHT: A moment of revelation; seeing that which was there all the time; knowing:

> The tree was a tree
> Before you could see
> The tree.

INSPIRATION: Energy fortified with intuitive knowledge.

INTELLECT: The computer, collector of information, facts, statistics, data of all kinds; should not function separately; part of an organic whole.

INTERPRETATION: Giving one's frame of reference as opposed to directly relating to events; adding or subtracting from a direct communication; might cause inability to meet a fresh moment of experience.

INTRUDING: Telling how to solve the problem; showing actors how to walk, talk, emote, feel, and read lines; meddling; inability to "play."

INTUITIVE: The X-area; an area to be prodded and investigated by everyone; unhampered knowledge beyond the sensory equipment (physical and mental); the area of revelation.

INVENT: Rearrangement of known phenomena limited by personal reality; from the intellect; solo playing.

INVOLVEMENT: Earnestly entering into the game or exercise; playing; discipline is involvement; involvement with object creates release and freedom to relate.

JUDGING: Playing safe before you can act; no choice made to act spontaneously.

JUDGMENT: Subjective placement of good/bad, right/wrong based on old frames of reference, cultural or family patterns (personal) rather than a fresh response to a moment of experiencing; imposition.

LABELS: Terms which tend to obscure their origin and block organic knowledge; the use of labels limits one to "things" and categories and neglects relationships.

LEARNED RESPONSE: A reaction rather than an action; keeps players from moving out into the environment; keeps players from exploration and self-discovery; "That's no way to do it!" "Why?" "My teacher said so!"; a shut door.

LEARNING: The capacity for experiencing.

MANIPULATION: Using problem, fellow actors, etc., for egocentric purposes; being opportunistic; manifests itself by resisting relating to fellow players.

MIND: Flows through the physical brain.

MULTIPLE STIMULI: The many things coming out of the environment at the player which he or she must be aware of and act upon.

NO MOTION: A series of stills (steps) that create movement; an exercise in which movement is broken down into held parts and then reassembled back into movement; an exercise which shows students that since present movement includes past time, they need not dwell on the past; can be used to heighten time; gives insight into compulsive action; helps student to see his or her present (on-stage) environment and make contact with himself or herself within it.

NON-ACTING: Involving one's self with a focus; detachment; a working approach to all the problems of the theater; keeping one's personal feelings private; learning to act through "non-acting"; showing, not telling; "Stop acting!"

NON-DIRECTIONAL BLOCKING: Sharing the stage picture; self-blocking without outside direction; developing the skill to see the stage (outward) picture while inside it; group assistance from fellow players in blocking; necessary technique for the actor in improvisational theater; player's skill in evolving stage movement from the progressing scene; a way to self-identity; helps break dependency on teacher-director.

NON-VERBAL: Teaching without lectures on techniques for the actor; language used only to present and clarify or evaluate a problem; not telling the student How to solve a problem; not "spelling it out"; breaks dependency on the teacher-director; non-verbal system of teaching as used in this handbook; another form of communication between players.

OBJECT: Object and focus may be used interchangeably; sets the actor in motion; used for playing, as a ball, between players; involvement with object makes relationship between players possible; mutual focus on an outside reality (the rope between players); a technique to keep actors from subjective response; meditation; a mutual problem allowing freedom of personal expression in solving it; the springboard into the intuitive; the physicalization of an agreed object, feeling, or event out of which a scene evolves.

OBJECTIVE: Anything outside a person; to be objective; the ability to allow an outside phenomenon its own character and life; not changing what is to suit subjective assumptions; being objective is basic to improvisational theater.

OBJECTIVE REALITY: That which can be seen and used between players; created by group agreement; a means of sharing our humanness; a changing theater reality that springs from group agreement.

OCCUPATION: The stage activity; that which is created by the actors and visible to the audience; that which the audience shares with the audience; the What.

ORGANIC: A head-to-foot response where mind (intellect), body, and intuition function as one unit; in one piece; part of everything, of itself; out of itself; functioning out of total humanness.

PANTOMIME: An art form related to the dance; not to be confused with "silent scenes" or a "scene without words."

PAUSE: Seeing what is happening right now! Giving full attention to what is at hand, free of the past.

PERCEPTION: Knowing without use of the intellect alone; osmosis; awareness of outside phenomena; ability to reach out into the environment; to become the object; intuition; X-area.

PERFORMANCE: Not to be confused with exhibitionism; letting go; a moment of surrender creating harmony and refreshment; a moment of personal freedom.

PERSONAL FREEDOM: One's own nature; not mirroring others; an expression of self free of authoritarian (approval/disapproval) needs; freedom to accept or reject rules of the game; recognition of limitation and freedom to reject or accept it; not to be confused with license; freedom from emotionalism; a moment of reality in which one has a part in the construction; freedom from survival clothes; a private matter.

PERSPECTIVE: Looking into; an objective view; detachment; the long view.

PHYSICALIZATION: Showing and not telling; a physical manifestation of a communication; a physical expression of an attitude; using self to put an object in motion; giving life to the object; "Physicalize that feeling! Physicalize that relationship! Physicalize that pinball machine, kite, fish, object, taste, etc.!"

PLAYER: One who plays; person skilled in creating the theatrical reality; pulling rabbits out of a hat; an actor; a non-acting actor.

PLAYING: Fun, enjoyment, enthusiasm, trust; heightening the object; moving relations with fellow players; involvement with the focus; the physical expression of the life force; a term usable instead of rehearsal in improvisational theater. "Let's play!"

PLAYING A ROLE: Playing as in a game; playing a role and not subjective playing of self; sharing a characterization and not using a character for emotional outbursts; keeping self-identity.

PLAYWRITING: Manipulation of situation and fellow actors; an unwillingness to believe that a scene will evolve out of the group playing; not understanding the focus; deliberately using old action, dialogue, information, and facts (ad-libbing) instead of spontaneous selection during improvisation; not usable in improvisational theater; "Stop playwriting!"

POINT OF CONCENTRATION: A chosen agreed object (or event) on which to focus; a technique to achieve detachment; the object around which the players gather; involvement with focus brings relationships; "trust the focus!" a vehicle that transports the player; it opens the student-audience to receive the communication; preoccupation.

PREOCCUPATION: The energy source; that which is not visible to the audience; by creating two-way problems, preoccupation eliminates "watcher" and thus makes playing possible.

PRE-PLANNING: Planning how to work a scene as opposed to "just letting it happen"; related to "playwriting"; a mental rehearsal; "the uncertain child"; pre-planning is to be used only for structure.

PRETEND: Substitution for reality; subjective as opposed to real (objective); "If you pretend, it isn't real"; imposing self on a problem as opposed to creating reality; thinking about an object's reality instead of giving it reality; improvisational theater grows out of objective reality; not accepting *any* reality.

PROBLEM: Not to be confused with conflict (an imposed tension and release); a natural tension and release resulting in organic (dramatic) action.

PROBLEM-SOLVING: A system of teaching acting techniques through solving of problems as opposed to intellectualizing and verbalizing use of material; puts student-actor into action (physicalizes); problem prefigures a solution; teacher-director and student-actor can establish relationship through problem as opposed to involvement with each other; within solving the problem is How to play; does away with pre-planning; presents a simple operational structure (as in a game), so that anyone of any age or background can play.

PROCESS: The doing; process is goal, and goal is endless process; there can be no final statement on a character, relationship, scene, system of work.

PSYCHO-DRAMA: Putting one's own emotion into play to create action; living story instead of "in process."

REACT: Withdrawal; self-protection; response to another's act as opposed to self-acting; attacking to avoid changing position; making thrust into the environment instead of moving out into it; fear of acting; fear of taking responsibility for an action.

RECALL: Subjective memory (dead); deliberately bringing back a personal, private, past life-experience to get an emotional or character quality; confused by many with acting; to use past experience, deliberately evoked for a present-time problem, is clinical and can be destructive to the theater reality and artistic detachment; in spontaneous selection, the intuitive gives us past experiences organically as part of a total life process; can be used by a director as a *device* (when nothing else works) for getting a mood or quality; bringing back a past memory through manipulation; related to psycho-drama.

RELATIONSHIP: Contact with fellow players; playing; a mutual involvement with an object; relationship grows out of object-involvement; allows players the privacy of personal feeling while playing together; prevents intrusion or meddling.

RESISTANCE: Manipulation of Where, Who, What; unwillingness to understand and/or explore the focus; indicated by jokes, playwriting, clowning, withdrawal, "acting"; fear of changing in any way; resistance is held or bottled-up energy; when resistance is broken, a new experience takes place.

RESPECT: Recognition of another; to *know* one another.

RIGIDITY: Held in; inability to alter one's point of view; inability to see another's point of view; armored against contact with others; armored against ideas other than one's own; fear of contact.

ROCKING THE BOAT: Unbalanced stage; refers to self-blocking; "You're rocking the boat!"; a term for very young actors in teaching them self-blocking.

ROLE-PLAYING: As opposed to playing a role; imposing a character as opposed to creating a role out of the problem; psycho-drama; dramatic play; artificial imposition of character on self as opposed to allowing natural growth to evolve out of relationship; subjective response to "what is a character"; using a character to hide behind; a mask keeping one from exposure; withdrawal; solo performance.

RULES OF THE GAME: Includes the structure (Where, Who, and What) and the object (focus) plus group agreement.

SCENE: An event that grows out of the focus; the results of playing; a fragment; a moment in the lives of people needing no beginning, middle, or end, biography or statistics; the scene is the game coming out of the rules; playing is the process out of which the scene evolves by involvement with an object (focus) and relationship with fellow players.

SEASONING THE ACTOR: Integrating all parts of the whole (theater techniques, playing, showing, etc.); releasing ability to meet all crises with certainty; making one's self comfortable in the stage environment.

SEEING: Seeing (objective) as opposed to believing (subjective); a term used as opposed to imagining or pretending; "See it!"; part of the sensory equipment; to see so you can show; to let the audience see a play as in a game; skillful playing; to look; looking at the phenomenal world and *seeing* it; seeing as opposed to staring; looking and seeing as opposed to pretending to look and thus staring; "If you see it, we (the audience) see it!"

SEEING THE WORD: The physical reality of consonants and vowels; the visualization brought up by a word; a sensory contact with words; the design and shape of sounds.

SELF: Refers to the natural part of ourselves; free of crippling mores, prejudices, rote information, and static frames of reference; that part of us capable of direct contact with the environment; that which is our own nature; the part of ourselves that functions free of the need for approval/disapproval; cutting through make-up, costume, rags, mannerisms, character, junk jewelry, etc., that make up the covering (survival clothes) of self; self must be found before one can play; playing helps find self. Right brain; X-area.

SELF-IDENTITY: Having one's own place and allowing others theirs; securely placed within an environment; where you are is where *you* are.

SENSORY: Body and mind; to see, taste, hear, feel, think, perceive; to know through the physical as opposed to the intuitive.

SET PIECES: Random furniture, blocks, props used to make the Where.

SHARE WITH YOUR AUDIENCE: Brings harmony and relationship between players and audience; making audience "part of the game"; used in side-coaching to develop self-blocking; the same as rocking the boat used for very young actors; "Share your voice! Share the stage picture! Share yourself!"; used from the first workshop to accomplish self-blocking and voice projection; removes need for labels; develops ability to see the outside view of the stage while inside of it.

SHOWING: Physicalizing objects, involvements, and relationships as opposed to verbalizing (telling); spontaneous experience; the actor brings creation or invention into the phenomenal world by *showing*; physicalizing.

SIDE-COACHING: An assist given by teacher-director as fellow player to student-actors during the solving of a problem to help them keep focus; a means of giving a student-actor objective viewing within the theater environment; a message to the total organism; a support in helping players to explore the emerging plays.

SIGHT-LINES: The clarity of vision of an *individual* in the audience to every single *individual* at work on stage.

SITUATION: A Where, Who, What, and Why which becomes the structure for a scene; the framework (skeleton play) in which problem is placed; the situation is not the problem.

SKELETON PLAY: A set form for which improvisation is used; a scenario; a way of building an improvised play; a series of beats/scenes which must be filled in by the players.

SPACE: Something about which we know very little; the stage area where a reality can be placed; space can be used to shape the realities we create; an area of no boundaries; without limits; the player uses space to bring reality into the phenomenal world; to make space for the object; the larger environment; the space beyond; a place to perceive or receive a communication.

SPONTANEITY: A moment of explosion; a free moment of self-expression; an off-balance moment; the gateway to your intuition; the moment when, in full sensory attention, you don't think, you *act*!

SPONTANEOUS SELECTION: Selecting that which is appropriate to the problem without calculation; a spontaneous choice of alternatives at a moment of crisis; since theater is a series of crises, spontaneous selection should be working all the time; selecting out of the "explosion" that which is *immediately* useful; insight.

STAGE BUSINESS: A stage activity used to implement, accent, intensify, or heighten; the manner in which one plays the objects in the environment; the way the "ball" is kept bouncing; stage business grows out of involvement with objects and relationship with fellow actors; GIBBER-ISH is a special exercise useful to this point.

STAGE FRIGHT: The fear of disapproval or indifference; separation of audience and actors, placing audience as viewers or judges; fear of exposure; when audience is "part of the game," stage fright leaves.

STARING: A curtain in front of the eyes to prevent contact with others; playing for one's self only; a self-protective wall; "See us!"

STATIC: A held moment having what has happened and what will and/or may happen within it; crises.

STATISTICS: Giving audience and fellow players facts, information, and/or biographies about each other; telling, not showing; expressing a character verbally; using facts, past information, etc., instead of improvising and letting the character come forth; "No facts, no information, no biographies. Show us!"

STORY: A story is an epitaph; the ashes of the fire; story is the result (residue) of a process; improvisational theater is process; for story (play) to live, it must be broken down into its separate parts or beats (disassembled) to become process again; a well-written play is process.

STRUCTURE: The Where, Who, and What; the field on which the game is played.

STUDENT'S PROGRESS: Any distance a person has traveled from his or her starting point.

SUBJECTIVE: Self-involved; inability to contact the environment and let it show itself; difficulty in playing with others; defensiveness which makes it difficult to understand how to play the game.

SUGGESTIONS BY THE AUDIENCE: A primitive audience involvement; overtly making audience part of the game.

SURVIVAL CLOTHES: Behaviorisms, mannerisms, dress, I.Q., affectations, makeup, personality traits, frames of reference, prejudices, body distortions, opportunism used to protect ourselves in living; must be seen for what they are to be freed for the learning process; status.

TEACHER-DIRECTOR: Teacher works for the students (unblocking etc.), director works for the overall stage; presents problems for both the individual experience and the stage experience.

TELLING: Verbalizing the involvements, Where, etc., of a situation rather than creating a reality and showing or allowing the scene to emerge through physical attitudes, relationships, etc.; inaction; nonplaying; results of telling are ad-libbing, playwriting, manipulation; imposing self on object, not letting object move self; "acting."

THEATER REALITY: Agreed reality; any reality the players choose to create; total freedom in creating a reality; giving life to a created reality; allowing space for a created reality.

THEME: The moving thread (life) that weaves itself into every beat of the play and unifies all the elements in the production.

TIMING: Ability to handle the multiple stimuli going on within the theater activity.

TRANSFORMATION: Creation; momentarily breaks through isolation, and actors and audience alike receive (ahhh!) the appearance of a new reality (theater magic); improvisation.

TRUSTING THE SCHEME: Letting go and giving one's self to playing.

TWO-WAY PROBLEM: Gives focus to the intellect and thus preoccupies the actor so as to remove any inhibiting or censoring mechanisms that keep one from playing; blanks the mind; "I didn't know what I was saying"; preoccupation/occupation; releases intuitive levels of new energy.

VERBALIZATION: Players telling the audience about the Where and the character relationships rather than showing; teacher-director giving *his or her* knowledge to the student; excessive verbalization of subject matter; suggests egocentricity and/or exhibitionism; excessive verbalization on the part of student-actor is mistrust of self-ability to show; a cover-up; teaching through words as opposed to allowing student-actor to experience; teaching swimming verbally without allowing anyone in the water.

VISUALIZATION (IMAGE): The deliberate use of an existing form (animate or inanimate) to aid in creating a character or a dramatic moment; evoking stimuli for a character or feeling through a device outside of the scene involvement. Not recommended.

WATCHER: A constant "eye" upon us; a restrictive control; one who judges; approval/disapproval; fear of the "eye" keeps self hidden from fresh experience and brings forth a "dummy" self through posturing, delinquency, apathy, stupidity, wordiness; "a watched pot never boils."

WHAT: A mutual activity between actors, existing within the Where; a reason for being somewhere: "What are you doing there?"; part of the structure.

WHERE: Physical objects existing within the environment of a scene or activity; the immediate environment; the general environment; the larger environment (beyond); part of the structure.

WHO: The people within the Where; "Who are you?"; "What is your relationship?"; part of the structure.

WORDS: Gibberish, chatter; verbalizing for lack of action; "Just words!"; playwriting; words as opposed to dialogue; words "in place of"; keep self hidden.

X-AREA: See "Intuitive."

GLOSSARY

OF

SIDE-COACHING PHRASES

All side-coaching is given during playing and rehearsals. Actors do not stop to consider what is being side-coached. They *act!* When side-coaching begins to work for you and your cast, it is rarely realized as theatrical directing; a symbiotic connection results. Side-coaching excites to action and hurtles everyone into the present.

Act! Don't react! Act goes forward; *react* is internalized before going out.

Allow the focus to work for you! Should *relax* player. Helps release obsessive control. An *outside force* is working and helping.

Camera! Head-to-toe camera on——! Putting full focus and energy on another player.

Contact! Vowels and consonants! Attitude! Spell! Reminders.

Expand that gesture! Pause! Widens experience.

Explore that object! Ideal! Sound! Thought! Puts player into a meditative observation as exploration is sought.

Extend the sound! Reinforces movement, sight, thought, character.

Feel that! In your back! Feet! Head! Shoulders! An emotion takes over the whole body.

Follow the follower! Players *reflect* without initiating.

Give! Take! Take! Give! Awareness of others.

Give the ball (the word, the pause, the look) its time and space! A pause given. Time/space can be a very emotional stage moment. The same is true of a look, a word.

Gibberish! English! No time lag. No "should I or shouldn't I?" Now! Off-balance is built in. No time to think.

Heighten that moment . . . that feeling! Brings a brighter, broader, intensified experience.

Help your fellow player who isn't playing! Awakens cast to others' needs. Produces much stage business.

Keep your eye on the ball! Your fellow player! Your prop! Anchors player in movement.

Let your sight flow through your eyes! Let the sound flow through your ears! Let your mind flow through your brain! Useful for SPACE WALKS.

No motion! Stops excessive head control. Puts action and thought on a back burner.

No Motion on the inner dialogue! A waiting (not waiting for, but *in* waiting). Peripheral thought, ambivalent thought, is nowhere to be found.

No Playwriting! No acting! Reminds players to get "out of the head" and "into the space!"

No urgency! Helps player get "out of the head."

Occlude your fellow player! Occlude the Where! Occlude the audience! Gives a new relation with the occluded; adds sight by bringing the occluded into sharp focus, as in a closeup; keeps a player from hiding. Can bring out hidden character qualities.

Out of your head, into the space! Open for the communication! Useful to get rid of attitudes. Players move out into the stage space. Frees the intuition (X-area).

Pause! Time and space are given a moment on stage.

Physicalize that thought! Gives physical (body) expression to a budding, emerging emotion.

Reflect! Don't initiate! To reflect is to include another; to initiate is to deny yourself.

See! Allow yourself to be seen! Come out, come out, wherever you are.

See the ceiling! The walls! Look out the window! Awakens the actor to the Where.

See in Slow Motion! Players see and feel what is going on.

See unlabeled! Fresh sight is called upon.

Share the space between you! Meet in the middle. The between space is where the individual energies can meet. Produces artistic detachment, makes visible to the players what is happening in regard to character and emotion.

Share your voice! Produces projection, responsibility to the audience. Not simply a direction to speak louder; it helps to alert a player organically, without the need for a lecture, to the need for personal interaction with the audience.

Slow Motion! Brings players into the moment of their playing. Details become sharpened.

Stage picture! Helps players to see audience view. Brings players and audience into the stage space.

Stage whisper! Reminds players to whisper audibly. Intensifies relationships.

Stay out of it! Stops interfering. Stops controls.

Take a ride on your own body! View the scenery! Creates great artistic detachment.

Touch! Allow yourself to be touched! Expands the sensual world.

Use your whole body! Helps to physicalize emotions, feelings, thoughts, character.

You name it! You supply your own side-coaching.

APPENDIXES

NEW EXERCISES

The exercises in this appendix are arranged alphabetically. Through cross-referencing to chapters and page numbers, the list below suggests where these new exercises, not formerly included in this book, belong in its curriculum. These games are also included in the alphabetized listing on p. xxxv.

Other exercises new to this edition besides those in the appendixes include:

NEW EXERCISES

BOX FULL OF HATS

FOCUS: on selecting costume pieces for character quality.

▶ Teams of two or more players agree on Who, Where, and What and then pick costume pieces from the box full of hats to fit the scene. Alternatively, players may pick costume pieces at random, allow the costumes to suggest character qualities, and then choose Who, Where, and What based on their selections.

Your box of hats is simply as many costume pieces and small props as you can readily collect: old gowns, jackets, a chef's hat, a sailor's cap, headdresses, helmets, shawls, capes, blankets, sheets, paper wings, tails for animals, gloves, canes, eyeglasses, pipes, umbrellas, etc. A prop table might display balloons, feathers, chains, a jump rope, bell, ball, rubber band, bean bag, horn, egg beater, triangle, etc. Hang clothing on a rack with the box full of hats nearby. Old neckties may be used for belts, making it possible to use any size dress or coat by taking up extra length and girth.

SIDE-COACHING: *Share your voice! Keep objects in space—out of the head! Show! Don't tell! Become part of the whole! One minute to play!*

VARIATIONS

1. Once players have randomly selected and donned costumes, audience players determine Where, Who, and What for players.

2. In ANIMAL IMAGES, p. 241, an exercise which originated with Maria Ouspenskaya, the characters must all be animals (though they retain speech and other human qualities).

3. CREATING SCENES WITH COSTUMES on p. 292 is a children's version of this exercise.

BUILDING A STORY

FOCUS: on full physical attention to the word being spoken.

Part I

▶ Group sits in a circle, with side-coach, who selects one player to begin telling a story. At any moment in the telling, the coach points at random to another player, who must immediately pick up as the first player leaves off, even if he or she is in the middle of a word. Story continues with all being chosen to participate until its conclusion is reached.

SIDE-COACHING: *Keep the story going! Stay with the word! Share your voice! Aim for one story, one voice! Stay with the word! Keep the word in the space!*

Part II

▶ Divide group into two teams. One team of story-tellers sits facing the team of audience players and the side-coach. Starting with the player on stage right, and flowing from player to player across to stage left and then returning again to the player on stage right, the telling progresses as side-coached. Players first build about two sentences "*One word at a time!*" and then give "*Full sentences!*" Coach allows all players a sentence, then coaches "*Stop mid-phrase!*" Then "*Stop mid-word!*" Finally, in the growing evolution of the story, the coach calls for players to "*Physicalize!*" The players will in turn stand and physicalize their telling of the story in stage space until the story concludes. Reverse teams after evaluation.

SIDE-COACHING: *One word at a time! Full sentences! Stop mid-phrase! No repetition! Mid-phrase! Stop mid-word! Physicalize!*

EVALUATION: Did players stay with the word as the story evolved or were they caught up in the idea of where the story should go? Did it become one story told by one voice? Did the story keep building?

POINTS OF OBSERVATION

1. To keep involvement in the process high, coaching seeks to catch players off balance, often in the middle of a thought or a sentence.

2. Pre-planning what to say fragments and alienates players. Spontaneity results only when players stay with the moment the story is being told.

3. While BUILDING A STORY, Part I, usually involves a story emerging in the telling, the exercise could also be played as a *retelling* of material that is in the curriculum of the group, such as a lesson, a fairy tale, myth, or history. Focus is the same.

DODGE BALL

FOCUS: on keeping the ball in space and seeing it as others see it.

▶ Large group of ten or more stands in a circle trying to hit a center player with a space ball. If hit, center player exchanges places with the player who threw the ball. It is a foul to be hit above the waist.

SIDE-COACHING: *Throw and catch with your whole body! Keep your eye on the ball! Keep the ball in space! No hitting above the waist!*

EVALUATION: Players, was the ball in space or in your imagination? Audience, was the ball in space or were the players pretending?

POINTS OF OBSERVATION

1. If players do not leave this game with all the excitement, physical warmth and out-of-breath state that they have after playing a game with a real ball, then the players were pretending. Ask students what makes them breathe more heavily after a game; why their bodies require more oxygen.

2. The rule of "no hitting above the waist" is an amusing one inasmuch as there is no material ball. The rule is followed, however.

ECHO

FOCUS: on picking up and diminishing a sound without letting it stop.

▶ Two large teams stand in columns facing each other. First player in column 1 calls out a word or phrase. This is repeated by the first player in column 2 and repeated in turn by each succeeding player in column 2 without pause. Each player diminishes the sound so that the sound finally fades away at the end of the line. Then, first player in column 2 calls out a word or phrase for column 1 to echo and the game continues back and forth as above.

SIDE-COACHING: *Let the sound flow through each of you! Let sound slowly fade as it passes through you! Each column is one body—one sound—the echo!*

EVALUATION: Audience, did each succeeding player pick up the words without pause? Did the sound flow as one echo?

POINT OF OBSERVATION

This is an excellent lead-in to SINGING DIALOGUE, p. 207.

EXPLOSION TAG

▶ This game is a natural lead-in to SLOW MOTION/FREEZE TAG, p. 212. Establish a relatively small area. A 20-by-20-foot space is about right for fifteen players. Half the group plays and half becomes the audience. Play a regular game of tag within boundaries. When energy levels are high, coach players to take a moment to *Explode!* when tagged, in any way they wish.

SIDE-COACHING: *Remember to play within boundaries! Play tag within boundaries!* When energy level is high: *When you are tagged, take a moment to explode! While pursuing another player, keep exploding! Explode in any way you wish! Fall on the floor! Yell! Explode!*

POINT OF OBSERVATION

Explosion is a spontaneous action at the moment of being tagged. It helps crack players' protective armor.

FOCUS ON THE WORD FOR READING

FOCUS: on full physical attention to the words being read aloud.

▶ A group of equally skilled readers all silently read the same selection simultaneously. Side-coach taps a player to start reading aloud. All follow along silently word for word. Side-coach will switch the reading aloud from player to player at random. New reader called may not repeat the last word spoken by the previous reader or skip any words in the text. To keep the game challenging and fun, tell players that changes may be called mid-sentence.

SIDE-COACHING: *Share your voice! Keep your eye on the word! Stay with the word! Aim for one voice!*

EVALUATION: Did you notice any words repeated or skipped?

POINT OF OBSERVATION

This exercise uses the same focus as BUILDING A STORY, p. 381. The side-coaching often catches players off-balance, heightening energy levels and involvement.

GIBBERISH/ENGLISH

FOCUS: on communication.

▶ Introductory Demonstration: Choose two players to select a topic and conduct a conversation. Explain to the group that players will be coached to switch from English to Gibberish and back again, even if caught mid-word. Proceed to side-coach. Conversation is to flow normally and advance in meaning.

When playing is understood, divide workshop into teams of three. Many teams, each with its own side-coach, play simultaneously. After a time, call *''change!''* for the side-coaches so that all team members have a chance to side-coach and to converse in Gibberish/English with both teammates.

SIDE-COACHING: *Gibberish! English! Gibberish!* (and so on).

EVALUATION: Did the conversation flow and have continuity? Was communication maintained throughout? Players, do you agree?

POINTS OF OBSERVATION

1. This game develops side-coaching skills within all age ranges.
2. If Gibberish becomes painful for any player, immediately change to English for a time. In all side-coaching, help the player who withdraws energy from the problem.

3. The moment of change should be when the speaker is off-guard, in mid-word or sentence. In the off-balance moment, the source of new insights is tapped.

4. A group of four can play, one as interpreter, the others speaking Gibberish, if the class size is uneven.

GIBBERISH INTERPRETER

FOCUS: on following the follower with Gibberish.

A. Interpreting a Lecture

▶ Teams of two. One player gives a speech or lecture in Gibberish to audience players. The second player is the interpreter for the audience. The speaker pauses for the interpreter's translations and then continues in Gibberish. The interpreter "follows the follower" by reflecting the speaker's sound and meaning spontaneously in translation. The speaker reflects the interpreter by taking in the interpretation as if it accurately translates what was meant.

B. Three-Player Gibberish Interpreter

▶ Two players who speak different languages are both understood by a third player who sits between them and interprets for them in English. Conversation between the two Gibberish speakers flows through the interpreter. After a satisfying exchange, the player on stage right leaves and the other two move over, leaving a vacant seat on their left for a new player. The player in the middle chair is now the interpreter for a new round of play, and the game continues until everyone has been an interpreter.

C. Gibberish Interpreter with Where, Who, and What

▶ Teams of three or more players agree on Where, Who, and What so that at least one interpreter is needed. Scenes on foreign borders, parties for diplomats, hiring foreigners are possibilities.

SIDE-COACHING: *Interpreter, know what the speaker is saying! Follow the follower! Know what is being communicated!*

EVALUATION: Players, did the interpreter pass on what you communicated? Interpreter player, were you following the follower?

POINT OF OBSERVATION

These Gibberish games carry a great deal of enjoyment for everyone and can be used publicly. As there is non-verbal dialogue going on, follow-the-follower between the Gibberish-speaking players and the interpreter appears to a marked degree.

GIVE AND TAKE FOR READING

FOCUS: on giving and taking the opportunity (to read aloud).

▶ Simultaneously reading the same passage silently, all players *give* the opportunity to read aloud to any player who *takes* it. Only one player at a time can read aloud. Whenever he or she wants to, a player may *take* from another player the opportunity to read aloud. Frequent give and take is desirable. Skipping words or repeating the last words of the previous reader is not allowed.

SIDE-COACHING: *Give when someone takes! Take when someone gives! Stay with the exact words being read aloud! Only one player reads at once! Share your voice!* (Side-coach only as needed.)

EVALUATION: Did the reading aloud become one flowing piece as though just one person were reading, or did it stop and repeat itself?

POINT OF OBSERVATION

See GIVE AND TAKE/TWO SCENES, p. 149.

GIVE AND TAKE WARM-UP

FOCUS: on trying to move within the rules of the game.

▶ Players stand in a circle. One (any) player may *take*; start a movement, and when any player takes, all other players must *give*; hold their own movement, waiting to move. Any player can take (move) at any time, in the space of the circle, but must hold if another player starts a motion. Sounds may be considered taking.

SIDE-COACHING: *Hold when another player takes! Give! Take! Even the slightest movement takes it! Hold your movement—ready to continue the flow of your movement when the chance arises! Take! Give!*

EVALUATION: None.

POINTS OF OBSERVATION

1. Even a beginning group can play this game successfully.
2. Players sensing another player taking are said to be giving.
3. The word "hold" is used instead of "freeze." "Freeze" is total stoppage; "hold" is waiting to move as soon as one can do so.

JUMP ROPE

FOCUS: on keeping a rope in space—out of the head.

▶ The rope is made of space substance. Have players count off into teams of four or more or allow random groupings. Each plays its own game of jump rope with some players turning the rope while the other players jump. Play until everyone has had a chance to turn the rope. The jumper who misses the rope must exchange places with a player turning rope, as in the regular jump rope game.

SIDE-COACHING: *Stay on the same rope! Keep the rope in space! Use your whole body to play the game!*

EVALUATION: Did players keep the rope in space? Or was it in their heads?

POINT OF OBSERVATION

Every age group enjoys jump rope. Variations are Double Dutch, High and Higher, Lindy Loop, etc.

MIRROR SOUND

FOCUS: on mirroring a partner's sounds.

▶ Teams of two players sit facing each other. One player is the initiator and makes sounds; the other is the reflector and mirrors the sounds. When *Change!* is called, roles are reversed. The reflector becomes the initiator; and the new reflector mirrors his or her sounds. Change-overs must be made with no stop in the flow of sound. Teams gather in different spots around the room and play simultaneously as all teams are side-coached at once.

SIDE-COACHING: *No pause! Notice your body/physical feeling as you mirror your partner's sound! Change the mirror! Keep the sound going! Reflect the sound! Change! Change!*

POINTS OF OBSERVATION

1. Players communicate orally but nonverbally. Sounds can be loud or soft, humming or shouting. Variety is desirable.

2. In both classical and jazz music, one hears theme or rhythm played by one instrument and then repeated with variations by others.

3. The next time you present this exercise, try dividing the group into teams of three. The third player side-coaches the other two. When you call "*New side-coach!*" the role of side-coach goes to another player. All teams play simultaneously.

MIRROR SPEECH

FOCUS: on mirroring/reflecting another player's words out loud.

▸ Teams of two players face each other and choose a subject to discuss. One player is the initiator and starts the conversation. The other player is the reflector and mirrors *out loud* the words of the initiator *at the same moment*. After a time, *Change!* is called and roles are reversed. Change-overs must take place with *no stop* in the flow of words. After a time, call more changes. Players will follow the follower in speech, thinking and saying the same words simultaneously and without conscious effort.

SIDE-COACHING: *Reflector! Stay on the same word! Reflect what you hear! Reflect the question! Don't answer it! Share your voice! Change the reflector! Keep the flow of words between you! Stay on the same word! Change! Change!* (When players are speaking as one voice, without time lag) *You are on your own! Follow the follower! Don't initiate! Follow the follower!*

EVALUATION: Audience players, did onstage players stay on the same word at the same time? Players, did you know when you initiated speech and when you reflected speech? Did you know when you were following the follower? All players, what is the difference between repeating speech and reflecting speech?

POINTS OF OBSERVATION

1. If a question is asked, coach reflector to *reflect*, not answer it. Coach initiators to avoid questions.

2. The whole body, the senses, must feel the difference between repeti-

tion and reflection of the words of the other player before "follow the follower" can take place. When true reflection takes place, the time lapse between initiator and reflector becomes very short, near nothing. In a sense, players connect with one another on the same word and become one mind, open to each other. Following the follower verbally creates dialogue.

3. If time is limited, teams of three (one being side-coach) can play simultaneously in different areas of the room.

4. This game can also be played silently. See MIRROR/FOLLOW THE FOLLOWER, p. 62.

OCCLUDING

FOCUS: on occluding as side-coached.

▶ Two or more players choose Where, Who, and What. During playing, they must stay fully with whatever they are side-coached to occlude. Occluding means *shutting out or shutting in*, not ignoring, that which is being occluded.

SIDE-COACHING: *Occlude the Where! Occlude fellow player(s)! Occlude the activity! Occlude the character!*

EVALUATION: Did occluding each other help players heighten their relation to each other? To the Where? To the activity? Players, do you agree?

POINTS OF OBSERVATION

1. The player, while occluding the subject, is at the same time embracing it. How can this happen? Like many other games, OCCLUDING is a paradox: the brain tries to figure out how to be aware of that which must be occluded (shut in or shut out). This produces a magical off-balance moment, one of the gateways into the intuitive. The invisible becomes visible.

2. What we want to make happen is the acceptance of the invisible as a connection between players and audience; connection (relating) being the real communication.

3. The player's mind is emptied (freed) of all manifestations of attitude or interpretations. This emptying allows energies to flow and players to become part of what is actually happening.

4. Occluding the Where, which was chosen along with Who and What, can be the focus of the scene. If coached to occlude the Where, players' relation (Who) becomes stronger than usual since there is nowhere to turn except to their fellow player.

5. A player in the pre-murder Macbeth scene, when side-coached *"Occlude Lady Macbeth!"* became a most dangerous character, a passive man with a dagger in his hand.

6. See SPACE WALK III (TOUCH & BE TOUCHED/SEE & BE SEEN), p. 83. OCCLUDING can be used as a side-coach in space walks.

PLAYGROUND

FOCUS: on keeping play objects moving in space.

▶ Full group divides into teams of differing size which move around the room and begin to play different games simultaneously as on a playground. Each team chooses a playground game requiring equipment or play objects, such as a ball game (baseball, basketball, volleyball, etc.) or a game using toys, like jacks, marbles, or tiddlywinks. All games are played with space-substance objects. All rules of the chosen game must be followed. Players must keep the ball or equipment in the space and out of their heads. The side-coach moves from group to group and joins in if needed to add to the playing.

SIDE-COACHING: *Use your full body to throw the ball! Heighten that movement! More energy! Heighten! Keep your eye on the ball!*

EVALUATION: Audience, was the playing object only an idea? Was it in the space or imaginary? Players, do you agree?

POINTS OF OBSERVATION

1. Players who are beginning to grasp the idea of playing with space-substance objects fill the whole playing area with excitement, energy, and fun. Viola Spolin reportedly saw as many as five innings of baseball played with space objects.

2. PLAYGROUND can be used often. It will benefit from audience evaluation (play it with half the group as audience) and allow audience teams to *side-coach*!

SPACE SUBSTANCE INTRODUCTION (FOR HANDS)

FOCUS: on the space substance between the palms of players' hands.

Part I

▶ Divide group into two teams—players and audience. Coach the first team, who work individually, to stand with the palms of their hands facing, and to focus on the space substance between the palms of their hands. Coach them to move hands up/down, close together/far apart, to feel the space material between the palms of their hands and to play with it.

SIDE-COACHING: *Focus on the space material between your palms! Move hands back and forth! Up and down! Anywhere! Keep palms always facing! Feel the space material between! Play with it! Let it thicken!*

Part II

▶ Two players stand opposite each other, two or three feet apart, with the cupped palms of one player facing the cupped palms of fellow player. Coach players to keep focus on the space substance between the four palms of their hands, and to move it about as side-coached. Many teams can play simultaneously if time is short, or divide the group so that a number of audience team players can have the benefit of watching the game played.

SIDE-COACHING: *Face a partner! Two palms facing two palms of partner! Feel the space substance between the four hands! Play with the space material! Move it about! Use your whole body! Focus on the space between your palms and let it thicken if it does!*

EVALUATION: Audience, did players let focus on space substance work for them? Did the players imagine the space material or did they really feel it? Players, do you agree? Did space material begin to become thicker for you?

POINTS OF OBSERVATION

1. The exercise quickly gives players an experience of space substance. However, players must in time let the partial focus on palms of hands dissolve in order to feel head-to-toe freedom to play with and respond to this most unique "stuff."

2. Students studying chemistry will be aware that air is a "substance" (oxygen mixed with other gases) which does not exist in outer space or on worlds like the moon, which has no atmosphere.

SPACE WALK/ATTITUDE

FOCUS: on walking without attitude, then on adopting the walk of others without attitude.

Part I

▶ All players form a line. One walks forward in a neutral walk (without attitude) however far the space allows and returns. The others move forward and return as a group, nonjudgmentally adopting the walk of the previous player. The exercise continues until all have walked, and their walks have been adopted by fellow players.

SIDE-COACHING: To solo walker: *Allow your own walk! Allow yourself to be yourself!* To group walkers: *Show us the head! The shoulders!* etc. *Don't hesitate to use slight exaggeration!*

Part II

▶ Divide the group; half play while the other half become audience. Coach players to "think of the physical body of someone you know as you walk: parent, friend, or enemy." Tell them to use slight exaggeration if necessary. Players work individually while walking.

SIDE-COACHING: *Think of someone you know! Take on his expression! Her rhythm!*

EVALUATION: Discussion: "I became my parent!"

POINT OF OBSERVATION

This game can produce great fun and laughter. It is useful for character development.

SPELLING

FOCUS: on communicating to another player.

▶ The whole group breaks into teams of two or three. They hold conversations, spelling their words.

SIDE-COACHING: *Spell sensually! See the letters! Physically see the words in your mouth!*

EVALUATION: How much of the conversation was understood by the listeners? Spellers, did you see the letters?

POINTS OF OBSERVATION

1. Continue as long as spirits are high and all conversing is fluent. The excitement of a connection with fellow players will appear.

2. After players are familiar with the game, choose a small section of a script to read, spelling.

STAGE PICTURE

FOCUS: on sharing the stage picture with the audience.

▶ Players move in and out and around each other until teacher-director calls out *Stage picture!* Instantly, players stop moving. If some part of each and every player is not visible to the audience, continue to side-coach *Stage picture!* Players then instantaneously move, doing whatever will make a part of them visible. Many random formations appear as players bend knees, raise arms, duck heads in response.

SIDE-COACHING: *Stage picture! Continue! Any part of you is all of you! Stage picture! Continue!*

Variation I

▶ Continuous moving stage picture. All players keep visible at all times while group stays in constant movement.

SIDE-COACHING: *Stage picture! Stage picture! Stage picture!*

Variation II

▶ Following one player. Players all move in and out and around one another. When coach calls one player by name, all other players follow this one player in space until *Hold!* or *Stage picture!* is side-coached.

SIDE-COACHING: (Name one player; when movement has led to formation): *Stage Picture!* (Name another player; when movement has led to formation): *Stage Picture!*

Variation III

▶ Divide group into two teams; one observes. The other team plays and the audience team infers a Where/Who/What from their positions as each stage picture appears.

EVALUATION: For Variation III: Audience, how did you reach your conclusions? Players, how does your sense of the stage picture match what the audience saw?

POINT OF OBSERVATION

The recognition that any part of you is all of you is given by this game, which also carries the implicit message that visibility is essential to stage life.

STAGE WHISPER WARM-UP

FOCUS: On releasing throat muscles and pouring full-body energy into an audible stage whisper.

▶ All players, seated, with both feet on the ground, are to pant out loud, trying to open their throats as much as possible. As throat muscles relax, coach players to add vocal sounds to the panting. (If a slight dizziness occurs, simply stop the exercise for a while.) When side-coached, players repeat simple words and numbers or rhymes using a stage whisper. For example: "Two, four, six, eight! Who do we appreciate?"

SIDE-COACHING: *Release throat muscles! Try to get that open throat! Add sound! Two! Four! Six! Eight! Push sound from the bottom of the feet on up and out!*

EVALUATION: Where did you feel the energy coming from for the stage whisper?

POINT OF OBSERVATION

A stage whisper is not a true whisper, for it must be shared with an audience and in a sense is "acting out" a whisper. If done properly, the voice will be resonant.

THREE-WAY CONVERSATION

FOCUS: for center player, on holding two conversations simultaneously; for end players, on holding a single conversation with center player only.

▶ Player A sits between two end players (B and C). Each end player chooses a topic and engages in a conversation with the center as if the other end did not exist. Center must converse with both ends, responding and initiating when necessary, fluent in both conversations and not excluding either end player. After allowing sufficient time to converse, rotate players by coaching *Next!* New player comes up and bumps one end player to the center and the center player to the other end, thus losing an end player. In this way, all players will have a chance to occupy both center and end positions. To make the game challenging, tell players they must avoid questions and answers to questions.

SIDE-COACHING: *Speak and hear at the same time! Take your time! No questions! Let conversations go where they will! Share your voice! No answers! Speak and hear at the same time!*

EVALUATION: Did players avoid asking questions? Did A stop hearing B while listening to C? Did ends pick up from each other? Did players reach the heart of their separate conversations? Did center player initiate conversation too?

POINTS OF OBSERVATION

1. Simple questions as to personal opinions and information are discouraged as these offer the center player a time lag which creates two separate conversations instead of two being held simultaneously.

2. This exercise develops alertness to multiple incoming data.

3. WANDERING SPEECH, p. 169, offers an earlier variation in which center and end players add Where, Who, and What to the above rules and play by that structure.

UNRELATED CONVERSATION

FOCUS: on extending full-body attention to the one speaking, and never agreeing, disagreeing, or answering.

▶ One player in a conversational group of two or more players begins speaking on any subject. Other players listen, giving full physical attention to the speaker. After a time, any other player may begin to speak on a completely unrelated subject. All players give this new speaker full body attention. Each player maintains his or her original subject when breaking back into the speaking role.

SIDE-COACHING: *Give the one speaking your full body attention! Listen with your feet! Listen with your eyes! Spine! Top of your head! Shoulders! Pick up the conversation whenever you want! Break in! Stay with your own unrelated conversation! No agreement! No disagreement! Physical attention!*

EVALUATION: Did you give the person speaking your full body attention? Did you feel a connection with that other person? Were you able to stay with your own unrelated subject?

POINTS OF OBSERVATION

1. This exercise shows that the full body is required in listening.

2. Body attention creates a flow felt among players. Side-coach everyone whose attention drifts away from the one speaking. Players are con-

nected by body attention to one another and not by language or sub-ject matter. This is excellent when used during rehearsal.

VOWELS AND CONSONANTS

FOCUS: on contacting the vowels or consonants in a word as it is spoken.

Part I

▶ Six or eight players stand in a circle or in two lines facing each other. Each player is to begin a quiet conversation with the player opposite (eight play-ers means four simultaneous conversations). Players are to focus on either the vowels or consonants, as side-coached, in the words they speak, with-out putting emphasis on them or changing speech patterns.

SIDE-COACHING: *Vowels! Consonants! Talk normally! Vowels! Feel the vowels! Touch the vowels! Let the vowels touch you! Consonants! Focus on the consonants!*

Parts II & III

▶ Keeping voices low, players are to move back away from each other as far as space permits and then forward again, as side-coached.

SIDE-COACHING: Part II: *Vowels! Move back from each other! Speak more softly than before! Consonants! Move as far back as possible! Vow-els!* Part III: *Now move in closer! Consonants! Speak more softly yet! Vowels! Close your eyes! Speak as quietly as possible! Consonants! Open your eyes! Move into your first position! Finish the conversation!*

EVALUATION: Did you have a sense of making physical contact with the word spoken? Was communication maintained throughout? Did meaning emerge in the space between the vowels and consonants?

POINTS OF OBSERVATION

1. Wait until players are attentive to partners before coaching them to move away from each other. Players actually can lower their voices considerably as they put distance between them; conversations can be held in a murmur from as far away as fifty feet.

2. The side-coaching to *Close your eyes!* opens players to the fact that they are not lip reading. The whole body, from head to foot is involved with the spoken word.

3. This exercise acquaints players with the physiological structure of lan-

guage, bringing a respite from subjective thought or interpretation. Have players think of words as sound which they shape or design into word patterns.

4. When coached to *Finish the conversation!* players usually have animated conversations.

WHERE WITH HELP AND HINDER

FOCUS: on helping or hindering fellow players' contact with objects in the environment.

▶ Two players agree upon Where, Who, and What, and also prepare a detailed floorplan. Players then make contact with every object in the Where while maintaining relationship and activity. When coached to *"Help!"*, players help one another make contact. When coached to *"Hinder!"*, players throw up obstacles to one another to prevent the other from contacting the objects. Helping or hindering must be integrated with the structure.

SIDE-COACHING: *Help each other make contact with the objects! Now keep each other from contacting the objects! Work on the problem! Help! Hinder! Help! Hinder! Integrate contacts! Integrate obstacles! Avoid dialogue!*

EVALUATION: Did players contact the objects through Who they were and What they were doing, or was contact random, made simply to touch the objects? When did the Where appear? Players, do you agree?

POINTS OF OBSERVATION

1. The game is over when both players have made contact with everything in the Where. However, it may be necessary to call *"One minute!"* to heighten the playing before achieving completion.

2. Ask for a great deal of detail in the floorplans.

3. No particular tension between players is necessary.

WHO AM I?

FOCUS: on involvement in the immediate activity until the *Who* is revealed.

▶ Whole group or large teams. One player leaves the room voluntarily while everyone else decides who the player will be, ideally someone who is often surrounded by much activity or institutional life. Examples include histori-cal characters or interesting professionals (union leader, cook in the Vati-can, circus barker, etc.) When Who is agreed upon and known by all pres-ent, the first player is asked to return. He or she then enters the playing area, sits stage center, and is told to "act as if you know who you are." The others enter in relation to the Who (one at a time or in small groups) and become involved in activity appropriate to Who and Where, until the player knows who he or she is.

SIDE-COACHING: *Who you are will become clear! Don't try to guess! Other players, give no clues! Show! Don't tell! Don't give it away! No hurry! Wait! It's not a guessing game! Show!*

EVALUATION: Did the player try to guess the Who or did she or he wait until what was happening made it clear? Player, do you agree?

POINTS OF OBSERVATION

1. *Who* will emerge if the player remains open (in waiting) to what is hap-pening and involved in the immediate activity. The most difficult part of WHO AM I? is to keep the unknowing player from making it a guessing game and the others from supplying clues.

2. The exercise reaches its natural ending when the unknowing player shows by word or deed that *Who* has surfaced. Players may, however, continue the scene after *Who* is known.

3. Choosing famous people might best be avoided until after the group is familiar with the exercise.

4. After the focus is clearly understood, WHO AM I? can be used in regular curriculum study of historical persons, scientists, engineers, inventors, authors, etc. Focusing on the immediate environment (Where) will bring greater understanding of the chosen subject.

5. WHO AM I? requires that players build a character through showing, not telling.

TRADITIONAL GAMES

The exercises in this appendix are arranged alphabetically as follows:

Beast, Bird, or Fish
Buzz
Concentration
Crambo/I'm Thinking of a Word
Don't Let Go
Dumb Crambo
Geography
Ghost
How Much Do You Remember?
My Ship Is Coming from London
Name Six
New York
Numbers Change
Object Relay
Ocean Wave
Proverbs
Pussy Wants a Corner
Red Light/Green Light
Rhymes
Rhythm
Singing Syllables
Single File
Streets and Alleys

Swat Tag

Transformation of Words

When I Go to California

In addition to the games listed above, the following traditional games appear elsewhere in this book as noted.

TRADITIONAL GAMES

Most of the traditional games included in this edition come from Neva Boyd's *Handbook of Recreational Games*.[1] Miss Boyd was Viola Spolin's key teacher and Viola has dedicated this book to her. No Spolin workshop ever started without a lively game.

As Viola has said, "A workshop is a sequence of activities with a theater game or group of theater games at its core. Each session has a beginning, a middle, and an end. Warm-up games and/or lead-in games prepare players for the day's offerings of theater games, and wrap-up games (like warm-ups) bring players together as a group and help focus energies for the next learning experience."[2]

In the foreword to her *Handbook*, Boyd states "The discipline of making judgments, often instantaneously, and of acting upon them within a static

1. Neva Boyd, *Handbook of Recreational Games*, foreword (New York: Dover, 1975; reprint of *Handbook of Games* [Chicago: H. T. Fitzsimons, 1945]).

2. Viola Spolin, *Theater Games for the Classroom* (Evanston: Northwestern University Press, 1986), p. 11.

frame of reference, i.e., the verbalized rules, is unique to the playing of games. While the game is an imaginatively set up structure into which the players project themselves psychologically, they act consistently with the demands of the situation, and thereby subject themselves to self-imposed discipline, which involves many aspects of social behavior."[3]

Some traditional games have been in this book since it first came out, but, as many readers are probably aware, most of the others now found here appeared first in Spolin's *Theater Game File*, her *Director's Handbook*, and her *Theater Games for the Classroom*. All are listed alphabetically above, as well as in the general alphabetical listing of exercises, p. xxxv. The games included in this edition were chosen because Spolin played them with her students. Whenever workshop energy flags, follow her advice: "Play a game!"

Neva Boyd also says in the foreword to her handbook: "The vitality of the game lies in the creative process of playing it. The omission of any suggestion of specific values is intentional. Games are the organized accumulation of play-behavior, and since play-behavior is centered largely in the thalamic region of the nervous system, and is therefore closely related to the outside world, every player has access to the stimulation of the dynamic process, and of necessity gets values out of his (or her) own experience. Because this is true, any attempts to set up values as goals for the players would tend to defeat the possibility of their experiencing these values spontaneously."

It is common knowledge that the spirit of traditional games is deeply rooted in our history and folk life. To quote J. Christian Bay, in his foreword to Boyd's *Folk Games of Denmark and Sweden*: "Every trait in the daily life, diversion and festive display of the people has grown out of centuries of usage. On the whole [these games] express ideals as old as the earth itself; and the fundamental thought in the life of any people is to keep the faith of the forebears." Viola added, "These games touch us, in short, where we are most human."[4]

---

3. Viola Spolin always said "Discipline is involvement!" See p. 264.
4. Viola Spolin, *Theater Games for the Classroom*, p. 24.

BEAST, BIRD, OR FISH   (Boyd, p. 101)

▶ I. Players sit in chairs in a circle with one in the center. The center player points to one of them and says, "Beast, bird, or fish?" and then repeats one of the three categories—for example, "fish"—and counts to ten.

The player being pointed to must name a fish before the center player finishes counting. Failure to do so, or repetition of a name already given, requires changing places with the one in the center.

II. Center player says "Beast, bird, or fish?" and adds, for example, "Vulture," whereupon the other must say, "bird."

BUZZ   (Boyd, p. 97)

▶ The players are seated in a circle. One player starts the game by saying "one"; the next says, "two"; the counting proceeds around the circle until the number seven is reached, for which the word "buzz" is substituted.

The players continue counting, always substituting "buzz" for any number in which the digit seven occurs, such as seventeen or twenty-seven. "Buzz" is also substituted for any number which is a multiple of seven, such as fourteen or twenty-one. Upon reaching seventy, the counting proceeds as "buzz-one," "buzz-two," etc. Seventy-seven is "buzz-buzz."

The player who says "buzz" in the wrong place, gives a number when he or she should have said "buzz," or calls a wrong number, drops out of the game. Counting continues from where the mistake was made. The game proceeds until all are out.

CONCENTRATION   (Boyd, p. 103)

▶ This game is played with a complete deck of cards placed face down in rows upon the table. The aim is to match the cards in pairs: two fives, two aces, etc. The first player turns up a card, lays it face up *in its place*, and then turns up another. If they make a pair, the player may take them, turn up two more as described, and continue until unable to make a pair.

The player then turns down the cards *in the order in which they were turned up*. This is done to permit all players to memorize the cards and their positions. The players continue in turn until all the cards are matched. Quiet and concentration are necessary in playing this game. The player who has the most cards when all are picked up wins the game.

CRAMBO/I'M THINKING OF A WORD (Boyd, p. 98)

FOCUS: on defining and on rhyming.

▶ The players sit in a circle. The first player says, "I'm thinking of a word that rhymes with 'sing' " (giving out any word that rhymes with the word kept in mind). The player to the left defines a word that rhymes with 'sing,' asking, for example, "Is it part of the equipment found on most playgrounds?" The first player answers, "No, it is not 'swing.' " Players, in turn, continue to define words that rhyme with 'sing,' and the first player answers each with, "No, it is not 'fling,' 'king,' etc.," until someone's question defines the word in mind. Then the first player says, "Yes, it is . . ."

If the player had *ring* as worn on one's finger in mind, he or she would say, "No, it is not 'ring,' " if asked by someone "Is it the tolling of a bell?" In other words, the *definition*, not the word, is the determiner. The player who defines the word that the first player has in mind gets the next turn to start the game.

If the first player does not guess the word that has been defined, the player who gave the definition begins the game again with another word.

Proper nouns are not permissible, and the word given by the first player must have the same number of syllables as the word of which he or she is thinking.

DON'T LET GO (Spolin, *Theater Games for the Classroom*, p. 29)

▶ Players form a single line, holding hands. The player at the head of the line begins to lead it around the room. By reversing, turning, and doubling back upon itself in a serpentine configuration, the head of the line crossing other points of the line, the line will tie itself in a knot, unable to move further. Now, the end of the line begins to unwind and continues to do so until the players have become untangled.

SIDE-COACHING: *Don't let go! Don't let go!*

POINTS OF OBSERVATION

1. The more interweaving and reversing the head of the line does, the tighter the knot will become.

2. This is a playground game quiet enough to be played indoors.

DUMB CRAMBO   (Boyd, p. 100)

FOCUS: on dramatizing a word.

▶ The players are divided into two groups (or three, if possible), one of which leaves the room while the other chooses a verb that can be dramatized. When the outside group is called back, they are given a word which rhymes with the verb that has been chosen. After consulting among themselves, the members of the group that left the room act out the verb they think is the correct one. If it proves to be so, the other group applauds; if not, they shake their heads. The guessing group continues to act out verbs until the correct one is discovered, whereupon this group chooses a verb for the other group to act upon. Should a group be forced to give up, that group must continue to act a new word chosen by the other group.

A variation is for a single player to be sent out while the group chooses a verb. The player then returns and, after being told a word which rhymes with the verb chosen, acts out verbs until he or she gets the correct one.

GEOGRAPHY   (Boyd, p. 96)

▶ Players sit in a circle. One begins by naming a city, Denver, for example. The next player must name a city beginning with "r," the letter with which the first player's word ended, thus saying "Rockford," and so on.

Any player who fails to name a city within a reasonable length of time is permanently out of the game. No name may be used more than once, even though there may be many cities of that name. The game continues until only one player remains.

GHOST   (Boyd, p. 103)

FOCUS: on not completing the spelling of a word, on penalty of becoming one-third of a ghost.

▶ Players sit in a circle and one calls out the first letter of a word that he or she has in mind but does not disclose. For instance, if the word is *which*, "w" is said. The next player, thinking of a word beginning with the letter "w," for instance, *work*, says "o." The third player may also think of the word *work*, and add "r." The fourth player must avoid saying either "k" or "d," which would complete a word, and think of another letter to follow "r" that will not complete a word, possibly thinking of *worst* and adding "s." The fifth player may be saved by thinking of *worship* and adding "h." The game continues until a player is forced to finish a word, in which case the player becomes one-third of a ghost but goes on playing.

A player who cannot think of a word and has to give up is thereby made one-third of a ghost. The next player continues. Anyone may challenge a player who is suspected of adding a letter without having a word in mind or misspelling a word. If found guilty, that player becomes one-third of a ghost; if not, the accuser becomes one-third of a ghost.

A player who ends a word three times becomes a whole ghost and is then out of the spelling, but tries to get others to chat. If successful, the victim becomes a whole ghost also. The game continues until all but one are ghosts.

HOW MUCH DO YOU REMEMBER? (Spolin, *Theater Games for the Classroom*, p. 133)

FOCUS: on being open both to reading and to hearing.

▶ This game has two players: a reader and a talker. The reader begins to silently read any story or article from a book or magazine, while the talker relates some incident directly to the reader.

Before reversing roles, the reader tells the talker what was read and what was heard.

Additional Memory Games

▶ The following three games can be played at home or with a few other players: OBSERVATION GAME, p. 64, IDENTIFYING OBJECTS GAME, p. 58, and THREE CHANGES, p. 73.

MY SHIP IS COMING FROM LONDON   (Boyd, p. 102)

▶ This game is played the same way as WHEN I GO TO CALIFORNIA, p. 412, except that in this game the articles are named in alphabetical order. For example, the first player may say, "My ship is coming from London laden with apples." The next player repeats this and may add "beans," and so on until the alphabet is completed. The player who makes a mistake must drop out of the game and does not add an object. The game continues until the last one fails or until the alphabet is completed.

NAME SIX

(Boyd, p. 99)

▶ All the players except one, who stands in the center, sit in a circle. The center player keeps eyes closed while the others pass any small object along from one to another. When the center player claps hands, the player caught with the object must keep it until given a letter of the alphabet by the center player.

Then the seated player must start the object on its way so that it passes through the hands of each player in the circle in turn. By the time it returns, six objects, beginning with the letter given by the center player, must have been named by the player.

If the player does not succeed in naming six objects in the time that the object makes the round of the circle, that player must change places with the one in the center.

If the circle is small, the object can be passed around two and possibly more times.

NEW YORK

(Boyd, p. 106)

▶ The players count off into two teams of equal size and stand on parallel goals twenty or more feet apart. The first team huddles, coming to a decision on a trade or occupation to be shown, and then advances toward the other team while the following dialogue takes place:

FIRST TEAM: Here we come!

SECOND TEAM: Where from?

FIRST TEAM: New York!

SECOND TEAM: What's your trade?

FIRST TEAM: Lemonade!

SECOND TEAM: Show us some! (if you're not afraid!)

▶ Coming as near to the second team as they dare, the first team's players, each in his or her own way, show their trade or occupation. Players on the second team try to identify the occupation by calling it out at first sight. If wrong, the first team goes on showing, the second team calling out. When someone calls out the correct trade, the first team must run back to its goal with the second team in hot pursuit. Those who are tagged must join their pursuers' side.

Now the second team chooses a trade and dialogue is repeated, followed by showing the trade as before. Both sides have the same number of turns and the team having the largest number of players at the end wins.

Variations of this game can be played showing animals, flowers, trees, objects, foods, etc., instead of trades.

NUMBERS CHANGE (Boyd, p. 116)

▶ The players stand in a circle with one player in the center. They number off consecutively, including the center player, or, the coach can whisper to each player a number in sequence. The center player calls any two numbers and the players having these numbers immediately change places, while the center player tries to get one of the places. If the center player succeeds, the one left without a place takes the center; if not, the game continues until the center player does succeed.

OBJECT RELAY (Spolin, *Theater Games for the Classroom*, p. 24)

▶ All players count off into two teams which line up side by side. The first player on each team has an object in one hand, such as a rolled-up newspaper or a stick. These first players must each run to an agreed-upon goal, touch it, run back, and hand the object to the next on their team in line, who must in turn run, touch the goal, run back, give the object to the third player on the team and so forth until all players have finished and a team has won.

OCEAN WAVE (Boyd, p. 118)

▶ All players arrange their chairs close together in a circle. One player goes into the center, which leaves a vacant chair. The center player calls "Shift right! (or left)," changing the command as he or she wishes. The players shift as directed, endeavoring to keep the chair on the right or left occupied, while the center player tries to get a seat. If the center player succeeds, the player who failed to shift in time must take the center player's place.

PROVERBS (Boyd, p. 96)

▶ One player leaves the room while the others collect a proverb, such as "Waste not, want not," "Faint heart never won fair lady," or "Better late than never." The words of the proverb are then distributed among all the players, who sit in a circle. Should there be more players than words, the proverb is repeated until all have a word.

The player who left returns and, beginning with any player, asks a question of each in succession. Each must use his or her word in a sentence, avoiding calling attention to the word. The player whose answer reveals the proverb becomes the next questioner and leaves the room.

PUSSY WANTS A CORNER (Boyd, p. 120)

▶ Full group stands around the perimeter of the playing space, except for one player (the pussy), who stands in the middle. The spot where each player stands is a "corner." Player who is "It" approaches any player and says, "Pussy wants a corner!" The reply to this is "See my next door neighbor." Pussy continues this dialogue with other players in turn, while trying to jump into a corner vacated by fellow players, whose business it is to dare pussy while trading places with each other, without pussy pouncing upon a corner. The odd player out in such a case is "It."

Players of all ages enjoy playing this excellent group warm-up.

RED LIGHT/GREEN LIGHT (Boyd, p. 115)

▶ All players line up on the starting line, with the one who is "It" fifteen or more feet ahead, on the goal line. All face in the same direction and move ahead while It counts any number up to ten and adds, "*Red light,*" e.g., "*One, two, three, four, five, red light!*" Immediately after saying "*Red light!*" It turns around. Any player who can tag It before It turns around becomes It and the game starts again. But if It is untagged, he or she sends back to the starting line any players who have been seen moving even slightly. After the offenders are back of the starting line, ready to begin, It turns and begins counting again.

RHYMES
(Boyd, p. 95)

▶ The group sits in a circle with one player in the center, who speaks a one-syllable word and points to any other player who must give a word that rhymes with it before the center player counts ten. A player who fails to give a word within the allotted time must exchange places with the center player; otherwise the center player continues. A player who uses a word once used by another player exchanges places with the center player.

RHYTHM
(Boyd, p. 104)

▶ Players sit in a circle and establish 3/4 (1,2,3) rhythmic movement as follows:

1. Pat both hands on lap
2. Clap hands together
3. Snap fingers of right hand

The game begins with one player starting the rhythm and all others joining in. On the third beat this player says "rhythm" and continues without a break until the following third beat, when he or she gives any letter to the player on the left. This player, on the following third beat, gives a word beginning with that letter and on the next third beat, a letter to the player on his or her left. This third player, in turn, gives a word beginning with that letter, and so on.

RHYTHM continues until a player fails to give a letter or a word on the correct beat, or repeats a word given by another player in the course of the game. When such occurs, he or she re-establishes the rhythm and begins the game again.

SINGING SYLLABLES
(Spolin, *Director's Handbook*, p. 107)

▶ All players sit in a circle. One goes from the room and the others choose a word—"Washington," for example. The syllables of the word are distributed around the circle. "Wash" is given to the first group of players, "ing" to the second group, and "ton" to the third group, so that all groups have an assigned syllable. To a familiar tune such as "Yankee Doodle" all players sing their group's syllable over and over simultaneously. The odd player

("It") walks about from group to group and tries to piece the word together, using as many guesses as needed.

The game may be made more difficult by having players change places after the syllables have been given out, thus dispersing the players.

SINGLE FILE   (Spolin, *Theater Games for the Classroom*, p. 57)

▶ A team of five or more players is to go from the room and run back in, one behind another in a line, and out again. All other players watch closely. Players return out of formation. Audience players then rearrange the runners, putting them back in their original order. When audience players agree that they have the runners back in original order, runners make any necessary corrections.

POINT OF OBSERVATION

This is an excellent warm-up for any observation game for all age groups.

STREETS AND ALLEYS   (Traditional game, not in Boyd)

▶ This is an excellent tag game to play in a restricted open space with a full group of fourteen or more players. Two players are selected to be "cat" and "mouse." All the other players form ranks by standing in equal lines with their arms extended sideways, shoulder high. The cat will pursue the mouse through the "streets" formed by the spaces between the ranks of players (see diagram). If the side-coach calls *"Alleys!"* all players in the ranks make a quarter-turn to their right, touching finger-tips with other players, to form a blockade of arms which cat and mouse may not crash through. When *"Streets!"* is called, ranks return to original positions and the chase continues through the "streets." When the cat tags the mouse, allow each of them to choose their own replacement.

Before the chase begins, practice the changes between streets and alleys a few times. Allow the side-coach to change at intervals.

As in other tag games, coaching all to play in *slooow moootion!* can heighten the excitement.

After all players have had experience with the game and are alerted to each other, it may be played without any side-coach, the ranks changing from streets to alleys, helping or hindering as the ranks non-verbally save the runner or allow the runner to be caught.

A variation is to give other character roles to chaser and runner: cop and robber; troll and young hero; villain and fair maiden or dog and cat, to name a few.

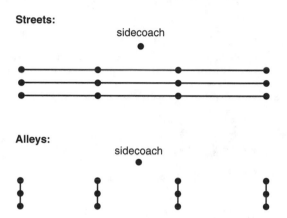

Streets:

sidecoach

Alleys:

sidecoach

SWAT TAG
(Boyd, p. 65)

▶ All players (except one who is "It") are seated in a large semi-circle. "It" (or A) is given a light rolled-up newspaper, firmly taped together, twenty or more inches long. A starts the game by lightly touching one after another of the seated players on the knee with the roll while moving around the semi-circle. Eventually, A strikes one of them, B, and then runs and places the roll on a stool centered 12 to 15 feet in front of the semi-circle. A then runs for B's seat. B, who has followed A to the stool, quickly seizes the roll and tries to strike A before he reaches B's seat. If B succeeds in striking A, she replaces the roll on the stool and runs for her seat while A goes for the roll and tries to strike her with it. If A succeeds, he places the roll on the stool and runs for his seat, pursued by B, who picks up the roll and dashes after him. This play goes on until one of the two players gets safely to the chair.

Most of this striking is delivered to the seat of the pants of the player being pursued. The one left standing starts the game again.

Should the roll fall from the stool at any time, the player who placed it there must replace it before he or she may be seated.

TRANSFORMATION OF WORDS (Boyd, p. 95)

▶ Players are given pencils and paper and assigned a word to be changed into another word. The process must be that of making a new word by changing one letter at a time in each word that is formed. For example, the word "pine" once changed as follows: pine, pane, pare, pore, pole, poll, pull, pulp.

It is interesting to experiment with words, not knowing whether they can be transformed.

WHEN I GO TO CALIFORNIA (Boyd, p. 102)

▶ Teams of ten to twelve players in a circle.

Part I

▶ The traditional game. First player says, "When I go to California, I'm going to take my kite (or any other object)." Second player says, "When I go to California, I'm going to take my kite and my hat box." Third player takes kite, hat box and adds something new. Each player takes in *exact order* all that has gone before and adds a new object. Player who makes a mistake is out and the game continues until only one player is left.

Part II

▶ Same team plays as above with a new series of objects, but instead of saying "take my shoes," for example, player *shows* putting on shoes. The next player repeats this action and adds a new object, perhaps showing a flute being played. As in Part I, each player repeats all that has gone before and shows a new action nonverbally.

Part III

▶ The game is played again as in Part I, with a new series of objects, and this time players take time to *see* each object as they listen.